The Captain And Mr. Shrode

The Captain and Mr. Shrode

A firsthand account of the voyage of *Maverick*

By Tony Johnson

Copyright © 2013 Tony Johnson

All rights reserved.

Library of Congress Control Number: 2013903832

ISBN-13: 978-0615651187
ISBN-10: 0615651186

For it seemed to me that I might find much more of the truth in the cogitations which each man made on things which were important to him, and where he would be the loser if he judged badly, than in the cogitations of a man of letters in his study, concerned with speculations which produce no effect...
—Descartes,
Discourse on Method

*My body's at home,
But my heart's in the wind.*
—Tom Waits,
"Shiver Me Timbers"

Captain's Prologue

One pleasant January day in a dead calm off the coast of Sri Lanka, the Captain was merrily piloting his craft towards a safe harbor when he espied an approaching vessel. It was brightly painted with a menacing dragon figurehead, but otherwise the boat was of the open, wooden type we had seen often, about 30 feet with a powerful outboard and a crew of eight or so swarthy gentlemen. Their behavior differed from the more common deportment of cheery fishermen selling their offerings from the day's catch, in that their smiles were of granite, and their main sales rep was more aggressive than we were accustomed to.

The spokesperson wanted to come aboard, which was odd, and even though there was a language barrier, it was clear he was insisting on it. He also didn't have the customary fish in his hand. The Captain's adept instincts told him that something was amiss. His knees, he noted in passing, were not so much trembling as attempting to jump overboard. He was reviewing in his mind his standard catalogue of suitable social responses, in the hope of deciding on one that would set just the right tone. Let's see, there's the sizzling riposte, the dismissive laugh, the impossibly dense philosophical analysis, the....When, to an operatic fanfare, manfully into the breach from the companionway strode Sergeant-at-Arms Terry Shrode to deal with these ruffians. Now the reader may presume that at this juncture Mr. Shrode would be armed to the teeth and ready to do battle. But we carried no arms aboard, and had we possessed them, there is not a high likelihood that this particular sailor would have been adept in their use.

No, Mr. Shrode countered with a thespian burlesque worthy of the great masters. Affecting an attitude of airy guilelessness, he projected a Forest Gump-like inability to comprehend the potential for evil. "Can't *we* get on *your* boat? That looks so cool! Are you fishermen? Do you have any fish? How do you catch them? Is it fun? Do you have candy?"

In the hands of a lesser man, this offering would have been transparently disingenuous. But Mr. Shrode is not a lesser man, and he relentlessly pressed on, not for an instant tipping his hand. Observing the fishermen's response, the Captain noted bemusement, curiosity, and a hint of empathy for one so diminished in apprehension. There is little doubt that if they had suspected he was putting on an act, or if we had assumed any kind of defensive posture, they would have stormed poor *Maverick*. These were not your professional pirates, however. Their only weapons were knives, and it would seem that, after a disappointing day, guided by one hawkish soul, they had sensed an opportunity. Yet Mr. Shrode's innocent exuberance had touched a deeper note that resonated with our common humanity. After five long minutes of Mr. Shrode's dissembling, they lost their focus and decided to head for home.

Of all the theatrical performances I have been fortunate enough to witness, this one had an unrivaled impact on my immediate circumstances. Of course, none of the rest took place in real life. But more to the point, none were better acted. Perhaps it's not one of the greatest pirate dramas of all time. But, on the other hand, perhaps it is.

The above story was mysteriously missing from the original email accounts of the adventures of the crew of the mighty *Maverick* on the high seas. These are now presented with modest editing from the original dispatches sent during a circumnavigation undertaken during the years 2001-2003. Welcome aboard.

Table Of Contents

Preparations

The Crew	1
The Boat	3
The Plan	9
Departure	11

The Pacific

Underway	15
Vomit	17
Marine Mammal Alert	19
The Northeast Trades	21
The Tropics	23
A Bath	25
Crossing the Line	27
Landfall Tomorrow	29
Landfall	31
Damage Report	33
Nuku Hiva	35
Contacts with the Natives	37
Departing the Marquesas	39
On to the Tuamotus	43
Terror in Tahiti	47
Other than That, Mrs. Lincoln…	53
French Polynesia for Gentlemen	59
Bora Bora Bora	61

DINNERTIME	63
WHAT'S NIUE?	65
FRIDAY NIGHT AT THE RACES	67
SO LONGA, TONGA	69
PRE-FRONTAL GEOMETRY	71
SAVUSAVU AND THE ROAD TO LAMBASA	75
KAVA JIVE	77
I TELL YOU NO LAU	79
MALOLO LAILAI	81
FIJIPHILIA	83
VANUATU TU	85
MISSIONARY IMPOSSIBLE	89
9/11	93
BEHIND CLOSED DOORS	95
MR. SHRODE'S WILD RIDE	97
THE KITE THAT TOOK FLIGHT	101
BONFIRE OF THE INANITIES	103
TORRES STRAIT, NO CHASER	107
ORIGIN OF THE SPECIOUS	111
FAITH IS THE PLACE	113
PARADISE LOST	115

THE MUSLIM WORLD

BALI, HI	119
AIN'T NO BALI HIGH ENOUGH	121
JAVA JIVE	125
GENTLEMEN DON'T DO IT	127
HOW WE RAN AGROUND	131
KUMAI	135
GILANG	139
THE RIVER	143
1000 MILES TO WINDWARD	147

Merry Christmas from Phuket	153
What Terry Missed	157
Ceylon	159
Hell on Wheels	161
A Measured Response	163
Uligan	165
High Wind, Heavy Seas	169
Pirate Plotting	171
Oman	173
A Fissiparous Fleet	175
The Bab El Mandeb	179
The Road to Asmara	181
The Night the Sea Turned White	185
The Full Red Sea Monty	189
Send Your Camel to Bed	195
Into the Valley of the Nile	197
Night Train to Cairo	201
Condo Made of Stona: The Sequel	205
Forward Progress	209
On the Hook in the Suez Canal	211

The Med

I Can See Clearly Now	217
Can You Hear Those Church Bells Ringin'?	221
Reunited	223
And a Bad Go-Getter	227
Meltemi	231
Delos	235
City-States	237
The Odyssey	241
The Battle of Salamis	245
Agoraphobia	249

CORINTH	253
ITHAKA	257
BEEN SUCH A LONG WAY HOME	259
THE WANDERING ROCKS	263
DISMASTED	267
ROCK THIS WAY	273
IN A LITTLE SPANISH TOWN	277
THE PILLARS OF HERCULES	281

THE ATLANTIC

THE MARRAKESH EXPRESS	285
THE MASTER	289
AND YOUR BIRD CAN SING	295
CHRISTOPHER COLUMBUS	299
HEAD OUT ON THE HIGHWAY	307
LOOKING FOR ADVENTURE	309
THE BUNG	311
THE DOLPHIN'S RINGS	315
IF IT'S GOING TO HAPPEN, IT'LL HAPPEN OUT THERE	319
HAND JIVE	321
HOUSTON, WE'VE HAD A PROBLEM	323
PARROT TALK	327
FIXING A HOLE	331
SEA TRIALS	335
A DIFFERENT DRUMMER	339
DREAMWORLD	343
LET US CROSS OVER	353
THE GREAT DIVIDE	355

THE FINAL LEG

HOMEWARD BOUND	361
THE OLD MAN AND THE SEA	363
HERE TODAY, GONE TAMALE	365
YOU'LL START OUT STANDING	369
TWO-LANE BLACKTOP	373
ACAPULCO	377
T-SHIRT WEATHER	379
WITH GOD ON HIS SIDE	381
ABASHED	389
JIGGETY-JIG	391
ALMOST HOMEBOY	393
THE GOLDEN GATE	397
BOTH SIDES NOW	399
APPENDIX	405
ACKNOWLEDGEMENTS	415

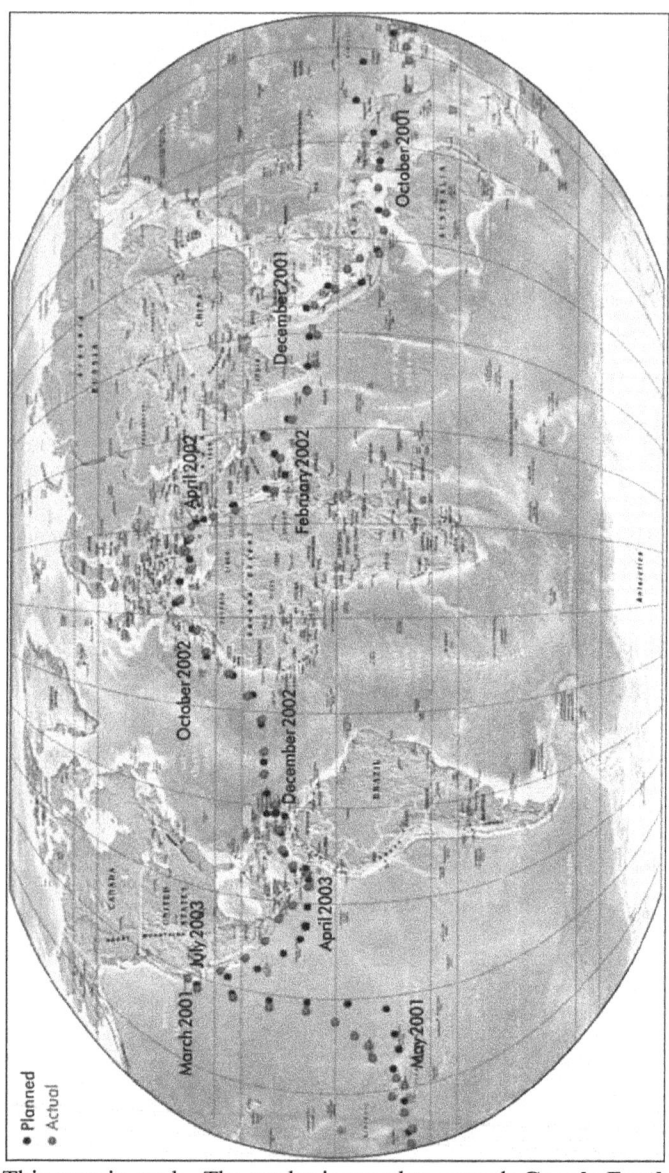

This map is crude. The reader is urged to consult **Google Earth** for orientation, using the place names or latitude and longitude found in the text. The positions that include minute indicators to three decimal points are accurate to about 10 yards, and the others to about one nautical mile.

Preparations

The Crew

That the sea is a dangerous place is sufficiently documented. The perils are well represented in film and fiction and include sharks, pirates, shipping containers floating invisibly just below the waterline, gales, unlit vessels, dengue fever, fire, rogue waves, gangrene, explosion, corrupt navies, food poisoning, infection, dismasting, hurricanes, sinking, rudder failure, burns, civilians driving nuclear submarines, contaminated water, scurvy, broken bones, tsunamis, rats, yellow fever, contusions, fog, saltwater crocodiles, dehydration, lightning, anchor failure, fishing nets, hypothermia, terrorists, whales, malaria, unmarked obstructions, strong currents, exposure, lee shores, waterspouts, reefs, large ships, seasickness, dementia, mutiny, dismemberment, and death. We need not speak of these here but will note that Samuel Johnson said that no man who had the wherewithal to get himself into a decent prison should consider going to sea.

We are not ashamed to say, however, that we find none of the above difficulties as daunting as the distress we fear as a consequence of our long separation from hearth and home, friends and family, and the comforts attendant thereto. Both skipper and crew live lives full of the common pleasures and amusements. Neither has a bone to pick with the world, nor the desire to bitterly rid himself of the problems of contemporary life. Perhaps the adventure will make homesickness moot, but perhaps not. We just have no way of knowing, and for this in particular we have no emergency back-up plan.

So where's to find them such as would sail? The captain must be a person of unshakable will and great personal discipline, and he should be possessed of the ability to lead and inspire men. He should be an able navigator, knowledgeable in all areas of the ship's operations, and have the ability to repair anything on board at sea, as the situation demands. He should be of positive disposition and be able to make swift and sound judgments with insufficient information even when ill and exhausted. He should be physically and mentally courageous. A flair for derring-do and a gravitation towards good luck will fill out the picture. Obviously, we don't know anyone like that, so we're just going to have to do it ourselves.

Our crew, Terry Shrode, is one of those stouthearted men about whom you've heard, and indeed one would have to search the pages of fiction to find a companion more boon than he. Unfazed by the prospect of going to the foredeck in a gale, dealing with engine problems, or loading 2000 pounds of fuel, water, and provisions aboard, he is withal a steadfast, gentle soul never prone to utter a discouraging word. Men, I have observed, are never named Faith or Hope or Charity. But Terry has all three.

About the Captain the less said the better, though it might be argued that his success in enlisting Mr. Shrode in this endeavor is a point in his favor.

As for onboard routine, it is natural to ask, "What do you do at night? Do you just go to sleep?"

And indeed, had we servants, we might. However, someone must stand watch 24 hours a day and there are only two of us. Sailors who undertake shorthanded voyages deal with this in different ways. Some just sleep when they feel like it, leaving Providence on watch. Others sleep for short spells, not more than twenty minutes at a time, which is approximately how long it takes between a large ship's appearance on the horizon and a collision. Our plan is to split the night into two six-hour watches and have shorter ones during the day, so someone will theoretically always be alert. We will experiment with this when we get out there but for now we think that, except in difficult conditions, this gives the crew a solid period of rest and is better than dividing the night into smaller increments. Nevertheless, the combination of less than normal sleep and the wear and tear on the body caused by the ceaseless motion of the boat means that fatigue will be a constant problem.

Entertainments at sea are rather limited. Although conditions can change abruptly, the typical experience is hour after hour of similar weather, where little needs to be done so far as trimming sails and adjusting the course are concerned. Steering will be done by hand only in harbor and close to shore, assuming that the vane and autopilot work. Navigation will be a daily and sometimes hourly job depending on how close we are to land. It is a pleasure when the weather is good and the boat is moving well but not so jolly as conditions deteriorate, which is, of course, the very time it is necessary to attend to it the more diligently. We will have books, musical instruments, a stereo, and the computer. We'll be talking on the radio with other boats and stations on land and will be emailing the folks back home with the latest dish. We'll have a fishing line out. But the vast majority of the time, there will be nothing to do.

THE BOAT

Our fine vessel, *Maverick* by name, is a 1972 Ericson 39 flush-deck sloop designed by Bruce King. Those whose appreciation of beauty runs to the superficial may say she has lost just a bit of her youthful charm and coquetry, but if there is a deficit in this regard, it is surely transcended by the haughty serenity of a street-wise veteran. Despite her hefty displacement (19,000 lbs.), she has a turn of speed that has shocked many an unwary competitor sailing one of those new, lightweight boats, and in her salad days she was campaigned successfully in Southern California. Her PHRF rating is 105. (Note that it is nautical tradition to refer to seagoing vessels as feminine. This remains mysteriously unchallenged by the occasionally ham-fisted logic of political sensitivity, to which logic of course I have no personal objection. Until a countervailing argument carries the day, therefore, we shall continue in this mode, notwithstanding the awkwardness of referring to a girl as "*Maverick*.")

Usually a skipper, save one of a sour disposition towards life in general, will maintain that his or her personal boat is superior to all other craft, much as one would defend one's child, mother, or spouse from ill-mannered criticism no matter what differences may otherwise characterize the relationship. On *Maverick* it is the same, but here we have objective proof of her superiority. (Of course, everyone has proof.)

A mathematically inclined scholar of naval architecture has computed a number of performance parameters for about 250 popular cruising boats from Swans to Catalinas, using well-established standards of boat design and his own screwy system. His completely objective scientific conclusion: the Ericson 39 is among the very best cruisers ever made. Though numbers may lie, it is somewhat reassuring for us to know that at the very least, according to some guy's idea of well-established principles of stuff, we are not setting out on a weird nautical experiment. You can look this up on the web, but don't bother.

The boat was originally drawn as an ocean racer but by the standards of today's race boats is quite luxurious below. Unfortunately, this means nothing at all, as even paint is considered too much extra weight these days. *Maverick* is quite Spartan in comparison to modern cruisers. She lacks hot and cold running water, refrigeration, a water maker, a microwave, a shower, a heater, a TV and VCR, and not a few other amenities now considered essential for persons whose habitat is not the Third World. That's where we're going, though, according to Terry.

On the other hand, she has received some significant upgrades from the original. These include increased tankage for fuel and water (about 72 gal. of each now), new Ballenger spars and rig, and considerably enhanced storage capacity for food and spares. We've added a Dodger, Bimini, cockpit cover, inflatable tender, solar panel, radar, SSB, and a beefed-up charging system. We will carry a 44-lb. Bruce on 250 ft. of 5/16" proof coil spliced to 125 feet of 9/16" nylon as our bower anchor and rode, handled by a power windlass. This is backed up by a 45-lb. CQR and 25-lb. Danforth for a stern anchor. All systems including the engine have been renewed. Well, okay, not the rudder. We will have a laptop, which, in addition to acting as a terminal for email, will receive weather faxes via the SSB radio and serve as a planetarium. We'll be able to look up worldwide trivia on two encyclopedias on the computer and edit digital photographs that we hope to send back home when we can get to an Internet café. The Encarta encyclopedia includes recordings of all of the national anthems of the world, so we hope to play the appropriate ditty through the ship's stereo when approached by the local constabulary. This, along with a substantial bribe, may help keep us out of jail and, by the by, enhance America's image in the world, I should think. The skipper has just qualified for a General HAM license so the amateur bands will be available to us for further email, weather, and emergency communications, and we have two VHS radios for short distances. We have two Garmin GPS units and if they both fail, we're carrying two sextants and the requisite tables, along with the standard navigation tools and charts. Steering will be done by a Monitor windvane while under sail and a Navico Wheelpilot 300-CX while under power. Sail inventory includes a newish Hood main, older Hood 135% on a furler, a nondescript 90%, a new Hood storm staysail on a removable inner stay, a ¾-oz. drifter/windseeker, and a new ¾-oz Hood cruising spinnaker named Luigi.

Safety gear includes an offshore life raft with strobe, personal strobes, a strobe at the masthead, a strobe that is deployed with the man-overboard pole, and a 406 EPIRB with a strobe and GPS interface, which in an emergency will emit a beacon notifying various agencies of a, like, serious problem and giving our position. It'll really be like the '60s with all those strobes going off. We'll have an extensive medical kit, and Terry's dentist gave him suturing lessons so brain surgery will not be a problem, as long as we limit ourselves to the part of the brain that has teeth. Fortunately, we will have email access to Dr. Frank Mannix, a friend from my youth who has become a professor of emergency medicine, to talk us through this sort of thing. We'll carry a drogue, which slows down the boat if following seas make her surf at uncontrollable speeds, although what's wrong with that? We'll have an emergency rudder and an emergency tiller. There are alarms, flares, and fire extinguishers and other regulation safety equipment.

In short, the boat has so much safety gear that the extra weight will no doubt prevent us from getting out of harm's way in the first place, thereby assuring its use; and in the interest of full disclosure, it may be relevant to mention that all of the gear we've listed was installed and will be operated and maintained by amateurs.

Maverick has suffered with equanimity these alterations to her original design, of which many place her squarely in the dowdy cruiser category. She has indulged us on the understanding that, at last, an adventure is afoot.

Luigi

Ericson 39

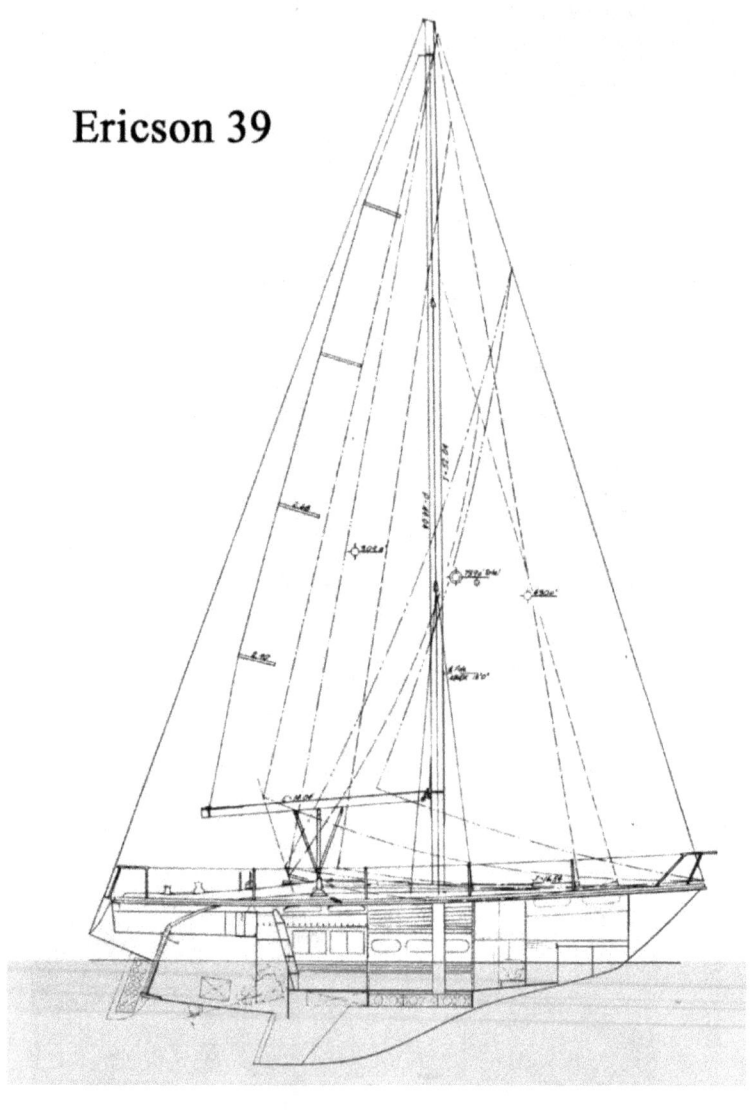

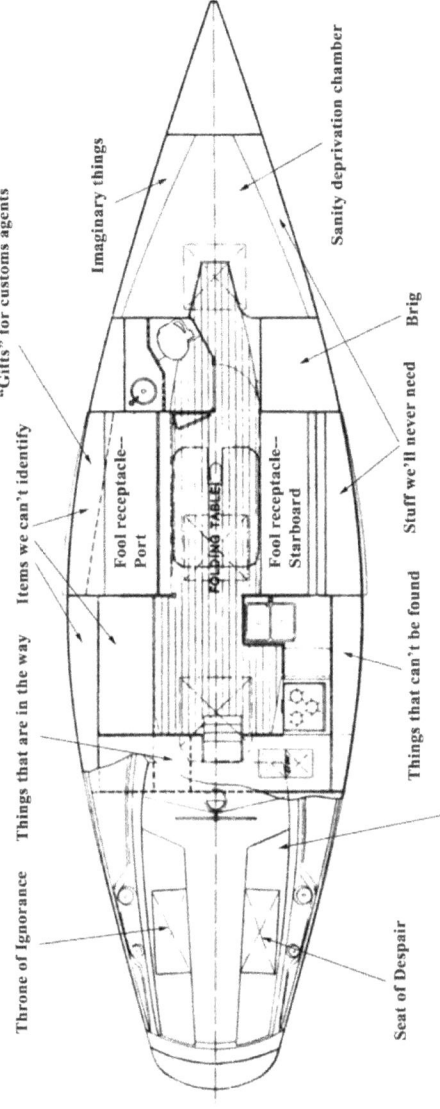

THE PLAN

The crew of *Maverick* is going to begin looking for a weather window for our departure about March 15 of 2001. The considerations guiding us to this date are poetic, as suggested by Tony's Theresa: *2001: A Sea Odyssey*. They are gerontological, as in most likely we won't live forever. And they are meteorological, based on the need to be out of the southern half of the North Pacific before hurricane season starts in June, and not to be at our intended first landfall, the Marquesas, before hurricane season ends in the South Pacific in April or May. We are pushing this second date just a bit, perhaps, to give ourselves the maximum amount of time in the South Pacific, since because of similar weather constraints we need to be in Darwin, Australia by fall. The plan was concocted by Routing Officer Terry Shrode, who in so doing eschews the tried-and-true procedure of coast-hopping down to Mexico in the fall, wintering in a suitable luxurious resort, and heading west in the spring. Mr. Shrode was inspired by the dictum of Admiral Nelson of the Royal Navy, who decided, "Damn the maneuvers, just go straight at 'em!" Unlike the strategy of those more cautious cruisers staying close to shore, our itinerary offers little hope for an easy return to a safe harbor once we leave.

We expect the passage to the Marquesas in French Polynesia to take a minimum of 30 days. The maximum could be double that. So assuming that we have perfect weather on the 15th of March, and we have favorable winds and no trouble en route, we'll be in the Marquesas in mid-April. After our stay in the Marquesas for reprovisioning, repair, and rest, we sail to the Tuamotus, the Society Islands, Cook Islands, Samoa, Tonga, Fiji, Vanuatu, the Solomon Islands, Papua New Guinea, and then to Darwin, Australia, with various stops in these areas depending on how things are going.

It is bad form in cruising, so it is said, to announce one's plans. This is because the likelihood of their successful completion is contingent on so many imponderables, and that once having announced a goal, one risks perceiving the whole enterprise as a failure if the larger target is not reached. Whatever.

We're prepared to say, disdaining tradition, that we'd like to make it around the world. Given enough time and enough money, brains and youth, the goal is certainly achievable. But of these we have quite finite amounts, and consequently I'd rate our chances at a bit south of even. Things can happen, even 20 miles outside the Gate. In the event something comes between us and our goals, you'll be there to share the pain if we come to a bad end—or not, if we come to a really bad end.

The idea is, then, to continue from Darwin up to Bali and thence across the South China Sea to Singapore. From there it's the Strait of Malacca, Malaysia, Thailand, Sri Lanka, Oman, Yemen (why not visit friendly Aden?), up the Red Sea, through the Suez Canal to the Mediterranean. We would like to arrive in the Med in late spring of 2002. The summer is to be spent transiting that fine sea, along the Turkish coast and through the Greek Islands, past Italy and France to Spain. In late fall we head through the Strait of Gibraltar to Madeira, then on to the Canaries and across the Atlantic Ocean to the Caribbean, the coast of Venezuela and the Lesser Antilles, the coast of Columbia and finally the Panama Canal. Arriving at last again in the Pacific, we must decide whether to sail along the coast of Central America and up the Baja Peninsula, or take the old clipper ship route 1000 miles offshore to Clipperton Island, where we would tack and make our way back to San Francisco and home.

We have allowed two and one-half years for the voyage. This is about as fast as it can be done unless one mounts an all-out racing program, which takes a lot of money and is for those with more of a blood-and-guts approach, and for that matter more hemoglobin and more internal organs. The schedule we must maintain restricts us to, by cruiser standards, short stops and little rest. Because we wish not to be caught anywhere in hurricane or cyclone season, it also means that should there be any major gear failures, health or family problems, untimely weather anomalies, or bad luck[*], we may not make a required weather window and will be trapped where we are for another year, perhaps putting the ultimate goal out of reach.

---

[*] All of these did, in fact, occur, as you will see.

Departure

12:22 PM, Saturday, March 17, 2001.
37° 54.394'N 122° 21.719'W*
Underway.

It is just after noon local time and the crew of *Maverick* is motor-sailing up Santa Fe Channel ready to fall off onto Potrero Reach. We cast off the lines at approximately 12:06 *(2006 March 17 UTC)* bound for the Marquesas. Until we get our sea legs, we'll likely not write, but we'll talk to you in a couple of days. Meanwhile, the following is a prerecorded message.

When a traveler approaches the Bay from sea, there is nothing at all to give a hint of the size and importance of the cities of San Francisco and Oakland. Sutro Tower is visible, and as you sail closer, you can see the understated Sunset District, which could easily be mistaken for a small coastal town, sloping towards the west. Otherwise, the cities are hidden by the coastal mountains and all the mariner sees is a rugged and undeveloped coastline, and in fact the Golden Gate is such a small opening that most early explorers failed to find it.

But as the sailor approaches closer to the rocks and cliffs of Land's End and finally passes under what is now the Golden Gate Bridge, the whole mass of humming activity suddenly reveals itself. This is startling at night, when it is reminiscent of the scene in a science fiction movie where a dark cave leads to a small door, which, when opened, reveals a vast, obviously powerful, alien civilization.

It will be the same in reverse for us. We'll make our way from the civilized calm of the marina in Richmond out Potrero Reach, give a nod to Red Rock, then turn left and passing Southhampton Shoal, proceed through Raccoon Strait, past Ayala Cove on Angel Island, the towns of Tiburon and Sausalito, then Yellow Bluff and the Bridge, taking a long look at the city of San Francisco. These protected and familiar waters, where so many beatific days have been spent sailing and at anchor, will then almost instantly be left behind. Exactly at the Gate, the swell from distant storms begins to be felt and if we glance backwards, much of our home waters will have disappeared from view; we're in the foyer of the Pacific Ocean. For a few minutes, the full size of the swell is dampened

---

* These positions may be viewed in Google Earth. The locations that include the degree and minute indicators are accurate to about 10 yards, and the others to about one nautical mile.

by the refraction around Point Bonita, but as we sail out past Mile Rock and the Point, we make the final transition to ocean waters and no land protects us from whatever sea is running. If it is at all large, the prudent sailor will not turn left until he's gotten himself through the shipping channel to the San Francisco Buoy.

At that point, the crew of *Maverick* will set its course on 180 degrees true, due south, from which, depending on the wind, it will try not to diverge for about 2500 miles. Soon the last shadow of land will fade, and we'll be all the way out there.

The Pacific

Underway

1:23 PM, Tuesday, March 20. 33 01 N 124 31 W
Temp. 65, Humidity 76%, Cloud Cover 100%.
Seas WNW 1.5 meters. Wind S 3k.
Fourth day at sea.

The boys got well throttled on the way out to sea on Saturday. As our friends were watching from a viewpoint in the Marin Headlands, we headed out past Point Bonita, and though the scene may have looked idyllic to them, what was taking place on the boat was a different matter altogether. Around the Point, our autopilot jammed up. This meant not merely that it wouldn't steer but also that we couldn't steer either. To disable the autopilot required taking off the steering wheel and removing the autopilot, which, it was immediately apparent, was the only solution. So in the middle of the shipping channel and with some lumpy seas, we took off the wheel and got out a hammer to get the autopilot loose with the boat carrying on pretty much as it chose. Necessity improved our efficiency tremendously and in a minute or two, mission accomplished. From shore, it just looked like another pretty picture. But we on board had another picture: no autopilot for the foreseeable future.

This was just the beginning of one of the most difficult 24 hours of sailing we've ever done. The seas in the shipping channel, though by no means the largest we've seen, were steep and nasty. As soon as we were able to turn left, after buoy #2, we pulled out the headsail and doused the engine. With the sea conditions as rough as they were, the best we could do was a beam reach—anything lower or higher than that was impossible to steer without flogging the sails, and even the beam reach was not easy to maintain. Meanwhile as the sun went down, both crew got violently ill and continued to puke for the next 24 hours, about which more next time, you lucky thing.

What we would have liked to have done was to head straight south but there wasn't a man-jack-boy aboard who was about to go forward to set the pole or do any other such foolishness. To make matters worse, because it was dark and we were sick and stupid from puking, we couldn't get the vane to steer so for the entire night we had to hand-steer in one-hour shifts, which sounds easier than it was as it entailed the challenging barfing-while-not-jibing maneuver. As a result of the enforced beam reach, for the next 12 hours or so, we went like a banshee on a course of about 240 true, which was unfortunate. We intended to make all of our westing south of the equator so as not to end up beating into the southeasterly trades for the last 200 or 300 miles of this passage.

Now it is incumbent upon us to, at the very least, not go any farther west for the duration.

On Sunday we managed to set the pole and head dead downwind, although there was still some sickness and we were exhausted. Now we could head south and we covered good mileage and when we passed Point Sur, the seas flattened out just a little. The wind went light and fluky on Monday, but settled for a direction today. In the last 24 hours, we've had to call Luigi (our spinnaker) in from the bullpen and then douse him in the middle of the night, to end up close hauled in about 4 knots of wind.

Through all the early rough stuff, *Maverick* was in her element, which is more than can be said for the crew, and she was just as indifferent to the discomfort of her charges as was the sea itself. Despite her heavy load, she was as fierce as ever, and if she had a complaint about the waves in the cockpit and over the deck, we heard none, so occupied were we with our own misery.

Vomit

(Sent with previous missive)
1:23 PM, Tuesday, March 20. 33 0 N 124 31 W
Temp. 65, Humidity 76%, Cloud Cover 100%.
Seas WNW 1.5 meters. Wind S 3k.
Fourth day at sea.

In our informal world, we often speak metaphorically, do we not? We might say, for example, "Play 'Cheeseburgers in Paradise' one more time, and there will be vomiting."

The reader is sophisticated enough to realize that having heard the above, it is not necessary to ring the triage nurse at the local hospital to arrange for care, nor run to the medicine cabinet for an antiemetic. The speaker is but having a little fun with language. A more appropriate response, perhaps, than medical care would be to change the music to something that obeys the letter, if not the spirit, of the plea—something that is not Jimmy Buffet but that might be equally repellent. Admittedly, the research required to achieve this end would be prodigious, and beyond the means of all but the most resourceful sadists.

On shipboard, however, predictions about bodily effluents need to be given sober consideration before being dismissed as metaphorical. When for example, above the rustle of the waves and rush of the wind rings the cry, "Verily, Captain, I am going to hurl," the prudent mariner will place himself at a generous remove and to windward of the afflicted, having made the seamanlike inference that no attempt at poesy is intended. And so it goes with other conversation in the environment in which "lowering the boom" on someone will produce a result more life-threatening than a flushed countenance.

On Saturday night last, when the crew of *Maverick* had made its way into the great Pacific, straight talk was called for. Soon after sunset, demonstrating the leadership that is both the privilege and the burden of his rank, the Captain tossed his cookies. Officer of the Deck Terry Shrode, than whom a man more willing to take up the task at hand would be difficult to find, soon came forward with a suitable hearty offering of his own. The Captain, in a fit of paranoia, perhaps, immediately saw a budding challenge to his authority and rebutted with alacrity. To this, Mr. Shrode had a ready answer. And so it went on through the night, each man unwilling to yield, as the spirit of competition comes as naturally to these two as their flair for ballet. Come morning, however, the Captain was ready to concede the match, which he had convinced himself was inconsequential, to the challenger. But Mr. Shrode was not done with him. He was simultaneously hungry and queasy, not sure which was the cause of which. So each time he felt unease, he would eat, with predictable results. By this stratagem, he was able to thoroughly put to rest any doubts about his mastery of this area, and the contest was settled.

On Monday we had light and variable winds; then Tuesday and Wednesday gave us light wind from the south, so we've been tacking on the shifts and earning every inch. The latest fax shows the high to be southeast of us, which would explain the southerly wind; and it predicts it will move to the west and below us in the next 24 hours. If this happens, we can expect favorable winds within the next day. According to the pilot chart, there's a high percentage of northerly winds in this quadrant this time of year, which went into our planning, so we'd like to see that happen. Three days of very slow progress has had little effect on our spirits, which are high.

Marine Mammal Alert

1:00 PM, Saturday, March 24. 27 19 N 122 58 W
Temp. 70, Humidity 62%, Cloud Cover 50%.
Seas WNW 1.5 meters. Wind S 4k.
Eighth day at sea.

Although we reckoned that sooner or later a morale problem would surface onboard ship, we were not prepared for its swift appearance, nor for its paradoxical complexion. The fact that so soon into the journey we would face our first challenge of this sort is perhaps a dark portent of events to come, or perhaps not. The issue is the following.

Since Tuesday evening, we have covered about 300 miles toward our goal, for an average of just over two knots. Watch Captain Terry Shrode and the Captain had a serious talk this morning, trying to examine our situation with the intent of discovering which points merit our serious concern—with unsatisfactory results. In any reasonable crew, this very poor progress would provoke an unease, nay, despair that we may never again see land, that other boats are going faster, that we are doomed, etc. So Mr. Shrode and the Captain went through a long list of things about which they should feel dismay, but the disturbing thing is that this only served to make the men rather giddy. So the effort was abandoned.

It is true that we must bear down and get on with it, as time and provisions are finite. Yet in Bowditch, Chapman's, and other texts, the mariner is cautioned not to rely on one means alone to establish his position. So in addition to the GPS, we have confirmed our progress by sensing the increasing temperature of the toilet seat in the morning. We're down to about one layer of fuzzies at night and t-shirts and embarrassing straw hats during the day. Last night we saw stars for the first time and could make out Orion between the clouds. An albatross and a tropicbird have kept us company today, and the dolphins have come to visit us many times now. The most chiseled heart must leap with a child's joy to see them dart under the bow. So we must be getting somewhere.

However, when we do get to what is rumored to be Paradise itself, there will be bugs and officials to deal with, fuel and water to find, provisions to carry, a crowded anchorage where earlier cruisers have chosen the best spots. We will have, like, a job.

Out here we can play the stereo as loud as we want. We can walk to the bow and declare that we are the king of the world, however pathetic that may be. You have my word that your Captain will never do any such thing. I do feel under some obligation however to inform you at home that nothing can stop me now, 'cause I'm the Duke of Earl.

THE NORTHEAST TRADES

11:00 AM, Thursday, March 29. 16 56 N 122 48 W
Temp. 73, Humidity 70%, Cloud Cover 100%.
Seas NE 3 meters. Wind NE 10k.
Thirteenth day at sea.

When we were last heard from, things were going quite well. Weather was improving and the Captain was enthusiastic about the chess game being played with the Pacific High, which was turning in the boys' favor.

It was key to traverse the high without using precious fuel, which must be preserved for the crossing of the Doldrums, so it was of some concern when the weather fax showed a high still to the southeast of us and moving west. If it parked below us, it might mean days of no wind. So we changed course to the southeast in anticipation of the high's progress, believing the position the fax placed it in 24 hours. And indeed as predicted, the high moved southwest of us the following day, and thus we were able to sail dead down wind and proceed south. On Thursday the 22nd we set the genoa and drifter on poles and sailed 180 true. Sunday the 25th the wind freshened as the high moved farther west, and we elected to hand the drifter and made good progress under the genny alone. Our spirits were high as we were going fast, and it would be only a short while before we would find the northeast trades, which would bring, we had reason to believe, good weather, long gentle swells, and a steady breeze. We were shortly to be disappointed.

On Monday the wind veered northeast and we dropped the pole, hoisted the main, and headed up to remain on our course of 180 true or so. Here were the trade winds we had anticipated. The wind freshened to about 30 knots and the seas became lumpy, with the main waves about 6 ft. every 4 seconds. *Maverick* was racing through this slop and beating the crew silly so we had to shorten sail, first one, then two reefs in the main, rolling up the furler one, and then two marks, and finally dousing the genoa altogether to get the boat speed down to 5 knots. Even at this, the motion on board was so violent that the crew got almost no sleep that night.

The sloppy seas were, reasoned the Captain, caused by the collision of the seas from the high, which were north, the seas from the trades, which were northeast, and the swell remaining from the storms in the Gulf of Alaska, which were northwest. This produced a mess that was uncomfortable and made ugly by the fact that, rather than clearing, the skies had turned to monotonous altostratus from horizon to horizon, and the mercilessly leaden aspect of the heavens made the seas that much less friendly. To add to the unpleasantness, the temperature had actually dropped now that we were nearer the equator, so the crew were back in their fuzzies at midday and our friends the dolphins had ominously ceased their visits.

We have made reasonable progress, but it is Thursday now and although the wind has decreased to 10-12 knots and the seas flattened a little, the situation is otherwise little changed. Now it should be pointed out that nothing about the present situation is the least bit dangerous. In fact, conditions are merely less pleasant than we would have liked, and they could of course be much worse. But unfortunately it seems they may become somewhat so, as the wind is predicted to lighten so we may have a long time to wallow in the bleak patch of ocean we have come upon. Fresh food has finally run out, having outlasted by several days our most optimistic projections; so it's canned goods from here on. Galley Specialist 1st Class Terry Shrode has announced that tonight we have a very nice "Sweet Polynesian Pineapple Princess Prepared Ham Parts Sauté with corn and water chestnuts soured by the crew, served over boiled domestic brown rice."

We saw our first flying fish today, so we're going to take that as a good omen, there being a scarcity of other candidates.

The Tropics

2:14 PM, Saturday, March 31. 12 10 N 122 50 W
Temp. 84, Humidity 75%, Cloud Cover 100%.
Seas N 3 meters. Wind N 14k.
Fifteenth day at sea.

Just hours, or perhaps minutes, after writing the last update, the conditions changed dramatically. The clouds dissipated, the seas flattened, the temperature rose sharply, and instantly we had the classic trade winds conditions. Although we had technically been in the tropics since latitude 23, this is the first time we felt we were really there. Now it was hot enough to bake one's brains, and since we had no designs to eat them, this did not seem a worthy plan. So yesterday we hoisted the Bimini, which is a Conestoga-type frame covered with canvas to shade the cockpit, and any illusions we retained of not looking the part of normal cruisers were abandoned. We were treated to a classic tropical sunset, which this correspondent will not embarrass the reader by trying to describe, and then a very bright crescent moon rose, accompanied by Jupiter and Saturn. Ordinary Seaman Terry Shrode commented that it would be perfect, if it weren't so fake-looking.

That night we also saw an object in the sky to the northeast about 10 degrees above the horizon; it was stationary and blinking red and green. It appeared again last night, this time off to the southwest. Now, this was an alien craft and we were abducted and operated on, but the point is that I can't understand why it was showing red and green lights. Our best guess, and we reached this after lengthy and earnest debate, was that the aliens, in their training, were required to read Chapman Piloting.

The dolphins have returned for more visits since our mood improved, and to take inventory we've seen to this point a black-footed albatross, some sooty shearwaters, several storm petrels, tropicbirds, and a few brown boobies, one of which took up residence on our bow pulpit for a few hours after spending the morning deciding where to land. This morning, both a flying fish and a squid were found on deck. Apparently, they were dead.

Gunnery Mate Terry Shrode has unaccountably taken up the job of conning us through the Intertropical Convergence Zone, the ITCZ, otherwise known as the Doldrums, which will be our next navigational challenge. This is a band of rising air parallel to the equator, which from the point of view of the sailor consists of very light to non-existent winds, high temperatures, and thunderstorms produced by huge convective clouds. From our weather reports, we gather that we will encounter it at about 8 degrees north and it will continue to 2 degrees north, a distance of 360 nautical miles. Its width, length, and zones of higher and lower intensity vary from day to day so the trick is to place oneself at a point on the northern edge of a thin area and go straight across.

Mr. Shrode has determined that we should make some westing to the 125th meridian and proceed south from there, basing his analysis on daily weather updates we get on one of the high-frequency radio nets. To that end, this morning the crew of *Maverick* doused the main and again hoisted our downwind rig, consisting of the drifter and genoa on poles. We are now moving along at about 6 knots, and making a course of about 250 true. When we reach longitude 125, we'll head up and tackle the Doldrums.

We have to this point sailed a distance of 1691 nautical miles. 2200 miles to the northwest, Hawaii beckons, and 2100 miles to the east is the great country of Nicaragua. The equator is 700 miles to the south, and the nearest land is about three miles straight down. But it's a long three miles. Depending on the route that we eventually sail through the Doldrums, we have 1400 miles or so to go, so arguably we're more than half-way to Paradise. But the other half might be the long one.

A Bath

3:00 PM, Thursday, April 5. 02 45 N   127 05 W
Temp. 85, Humidity 81%, Cloud Cover 20%.
Seas NE 2 meters. Wind NE 10k.
Twentieth day at sea.

We continue through the NE trades, and for the vast majority of time since the 27th of March, we have been on a port tack broad reach with 10-20 knots of wind and 6-9 ft. confused seas. We can't figure out why we are still getting seas from three directions.

We of course have tried to plot a good course through the Doldrums. When we were up at latitude 12 north or so, the best information we had put them beginning at 8 north. The next two days we couldn't get the weather report from a land-based operation that gives sailors the best route through the ITCZ, so we just kept heading south, based on the two-day-old prediction. We went past 8, then 7, and now are below 3 north, and still we are getting the trade winds; the Doldrums keep moving south ahead of us. They are still 300-500 miles wide, but we have hopes that they will move north to their normal position while we move south, and we'll have a quick passage.

Two nights ago we had a 45-knot squall. We had reefed down pretty well since we were seeing these things frequently but the earlier squalls had been only about 25 knots. This one was a bit of a bad boy, but the worst damage was that the lid of the barbecue blew off, which, as it is on a stainless steel lanyard, we easily retrieved. That morning early it began to rain and kept it up for about 36 hours, with a wind shift or two.

During the rain, we collected almost 30 gallons by using our excellent water catchment system. This consists of port and starboard deck fills at a low spot on the deck, which are connected to quick-release garden hose fittings in the cabin. To these we attach a short length of hose with a valve, and then run this to a collapsible 5-gallon water jug in the galley area. After the first bit of rain, which washes the salt off the deck, we block the scuppers and make a dam around the deck fills with modeling clay. Then we take the caps off the deck fills, open the valves, and get water that is quite pure, save the odd squid part. After we're done collecting about five or six containers, we empty them into the boat's water tanks, and there you have it.

Water conservation aboard is of course paramount, as we started with only about 80 gallons for what could be a long trip to take care of cooking, drinking, and cleaning. Vegetables can be steamed with salt water. For washing dishes we have a faucet at the sink fed by an electric pump from a saltwater intake, as there is no shortage of the stuff. Most of the washing is done with salt water; and then rinsing is accomplished with fresh water, which is pumped with a foot pump to constrain use. As regards bathing, the chief method of conservation is of course its infrequency. This works out fine, as our social obligations are fairly rudimentary, and one who might attempt bathing every day risks putting himself under some suspicion of being a girly man.

When appropriate, however, it is accomplished by heading to the foredeck rather more naked than a jaybird, with a bucket and a bottle of Joy, a brand of detergent that does a fine job of making suds in salt water. Salt water is fetched from the ocean and, co-mingled with the Joy, is used for washing. Then as many buckets as the bather deems appropriate are dumped over his head. Final rinse alone is carried out with fresh water, from a sun-shower placed there earlier in preparation for the glorious event. Those considering the cruising life should spend some time in contemplation of the image of a nude, middle-aged man comporting himself in the manner described before embarking on this exciting adventure.

CROSSING THE LINE

8:00 PM, Tuesday, April 10. 05 59 S 134 20 W
Temp. 85, Humidity 84%, Cloud Cover 50%.
Seas SE 2 meters. Wind SE 18k.
Twenty-fifth day at sea.

As we write, we are doing about 7 knots under full sail in the southeast trades, and Hiva Oa, our destination, is about 344 miles away. We've actually gone to the chart tubes and pulled out a chart for the Marquesas and for Hiva Oa. Until now we used an inflatable globe for navigation.

Last night at about 2300 we saw lights from another boat, probably a sailboat. The Captain saw the lights on his watch for about 20 minutes, and then they were gone. Since the night of our departure, the night of the big barfennany, this is the first time we have seen anything in the ocean besides a few bits of flotsam and the critters who live here. The only other visual evidence of the existence of human beings was a couple of contrails we saw as we were sitting in the Pacific High.

Since we last wrote, we had a little bit of fluky breeze and then the wind veered to the southeast and we had found the beginning of the southeast trades, north of the equator. The Doldrums had evidently parted before us, as we never encountered the classic glassy seas and complete lack of wind.

But what's wrong with glassy seas, anyway? I'm going to buck the crowd and put in a word for the calms one occasionally encounters at sea. The wind has ceased, and you're alone in a vast, primordial wilderness far from the chatter of civilization. It wasn't easy getting here. The ocean is quietly resting, though you sense the uncanny power of her languid, Brobdingnagian undulations born of distant, violent storms. In this desolate and dreamlike domain, you can read, contemplate, and swim in perfect serenity and solitude. Your cup and plate sit calmly on the table instead of unsociably flinging themselves to the cabin sole. The sunset beams across the anvil tops of thunderheads a hundred miles away. Soon enough, you'll be in a city with all the normal folks. What's the hurry?

We crossed the equator in the middle of the Captain's watch, 0027 on April 7. The Captain awakened Fleet Archivist Terry Shrode, who got out the camera to take a picture of the GPS. The Captain is quite skeptical that this really proves anything to anyone, and in any case it's not really much of a picture. Because of his mature years, Mr. Shrode had difficulty manipulating his various eyeglasses and the camera, and as the camera has an infuriating wait between pushing the button and getting an exposure, he didn't actually time it well enough to get 00 00 000. The GPS, after all, reads out in thousandths of a minute or about six feet (which is a higher degree of accuracy than it can reliably sense, so even if you caught it at zero, you're not that close), and *Maverick* was screaming through the night at about 7 knots at the time, which is about 12 feet a second. And how accurate is that line, anyway?

As one crosses the equator for the first time, so goes nautical tradition, one ceases to be a "pollywog" and becomes a "shellback." There is hazing. Alcohol, a bit of everything on board, must be drunk. Unpleasant substances are rubbed all over one's body and a dip in the ocean is made to cleanse oneself. On *Maverick*, a new tradition was begun, and we commend its adoption. The Captain said, "Good work with the camera," after which Mr. Shrode, shellback, repaired to his bunk. One detail of note: As Mr. Shrode was at the nav station and the Captain was above watching the radar, Mr. Shrode crossed the line first by about two feet and is the senior shellback.

The next day or so the wind went light and then picked up again from the southeast. Sunday brought nasty, lumpy seas, reminiscent of the seas we had at the beginning of the northeast trades. We had swells of about nine feet from the northeast and also from the southeast plus a lot of chop from the wind. It's hard to say exactly what makes seas really unbearable. Saturday night we had a rough time of it and the boat and rig took quite a beating, yet neither skipper nor crew felt any the worse for it. But on Sunday afternoon, all either of us wanted to do was to take to the bunk and hope for unconsciousness.

The 344 miles to Hiva Oa present a challenge. Our understanding is that we can't check in with immigration on the weekend, and this particular weekend being Easter is three days long. This means that if we don't get there by the end of office hours Friday, it is quite likely that after 3400 miles and 27 days at sea, we will be confined to the boat and unable to set foot on land until Tuesday morning. And to get there in time to anchor, pump up the dinghy, fire up the outboard, get ashore, and walk a half-mile to the gendarme's office before he closes, we'll have to arrive by about noon. Unless the wind stays fresh and constant, we don't stand a very good chance.

LANDFALL TOMORROW

9:27 AM, Thursday, April 12. 08 44 S 137 29 W
Temp. 85, Humidity 83%, Cloud Cover 10%.
Seas ESE 1.5 meters. Wind ESE 12k.
Twenty-seventh day at sea.

We are about 100 miles from the Island of Hiva Oa. It's about another 20 or so to Traitor's Bay and the anchorage off the town of Atuona. We want to arrive there in about 24 hours, Friday morning. Our concerns about not making it by the end of the work day on Friday have been resolved on two counts. One, it is after all possible to do an informal check-in any day of the week. And two, we've been going so fast that we've actually had to shorten sail and will have to slow further so as not to get there in the middle of the night on Thursday. On *Maverick* we wish to avoid entering unfamiliar harbors at night, and from here on out, they are all unfamiliar.

On the day before arrival, there are suddenly a slew of new tasks to accomplish. The Captain, who has avoided reading about anything we are about to do, must do his homework on the approach to the harbor and anchorage, along with the entry formalities. The chart will be studied and guidebooks consulted. We understand the small anchorage is rather crowded, though only about 15 boats are there, so it will be necessary to anchor bow and stern and we need to check and mark our stern rode. We will take baths and perhaps trim the facial hair to take the edge off that "been to sea for awhile, eh?" look and fragrance.

We're of course curious about what it's going to be like, but we're not frantic to get there. We've heard it's hot and sticky, the anchorage is rolly, and there are bugs. Except for the bugs, it doesn't sound too different from out here. We pick up a little sense of urgent anticipation on the radio from other boats, and some frustration at the long passage. The feeling aboard *Maverick* is one of equanimity, and also expectation, not frustration. But tomorrow will be a day very much different from the last 26, we can be sure of that.

LANDFALL

*5:00 PM local time, Friday, April 13. 9° 48.233'S 139° 1.883'W
Baie Taahuku, Hiva Oa, Iles Marquises, French Polynesia.
Temp. 84, Humidity 84%, Cloud Cover 100%.
Seas calm. Wind calm. Anchor down.*

Lookout Terry Shrode spotted land on his watch at first light this morning. He had seen it on the radar and the GPS told us we were here, but he rejoiced at seeing Cape Balguerie with his own eyes. The Captain was informed upon rising about 0645. The wind had perversely gone light the previous afternoon, and after having taken it too slow for a day, the crew was forced to motor for six of the last twelve hours of the passage, which was equivalent to all the motoring we had done up to now combined, with the exception of the day of departure.

We anchored bow and stern and recorded it in the log at 0951, or 9:51 AM Marquesas time, 1921 Greenwich Mean Time. (Greenwich Mean Time or GMT, also known as UTC for Coordinated Universal Time, or Z for Zulu, is the international standard for many things, including navigation and weather.) The time underway was 26 days, 23 hours, and 15 minutes. We had sailed 3492 nautical miles from the San

Francisco channel, or about 3512 from the dock, at an average of 5.4 knots. The time of passage is quite respectable, we feel, despite the fact that in order to avoid the Pacific High and also to avoid sailing against the southeast trade winds, we had sailed 505 miles farther than a great circle route, the shortest path between two points on the globe. We do not regret the course we chose, having had a good look at the southeast trades.

In the small anchorage were 19 other cruising boats, and many crews we had spoken with on the radio came to greet us. All had departed from Mexico. We immediately prepared to go to the village of Atuona, the largest on the island of Hiva Oa and home to a big percentage of the 1500 people who live there, a mile or two up the road. A cruiser recommended a shortcut that looked like a page from a child's adventure book and involved crossing a stream. We took off our shoes but needn't have bothered. Ten minutes later the heavens opened and in the next three minutes we were soaked through, shoes and all. The deluge continued for the next four or five hours, but our walk was not a whit the less beautiful for it.

It was Good Friday and when we got to town, it appeared that everything was closed. We had a powerful yearning for cold drinks and ice cream and civilization, so we were quite disappointed. But farther into town was a snack bar, the only establishment of any kind open for business, where we were thrilled to get a couple of beers or maybe more and lunch. We were relieved of $50 US for the privilege, and considered it an extremely prudent use of our cash.

About the mood aboard: Suppose you were an 8-year-old boy with a bike and you had the dreams that are mostly restricted to 8-year-old boys about becoming a space pilot or war hero or sailing to the South Pacific, but you didn't know how to tie a constrictor knot or cut a dovetail, and you didn't know about apparent wind or how to take a fix or figure winch ratios or what kind of hose to use in the head or what a passport was. Plus, you only had $7 and the farthest your parents would let you go was to your friend Bruce's house, so you just, like, grew out of it. Then imagine that the next thing you know you're a grownup and you don't have any parents and you've done some stuff that turned out pretty good and some other stuff that didn't and you've learned all those things the little guy didn't know and some others too, and saved some money, not much, really, by American standards, and then one day you actually back the boat out of the slip and you sail it all the way across the Pacific Ocean and you get to a little harbor that looks just like the ones in the pictures, and the 8-year-old boy isn't disappointed a bit. He thinks it's just as cool as he imagined it would be. Wouldn't that be excellent?

Damage Report

*8:00 PM local time, Easter Sunday, April 15. 9° 48.233'S 139° 1.883'W
Temp. 82, Humidity 85, Cloud Cover 20%.
At anchor in Hiva Oa.*

"Scotty! Damage report!"

"Aye, Captain. The light in the head has been fixed and we planed down the cabinet doors, which were sticking. The autopilot turned out to need just a wee belt, which we expect to have sent ahead to Papeete."

The Captain, who has provided the ship with spares of just about everything, including even the guts to the stereo, is somewhat embarrassed at not having a belt for the autopilot on board. The manufacturer was consulted on this issue and told the Captain the belt couldn't be replaced by amateurs and anyway it was Kevlar and would last until the universe had gone through almost an entire cycle of death and rebirth and had gotten back to where *Dobie Gillis* had gone off the air but *Gilligan's Island* hadn't started yet. The Captain was persuaded by this quite reasonable projection and decided against ordering a spare.

One thing that 8-year-old boy of the last missive could not have enjoyed was the pleasure of alcoholic beverages, which is just as well since he would inevitably have lacked the self-discipline to consume them responsibly, and in moderation, the way their manufacturers recommend. This, of course, is without doubt the way the crew of *Maverick* imbibed them on Saturday night last, after doing some very pricey grocery shopping in town. Easter morning dawned, however, with the boys still in their bunks and it was quite some while before they summoned the energy to arise and begin the day's chores. These included doing the laundry at a faucet on shore where we also took showers, and then hanging it all on the lifelines and genoa sheets to dry.

We hitched a ride into town from a Marquesan, harboring a slim hope that we would find an open store or snack bar where we could procure ice cream with which to celebrate Easter. We were surprised and pleased to find that the same solitary snack bar, run by a French couple, was open, and we had our fill of ice cream and then some. We took a walk outside of town, to the countryside, as it were, and viewed a landscape that was extravagantly verdant and psychedelic quite beyond the Captain's powers of description. In many places, palm trees climbed the steep hillsides, which seemed peculiar though lovely, and we surmised that these must have been planted as coconuts don't roll uphill. Later, we were directed by a very nice gendarme up a steep incline to a cemetery where we found the grave of Paul Gauguin, which held fresh flowers, seashells, and other offerings. We did not locate the grave of Jacques Brel, but it's there someplace too.

When we returned to the boat, the clothes weren't dry as there had been a couple of showers since we left, so they're still outside as I write. Tomorrow we're going to check our halyards, see about some fuel, and then sail about ten miles to the island of Tahuata and an anchorage, which, according to Eric Hiscock, is one of the three most beautiful in the South Pacific. But the crew of *Maverick* feels that it is hard to believe it could improve upon our first landfall.

NUKU HIVA

9:30 PM local time, Saturday, April 21. 8° 54.931'S 140° 6.076'W
Temp. 85, Humidity 78, Cloud Cover 90%.
At anchor in Taiohae Bay, Nuku Hiva, Iles Marquises.

Since our last post from Hiva Oa, which by the log looks to be about a week ago, the crew of *Maverick* has kept steadily on the move. The day after Easter we had a short sail to the neighboring island of Tahuata and anchored with four other boats off an uninhabited tropical beach. We left at dusk the next day for an overnight sail in light wind to Ua Pou (pronounced wa-po, as if you didn't know) so we could arrive in daylight. We anchored bow and stern in a cross wind in the small harbor off the village.

After doing some reconnaissance of the town and its inhabitants and determining they were not hostile, we set sail in the morning for the island of Nuku Hiva and Taiohae, the largest town in the Marquesas, about a five-hour sail in pleasant conditions. We anchored, went ashore, and found a restaurant overlooking Taiohae Bay, quite a large bay by comparison to the others we've visited. Pizza was the big attraction, but this did not suit us, so we guessed at the French menu and were not disappointed.

The next day, Friday, was filled with not a few chores and our first seriously boneheaded moves. The Captain takes full responsibility, as he must, for the buck stops with him; and the fact is, if he were looking for where it started, he wouldn't have to get up out of his seat.

The first involved the mysterious refusal of our credit cards by the local bank, which could obtain an OK for no more than $50 while we needed about $800 each to post a bond permitting us to stay in French Polynesia. At this time the Captain got to thinking his second card had been left at the last island. All was worked out after a couple of hours and a fine fit of paranoia. Later, after taking the dinghy over to the fuel dock to get four jerry cans of expensive diesel, we discovered we were out of water in two of three tanks. The story is too tiresome to convey in detail but included leaving a valve in the wrong position and creating a siphon, when heeled underway, in one of the tanks after modifying a vent line's placement. However, though none is available here in Taiohae, we understand there is good water to replenish our supply on the other side of this island, and we plan to sail there tomorrow. But putting it on the boat isn't just a matter of hooking up a hose to a faucet. We also discovered we forgot to bring in the fishing line when entering the harbor and it is now around the anchor chain, which is a pretty good boo-boo, but none of the above compare to the really perfect mistake of the day.

We had lugged groceries and ice half a mile to the dinghy dock and were loading them onto the boat in a hurry because while we were gone to the store, an 85-foot ketch was attempting a Med-tie and his stern line was under our dinghy, threatening to lift it out of the water. We managed to get out of there just in time. But about 8:00 last night, a very nice French couple rowed up to our boat and handed us a backpack. The bag, which we had in our haste left on the dock, contained the boat's document, our entry papers and bond certificate, driver's licenses, radio license, all credit cards, and our passports. Our benefactors had seen it on the dock, realized its importance, and rowed around the harbor from boat to boat looking for the Americans who didn't even know it was missing. Nor was this the first time French people have been kind and courteous far beyond the norm to the Captain, who does not share the views of some of his fellow citizens in regard to this fine country. How can you thank a culture that has brought the world Rimbaud, de Sade, Genet, and Chevalier?

The Captain, partly by reason of his disposition and partly because he is the Captain, lives in daily fear of making the error that puts the boat on the rocks. For every voyage that comes to a bad end, there is what seems in retrospect to be a quite obvious mistake that, when hearing about it, one thinks he would never make. The problem of course is that there are a lot of things to keep in mind and that particular one is never seen coming. But this is one of the charms of an adventure, is it not?

Today, Purser's Mate Terry Shrode went to town looking for fresh fruit, which can be found, oddly, not in stores but only in the private yards of residents. Having been coached by the Captain to fortify his French vocabulary, he approached a local woman but did not achieve his goal, as he apparently asked, "Madam, could I please understand your dog?"

Contacts with the Natives

7:30 PM local time, Monday, April 22. 8° 54.931'S 140° 6.076'W
Temp. 81, Humidity 80, Cloud Cover 90%.
At anchor in Taiohae Bay, Nuku Hiva, Iles Marquises.

The more anthropologically inquisitive of the Captain's readers are no doubt wondering what he can tell them from his experience in the Marquesas regarding the primitive natives of this far-off land and their customs and situation. The Captain is, as it turns out, quite an acute student of human culture and is happy to share the results of his research in this area with all.

The practice followed aboard *Maverick* is one of treading lightly and making furtive observations. It is acknowledged that Margaret Mead's research efforts were compromised by her actions and indeed her very presence among the people she was studying, so we aboard *Maverick* accept the principle of observation's corrupting influence as fundamental to our restraint in its use.

It was the noted student of anthropology, Mark Twain, who argued that you should, "Get your facts first, and then you can distort 'em as you please." As sensible as this seems, Twain was writing before the discovery of quantum mechanics and the special theory of relativity, so we believe his approach to be short-sighted. The theory of quantum mechanics predicts that, at the quantum level, the observer changes the events observed merely by the act of observing, and although this principle runs contrary to common sense, it has been well established by experiment. It remains controversial whether the same limitation applies to events in the world visible to the eye, but nevertheless aboard *Maverick,* we feel that its cautious application to our methodology is prudent. As a consequence, the reader may have confidence that our conclusions, based as they are on a statistically insignificant amount of empirical data, are authoritative.

There are two main concerns often expressed about such peoples and their present condition. One is that they may not have the benefits available to those living in the industrial societies; and the other is that they may. The Captain is very happy to be able to report that in both respects he has satisfied himself that things are much better than many have feared.

The natives, who, by the way, are somewhat less naked than one might have had reason to hope, do not as a rule live in poverty. By some system, which the crew of *Maverick* was unable to discover despite much delicate questioning, everyone, or as the French say, *tout le monde*, drives around these rather small islands in $30,000 four-wheel-drive vehicles that are quite new; and yet we could not find the source of income used for the purchase thereof. The towns may be, in all, five blocks by five blocks, and these SUVs as superfluous as they are common, yet employment seems sparse. Actually, adults in general are not plentiful and we wonder whether they arise before dawn to go to their employment in some mysterious industry and return after the crew of *Maverick* has retired to quarters. Or, as the Captain is rather fond of thinking, they don't work at all and have no need to leave the house. If the latter, the wisdom of this arrangement should be apparent to anyone, and we commend it to the industrialized nations for further study.

Having satisfied themselves that poverty is not a problem, the crew set about to find out whether these unfortunate people have been culturally destroyed by modern influences. They speak in odd grunts and howls that the Captain is quite certain cannot be translated into a civilized language, much like their French governors (here we make a little joke at the expense of the French who, the Captain does not tire of repeating, have never failed to treat him with unequalled courtesy and friendliness), and this by itself is reason for hope, since they can say neener-neener-neener without outsiders comprehending. And to the question of adverse cultural influences, there is again a happy answer, which is that, while there is evidence that Western culture has indeed found its way here, there still is much canoeing and tattooing, to everyone's delight.

Signs of Western influence are abundant and varied but select. The proprietress of a corner store we patronized was biding her time by viewing a Cheech and Chong movie dubbed in French. Later, the same woman was observed intently studying a Janet Jackson video. There was in evidence in another store an impressive display of Britney Spears posters, more extensive than even the Captain's own rather complete collection, and Celine Dion was heard in the background to enhance our shopping experience. At dinner at a modest restaurant, the small local crowd was entertained by *Friends* on TV, dubbed in French, which was followed by a quite sophisticated Parisian program of the *Jerry Springer* ilk. No one was observed watching that stupid PBS stuff.

In sum, these people, attractive and of noble bearing, while retaining their native traditions, have an innate desire and appreciation for the highest achievements of the modern societies and a subtle and discriminating understanding of what these have to offer. In these respects, it is quite accurate to conclude they are not more culturally deprived—nor corrupted—than the average Marin County resident, but have in fact similar tastes, and better skin.

Departing the Marquesas

9:30 PM local time Wednesday, April 25. 8° 49.275'S 140° 3.857'W
Temp. 85, Humidity 75, Cloud Cover 40%.
At anchor in Anaho Bay, Nuku Hiva, Iles Marquises.

In need of water, the boys from *Maverick* sailed around the windward side of Nuku Hiva on Sunday and had quite a bumpy time of it. Given the conditions, we had to stand well off not to scare ourselves, and this made the trip about seven miles longer. We arrived in Anaho Bay that afternoon and primarily rested as the Captain was, in his weenie little way, beat. We got up Monday and surveyed our surroundings. Anaho Bay is the most spectacular place we've visited, which is a fair compliment, and our last stop in the Marquesas. Imagine sailing into Yosemite Valley, filled with a large lake, but on the shore is exotic vegetation and sandy beaches. A stiff warm breeze is blowing, and as the humidity is down into the 70s, it feels like a desert wind. There is one other boat, French, at anchor and perhaps a dozen small dwellings ashore, almost all unoccupied. We rowed in through a pass in the coral surrounding the beach and found the promised hose bib a short walk away. We filled five collapsible 5-gallon jugs, took showers using the hose attached to the spigot, and made two more similar trips, transferring the water to the tanks on board.

Yesterday we set out on foot for another bay just over a ridge, Hatiheu, but couldn't find the fork in the trail, so we continued around the bay and east over a ridge in search of an archaeological site. We didn't find this either. But it was the bomb hike, primeval, luxuriant. Then today with some false starts, we did find the way to Hatiheu, a jungley trail up a steep ridge and down again. The village there was very cute in that South Pacific way. A dirt road parallel to the beach, complete with roosters, was the main street, on which we found a simple but lovely church and a restaurant with a thatched roof.

The restaurant, where we had a great meal of lobster and grilled tuna, was a bit large, we thought, given the size of the village. Tourists may come from elsewhere and this might explain the unexpected luxury but really, it isn't that easy to get here. At lunch we hypothesized that the food, along with several beers, would fortify us for the trek back over the hill. You might think the Captain will have a little fun with this and say the experimental evidence did not support the hypothesis. But no, quite the contrary. In fact we thereupon resolved that, hereafter, every outing should begin thusly.

Mr. Shrode, naturalist and fruit-lover, is always on the lookout on these walks for some exotic fresh mango, guava, papaya, or better yet something unheard of and possibly never eaten before, to sample. The Captain tries to remind him that if any such thing existed, it would be on the shelves of Safeway, as this is not the 15th century and trade to the tropics is well established. Take bananas, for example. Do they grow in San Francisco? They do not. Why are they so abundant at Safeway if they come from so far away? Because they are yummy. They are well packaged. People like them. Believe me, if the same were true of the durian fruit, we'd see a lot more of them. But Mr. Shrode is not easily put off his mission, which on this particular day was unsuccessful.

The Captain was sent aloft today to inspect the rigging, which he pronounced "good enough." We created ratlines using Prusik knots and 1/4" braided line for Lookout Terry Shrode to climb. This was done for the reason that our next destination, requiring a passage of over 500 miles, is the Tuamotu or "Dangerous" Archipelago. The Captain is not fond of discomfort of any sort, and he is particularly cool to "Danger."

We have been told, those of us who sail on the San Francisco Bay, that if we can sail there, we can sail anywhere. And so it is that the crew of *Maverick* takes its extensive experience sailing in San Francisco Bay, where there are no reefs or atolls, to this next adventure, which involves reefs and atolls. We have been advised not to go with the main flow of cruisers through Rangiroa by the very same French couple that saved our bacon back in Taiohae Bay, but instead to visit an atoll named Fakarava. We have looked at charts. We have entered waypoints into the GPS. Nevertheless, when we get there that morning, having passed close between two islands that will be invisible in the middle of the night, we will have to negotiate a pass to get inside the reef.

Atolls are irregular rings of coral around a sunken volcano. They have little elevation, say ten feet, plus the height of the palm trees, and some of them have "passes" or breaks in the reef where a boat can make its way through. But there are often powerful currents running in or out, at times in excess of the speed your boat can manage. To either side of the pass are large breaking waves, and even within it, there may be coral just below water level. So the idea is to time your approach with the sun behind you at slack water (the time of which has been difficult to establish, but we hope our information may be adequate), then send the eagle-eyed Mr. Shrode up the ratlines so he can see where the coral is under water. Arranging for the sun to be behind us at slack water with no clouds on our arrival day wasn't easy, folks. We won't be exactly fresh, either, having spent several days at sea. We view this operation with some trepidation.

And so tomorrow we bid farewell to the Marquesas. It is poignant to view the things we see around us and know for a fact that we can never come back. Our stay has been not less beautiful than we might have hoped and of course included much that we could not have foreseen. But it is in the going, and not the staying, that the adventure reveals itself. And this adventure has just begun, I do believe.

ON TO THE TUAMOTUS

7:15 PM local time, Tuesday, May 1. 14° 57.974'S 147° 38.474'W
Temp. 86, Humidity 75, Cloud Cover 40%.
At anchor in Rangiroa, Archipel des Tuamotus, French Polynesia.

Our passage to the Tuamotus began scarcely less roughly than our departure from San Francisco. On the last day we had each collected in a very short period of time, perhaps ten seconds, a rather impressive number of no-see-um bites, which certainly exceeded 100 apiece though the Captain didn't bother to count. So we had a souvenir that lasted the whole passage and beyond to remind us of our wonderful time in the Marquesas. The reader may recall, from the chapter entitled "Vomit," the crew's way of handling what we sailors euphemistically call lumpy seas, and there was more of that at the beginning of this passage. Perhaps the Captain may take the time in this issue to give the reader a closer look at how rough things were or were not, so he can judge for himself exactly where on the weenie scale to place our boys. Sitting in a cozy bar and discussing at some length the idiocy and weaknesses of one's colleagues is among the most venerable and pleasurable attractions of the sport, and if the Captain were there with you, as sometimes he wishes he were, he would be the first among equals in giving no quarter to the embarrassing whining of our *Maverick* boys.

At any rate, when we left San Francisco, there was a small craft advisory for hazardous seas, and when we left Anaho Bay, we had similar seas but were spared the advisory. We took four waves into the cockpit, say 10-15 gallons each, two of which were over the transom. We sailors call this *being pooped*, in this case just a tiny bit pooped, and if this makes the little ones laugh, what's wrong with that?

We had decided to go to Fakarava in the Tuamotus, on the advice of our French saviors, who were quite familiar with the entire area. Their complaint about Rangiroa, the normal cruiser stop, was that it wasn't the real Polynesia as there were dive shops, glass-bottomed boats, and tourists. So after clearing the bumpy lee of the Marquesas, which went on forever and was caused, we supposed, by the steep seas refracting around the island and then rejoining one another at a 90-degree angle on the other side, just where our heroes happened to be, we set a course for Fakarava, 207 degrees True. This was a beam reach in 6-10 ft. seas—let's call them 8 feet, with a frequency of 4-6 seconds—which had now straightened themselves out but were crossed by, from two directions, 2-3 ft. wind waves, even though the wind is all from the same direction. The Captain gave this matter his full attention for quite some time while using the accurate one one-thousand, two one-thousand method and feels these are fair descriptions. The reader may wish to consult the buoy page on the NOAA website for comparison purposes; clearly, it's the frequency, not the size, that is the bother.

After about 30 hours of this, the crew had a conference about the plan then in effect. We weren't really ill, but it was too rough to cook with the rolling and difficult to sleep. About every five minutes, someone thwacked *Maverick* on the beam with a large baseball bat, the boat shuddered, and a couple of buckets of water were thrown into the cockpit. One didn't really want to be sitting out there. Not that one can't take a little dousing now and again. It just...got old. That hatches had to be dogged down in 85 degrees and 85% humidity to avoid the same treatment in the cabin meant things were not so comfy below either. We started to think: Tourists? What's wrong with tourists? *We're* tourists! Glass-bottomed boats? I *love* glass-bottomed boats! And we fell off to Rangiroa, 240 True.

We could now sleep and eat better. After a day or so, the skies filled up with cumulous, the seas diminished, we had lots of squalls, and finally, the wind died completely and we ended up motoring all night in glassy seas to make it to the entrance to Rangiroa at what we thought would be low slack. Motoring all night is less fun without an autopilot.

As we mentioned in our last post, even though the Captain is, it goes without saying, expert in all things maritime, he had never been to a coral atoll before. He had made the large mistake of thinking that somewhere in the Marquesas we could get tide charts for the Tuamotus, since they don't have them at, like, West Marine. There are several harbors with towns, after all. But no. We made do by copying, back in Nuki Hiva, some computer printouts from other cruisers of several of the Tuamotus, but these people didn't have tides for where they were going, either, and had not been able to find them anywhere although they must exist.

What we ended up with was three different tide charts (no current charts were available) from two different computer programs for three islands we did not plan to go to. After comparing them all, we came to two conclusions. One, they didn't make sense. The earliest low on the 30th was put at the westernmost island, the next at the easternmost, and third low was at the one in the middle. Two, even though they didn't make sense, the lows all occurred between 0320 and 0530. Since our atoll, Rangiroa, was somewhere in the middle of the three, we reasoned that we could expect low slack to occur there between about 0630 and 0830, unless both computer programs were wrong, or the Captain misread them, or currents don't work that way in atolls. But he had looked at them with the people owning the software and they agreed with his understanding of them after extensive review. They had a vested interest, too, in getting it right, as they would be right behind us.

The issue is that you want to enter the pass at slack, and low slack if possible, because the currents might run, say, 10 knots or more. *Maverick* can only do about 7 in calm seas with a tailwind flat out under power. (For you non-sailors, and perhaps some of you sailors as well, "low slack" is the term used for the time, in an enclosed body of water, at which the water stops flowing out and starts flowing in.) If you go in at the wrong time, the outgoing currents can kick up standing waves against the incoming swell, or overpower your ability to steer your course and put you in a nasty place, both geographically and emotionally, as the pass is a narrow slot with breaking seas and coral on either side.

We get to the entrance at dawn as planned. We figure at least we can raise someone on the VHF to confirm our tides, some cruiser or dive outfitter or gendarme or harbormaster. Nada. Look, I see cars and there are boats running around in there. Try again. Nada. So we looked at it. The Captain said, "I dunno, what do you think?" and from up the ratlines, Lookout Terry Shrode said, "I dunno, what do you think?" Then the Captain said, "I'm not sure, what do you think?" and so on. So we circled, and we looked, and we saw riffles on the outside of the pass which indicated to us that there was probably an ebb running. We thought, this makes sense, it's supposed to be a dying ebb according to our info, so we'll just kind of sit out here until it's slack. So we putted around, hoping that someone would come up on the radio or a local boat would enter or leave so we could get a sense for what was going on. Nada. Rien. About this time the engine died. Has anybody looked at the fuel gauge recently? We switched tanks and bled the diesel but it didn't help our confidence to think that, had we gone in a few minutes ago, we would have lost power right in the pass. We've used up another of our nine lives.

Then the Captain says, "It doesn't really look that bad to me, does it to you?" and Mr. Shrode says, "Not really," and the Captain says, "But what the heck are we supposed to be looking for?" and Mr. Shrode says, "You're asking me?" etc.

So the Captain just starts steering for the pass, thinking, if it's an ebb, which we'll be able to see by observing our progress along the shore and comparing the GPS with the knotmeter, what's the worst thing that could happen? OK, well, that's not gonna happen, so what's the next worst thing? OK, and the next worst thing? We'll just get flushed out! No big deal.

So here we go. It's soon apparent it's an ebb, for sure, and actually, kind of a strong one at that, and as a matter of fact, we're not there yet and it's getting stronger, and we're now motoring at full throttle and the

GPS shows a little under 2 knots while the knotmeter shows 6 1/2, and the current is twisting the boat this way and that, but we're still moving so we keep going, and by gum, after a long five minutes we make it through and the Captain faints dead away.

We went back to look at the pass after we anchored and got our dinghy inflated. All the tide charts were wrong, or, perhaps our assumptions about how high and low tides affect the time of slack in an atoll were confused, or our extrapolation from the other islands was misguided, or all three. We had actually entered a bit after high slack and were in a building ebb. Another hour and there's no chance we would have gotten in and, we'd like to think, would have had the sense not to try.

Back in the bar at the Richmond Yacht Club, where the Captain is not exactly a member *per se,* someone is saying, "Sheesh. The currents in Rangiroa are on the web at rangiroacurrents.org. Any idiot knows that and shouldn't take a boat out of the Gate unless he can figure it out. That fuel thing, I'm sorry, he just isn't up to the job. He's a danger to his crew and everyone in the anchorage. And lumpy seas, my ass. Why, I remember the time I was...." And the Captain, were he there, as he sometimes wishes he were, would shake his head side to side, sigh, roll his eyes, sneer, and order another Red Tail Ale from the goodly barman, Charles.

TERROR IN TAHITI

10:00 AM local time, Saturday May 12. 17° 34.978'S 149° 37.113'W
Temp. 79, Humidity 82%, Cloud Cover 95%.
At anchor at Faaa, Tahiti, Iles de la Société, French Polynesia.

Our trip from Rangiroa proceeded without incident, except for a 35-knot squall in the wee hours of Saturday, and by that morning, the 5th of May, we were anchored at Papeete, Tahiti. We went ashore and the Captain called his girlfriend Theresa, who had come to meet us, and whom he was more thrilled to see than he would have allowed himself to contemplate. Perhaps tears were shed, but certainly, one should think, not by the manly Captain himself. Terry's wife Caroline came in the next evening. We decided not to try to get a berth on the famous quay, as the motion of the boats against one another and the wharf is pretty impressive when the huge Moorea ferries come and go. Instead we chose an anchorage in Faaa near the airport where we were soon joined by some boats we met in Rangiroa. The Captain stayed at Theresa's hotel on Saturday night while Mr. Shrode assumed full command. When cruisers talk about the wonders of a hot shower, they do not exaggerate. You may have the Captain's word on it.

The next night, as Mr. Shrode had been approved for two days' shore leave with Caroline to enjoy for himself the pleasures of a hot shower, Theresa and the Captain were alone on the boat when there was a buzz on VHF about a deepening low, which was being called a tropical disturbance. It was 300 miles west moving directly towards us, and was the third in a series of these, each deeper and larger than the one before. It would be rare, but unfortunately, not metaphysically impossible, for a tropical storm or even a cyclone to form this late in the season, and since this is how they are born, it was making the cruisers nervous. The weather had become unseasonably squally and rainy as a result of this low and was causing our stay to fall short of picture-postcard Tahiti. So the Captain set alarms at various times and arose during the night to check weather faxes and the anchor.

French weather estimated that during the next 48 hours we should see squalls of 35-50 knots with heavy rain, which would be part of this weather pattern, but they did not yet make any mention of something bigger. At this point the Captain focused on his anchoring strategy. It is quite bizarre, for one used to anchoring in normal harbors, to anchor behind a coral reef. There is the ocean; there is the reef, reaching from the depths nearly vertically to the surface; there is a deep anchorage inside the reef, say 50-60 feet; then there is more coral next to the island. So you are anchored in 50 feet of water with large waves breaking over a reef quite close by in clear view, to seaward, and another reef on the landward side. Since the reef takes the energy out of the ocean waves, one need not fear the surge, but to someone unaccustomed to it, it is quite a disconcerting sight and sound.

The Captain was satisfied his anchor was stuck. But as the weather was cloudy and the anchorage choppy, it was difficult to see even with the dinghy the exact limit of the reef to landward of us, which was also at this time to windward. Perhaps the reader can appreciate the difficulty of estimating without fail a radius of 250 feet from the place where the anchor was dropped and determining the extent and relationship of the reef to the anchor without surveying gear. The crew of *Maverick*, accustomed to anchoring in 20 feet or less, hadn't practiced its eye for estimating this large a swinging radius. But in this tight anchorage, we had taken some care in choosing this spot, and thought we had ourselves safe and sound. Given the concern about the squalls, however, the Captain veered an additional 25 feet of chain. It would be a decision he would come to regret.

The next day the Captain and Theresa took a high speed ferry to the splendidly dramatic Cook's Bay on nearby Moorea. We returned to *Maverick* that evening and though we saw a powerful squall come through while we were on our excursion, everything remained quite snug at the anchorage. The Captain checked weather faxes, which had not changed much, and the anchor rode, before retiring.

At about midnight, there was a violent, explosive, scraping sound that had the Captain on deck before he was even awake. There he confronted a blinding squall, with winds in the high 30s and higher in gusts and visibility down to about two boat lengths in the heavy rain. Even though he had never heard this strange, awful noise before, he had not the least doubt what it was. *Maverick*, our home and protector, who had charged with us so many times up to Drake's Bay, who saw to it that we made a respectable job of it in numberless races, who calmly watched over us if we had too much to drink in Ayala Cove, and who had brought us safely all the way down to the South Pacific: *Maverick*, our trusty old friend, was on the reef.

The Captain has been aground many times before, in San Francisco Bay, the place about which it is said, if you can sail there, you can sail anywhere. Running aground there goes something like this:

"Oh, dear, I'm afraid we might have run aground."
"My, that's a bother."
"It is a bit of that."

"It's especially troubling, since we made arrangements with Pat and Ted to have dinner at the club. I certainly hope this won't make us change our plans. That would really be quite a nuisance, but if you think it's necessary, I'll ring them on the cell phone."

"Never worry, pet, I'll just start the motor and back off the mud. We'll not be a minute late."

The feelings aboard *Maverick* that night were somewhat more intense. Though there were no appreciable swells in the anchorage, the wind had developed quite a chop that pounded *Maverick's* keel horribly, meaning in a manner that in the hearer produces actual horror, on the hard coral. The Captain determined quickly by the feel of the wheel that the rudder was also involved. It was not immediately apparent what caused us to be on the coral. Had we dragged or swung into it? There had been a wind shift of 180 degrees, and if in fact the anchor wasn't holding, this would make the situation significantly more difficult.

Poor Theresa, who had looked forward to sunny skies and calm walks on the beautiful islands of Tahiti and Moorea, was now, in the absence of Mr. Shrode, pressed into service in a frightening gale in the middle of the night in the desperate effort to save *Maverick*. She had no experience driving the boat under power and was taking direction from a rather distraught skipper. Yet she was as brave and steadfast as ever an old sea dog could have been in such circumstances.

The Captain fired up the engine, always left ready to start, and put the boat into gear. Telling Theresa to hold the wheel and try to drive us forward, he rushed to the bow, naked as a trout, if you must know, to see if anything could be accomplished by use of the windlass, which is of course not designed to pull a boat off a reef. He was able to gain some inches and that was all, but this and the tension on the chain showed that the anchor was holding. What had evidently happened was that the boat had swung on its anchor, whereupon the increased wind had done a good job of stretching out the rode nearly to its limit and over the reef. Running back to the dodger, he told Theresa to increase the power and then went forward to try to pull some more chain up.

A couple of times through this process seemed to be earning us some limited progress, but there were terrible grinding sounds and stresses on the rudder, which could not but put dread into the skipper's heart. And in another minute or so, a new sound was heard that made his blood freeze in his veins: The prop had found the reef. This seemed almost impossible but meant one of two things: Either there was a coral head between the keel and the rudder tall enough to interfere with the prop, or *Maverick* was up against a shelf that ran alongside the keel. It was hard to say which was worse, and although the skipper knew that a calm assessment of the situation was called for, the number of calm persons whose analysis could be conveniently brought to bear was negligible. What was clear was that if the prop was damaged to the point that it could not move the boat, and the windlass by itself hadn't the power to get us off, *Maverick* would most likely suffer fatal damage before other measures such as launching the dinghy and running out a kedge—a very tough process in those conditions—could be effective.

It was at this point that the Captain had the nautical equivalent of his entire life flashing before his eyes. The whole adventure might well come to a halt right there and then, and he and Terry Shrode would just be two more hapless dudes who thought they could sail to the South Pacific. This is not to mention the inconceivably awful and unlikely but nonetheless real possibility in the skipper's mind that there could be some injury, or worse, to the precious Theresa, who does not swim. In the next few minutes, we would find out whether what was going on right then would become a life-changing experience or merely a really bad bummer.

We continued attempting to gain ground with the windlass, afraid to try the prop. This seemed to have some little effect and we gained a few more inches. The Captain took a deep breath and put the engine in gear. There was more awful buzzing as the prop hit the reef, but before he could throttle down to limit the damage, the noise stopped, and we were off the reef. *Maverick* was free!

The whole incident to this point had probably not lasted more than 15 minutes, but it is impossible to describe the relief we felt at that moment. Nonetheless, it was also clear to the Captain that we were not by any means out of the woods. We had to re-anchor the boat with a damaged rudder and prop, we might for all we know have a breach in the hull, we were surrounded by other boats in a tight anchorage, there were coral reefs that could not be seen at all at night, and it was still blowing hard with torrential rain and little visibility.

We picked up the anchor and drove around the vicinity trying to find another spot to drop the hook. As the Captain took the helm, he found that the rudder felt okay and we could move the boat forward seemingly normally, but there was some vibration of the prop in forward that became quite worrisome in reverse. Also, in the given conditions it was difficult to make reasonable judgments about other boats' anchoring situations. Were they on chain or rope? Hanging on a mooring? The Captain had an idea from previously assessing these points, but he certainly did not want to make matters worse by making another mistake and swinging into someone.

The wind finally diminished to about 20, then less, the rain eased up a bit so we could see, and we dropped the hook at last in a place that we were certain was clear of coral and other boats but a little in the channel.

We didn't like this but since it was not a shipping channel and it was the middle of the night, we figured we were safe until morning. We went back to bed exhausted, but the Captain was not able to find any solace in sleep.

The next morning we went to a pay phone ashore to try to contact Mr. Shrode, provisional landlubber, a person who can always be counted upon to add a positive outlook and who, unlike the Captain and Theresa, would have been rested. The hotel said no such person was in residence there. Since after repeated insistence, the receptionist could not find Terry or Caroline in their records, we had no choice but to abandon the effort to contact them. Of course, they had been there awaiting our call all the time, and indeed Mr. Shrode could see the boat from his hotel, had watched the weather with concern earlier that last evening and noted in the morning that the boat had moved but had no idea what had transpired and no way to contact us. Theresa and the Captain returned wearily to the boat.

We had checked the bilge in the night and ascertained that no water had come aboard, and the Captain now dove under the boat to see just what the damage looked like. The prop appeared scuffed and there were plenty of gouges and scrapes in the keel and rudder. Beyond this, as Mr. Shrode confirmed on his dive the next day, it seemed that our folding prop had been put out of balance so that it produced a vibration in both forward and reverse. We are concerned that the prop shaft or cutless bearing may be compromised, and we will have to look into it further. But *Maverick*, while battered, is, we feel to our great relief, going in the end to be okay.

The dismasting we suffered two years ago in the Doublehanded Farallones Race in 15 ft. seas and 30 knots of wind was very tough, but emotionally quite a mild experience compared to this one. Nick Nicholson reported in a recent issue of *Practical Sailor* that two days after the grounding of his boat in the Red Sea, his hands still shook. The Captain was not able to sleep or eat normally for a similar two days after this bump in the road.

But the fact is that like it or not, incidents like this are sometimes part of the adventure, and they can happen ten feet from one's home slip. Few cruisers escape the experience without some dodgy escapades, and some of our colleagues here in Papeete have, by the way of offering condolences, come forth with stories of their own mishaps and mistakes. Already the sting of this night has dimmed, and soon we'll be on our way again.

Other than That, Mrs. Lincoln...

10:00 PM local time Wednesday, May 16. 17° 30.173'S 149° 51.376'W
Temp. 83, Humidity 79%, Cloud Cover 70%.
Baie d'Opunohu, Moorea, Iles de la Société, French Polynesia.

We have finally left Tahiti and had a very nice short sail to Moorea today. We are glad to be quit of Papeete and on the move again. Papeete is a rather large city, by far the largest in French Polynesia, with traffic and pollution and crime. (The word "Polynesia," as romantic as it sounds, comes from Greek and simply means many islands. I don't know what the word "French" means.) In addition to our other stresses, we had to be wary of leaving the boat at night and also had to take precautions with the dinghy.

But as compensation, we were anchored in such a way that we had nothing but a reef and open ocean separating us from a sunset over Moorea. There were not even any other boats in that direction. James Michener defended the much-maligned Papeete by saying that any place one can see Moorea from can't be all bad. So for all that it would have been fine, but we were restless and wanted to get down the road.

We removed the damaged folding prop and shipped it back to the States for repair as everyone here gave it the RCA dog look. We had no nut to hold our spare prop, a standard two-blade, on the shaft because the Captain had not taken into consideration the fact that our folding prop had a special nut that is not appropriate for holding anything but itself, and he had therefore failed to provide a nut among the spares. The less creative of you may feel free to insert a joke here. In Tahiti it is not possible to buy a bronze or stainless ¾" S.A.E. nut, since the French, so exemplary in every other way, go by that ridiculous metric system. So we had two made at a machine shop. Because of the Captain's limited command of French, we ended up with two bolts instead, and had, in effect, to pay to have the nuts made twice.

We hired a local diver to pull the folding prop and replace it since even both of us put together can't hold our breath that long. Frogman Terry Shrode was able to replace the shaft nut and lock nut, however. The spare prop seems to rob us of about 1 knot of boat speed while under sail, and although this is probably an exaggeration, it sure feels slow.

All this was more complicated than it sounds, which is why we spent what to us was an excruciatingly long time staying put. We fixed the autopilot, though. We also filled the propane tank with butane and, after we got it filled, carried it all over town looking for that unavailable S.A.E. nut. Ship's Trainer Terry Shrode is persuaded that carrying things is good exercise, and the heavier and longer the better, so why not fill the tank *before* you have to walk long distances. On his theory, then, not a few benefits were enjoyed by the crew of *Maverick* during this episode of our adventure.

We are presently anchored in Opunohu Bay on Moorea, the same bay used for the setting of the movie *South Pacific*. The spire of nearby Mont Mouaroa, visible from the boat, was, in the movie, called "Bali Hai" and the Captain has been unable to dissuade Ship's Film Historian Terry Shrode from, at all hours, breaking into an operatic rendition of the song of the same name.

We had planned to anchor in Cook's Bay, named after that famous Captain, the one, that is, named Cook, not to put too fine a point on it. However, we had earlier visited that bay by ferry and, aside from the fact, which the careful reader might deduce, that this means that ferries go into that bay, today there was an actual big old fancy cruise ship in there. We reckoned that there were probably a lot of people on that boat, and since we don't like them, people that is, we changed our destination to Opunohu Bay. This bay is in every way as absurdly dramatic as Cook's Bay, and unlike Cook's, is a movie star. Yet instead of ferries and cruise ships, tonight it harbors merely three little old cruising boats counting *Maverick*. We'll have to take a bus or hitchhike to get to the t-shirt shops and tattoo parlors.

Tahaa Ha Ha

7:00 PM local time, Thursday, May 24. 16° 38.209'S 151° 29.283'W
Temp. 82, Humidity 67%, Cloud Cover 25%.
Baie Haamene, Tahaa, Iles de la Société, French Polynesia.

We weighed anchor Sunday the 20th at Moorea heading for Huahine. We had pleasant conditions and cleared the pass through the reef about 1:00 PM. It seemed a perfect day to sail there. As we have mentioned before, the weather since we left Rangiroa has been troublesome. There's been a big S-curve in the isobars around Tahiti for three weeks caused by various lows passing to the south and the wind has, as a result, been coming from the WNW. The pilot chart says this happens about 5% of the time, or approximately 1.5 days on average in the month of May, so we feel mistreated to have had the corresponding wet, squally, and unpredictable weather for over three weeks straight and we are writing for a refund. But Sunday we had wind from the NE, and since our destination was NW, we could fetch this easily.

By about sundown, though, we had been headed to the extent that it wasn't even possible to lay Huahine close-hauled. We were in fact ready for this since we didn't trust the good-looking weather yet, and as a result we had left on the 90-mile passage at noon, giving us 24 hours to be there early the following afternoon. This would only require that we average a little over 3.5 knots, so we could tack and still make it.

But as Mr. Shrode retired that evening and the Captain began his watch, the wind kicked up a notch and some squalls began blowing through with heavy rain. To the west was seen a tremendous amount of lightning. Lightning means thunderstorms, which means a lot of convection, which means unsettled and possibly troublesome weather. The Captain went below to view a weather fax that had just come in, and he saw a picture that set off the little alarm bell he keeps next to the bats and the picture of Annette Funicello in his belfry. To the west of us, a low. To the east of us, a high. We were in a newly formed "squash" zone, as the meteorologists call it, where winds from a low are amplified by winds from a high. It could get dicey, said his paranoid little mind.

Mr. Shrode was awakened at 0100 and for the first part of his watch saw the wind and rain ease a bit. But by morning, rainy, windy weather revisited us. We were about three miles from our waypoint about two miles off Huahine when a blinding squall hit and the Captain decided to heave-to until it passed, since visibility is desirable when approaching coral reefs.

Looking in our semi-reliable guidebook during this time, the crew found that the harbor to which we were heading on Huahine was not an "all weather" anchorage. Let's see, we said. High wind from a direction for which the anchorage gives little protection. Rain. Lightning. Thunder. Heavy chop. If that isn't all weather, it's a pretty big majority. So after an hour of no letup in the "squall" with the rail being put well under in the gusts so that we saw little fishies in the galley windows, we decided it might not pass and determined to head for Raiatea, which we were assured had better shelter.

We realized that by now, even motor sailing, we would be lucky to reach Raiatea, which was still 20 miles distant directly upwind, by mid afternoon and would still have to find an anchorage. The Captain felt it was not cause for terrible concern if we didn't make it in daylight, but it would be a genuine drag. We would probably get in the pass okay as it is well lit, but we had very poor American charts for the island and reef once we got inside and would face a crapshoot navigating. As we would not, therefore, want to enter the pass after dark, we could heave-to all night, which would take us at about two knots in the wrong direction, but we would not be in danger of hitting land. On the other hand, if the squash zone strengthened during this time, staying at sea would not be a good thing in still higher winds. So we really did want to get there.

Perhaps I failed to mention that the new belt for the autopilot we installed in Tahiti failed after only about two hours, so motor-sailing for all we were worth to Raiatea, we steered by hand. And after a sloppy, slow ride, we got to the pass into Raiatea about 3:00 PM.

Our US charts are far inferior in this area to the French ones, but we didn't have those. So we stopped at the fuel dock, asked advice from a local cruiser, and found our way through the marks to the anchorage he recommended. To our horror, the only spots available were in excess of 100 feet of water. This is the equivalent, for you Bay Area sailors, of dropping the hook in the middle of Raccoon Strait: 100 feet is eight stories down. But it was getting late, we were very tired, and finding another anchorage with our useless charts amidst a coral reef in the dying light was also out of the question. So we dropped it down there. Kinda creepy, if you ask the Captain, like sending your anchor off to a different universe.

We put out a scope of 3 to 1, which is 300 feet for you math buffs. We like to have 5 to 1 but let's get serious. That's 500 feet of chain. A very experienced cruiser near us told us that it doesn't matter how deep your anchor is, your swinging room remains the same when you're on chain. There is some truth to this if one can assume less than 5 knots of wind, but I inferred from his explanation that there also may have been a misunderstanding of the Pythagorean Theorem involved.

The Captain and Mr. Shrode

We thanked him, but since the Tahiti incident, thinking about swinging room had become somewhat of a sickness with the Captain to the discomfiture of Ship's Psychiatrist Terry Shrode. At about 1:00 AM the Captain made the calculation that the theoretical swinging radius for 300 feet of rode in 100 feet of water is 282.84271247461900976033774 feet, which means that after you set the anchor you need to estimate a diameter of, to round off, 565.68542494923801 feet and make sure nothing is there to hit. But that's not the end of it. The boat is 39 feet long, so if we add double this figure to the diameter, we get 643.68542494923801 feet, and this will keep the rudder off the reef. Of course, you must know exactly where your anchor is to make the appropriate judgment. 643.68542494923801 feet is, again rounding off, 16.50475448587789 boat lengths for *Maverick*.

The Captain awakened Mr. Shrode with this information. He added to Mr. Shrode of the raised eyebrows that due to catenary, the actual swinging room would depend on the wind strength and would probably never reach the above figure, but this added analysis failed to stimulate Mr. Shrode's full attention. The Captain, undeterred, suggested an anchor watch, to which, to be rid of him, Mr. Shrode readily agreed. We didn't drag that night, nor has *Maverick* on our watch ever dragged its anchor...yet.

Ashore in the Raiatea Carenage, we found the boat owned by the late Bernard Moitessier after *Joshua* was driven onto the beach in a hurricane. It was a very funky boat with mismatched galvanized rigging that was being worked on, I believe, by his girlfriend. The island itself was very charming, complete with a rainbow, if that's what it's called, that appeared along the side of a mountain and seemed to lie in the valley next to it instead of the sky where rainbows belong. But we were tired and the Captain was cranky and it seemed unnatural to be in that much water, and we wanted out of there. He wished for three days of settled weather, that's all.

We visited the Moorings dock, which was nearby, and bought their charts of Raiatea, Tahaa, and Bora Bora, and as they were very good, they eased the mind. We saw on the fax that the squash zone had strengthened but had moved south and west and was squishing the folks down there. We are now anchored and relaxing in Haamene Bay, Tahaa. We've decided we need some rest and fortunately the conditions seem to be giving it to us. The accumulation of three weeks of unsettled weather and dodgy anchorages and that nasty, short passage to Raiatea had taken their toll on the Captain's patience and this in itself is a lesson. But the Captain is aware that boats rarely come to grief because the skipper is too paranoid, although the crew very well may.

French Polynesia for Gentlemen

7:00 PM local time, Tuesday, May 29. 16° 36.942'S 151° 32.915'W
Temp. 86, Humidity 71%, Cloud Cover 35%.
Baie Vaiorea, Tahaa, Iles de la Société, French Polynesia.

Since departing Raiatea for Tahaa, we've heard the weather girl on the radio predicting "pretty skies," an aesthetic judgment we never get from NOAA, and indeed the weather has been very nice with light wind. We have been enjoying the sybaritic pleasures of normal cruising and are getting quite fat and listless. A man comes alongside in the morning with fresh croissants, fruit, baguettes, and a roasted chicken we can heat up for lunch. Much of the time we have fresh food and cold beer.

The reader will recognize to his dismay that this is not really the *Maverick* way, and indeed, the boys are a little out of sorts. Our long delay here is dictated by the fact that we expect our repaired prop to be shipped to Bora Bora, where we will sail tomorrow, and so, alas, we are for the nonce captive in French Polynesia. The Captain will leave it to you, our friends in this time of need, to conjure an image of our despair.

The Captain is quite aware that nothing one can imagine could possibly be less interesting to our readers at home than descriptions of snorkeling at coral reefs, relaxing on the beaches of small islands the locals call *motus* for who knows what reason, and having a sundowner before the beautiful tropical sunsets. What is wanted, we all feel, is adventure, and that won't be had sitting here in a nice anchorage with balmy weather. Soon, we will be puking over the side and eating out of cans, and when I mentioned this to Ship's Enthusiast Terry Shrode the other day, his eyes lit up like a Nintendo game.

In the meantime, the Captain will do what he can to entertain those of you following along at home with the results of his various ongoing scientific researches, and hopes this will serve as a yo-yo where a bungee jump is wanted.

First we have a report on the sociology of the Society Islands. The Captain has wondered about the tone of the relationship between the native islanders and their French governors. Can it be described as cordial? We approached cruisers with extensive experience in the area, and asked them if they would be so kind as to give us the benefit of their wisdom on this question. One of them reported that there was much hostility towards the French on the part of the Tahitians. The other reported there was very little hostility. The Captain and Mr. Shrode feel this about covers it, and have, therefore, closed their inquiry into the matter.

Now on to the flora and fauna. There is the issue of island dogs. No, not us, and that isn't even funny. We speak rather of *Canis lupus familiaris*. The dogs of French Polynesia we have observed since Hiva Oa are quite a depressed bunch, by normal dog standards. Do they wag their tails when you approach, and sniff and lick before asking? They do not. They regard your passing woefully, with a disinterest that verges on disdain. Nor do they chase the many chickens running about free but rather regard them also with a barely veiled contempt. They seem to be all of the same breed. Uncharacteristically, the Captain has no explanation for this.

We have found some very serious ivy, if one may use that botanically imprecise term, on the island of Tahaa. On yesterday's hike (which by the way ran to about 18 miles instead of six because of the *Maverick* crew's overestimation of the delight the locals might find in offering them a ride), ivy was observed in the act of devouring large coconut palm trees. The vine, as we saw it in various stages on different trees, climbs the trunk, puts out tendrils on the fronds, covers first one palm and then the others until only one terrified frond waves vainly, seemingly in a desperate plea, barely above the mass of growth, and then...silence. If Harvard and Yale had ivy like this, the professors would have such a job fighting it off, they'd hardly have time to strut around in their smarty-pants.

Roosters. They are everywhere here in this world the French call "Polynésie." How did they get the reputation for crowing, as Bob Dylan says, "at the break of dawn?" Roosters have the most ill-adjusted sense of time of any bird commonly encountered, and they will in fact crow quite without reason at any hour, day or night, while other more sensible birds are asleep or busy with the important business of life. Songbirds of various persuasions are far more reliable and can be trusted to sing, accurately, just at or before the break of dawn, depending on species. Please, Bob, consult the proper ornithological texts if you're going to call yourself a writer.

At long last the final item, the Tupa, or as we poetic Americans say, land crabs. We thought there were lots of gophers in French Polynesia until we saw crabs dash into their holes when we approached, which, by the way, gives one an immense feeling of power. The crabs live in these holes and, the Captain speculates, do a crab version of what gophers do, and here the imaginative mind boggles.

Bora Bora Bora

4:00 PM local time, Monday, June 4. 16° 30.036'S 151° 45.225'W
Temp. 85, Humidity 67%, Cloud Cover 65%.
Bora Bora Yacht Club, Bora Bora, Iles de la Société, French Polynesia.

Wednesday we left Tahaa for Bora Bora and anchored in front of the town of Vaitape a few hours later after an easy sail. The name Bora Bora, as you know, is but the native pronunciation of the venerable Yale fight song. The island's glamorous looks and large lagoon attract an army of admirers, who literally sit at her feet. Tahaa's sleepy, peaceful little villages are no match for the expensive resorts and hustle and bustle of her glitzy big sister, who is festooned with thatched huts over the water, chartered sailboats, helicopters giving rides to tourists, cruise ships, dive boats, and jet skis.

Chief Surgeon Terry Shrode has caught a bit of a bug, has a fever, and is resting in the Captain's quarters, which we have turned into sickbay. It seems odd not to have him up and around.

6:30 PM local time, Sunday, June 10. 16° 30.036'S 151° 45.225'W
Temp. 85, Humidity 73%, Cloud Cover 10%.
Bora Bora Lagoon, Bora Bora, Iles de la Société, French Polynesia.

Here in Bora Bora, the trade winds caress the hillsides and charm the lovely coconut palms into swaying fetchingly as though singing and dancing in harmony. Turquoise lagoon waters lap at the hull while majestic Mount Pahia benignly oversees the play of happy native children. Tourists take their ease at fabulous restaurants or join a mesmerizing dive with sharks and manta rays.

Down in the cabin, the Captain is focused on one thought: Is there no way out of this hellhole?

We have been stuck here since the 30th of May. The earliest we may leave, for a few reasons, is June 13. Although we've outrun, by quite some distance, every boat save one that left North America this season, we feel like we're getting behind. The prop arrived, but because of some admirable, but in this case overzealous, care on the part of FedEx, it sat in Papeete for four days before being shipped to Bora Bora, as they were unable to confirm we were here. This turned out to be a blessing in disguise, sort of, because on Sunday Terry came down with a fever that put him in bed for five straight days. He is just now recovering his strength. We are not sure what he had, but the best guess is the dreaded dengue fever, also know by the spooky and descriptive title, "breakbone fever," for which there is no treatment. In any case had there not been a delay in getting the prop, we would very likely have been at sea when he became incapacitated.

In the meantime, the prop, which, although improved, could not be returned to its pre-coral state, did arrive and a diver was hired to put it on. By this time, however, yet another problem had revealed itself in that the outboard motor, which had been giving us some trouble, started behaving in a way we could not diagnose. A very pleasant Tahitian outboard mechanic determined that the rod bearing was shot, and as we were not willing to spend the time to wait for yet another shipment from the US, a new motor had to be ordered from Papeete. Bora Bora is not, as the reader may imagine, an ideal location for discount shopping in boating supplies, but the alternative as we head to more remote areas is so indeterminate that this is the only reasonable option.

Perhaps Wednesday morning, if all goes well with the new outboard, dealing with the bank about our bond, and Terry's recovery, we may finally head to sea. The delays here and in Papeete mean we have crossed both Raratonga in the Cook Islands and Samoa off our list. At this moment the thinking is to go straight to Tonga, with a possible stop in either Nuie or Suwarrow, two rather exotic destinations on the way.

Dinnertime

9:25 PM local time, Saturday, June 16^h, 2001. 17 43 S 159 16 W
Temp. 82, Humidity 84%, Cloud Cover 20%.

We finally got out of Bora Bora Wednesday morning. After a nice start, a front came through with 40 knots and 15-foot seas for about ten hours, then left us with rain, no wind, and a bumpy sea. It's now Saturday night, the skies have cleared a bit, and we're close reaching in light air. It's dinnertime in this odd piece of the trade winds.

Ship's Culinary Specialist Terry Shrode has taken on the preparation of dinner as one of his many contributions to the ship's well-being, partly in self-defense. His Pineapple Princess Ham Parts, mentioned in an earlier episode, was a great success, as are all, or at least many, of his meals, born, most often, of canned goods assembled in quite a merry fashion. Cooking while underway is not easy, and we can liken it to strapping a small kitchenette to oneself like a hot dog vendor at a ballpark, then mounting a horse and trotting around in a circle cutting up vegetables and stirring a boiling pot.

If conditions are benign, as they sometimes are, and the weather is balmy, as it often is, onto the stereo goes some music, which can vary widely, although not so widely as to include Jimmy Buffett, and this immediately changes the feeling aboard. Perhaps a tape of oldies is put on, and we may hear the Penguins or Little Eva or the Dovells or Little Shorty Long (who looks as if he may never have been to sea before), and the Captain is transported to a time when he thought if he just concentrated hard enough, the girl next to him at the beach party, for whom he was willing to endure the sand grinding his sunburn, might realize that she ought to give him some signal that she wouldn't mind if he held her hand, and whatever might happen next he could not think as the hand-holding itself was so great a thing to imagine he couldn't visualize anything beyond it, and for all he knew it would cause him to vanish into the sky and become a constellation. Or when those girls on American Bandstand used to sit in their seats and bounce and twirl their hands to the music, between clapping on the backbeat, in a manner thought-provoking for a person of his age, and wear their hair all teased, which didn't help every girl but was used to limb-loosening effect by Brigitte Bardot and Britt Ekland and Elke Sommer, and—in the interest of full and complete disclosure—lovely Theresa Fisher, our very own email monitor, and Terry's beautiful wife Caroline. I'm not lyin'.

Then we're back on a small boat in the Pacific Ocean, and out comes some delicious concoction from Mr. Shrode and as the sun sets and we eat our meal, we hear "Running Bear" (the tragedy of which song could have been averted had the two lovers but worn their life vests), and "For Your Precious Love" and "Stranded In The Jungle" and "One Fine Day" and "You Talk Too Much" and "Lavender Blue" and it is difficult for the Captain not to compromise his level of military alertness by falling into a reverie upon the puzzling bounty of life. It seems it ought to be possible to put all of the hilarious, amazing, sexy, revelatory, soulful, untethered, ecstatic, and sensual things you've ever experienced together in your mind at the same time, like a computer uploading a significant portion of the hard drive into RAM and displaying it all on the screen simultaneously. But if you could do that for even 1/100th of all the good things, your brain would just pop like a balloon.

Mr. Shrode has retired now and the Captain is left with just Luigi (our spinnaker) for company. We don't always have a moon out here anymore than you do on land, but tonight on the second watch we will, so in honor of that we'll put the needle down on a Blast from the Past Built to Last, a Solid Smash That Brought Home the Cash, a Golden Nugget cuz You Dug It, a Groove That Time Could Not Improve: one from the Capris entitled "There's a Moon Out Tonight" and this one goes out to Theresa from Tony, to Caroline from Terry, and to all the rest of our friends, especially the ones out there sailing their ships alone tonight, from the crew of *Maverick*, ghosting through a starry night, in a quiet neighborhood of Paradise.

WHAT'S NIUE?

6:35 PM local time, Saturday, June 23. 19° 3.240'S 169° 55.397'W
Temp. 83, Humidity 80%, Cloud Cover 80%.
On a mooring at Niue

We had a 10-day crossing from Bora Bora to Niue, which is a little over 1,000 miles. Nothing particularly awful happened to entertain you with.

Few people come here because it's a bit weird for a yacht and the airlines don't have regular flights. It's sitting out here by itself, measures about 6 by 8 miles, is politically affiliated with New Zealand, and they call it "The Rock of Polynesia," and I mean, on the VHF radio they say, "Welcome to the Rock of Polynesia." It seems to be kind of the Mayberry of the South Pacific. You call Radio Niue, which is associated with the AM radio station, on the VHF to ask them, of course, how to arrange for customs, and they tell you to stand by, while they call up the customs guy and tell him to get down to the office. Then they come back on and say fine, come on in. When you go to customs, you notice there's an open door between them and the liquor store, which the customs guy is kind enough to give a plug, not failing to mention our duty-free status.

On the radio we call the Niue Yacht Club, which is also the car rental place, and we ask the nice lady there whether it's too late on Friday to get New Zealand dollars from the bank. She says the bank closes at 3:00 and we've already missed it but come on by and she'll take care of us for the weekend. We go by and she gives us New Zealand dollars, which by the way have a window in them, and charges it to our credit card, plus of course a little fee and who knows what exchange rate. Can she do that? Is that a black market thing?

There's not really a yacht club in the sense that there is a place that is the Niue Yacht Club, unless you call the car rental place a yacht club. There's not even a bar at the car rental place, so you can tell it's not really a yacht club. Nonetheless, your correspondent, the Captain, now possesses a burgee (a small banner with a yacht club's insignia), so it must exist. And indeed we were better taken care of there than at the yacht clubs with bars that don't let us in.

Now Mary at the car rental place/yacht club is also a wealth of information and connections. She says, anything you need, if you can't get us on the radio, just call up Radio Niue on channel 16 and they'll call us at home and we'll call you on the VHF. No problems, mate. We ask her about where to get a bite to eat, and she recommends a place or two and then we ask her if they're serving yet. She says, wait, and she tries to call Lava. Hot Lava, as it turns out she calls herself, runs a snack shop. She calls the snack shop but it's disconnected, so she calls Lava's home number, which is also disconnected, and so she calls somebody else, I don't know, Lava's boyfriend, or sister, or aunt, and asks where she is and whether she's at the snack shop and when she's going to open for dinner. Well, the best she can do is say, I think she opens at 6:00 so just go over there and find her and tell her to feed you. So we go over there and no one's around but the neighbor across the street says, Lava's downtown, and folks she's exaggerating since there can't really be a place here they call downtown, can there?...but anyway, she'll be back in a minute. Which was about a half hour, but Terry and I, we're starving to death cuz the last two days were pretty rough and we ate, maybe one bowl of soup each for 48 hours. So while we wait, we go to the auto parts store, which, of course, has ice cream cones. As we're walking there and back, no one at all fails to wave first.

Friday Night at the Races

8:15 PM local time, Saturday, June 30. 18° 39.424'S 173° 58.987'W
Temp. 78, Humidity 67%, Cloud Cover 80%.
On a mooring at Neiafu, Vava'u, Tonga

We left wonderful little Niue about 0200 Monday morning. After studying the fax, we expected light wind and had planned two and a half days (plus a very short one for the international date line) to make the 225 miles to Tonga. Unfortunately, the wind soon built to 25 knots, so we went fast and ended up having to stand off for 12 hours, which was pretty ugly. When we got into the harbor, there was quite a boating scene and we checked a weather warning posted at the local yachtie hangout. It said it was blowing 25 and seas were rough. Now we know. I may have occasion to expand on this at some other time, but for now let's just say if you're wondering where we are, dial up a weather fax of the South Pacific. If there's a low between 10 and 20 degrees south, we'll be under it.

The check-in wasn't so delightful and involved some tight maneuvering around a container ship and tying up to a pretty nasty wharf not meant for little boats. Customs had to inspect the boat and would not come out by dinghy.

The next day the *Maverick* boys were minding their own business at the fuel dock, having just topped off the tanks and filled the jerry cans, when a middle-aged woman who was bending sails on a nearby 25-footer asked us if we were going to be racing that night. We had heard something about there being races here on Friday nights but had just gotten in Thursday and hadn't gotten all the facts.

"When is it?"

"Well, the skipper's meeting was at 4:00 and the warning is at 4:25."

I looked at my watch. It was 4:18.

"We're gonna have to pass. We'll never make it."

Liaison Officer Terry Shrode began to explain that the deck was strewn with unsecured gear, including all of our jerry cans, fenders, and fender boards, while I went below. Mr. Shrode came into the cabin about a minute later and briefed me on the rest of the conversation, as is SOP after contacts with hostiles.

"She said, 'Yeah, we always try to get the cruisers to race, but (here the Captain must unfortunately sacrifice his ordinary standards of decorum in the higher interest of veracity; women and children should avert their eyes) they're such pussies they never do.'"

A meaningful look was exchanged. I shook my head and sighed a sigh of resignation. I disembarked and asked the attendant at the dock whether it would be possible to leave some gear there temporarily while we participated in the race. At his okay, the above-mentioned items were summarily ejected from the boat, the engine was started, and I took a glance at the hand-drawn chart of the race course the enemy had in her possession, which she was sporting enough to offer. Noting which marks were to be taken to starboard, which to port, I returned the chart, jumped behind the wheel, and we were off. I shouted the boat name to the race committee at the dock, and they put us down. On the way out to the line, where the participants were already maneuvering for the start, we tore down the Bimini, doused the lazy jacks, hoisted the main, unfurled the genoa, and manned our stations. The American flag was proudly flying as *Maverick* prepared for baneful war.

The start itself was exciting, with a lot of boats on the line and much yelling. We could almost hear this from our position some distance back. Even though we had seen the chart, as we crossed the line, we had absolutely no idea where the first mark was, but the good news was the rest of the boats knew, and they were all in front of us. Unfortunately, at the windward mark, we had reason to worry, as there was only one boat left to pass.

Now most of these boats were chartered Beneteau 38s and 41s from Sunsail and the Moorings with some locals, actually Kiwi expatriates, driving, but there were some other local boats and one or two other cruisers. You can be sure the Beneteaus were sailing on their marks and not six inches below their waterline, as a result of not needing hundreds of pounds of fuel, water, food, spares, and other junk aboard. They also owed us anywhere from three to 35 seconds. But never mind, we're from San Francisco.

We gave chase to the leader and left the rest well behind. We gained on him the whole race but in the end were beaten by a boat length, much of which could have been made up if we had known on which side of the pin we were to finish. The winner, to whom, not to brag, we gave 15 boat lengths, was the local ringer who wins every week. We got breakfast at a local eatery, which turned out to be terrible, I'm afraid. However, we're lucky we didn't win, because the first prize was two bottles of wine, and we'd sure feel worse today after that. If we're here next Friday, we'll go to the skipper's meeting.

So Longa, Tonga

7:40 local time, Tuesday, July 10).
18 04 S 175 49 W
Temp. 84, Humidity 72%, Cloud Cover 20%.
Seas S 1.5 meters. Wind S 6k.

We're at sea en route from the Kingdom of Tonga to Fiji and hope to arrive this weekend. There's very light wind and we're making about 2.5 knots.

Last Friday night there was another race. We still blew the start, as the race committee decided to use some unusual timing for the shapes and we didn't pick up on it. Still, by the second leg, we had put away the Beneteaus, and with Master Helmsman Terry Shrode at the wheel on the third, downwind leg, we passed the only boat that gave us trouble, another cruiser, a half mile from the finish. We got the two bottles of wine for first but fortunately had to share them with two extra crew, some Kiwis we invited along, who of course claimed credit for the win when all they really did was talk in that silly accent.

Tonga is quite a bit poorer than Niue or any other place we've been, yet in the countryside the native people are just as friendly. In the small city of Neiafu, however, they are often quite curt at the commercial establishments. We have come to believe that Polynesian culture does not easily bend itself to the demands of commerce. There are traditional, pre-capitalist customs here about how trade is carried on. They make as much sense to the people here as our culture does to us, but they are not particularly conducive to the efficient operation of small businesses. Whether the efficient operation of small businesses is the *sine qua non* of civilization is a question that is beyond the Captain's mandate. In any case, the result is that Europeans run most thriving shops, even on the islands like Niue and the Tonga group which are governed by the native people.

We rented bikes to have a look around. In the countryside of Vavau, people come out of their houses to say hello as you pedal by. We came across some young vintners, who gave us a sample of the latest batch of what they called "brown wine." The Captain cannot share with his readers the ingredients, which, even though they gave them to us, are secret, but in any case a feeling of general conviviality was the result.

We also took in a native feast on Tonga. The Captain prepared himself for the worst sort of tourist spectacle but what we got was the most unaffected entertainment imaginable. There was great singing, primarily by a quartet of middle-aged men featuring very pure harmonies but often joined by the ensemble. The dancers, mostly between the ages of 4 and 15, were in all stages of learning the moves but this in no way detracted from their charm, particularly considering we didn't know what the moves were supposed to be either. The food was interesting if unidentifiable, and the Captain was discovered trying to eat one of the utensils. After we dined, we were serenaded by the quartet who joined us in drinking kava, about which the Captain may have more to say anon.

In addition to these amusements, we enjoyed the many interesting features of the island group including a place called Mariner's Cave. In order to get inside, you swim up to a cliff face in the open bay and dive down about three feet where you find a tunnel through the rock. You must swim through this for about 20 feet in blackness underwater, gaining the surface again on the inside, where you find yourself in a large cavern. The ceiling towers overhead, and the bottom is visible deep in the water below. As the swells cause the water to rise, increased pressure creates a fog, which disappears as the swell recedes. The Captain was too blind without his glasses to enjoy this phenomenon, but eagle-eyed Shrode has verified its existence.

Pre-Frontal Geometry

2:00 PM local time, Sunday, July 15 (0200 July 15th UTC).
16° 46.643'S 179° 19.908'E
Temp. 82, Humidity 76%, Cloud Cover 40%.
On a mooring at the Copra Shed Marina, Savusavu Bay, Vanua Levu, Fiji.

We picked up a mooring here Saturday. The careful reader will have noticed that our longitude now puts us east of the 180th meridian, no longer in the western hemisphere. We are almost 60 degrees west of San Francisco, or nearly 1/6 of the way, in longitude, around the globe. [For archivists and academics, we will henceforth try to remember to include our date and time at Greenwich, England, in our chapter headings. This is either to avoid confusion, or create it. I can't be sure. Our local time, since departing Tonga and crossing the International Date Line, is now ahead of, not behind, Greenwich Mean Time.]

Our passage from Tonga continued a pattern we have adhered to without exception since Papeete. We leave on a splendid day with either light wind or none at all and have good weather information that our passage will be benign. Two days before arrival, we have 30 knots and rough seas. The most crucial time of the passage is closing the coast and entering a strange harbor. One would like to be fresh and rested. This is particularly desirable when approaching Fiji, where the distance between being near the first islands and actually in the harbor is over 100 miles of islands and coral reefs. As a sailboat can't make more than 6 or 7 knots, it is impossible to do all of this part of the passage during daylight hours. At night one must rely on radar, GPS, and charts that are not very accurate in this area. The Captain shudders to think about doing this run into Fiji with a sextant. Even with modern instruments, when the weather is gentle and one is rested, it is somewhat of a challenge to make it safely. But the crew of *Maverick* was tired before we entered Fijian waters, and the weather was rough.

On the morning of Thursday the 12th, we were in 8-10 knots with Luigi overseeing things, and we were sailing along at about 4 knots in smooth seas, without a care in the world. The Captain noticed to the south an impressive bank of clouds stretching from horizon to horizon, paralleling our course. He reasoned that clouds mean weather, and there was an occluded front on the weather fax in that vicinity, so here was a care for you. But we had a very specific and impressive forecast for mariners from the day before, predicting that for the next 48 hours and probably beyond, we would have light winds from the NE, which is what we currently were seeing. The weather forecast was so detailed, authoritative, and elegant, in fact, that we could almost forgive its being dead wrong.

By noon on the 12th, we had 30 knots from the south and building seas. We soon realized that we had a problem in terms of timing our approach to the islands. It's about 115 miles from the approach from seaward through the islands and reefs of Fiji to get to our port of entry at Savusavu. But we do not want to attempt navigating through the pass in the reef surrounding the harbor in darkness, and we do not want to be hanging around in the vicinity of reefs near the pass, which are poorly marked if at all by aids to navigation, through long hours at night in heavy winds. Complicating the situation, the speed and direction of the wind for the duration, which will determine our progress, can only be guessed at, as our confidence in the weather broadcasts has been shattered. So the Captain laboriously figured the speed/time/distance calculations to come up with a safe time window to attempt the passage through the outer islands, the objective being to arrive at the harbor entrance in daylight.

The result was that the conservative move, the prudent move, the unpleasant move, was to heave-to well off of the islands of Fiji, in the open ocean where there's nothing to hit, and then to proceed to the waypoint where we would turn into the islands. This is what we did, in 30 knots. It would be the second time in a row we had to stand off all night in 25+ knots at the end of a passage. Now the Captain must calculate how long to heave-to so that we don't get there too early on Saturday, and we don't get there too late. And, incidentally, so we don't die, as a sailor did here in March.

As the Captain sat in the cockpit on his watch running through these dreary but necessary scenarios and making the calculations in his head, his stomach engaged in *Maverick's* weight-loss program because sailing in light air doesn't set your tummy for the rough stuff. He determined we would heave-to until 0400 and go for it, leaving, he hoped, a safety margin in either direction, and this information was passed along to Officer of the Watch Terry Shrode as he was awakened at 0100. The Captain retired.

Dutifully, Mr. Shrode began sailing for the waypoint at 0400. We were there at around noon on the 13th, and indeed, by that time the wind had changed direction. We headed up to just above a beam reach, but to keep the speed down to our target of 5 knots, we had about ten feet of jib unfurled, and two reefs in the main.

Then, soon after we made the turn, there was an awful vision. After spotting the first Fijian island, we saw a ketch that at first looked like it was heeled over, but as we stared at it we realized it was on its side, on the reef. We had seen this boat back in Tonga. It had left a couple of days before us, and now it had foundered and was never to sail again. The skipper, a very experienced single-hander, saved himself, but not the boat that was his only home. (The boat's name was *Fearless*, and some sailors discussing this later in the safety of the bar at the Savusavu Yacht Club thought, as sailors will, that perhaps the name itself foreshadowed her doom.)

There is no question that at this point the crew of *Maverick* was tired and unwell, and had lost their sense of humor. We thought about being home, clean and warm, and snuggled up and safe in a comfortable bed. Mr. Shrode considered reminding the Captain of our oft-repeated saying, that when you really would vastly prefer to be back at home sitting in traffic on the way to work, you know you're on an adventure. And yet he decided, with his characteristic wisdom, against so reminding him. As we worried about the fact that things could indeed get much worse, we refocused our attention on the task ahead. We had to keep a close watch for the next 24 hours, and all would be well.

As Mr. Shrode retired for a nap, the weather cleared, the wind eased, the seas flattened, and the front headed north of us in a definite line. All was right again with the world. Then something happened that is probably not new to weather but was new to the Captain. The front looked down on *Maverick*, thought, "Did we miss those guys?" and backed up and ran over us again, like the old joke, just to make sure we were dead. And it blew hard all the way to Savusavu.

Savusavu and the Road to Lambasa

8:30 AM local time, Saturday, July 21 (2030 July 20th UTC).
16° 46.643'S 179° 19.908'E
Temp. 79, Humidity 87%, Cloud Cover 80%.
On a mooring at the Copra Shed Marina, Savusavu Bay, Vanua Levu, Fiji.

If, during the long, dark last night of the passage to Fiji, it seemed to the boys as though they were in a dungeon of physical and psychological purgatory, when they arrived in Savusavu, they felt, as they often do at the end of a passage, like they had landed on the very doorstep of paradise.

Upon entering Na Kama Creek, a boat came out to greet us and lead us to a mooring. It was manned by Geoff Taylor, an Olympic Finn sailor and the energetic kingpin of the small but vibrant local yachting scene. He helped us with formalities and at a meeting the next night, he and the rest of the Savusavu Yacht Club officers apologized for the lack of festivities upon our arrival. They have graciously scheduled a regatta and welcoming feast for this coming weekend, complete with native dancing and food. Okay, it's not really just in *Maverick's* honor but the truth is that the welcome we've received here outshines that of any other country where we've made landfall, even Niue. Geoff is scheduling two races. In the morning, the cruisers will be at the helm of Optimist dinghies and local kids, who have become hotshot sailors under Geoff's coaching, will be in the boat calling tactics. Later, the kids will crew on the cruisers' boats for a big boat race.

Speaking of races, Fiji seems as integrated as anyplace the Captain has ever been. During the recent coup, rebels took over the local police station and when the army came in to retake it, the rebels were viciously beaten. Yet today we see no extra security on the streets, and the native Fijians, East Indians, and whites (who are a very small minority) seem on quite friendly terms. You will see all cultures drinking together at the bar at the Savusavu Yacht Club, which is more than can be said about any yacht club in oh-so-liberal San Francisco. As it stands, the political tensions haven't hampered our visit. Next month, however, there are elections, and we'd like to be out of here by then.

Fiji consists of two large islands, Vanua Levu, where we are, and Viti Levu to the south, where we'll soon sail. In addition, there are 330 more islands that are much smaller. The big islands are larger than any others we've visited, more than twice the size of Tahiti, for example, and they are big enough to have different ecosystems. Ship's Tour Guide Terry Shrode and the Captain took a three-hour bus ride over the mountains from Savusavu to Lambasa that began with the silly redundancy of verdure that reminded us of Tahaa. But soon we were in a high valley reminiscent of Wyoming, even though the pines were mixed with tree ferns. Down on the leeward side of the island, there were rolling hills of farmland given over to the cultivation of sugarcane. Throughout, the beauty fell on the Captain's eyes in cloudbursts, like sheets of rain. The town of Lambasa was dusty and worn, and apparently populated mostly by Indians. Fiji is the first country we've come to in the South Pacific that is not uniformly Christian, and along the road and in town we saw examples of Hindu art and architecture. We didn't linger in the city but after a lunch of curried lamb, took the first bus back, and the return trip was just as mesmerizing as the trip out, as we passed small villages where women sold refreshments to bus passengers through the windows much as is done at train stations in Europe.

At the yacht club bar the next day, your correspondent met Malcolm, a 60-year-old retiree from the communications field in England. Three years ago he met and married a local woman of Fijian and Chinese descent and moved to her family place in the country (the "bush") to farm grog, which is slang for kava. Malcolm's wife's farm is barely self-sustaining for the eight people who live there under a tin roof. There is no electricity and water is brought in from the creek, where laundry is also done. Malcolm is well educated and sophisticated, articulate, very pleasant, a good drinker, and he and his wife seem about as happy as anyone anywhere might hope to be.

Kava Jive

10:00 PM local time, Monday, July 23 (1000 July 23rd UTC).
16° 46.643'S 179° 19.908'E
Temp. 76, Humidity 89%, Cloud Cover 90%.
On a mooring at the Copra Shed Marina, Savusavu Bay, Vanua Levu, Fiji.

A local historian here told your correspondent that Fiji was originally colonized by Yale University in the third century, but the colony was pillaged by a seagoing band of Picts a few hundred years later and destroyed. I tended to dismiss this until I met a Fijian from the bush who otherwise spoke no English but could give a perfect rendition of the Whiffenpoof song. The clincher is that the universal greeting of Fiji, usually repeated, is "bula," for "hello."

And there were many "bulas" on Friday night last when the Savusavu Yacht club hosted a traditional welcoming ceremony for the most recent arrivals, perhaps six boats. Presided over by a village elder, the "sevusevu" ceremony involves primarily a ritualized preparation and serving of what the common folk call *grog* to honored guests. Grog, which is English slang for the pepper plant *piper methysticum*, is also known as *kava*, which is the more common Tongan word for the Fijian *yaqona*, pronounced "yanggona."

Grog is an important part of Fijian life. It might seem weird to a westerner that even sessions of the legislature here begin by drinking an intoxicating beverage, but then the elder Bush will be remembered by some of us for barfing after a toast at a Japanese banquet among heads of state. Smoking a pipe was a ritual in Native American culture, and of course alcohol, pot, coke, and tips on IPOs were ritualized offerings in, respectively, the 1950s, '60s, '70s, and '80s in, let's face it, mainstream American culture. The drinking of yaqona, like the use of the above substances, is also enjoyed in Fiji on informal occasions.

Your correspondent, the Captain, in his singular quest for a full scientific account of the Fijian experience, subjected himself without regard for personal safety to this ritual. He joined others in a circle around a special bowl, the *tanoa*, wherein the yaqona was prepared. Upon the guest's clapping once, which essentially calls for a round starting with himself, the host passes to him, with great ceremony, the *bilo*, which is a half coconut shell filled with the yaqona. The beverage tastes like ground-up parts of a bush, which of course is just what it is. The guest drains it in one draft and the others of the assembly clap three times, in apparent approval of his effort, and this is repeated around the circle throughout the evening as appropriate, or until there is no more yaqona, or, one presumes, until there is no one left who is conscious.

Kava, as it is more widely known, is a mild soporific. During the worldwide search for legal drugs which went on in the '60s, kava apparently seems to have escaped the notice of the hippie movement as well as the authorities. It's still legal, sold in health food stores, and not controlled in the US. In fact, a man was arrested in the SF Bay Area for driving under the influence of kava, but the case was dropped on the quite reasonable grounds that, as his lawyer pointed out, there is no law in California against driving under the influence of kava, not to mention no legal standards for the point at which one becomes "drunk," and that the state can't go around arresting people for things that aren't against the law.

The Captain, in his effort to provide the reader with an accurate report on yaqona's effects, drank about 12 cups, which is not a trivial amount and indeed quite a bit more than the amount consumed by the rest of the yachties, who wandered off after two or three cups, thus proving themselves to be mere tourists. As the session developed, the Captain followed his kava quaffs with beer chasers as his hosts were doing and which they told him was fine, even recommended. The Captain confesses—and would appreciate the reader's keeping this to himself or herself and especially not sharing it with the youngsters—that he has been, on more than one occasion in his life, more intoxicated than he was that evening. Nevertheless, he would fall short of adhering to the standard of professional reportage that his readers have come to expect if he claimed that he was not "toasted." In the wee hours of the morning, the Captain awakened from his stupor and allows he felt quite strange.

The next day the scheduled regatta was cancelled because of lack of wind and as the Captain was feeling the effects of the previous night and in addition had seen the frightening talent of the young Fijian sailors, he will admit to having been a bit relieved. But that evening a native feast called a *lovo* was offered, which did not depend on the wind. Linguists may theorize on the word's derivation from the same root as "luau," for the meal was similarly prepared on hot stones in a shallow hole in the ground upon which food was placed, then covered with leaves and left to cook. The result was quite delicious, with, the Captain must say with apologies, the exception of taro, which really needs a sauce or something.

I TELL YOU NO LAU

10:00 PM local time, Tuesday, July 31 (1000 July 31 UTC).
18° 7.352'S 178° 25.481'E
Temp. 78, Humidity 78%, Cloud Cover 10%.
At anchor at the Royal Suva Yacht Club, Suva, Fiji.

We arrived in Suva, Fiji's capital, Wednesday at about 4:00 after a 26 hour, 120-mile sail from Savusavu. Suva is a big city, the most modern we've seen since leaving California.

Our obituary of *Fearless*, the boat we saw on the reef as we entered Fijian waters, was premature. Some cruisers who had a powerful pump came along, after the owner had salvaged sails and gear and abandoned the yacht, and managed to pump it out, fix the leak, and refloat it at high tide springs. It was a stoutly built steel ketch or it never would have survived. The owner, who handled himself with great dignity through the whole ordeal, seemed near tears when he gave me this news the day he heard it. He and another cruiser headed out with sails, a handheld VHS, and a handheld GPS, and managed to sail *Fearless* back the 120 miles to Savusavu without engine or any electric power. His companion reported that taking it through the reef into Savusavu Bay, which the skipper decided to attempt at night with no engine or radar, was one of the most stressful things he had ever done.

On the topic of driving under the influence of kava discussed in the previous post, apparently there has been another arrest in California. It turns out that the law against driving under the influence, at least as interpreted by San Mateo County Superior Court Judge Quentin Kopp, not a liberal, does not in fact require that the substance in question be actually named in the statute. He ruled that "actual notice of each drug constituting a basis for prosecution under Section 23152(a) is not required if a person is reasonably made aware of the proscribed conduct, namely, impaired driving ability resulting from ingestion of some substance." Watch out, Sudafed users.

On to some general culture notes. By now it will come as no surprise to our readers that western arts have a fan base in the South Pacific. Three very popular TV shows in Fiji are *Oprah, ER,* and, right before the Fiji news, *Get Smart.* While we were waiting in the Australian consulate for our visas, we watched MTV and were entertained by Destiny's Child, O-Town, and N-Sync. Today in the hardware store we heard a Dolly Parton tune. A couple of days ago we went to a very modern Cineplex and saw a movie called *Captain Kangaroo's Mandolin* or some such starring Nicolas Cage, of whom Ship's Movie Critic and Historian Terry Shrode is a fan, and Penelope Cruz. In general we could have been in Ohio, so sophisticated was the presentation.

On the other hand, there is an island group in Fiji called the Lau Group, where, to hear some tell it, people really do run around in grass skirts and live in thatched huts. We cruisers are currently prohibited from going there, the reason vaguely being something about modern people corrupting the natives, so of course the Captain's interest has been at a high pitch. We have heard that if you have enough money, you can pay the right people who in turn pay the right people and as a result your going there will not be reported to those who like to have such things reported to them, or if it is, they might be watching *Get Smart* just at that moment and not hear about it. This, of course, is *not* seen as corruption of the natives. In any case, the Captain is quite beside himself with shame to have to admit to our readers that, because no provision was made for this sort of expenditure in *Maverick's* budget, he is unable to provide a report on the Lau Group of Fiji.

But it just seems plain odd that we can't go there. Exactly what do they think? Do they think that if the Captain and Mr. Shrode do not visit these precious places, the people residing therein will never, ever hear of our Britney? And is that a good thing? Are they Christian? Is that a traditional Fijian religion? Are they an exhibit, these primitives, with no audience permitted but an odd assembly of missionaries, anthropologists, and Greenpeace activists? Aren't they smart enough to decide for themselves if the crew of *Maverick* are a corrupting influence, as so many others have? Does the chief make these decisions for them?

Aren't they just like real people? And don't they have relatives in the big city? Most folks do. Don't they tell them anything about, like, the latest stuff? So maybe they don't want to hear about it. Don't you think they have some brother-in-law who wears loud shirts and just won't stop going on about Jennifer Lopez or his new cell phone? Do they put their hands over their ears and yell so they don't find out who won the rugby match against Australia or about the fact that, with a computer and a telephone line you can now sit on your island, check out a fishhook catalogue, and get back to your brother-in-law by email if and when you feel like it? Do these people know that the earth revolves around the sun? That many diseases have cures? Maybe I'm whacked, but let's go tell them, that's what I propose, and then see what they think. The Prime Directive is SCIENCE FICTION.

PS: It just occurred to me, after re-reading the above, that maybe they just keep us out because we're annoying.

Malolo Lailai

8:30 PM local time, Sunday, August 12 (0830 August 12 UTC).
17° 46.280'S 177° 11.286'E
Temp. 78, Humidity 62%, Cloud Cover 0%.
At anchor at the Musket Cove Yacht Club, Malolo Lailai, Fiji.

On the 4th of August, we weighed anchor in Suva just after noon for an overnight sail to the west side of Viti Levu, the southernmost of the two largest Fijian islands. After clearing the reef at Suva, we had about a 100-mile sail to enter the pass through the reef on the western side, and as usual we tried to plan it so that we would not leave or enter either pass in the dark. A front passed during the night and we had lots of rain and lightning, but the wind never went above 20 and the seas were moderate, so we counted it an easy passage. There was plenty of navigation to do through the night and several major wind shifts, so the watches never got boring.

We worked our way through the reefs surrounding Malolo Lailai Sunday morning and anchored in 60 feet, half a mile from the famous Musket Cove Yacht Club. The Captain and Mr. Shrode became life members of the yacht club, and for this privilege the Captain paid $1 Fijian while the crew had to pony up $5. We now have full use of the facilities at the Musket Cove Resort, which include showers, swimming pool, laundry room, lounge chairs on the beach, and access to the stores, bar, and restaurant. Got a burgee, hat, and shirt, too, though these were extra. The island of Malolo Lailai has no native villages and is occupied by several large resorts. If you were to fly to the South Pacific for a getaway, most likely this kind of resort would comprise the majority of your holiday experience. The only Fijians you would see, for the most part, would be employees. Once again this reporter has sacrificed personal preference and safety, this time to subject himself unrelentingly to the total resort experience, strictly for the purpose of providing you, the paying customer, with the most up-to-date, reliable data available. It's not something we're proud of, but it comes with the territory in our line of work.

The Musket Cove Yacht Club sponsors a race every year from here to Port Vila, Vanuatu, in September. The tone of the race can be inferred from a few of the rules. For one, the boat that crosses the finish line first is automatically disqualified, unless its skipper can provide credible proof of blatant cheating. Penalties (and possible disqualification if the infractions are serious enough) may be incurred by yachts whose crew wear Sperry topsiders or hoist light air sails. Fortunately, the crew of

Maverick will be well on its way by the time the race starts, for this is just the kind of foolishness we, as the reader well knows, disdain.

From the day we got here, we have had the most perfect weather we have seen in the nearly five months since we began our voyage. Sunny days and mild breezes have affected the crew like heroin, giving them a feeling of euphoria without their having to do a thing to merit it. The listlessness they experienced back in Bora Bora was at least interrupted by squalls and fairly strong winds at the anchorages, but here there is nothing to challenge even the most rudimentary consciousness. Malolo Lailai sure rolls off the tongue, though, doesn't it?

As has been noted before, nothing could be more annoying, nay, infuriating to read about than the happy times of others, so we will leave the specifics to the reader's imagination, and ring off until time provides us with more serviceable material for stories of the high adventures of the crew of *Maverick*.

FIJIPHILIA

7:30 AM local time, Thursday, August 23 (1930 August 22 UTC).
17° 38.690'S 177° 23.541'E
Temp. 79, Humidity 71%, Cloud Cover 90%.
At anchor at Saweni Bay, Viti Levu, Fiji.

The South Pacific Convergence Zone is a trough of low pressure that appears and disappears mysteriously over our whole route from Papeete through Tonga and Fiji up to the Solomons, sometimes extending 50 degrees in longitude and 20 in latitude. Not to be confused with the Intertropical Convergence Zone (the Doldrums), this zone brings unpredictable bad weather and wind, and has bedeviled Ship's Weather Forecaster Terry Shrode and the Captain since Papeete. Some years it appears more often than others, or is stronger, and this is one of those years, it seems.

Last Thursday, the weather services predicted 30 knots from the north. Since Malolo Lailai, where we were, is a well-protected anchorage from that direction, we delayed our departure to Viti Levu, as the anchorages we were headed for were open to northerlies. On Thursday we got torrential rain but little wind, and on Friday morning the wind built to 35 with gusts to 45, but it was from the *south*. In the Captain's weaker moments, he thinks the weather services would be doing us a big favor if they just said, "Tomorrow there will probably be more wind than usual from one direction or another." At least we would not get the idea that they actually know something that no one really knows. But they're trying their best, in their warm, dry little offices.

So instead of moving to Viti Levu, where we would have been well protected from a southerly, we stayed put. What happens in an anchorage protected from the ocean by reefs, like Malolo Lailai is to the south, is that at high tide, the protection is minimized because the reefs are four to five feet beneath the surface and thus do not blunt the ocean's energy. On Friday we were right before a new moon so with high winds all day—to reiterate, from the south—it got stressful, with two to three feet of chop. Two boats had their mooring lines part and very quickly fetched up on the reef. One boat was pulled off by some fast action by local boats, but the other, a 100-year-old wooden boat named *AnneBeth*, is holed and is still aground, full of water at high tide. *Maverick*, with 250 feet of chain out in 50 feet, stayed put but our snubber, a nylon line that takes the strain off the last 20 feet of chain or so, did break with a bang. We stayed on the boat for 48 hours to keep watch.

On Monday we moved ourselves 20 miles to the east, to the west coast of Viti Levu. Here we've spent a couple of days checking out the towns of Lautoka and Nadi and environs, and also doing some provisioning for our passage to Vanuatu. On the 24th, elections begin here, and though everything is being done to ensure they are fair and peaceful, there is a bit of nervousness in the air and it is not out of the question that there will be some civil disturbances following the announcement of the results, or efforts by some elements to disrupt the process entirely. We have no reason to fear for our personal safety, but to avoid any disruption that could possibly be caused in government services, we checked out of customs and immigration yesterday and will sail today.

Fiji has proven to be a difficult place to leave for all the reasons you might imagine. It's also a democracy, or at least one in the making, and they have what seems to be a free press including radio and the evening television news. It feels like this gives the people a different outlook than French Polynesia or Tonga. English is universally spoken and that has made our stay more interesting. The sailing is challenging but has its rewards. Undoubtedly, our departure will be the most bittersweet of the trip so far.

But it's time to go. As much affection as we have for all the countries we've visited, the excitement begins when we say our farewells and set our course for a distant harbor, a place we've barely heard about, and despite our charts and books and sailing directions, it'll be someplace we can't imagine. We've charted our course to Port Vila, Vanuatu, our last stop in the South Pacific and a passage of about 500 miles, and entered the waypoints into the GPS. The tanks have been topped off and soon we'll deflate and stow the dinghy and its gear, put away books and dishes, check the lashings on the jerry cans, take the cover off the mainsail, make the halyard fast to the headboard, and start the engine. The Captain will declare, "Mr. Shrode, our work here is done. Raise the anchor, if you please, and we'll be off to show the flag and share the magic that is *Maverick*, in a new land."

Vanuatu Tu

10:30 PM local time, Friday, August 31 (1130 August 31 UTC).
17° 44.659'S 168° 18.744'E
Temp. 79, Humidity 67%, Cloud Cover 10%.
On a mooring at Port Vila, Efate, Vanuatu.

We did, as promised, say goodbye to Fiji on Thursday. The prediction called for 15-20 knots of southeasterlies, but we got about 6 knots. The seas were lumpy enough that we couldn't fly the light wind sails, and we elected to motor-sail until we found the breeze. On the third day we still had little wind but decided to leave a reasonable amount of fuel for our approach to Vanuatu, and we turned off the engine. By then the seas had flattened out somewhat so we hoisted the drifter and managed 60 miles in the next 24 hours.

San Francisco sailors will know that if you sail to Drake's Bay in 25 knots and the wind dies overnight while you're at anchor, the next day upon clearing Pt. Reyes, you will find glassy seas with a long, low swell. Here the ambient seas were still a mess, 4-6 feet from three directions, after two or three days of less than 8 knots of wind. Now you see how it can get rough if you add a fairly serious breeze. But on the fourth day, we had a truly beautiful day of sailing with sunny skies, 3-ft. seas, and a 12-knot northerly on our beam. If the sea were always like this, the oceans would be crowded with boats. It was good for almost eight hours; then the wind headed us and finally died completely, so we put together 130 miles or so between motoring and some light air close-hauled sailing to arrive at our destination.

We got into the harbor on Tuesday, a day later than expected, with about four gallons in our tanks. We blame the lack of wind on the fact that, after five months of strong breezes where our larger headsail was constantly reefed, we had finally decided to douse the genny and put the smaller working jib on the furler.

Port Vila is pretty sophisticated and another yachting center like Neiafu, Tonga. It's a very pleasant place and we wish we could explore the outer islands, but we need to move along. The life is quite stone-age there, we've heard. Gentlemen who dress traditionally wear only a belt-like device made from leaves that holds the penis away from the body. The testicles, known colloquially as balls, nuts, cojones, the family jewels, or the Bobbsey Twins, are not covered as they might be in San Francisco by an athletic supporter, briefs or boxers, knickers, trousers, kilt, sulu, or petticoat but are left uncovered and unprotected from the depredations of bees, wasps, spiders, snakes, rats, opossums, raccoons, weasels, coyotes, owls, cats, dogs, alligators, big horn sheep, wolves, kangaroos, cassowaries, mules, cougars, lions, tigers, and bears, not to mention lightning, landslides, tsunamis, meteorites, and car doors. Yet, these hardy people carry on, though it is notable that no famous jockey or big league catcher has issued from their ranks. A fellow cruiser who visited these islands found himself in a conversation with the chief about youngsters straying from traditional ways and reported that he felt very much like saying, "My good man, I'm sorry to say that because of your attire, I find it altogether impossible to give this matter the serious consideration it undoubtedly deserves. Put your balls away, and then let's talk."

As the young men of the more remote islands grow up, they face the difficult decision on whether to carry on the customs of their forebears or to adopt modern dress. The Captain, with humility, suggests that, when faced with this sartorial quandary, one that implies layers of other ethical, metaphysical, and personal hygiene questions, the more serious among them should do as the Captain does when deep issues find him at sixes and sevens, and ask themselves, "What would Britney think?" If you showed up on your first date in that penis holster affair, would she be a) extremely pleased, b) not very pleased at all, or c) quite displeased indeed? Frame your query thus, and you'll never go far wrong.

On the other hand, the large town of Port Vila is perfectly civilized, down to bocce ball tournaments and people who pretend to be working at a computer terminal but are actually playing games or surfing the web. SUVs, posters for AIDS awareness or prevention of spousal abuse, and French restaurants fill out the picture. People all recommend visiting the other islands, but I notice they make their homes here, where they can watch TV, buy ice cream cones, and shop for clothes.

Not everything is as up to date as we might wish, as we saw when we had occasion to visit the local hospital in search of the most up-to-date information on malaria, a big problem here. It was disconcerting to go to the lab and see the pathologist sitting in a cluttered and not particularly clean room, wearing shorts, flip flops, and a polo shirt, examining a pile of slides of potentially lethal diseases without availing himself of the protection of surgical gloves. He was as helpful as he could possibly be, but the finicky Captain, as he left, wondered what microbes might have been transferred to his person when he shook this very nice man's hand.

Back on the boat, I can hear from our mooring here in Vanuatu the cover band on shore at the Waterfront Bar & Grill playing "Brown-Eyed Girl," and this reporter reflects that the real brown-eyed girl, the one about whom the song was written, is an old friend, and that the world, penis belts notwithstanding, has become a familiar place indeed.

The other day we were remarking that even though we are now not as far away from Asia as we are from the US, we seem to never see anyone from Japan or China out cruising. Soon after that we were sitting at the local yachtie watering hole and an Asian couple came in from the dinghy dock. We waved and asked them what boat they were on. They said they were from *Balmette* and Ship's Sinologist Terry "the Asian Liaison" Shrode and the Captain instantly understood from their accent that they were not Australians of Chinese descent, which wouldn't be so uncommon. They were Chinese.

The man told me his name was Wei and introduced his wife, Jane. Their full names are Zhang Wei and Gu Xiu Zhen, which she shortens to "Jane" so we unilingual westerners can pronounce it. Also aboard *Balmette* is their 14-year-old daughter, Zhang Shan Shan. I asked him where he was from and he said "Peking" (he called it "Peking," not "Beijing"). "THE Peking?" Yep, that's where he's from.

Wei and Jane were in Fiji where he was working and one day he sailed a Hobie Cat and decided on the basis of that experience alone that he would get a boat and sail with his family around the world. He bought a French steel centerboard sloop and worked for a year to get it ready to cruise. In May of 2000 they set sail for Vanuatu without VHF, depthsounder, or self-steering. They hit the reef on the way out of Fiji but "not too hard." Wei said before he launched his boat, that day on the Hobie Cat was his entire sailing résumé.

The Captain, who is quite skilled in the area of Far East diplomacy, was forming a response to Wei's story as he listened to him. I quote the Captain word for word so that those at home can appreciate its subtle nuances. "You've got no brains!" There was a slight pause, then Wei laughed, and nuclear war was averted. Admittedly, it's not really so hard to get Wei to laugh.

Wei is still having trouble registering his boat in China. He claims he finally had to write the "president" (that's the word he used...is there a president in China?) and supposedly they're going to register the boat, though the government of China is having to create the procedure for him. "It's never been done for a private yacht before" is what he said, and as hard as that is to believe, if Wei said it, it's true. So his boat registration alone makes him one in a billion. As a result of his lack of proper paperwork, Australia would not let him in, but New Zealand would, so he spent the last hurricane season there. On the way to Port Vila six weeks ago, his boat suffered a knockdown in 30-foot seas. The battery hit the roof, everyone was thrown around, a lot of gear was ripped off the deck, and Wei and Zhang Shan Shan were injured. Wei just wiped the blood off and put the battery back. He now has a wind vane and a VHF radio, but no HF communications, no fax, and not a lot of other things either, except guts and his own good nature and that of Jane and Zhang Shan Shan.

Our stay in Vanuatu must needs be brief, and we'll depart tomorrow. We lingered too long in Fiji and as a result, we're going to have to skip the Solomons and go directly to Australia. The next leg is the longest passage since the trip down to the South Pacific, about 2400 miles unless we call at Port Moresby, and it takes us through the Great Barrier Reef and the infamous Torres Strait. This will involve weaving our way through an intricate maze of passes and will also have the added danger of being full of large and small ship traffic. It's a challenge the Captain and Navigator Terry Shrode have been looking forward to.

Missionary Impossible

11:00 AM local time. Sunday, September 9 (0000 September 9 UTC).
14 05S 157 26E
Temp. 85, Humidity 71%, Cloud Cover 10%.
Seas SE 1.5 meters. Wind SE 10k. Crossing the Coral Sea.

We left Vanuatu on Tuesday, one day later than anticipated, because we decided we may want to make a pit stop in Papua, New Guinea, and we had to get a visa from the High Commissioner in Port Vila or they wouldn't let us in. We're about 650 miles out now, with about the same to go to Port Moresby, and both the weather and sailing have been quite pleasant. We currently have 10 knots from the SE, and we're heading NW under poled-out headsails doing about 4-5 knots. The Coral Sea is a place where we expected strong winds, but we got these in the eastern part of the South Pacific where winds were supposed to be lighter. As of yesterday the wind freshened for a while and a swell came up on our beam as well as what we had from behind, and as we were dead downwind, it got a bit rolly, making it hard to stay in one's bunk. We tried a trick we'd read about and hoisted the main with a double reef and using the mainsheet, preventer, and traveler centered it so that the leach points directly into the apparent wind. This really did do a good job of dampening the roll a bit.

In this post we will review a letter from old friend Bob Riedel to see what wisdom we may find therein, and in doing so will hope to shed more light on the issue of bare-breasted native women in response to a plea from Mr. Shrode's father-in-law, Paul, and by the way, thanks for the inquiry about this important topic.

Mr. Riedel, who does not share the Captain's enthusiasm for less-is-more anthropology, actually spent quite some time in this area of the Pacific and among its residents, and he can speak therefore with some authority on the topics of local healthcare and customs. On the former subject, he points out quite rightly the astonishing fact that surgical gloves weren't used in our fancy western hospitals either, until the AIDS scare.

In Mr. Riedel's letter, he also brought up the subject of penis belts or sheaves or whatever, so recently covered by your correspondent. He said, among other things, that "a penis sheath is surely little worse than a codpiece, and serves the same purpose." This is quite an interesting point of view, on which we will be commenting next time. First, let's recall a little history.

The belief that the soul, or the spiritual and mental part of the human being, is its most important or essential aspect has an ancient provenance. The doctrine that the body is, on the other hand, a source of misinformation and cause for bad judgments seems to be more recent but can be traced back at least to the pre-Christian thinker, Plato, in his depiction of Socrates' last day on earth in the Phaedo. In that dialogue, Socrates recommends paying little heed to the body, a temporary vessel, and concentrating on the soul, which, he argues at some length, is eternal.

That the body is a source of actual evil is a more radical doctrine that can claim as its defenders personages no less imposing than Saints Paul and Augustine. It is less clear what Jesus taught on the subject; he is better known for miraculously making wine and defending a woman of ill repute against her accusers. But Augustine takes the austere view that spicy foods, bright colors, and even the love a father has for his son, not to mention sexual impulses, are temptations the world offers to misguide the soul onto a false path.

This doctrine spanked its way down through the centuries, shaking its bony index finger at many a lustful teenager, until, through the efforts of courageous European missionaries shortly after the voyages of discovery initiated by James Cook, it finally flopped down exhausted on the beaches of the native peoples of the South Pacific. Like many societies, including those of ancient Greece, Rome, and India, some of the South Pacific cultures had until that moment venerated fertility and the instruments thereof. In the golden age of ancient Athens, the god Hermes was represented in statuary with an erect penis. Assuming that this hadn't fallen out of fashion by the first century AD, St. Paul would have passed many of these popular figures as he traveled to the agora to preach. Perhaps Paul would have taken this in stride, but we prim heirs of his thought would be shocked to see the same thing decorating middle-class houses in our day.

When the people carrying on St. Paul's mission came to the South Pacific, they brought with them, among many new beliefs, doctrines prohibiting cannibalism (which, not incidentally, was in the self-interest of the missionaries but also, I mean, get real), the display and enhancement of male genitalia, and the uncovered female breast. The Captain, also a product of the culture founded by the above-mentioned sages and other worthies, heartily concurs with the first prohibition, is a strong supporter, so to speak, of the second, and has heard of the third. Presumably, the native people were taught that among other things, observing these prohibitions would contribute to their being given eternal life. Not doing so might send them to hell. It's a carrot-and-stick kind of deal.

Now the Captain would like to offer a couple of puzzles which may be emblematic of the fragile and fickle nature of human morality, once a favorite subject of the Great King, Darius of Persia. Your correspondent would like the reader to put himself in the position of the thoughtful South Pacific islander and imagine what his conclusions might be when pondering these same curiosities.

1) When foreigners come to visit this area, they are often cautioned to dress conservatively, and particularly not to go bare-breasted or wear skimpy bathing suits near villages where native people may be worshipping fully dressed as their missionaries have taught. Who *are* these people who sent missionaries with puritanical rules but need to be admonished thusly, appearing to have no such prohibitions among themselves?

2) When tourists come to visit, they are offered a variety of activities and one of the most popular is attending native dance ceremonies. In these performances, local people, who usually wear Nike t-shirts and shorts that cover their naughty parts, will dress in traditional attire, and this sometimes means the men wear penis sheathes and the women perform topless. They do dances that have various themes, many based on animism—a set of beliefs inconsistent with the teachings of Christianity. Who *are* these people who sent missionaries to "civilize" them and now pay the natives to do the things these missionaries taught them were evil?

And that's not all. It took relatively little time for the missionaries to convince the Polynesians and Melanesians to adopt the teachings of the Christian tradition. But the very Catholic French, for whom the reader is well aware the Captain has nothing but praise, have turned a deaf ear to the teaching above about female breasts, notwithstanding the fact that they've been Christianized for well over a millennium. So to Mr. Shrode's father-in-law Paul, namesake of the other Paul mentioned above, the report is, the crew of *Maverick* has seen a number of bare-breasted native women in our travels, but unfortunately that number is zero. Join us in France, where the real primitives still haunt the shores of Cannes and St.-Tropez and ignore the mighty Augustine.

9/11

11:00 AM local time, Thursday, September 13, 2001 (0000 September 13, 2001 UTC). 10 30 S 148 12 E
Temp. 82, Humidity 81%, Cloud Cover 10%.
One day out of Port Moresby, Papua, New Guinea.

We heard about the events back home of September 11 when we checked email on Wednesday morning here, which would have been Tuesday afternoon for you. Caroline had written Mr. Shrode a short email that included the basic facts, which we of course found beyond imagining. We soon made our customary radio contact with a HAM net, where we were able to find out the frequency for a New Zealand shortwave broadcast of the BBC and Voice of America. We normally don't follow these, but we spent the day around the radio listening to the voices crackling over the airwaves and describing one incredible fact after another, much as people did in World War II.

We do not normally fly the Stars and Stripes at sea, but we raised it today to half-mast. We are safe and our thoughts are with all the people back home, particularly my brother in Washington, our friends in New York, and webmaster Jim Mead, who works for the FAA and probably had a tough day.

On my night watch last night, I spent a long time looking at the stars, mindful of the thousands of eyes that will never see them again.

This time it's us wishing you to take care and Godspeed.

Behind Closed Doors

6:00 PM local time, Thursday, September 20 (0800 September 20 UTC).
9° 27.976'S 147° 9.185'E
Temp. 86, Humidity 73%, Cloud Cover 60%.
In a slip at Port Moresby, Papua, New Guinea.

The President has told Americans to get back to work. We saw the Yankees on CNN the other day saying that, with mixed feelings, they will play, in the hope that their efforts will provide some respite to a nation in need of diversion and something to cheer about. With the exception of the Oakland Athletics, I don't think there's anyone I'd rather hear it from. As our particular job is reporting on how things are out here, we will take the President's encouragement to heart and begin once again. Those of you who find our stories now even more insignificant and irrelevant than before will not miss much if they pass them up for the nonce. But the Captain, whether through lack of will or lack of talent, will not substantially alter his tone. If these missives seem to be written with a tin ear for the feelings of the day, as one very close to the Captain has suggested with a resultant frank exchange of ideas, consider my apologies offered.

We arrived in Port Moresby Friday morning. Ironically, while all hell was breaking loose at home, this was the first passage of our voyage that was peaceful from beginning to end, with fair winds, never over 20, regular, following seas, and blue skies with nothing other than puffy little clouds and an infrequent hint of a shower. We've been experimenting with some unusual sail configurations. We have previously mentioned sheeting the main amidships to control the roll while running downwind with poled-out headsails, which we are now addicted to as it works so well. We also found a solution to the problem of sailing about 130-150 degrees off the wind in light air when the seas are lumpy. Generally, this is a tough point of sail because the headsail is always on the verge of collapsing. Once it does, you lose boat speed and the vane gets confused and can't find its way back up. What we've done is pole out the drifter, which is about a 120%, ¾-oz. and pretty flat, to windward, and leave the full genoa to leeward, not on a pole but sheeted in rather tighter than usual when off the wind. It is filled by the exhaust from the drifter and not blanketed by the main. That way we can put up over 1000 square feet of sail, all drawing well, and the combination works like a main with a spinnaker, yet is much more forgiving and easily steered by the vane. I've never heard of this arrangement before, but we couldn't be the first ones to think of it.

We planned to stay three days here and would have left by now but the winds have strengthened with the passing of a substantial high in the Tasman Sea. In the harbor, the resultant williwaws blast down the hills like cannonballs, gusting over 40 knots, causing *Maverick* to strain at her lines. With lighter air, we hoped to have less trouble negotiating the shoal waters and reefs of the Torres Strait, a maze of navigational problems 200 miles from here and about 140 miles from entrance to exit. We also know as the days progress, we will be further from spring tide, when currents can run up to 8 knots in certain sections. We would like to avoid an 8-knot current against 25 knots of wind in a shipping lane at night; and as there is no sign of the winds decreasing in the immediate future, we'll stay here for now.

Port Moresby is pretty crime-ridden. We are staying at the Royal Papua Yacht Club, which has intense security, not so much because we are afraid but because there are no other suitable options. If you go out of the complex, even locals will come up to warn you to be careful of the "raskols," who are mostly pickpockets but it's possible to get mugged. The unemployment rate is, according to the government, 80% in Port Moresby. Some of those who are employed are still searching for unexploded ordnance from WWII, which they call "goodies," and detonating it. Sorcery has regained its popularity here, and there have been murders of those suspected of being sorcerers. We haven't ventured out at night.

On Saturday we went to an independence day celebration on the beach where we saw traditional boats and traditional dancers in traditional costume. We were told that last year the girls who work as checkers at a local supermarket, and are all from provincial villages, were competing. After the dancing, they showed up for work and did the checkouts in native dress, which no one, oddly, takes any notice of whatsoever. Except, of course, Europeans. Apparently for the natives, when one is clothed in western dress, even a short skirt, say above the knee, is indicative of a loose woman. But for the same person in native dress, a grass skirt with nothing underneath and nothing else at all but beads and a headdress is considered completely proper and chaste attire.

Mr. Shrode's Wild Ride

11:00 PM local time, Monday, Sepember 24 (1300 Sept. 24 UTC).
9° 27.976'S 147° 9.185'E
Temp. 83, Humidity 78%, Cloud Cover 60%. Windy.
Royal Papua Yacht Club, Port Moresby, Papua, New Guinea.

On Sunday we were introduced to Paul and Francis of Paul's boat *Okiva*, a 41-ft. Freeport ketch. Paul is from Santa Barbara, is about 45, and is quite mad. He met Francis, a native of Fiji who has worked as a professional skipper on other yachts, in Fiji, where he had singlehanded from California. They are planning a world cruise, adding other crew, including Paul's wife, Paula, like the song, here and there. They invited the Captain and Ship's Harmonica Stylist Terry Shrode over to the boat and broke out a bottle of rum. Actually a number of bottles of rum: four or five was the official total as close as could be determined. They played the impressive stereo really loud, and soon we broke out guitars and harmonicas and were jamming.

As the day wore on, Paul suggested to the Captain that we go see what was going on in the boat next door, a large charter powerboat where a party was underway. Paul got on board and immediately went to the helm. He told your correspondent, authoritatively, that we would be taking the boat out, and that an announcement should be made informing everyone of that fact.

"How soon shall I tell them we're leaving?" I asked.

"Oh, fifteen minutes."

So this reporter announced loudly and clearly so everyone present could hear, in a voice that to him sounded quite official, "Ladies and gentlemen, in fifteen minutes we will depart on a harbor cruise. If you'd like to come along, you're welcome to stay aboard, but otherwise we need you to disembark as soon as you can."

I returned to Paul and told him the announcement had been made. He was having a hard time getting the boat started and told me he needed a screwdriver to hot wire it. I went back to Paul's boat and told Francis we needed a screwdriver to start the powerboat. Francis instantly realized that what Paul was up to, with my assistance, was stealing a $750,000 yacht. This took me rather by surprise, for at no point had your correspondent recognized that there was anything untoward about our plans. Rum connoisseurs may recognize this syndrome.

Francis said, "Tony, you stay right here. Do not move." He went over to the other boat to try to save Paul from further misadventures, but by that time security had been called and he was persuaded to leave the boat without further incident.

Later, about 2:00 in the morning, after the Captain had, shall we say, retired, Mr. Shrode was enlisted by Paul to join him in his very fast dinghy on a joy ride around the harbor at suicidal speed. Paul was sitting in the bottom of the stern of the dinghy where he could not have seen where he was going even if he were sober—and he was driving. Mr. Shrode, on the bow when he could keep his balance, could dimly see through the spray and shouted commands. They stopped at various container ships and pounded on the side trying to wake up the crews to see if anyone aboard might be in the mood for a cocktail. In this, they were unsuccessful but they did run into a few things. One might, gaining some distance on the evening, wonder at the wisdom of strangers approaching large ships in a dinghy so soon after the events of 9/11.

The staff here at the Royal Papua Yacht Club has made no mention of this and in general one is treated as one imagines lesser royals are treated, and that includes having one's lapses in behavior ignored to an almost surreal degree and never spoken of again—unless it's a violation of the dress code, which is of course not to be tolerated. Like the Royal Suva Yacht Club, its use of the word *Royal* is an honor officially granted by the Queen of England. It's a very elegant club and meticulously maintained, as befits something royal in the British Commonwealth. There must be a full-time, paid staff of 100, so the yachting community is doing what it can to support the local economy. The membership fee and dues here are no doubt substantial, but voyagers like us are welcome to have complete use of the facilities at this and all similar clubs for next to nothing. It's amazing, really.

It's not a little odd that a couple of grotty Americans have found themselves hanging with the swells since we left French Polynesia, where one would have thought things might be rather more organized than they were. There is really nothing worthy of the name *yacht club* until you leave there and go farther west, where one, being ignorant of such things, would have thought the situation might have been a bit more primitive. But the influence of British, Australian, and Kiwi colonialism has left its mark, and in addition there is a steady flow of yachtspeople from the latter two who sail no farther east than Tonga on their adventures in the South Pacific.

We don't go to the yacht clubs because of our affection for colonialism but because in every locale, they furnish the exact things we need: a safe anchorage, information on how to clear customs or to fix your boat, laundry, showers, and the company of other cruisers, the majority of whom have better local knowledge than you could find from any other source. And like Dave and Ros of *Arafura Maid* here, they are not infrequently spectacularly generous with their help.

But back to Paul. A few days later Paula had arrived and they had us over for dinner. As I left, Paul walked me up the ramp, raised his arms, and confessed to me as one skipper to another, in a voice that could have been heard throughout the marina and perhaps throughout Papua, New Guinea, "I'm the captain of a boat that is sailing around the world. I've got the best fucking job in the universe!"

The Kite That Took Flight

10:00 AM local time, Thursday, September 27 (0000 Sept. 27 UTC).
9° 27.976'S 147° 9.185'E
Temp. 81, Humidity 86%, Cloud Cover 100%.
Still caged at the Royal Papua Yacht Club, Port Moresby, Papua, New Guinea.

The other day Ros of *Arafura Maid* was racing with some people on a 10-meter boat and they needed extra crew so the Captain, bored a bit by our enforced stay here, jumped at the chance. I got on board and met the rest of the crew, and we motored out to the start. The skipper, Ron, is a pro who has done the Whitbread (Volvo) and skippered a boat in the fateful Sydney-Hobart race. As it turned out, we were lucky to have someone that good.

It was blowing in the low 20s, but Ron decided to go with the full main, as did many other boats, and their number three. The conditions were not unlike racing in the slot in San Francisco Bay, except it was warm. Our start wasn't spectacular but we hung in with the crowd. The race was perhaps 20 miles, with maybe six roundings. After a leg or two the wind came up a bit, to 30 and above, and boats started having problems and blowing out sails. Our headsail (they call them *headies* here) went bye-bye, so we hoisted the number four. Spinnakers started to shred. As a result of all the mayhem, we caught the leaders. We were feeling pretty good on the last downwind leg, hitting 11 knots surfing, and were just about ready to hoist the headsail and douse the spinnaker at the leeward mark when things suddenly went wrong.

The afterguy (they call it a *brace*) let go and the pole went forward, banging against the headstay. Ron immediately called for the sail to be doused, but the halyard got jammed in the clutch and wouldn't let go. In 30+ knots, with four feet of chop, we had to get it down so the skipper yelled "Cut" and the halyard was cut away. The sail fell into the water and the bowman and a couple of crew grabbed the sheet to try to pull it in as we sailed by. But the frayed end of the halyard had stuck in the mast somewhere and hadn't let completely go. A puff came along, the boat heeled suddenly to windward, and the halyard came taut, pulled up the kite, and it filled, propelling the bowman, who had the sheet around his arm, right past the shrouds (which he was very lucky not to hit) and shooting him into the water like a cannonball. During this whole mess, the boat jibed and a woman was hit in the back with the boom.

Okay, you're the skipper. It's blowing like snot, there's heavy chop, you've got the spinnaker flailing and maybe 50 feet to leeward of the boat, there's someone hurt and a man in the water, who'd somehow managed to grab something and was holding on. About 200 yards farther to leeward is a reef. Less than a minute ago, everything was great. Nobody freaked, but a lot of nasty images ran through your correspondent's mind.

Ron hove-to and stopped the boat with the spinnaker flying madly and the sheet tailing behind it, way up there in the sky like, one might say, a kite. The halyard was now fully extended but still jammed in the mast so the sail was nearly 100 feet from the boat and 45 feet in the air. The bowman was holding on to something for dear life, and in this case "for dear life" was not an overstatement. He was not wearing a life vest. He was beside the boat and was a big guy, and fortunately for him a strong one, so I yelled to him to try to work his way back to the transom, which was open. We could never have gotten him over the side. I was very conscious, as I'm sure the skipper was, that in the meantime we were making quite a bit of leeway towards the reef. Another crewman and I wrestled the man back on board over the transom. He had a big gash in his leg, which it turned out was actually not a cut but had been abraded away by rope. We got him below and lying down, and he yelled to the skipper, "We're still racing!" This meant he didn't want us to withdraw from the race on his account.

We managed somehow to retrieve the spinnaker, which was important because we couldn't sail upwind to get home with it flying like that. We got the headsail up, but the top three feet of the luff ripped out. Luckily, the tear stopped there because with an old main, we needed that jib to get us home. We finished the race but weren't up there in the money anymore.

Ron kept the crew focused the entire time and was very quick to make decisions and tell us clearly what he needed done. As a result, what could have been really awful was reduced to a couple of relatively minor injuries and a lost sheet. Relatively minor, but the bowman was treated by a doctor (Dave, Ros' husband) as soon as we got the boat tied up and he will require stitches and some recovery time. Dave said the man had gone into shock, but he was seen later in the bar hoisting something a bit less dangerous than a kite.

Bonfire of the Inanities

A while back, before *you know what* happened, the Captain promised, in the dispatch entitled "Missionary Impossible," to comment on a remark, contributed by one of our readers, on the penis sheaths worn by the men of Vanuatu. The editors held this back for a spell as being too frivolous, but we now pick up where we left off and offer it as part of our ongoing dialogue on matters of consequence.

So on to the argument of old friend and reader Bob Riedel that "a penis sheath is surely little worse than a codpiece, and serves the same purpose." Mr. Riedel is, as we can see, a man of the world, but he is also a man of the cloth, a consequence, no doubt, of his faith and of his sensitivity to profound religious and moral questions like the meaty one we consider hereunder. It is no small matter for the Captain to presume to gainsay a man of his stature, as the Captain himself, since Little League, has sometimes been called but seldom chosen. But if by chance our inquiries lead us towards the unhappy burden of taking exception to the good pastor's theory, and if, having dared to contradict our friend, the Captain is found at fault in his analysis, he has little doubt that his hubris will receive its proper comeuppance on That Great, Gettin'-Up Mornin'.

Pastor Riedel's argument was offered, we believe, in defense of the practice of the peoples of Vanuatu and Papua New Guinea, and to sound the bell of racial and cultural fellowship, by showing that penis sheaths, worn by what some would call the primitive (and non-white) inhabitants of distant lands, are really of the same category as codpieces, worn by…ah…here the Captain must confess that the pastor has the advantage of him, as he cannot claim to know who exactly wore or wears codpieces. For the sake of argument, however, let's stipulate that except for Mick Jagger and perhaps the more flamboyant members of the gay and/or leather communities, they were (white) Europeans of the 15th and 16th centuries. If Mr. Riedel is to be counted among their number, he will be happy to learn that his secret is safe with the Captain.

We will begin, as we should, by determining what features of this argument deserve our praise. In this we will not be disappointed, for the form of the argument rests squarely on that most solid of moral principles, the Categorical Imperative. "Act only on that maxim which, by thy will, could be made a universal law," said Kant, or words to that effect. This means that if it's okay for me to do it, it's okay for you to do it.

As the reader surely knows by now, the Captain is no relativist. (Relativism, a boring but popular view with an ancient heritage, cannot actually be unhypocritically practiced for reasons the Captain will forbear explaining here, but be assured he could if he wanted to so consider yourself lucky.) He believes that if education is good in Kansas, it is good in Vanuatu, no matter how or to what extent it may cause villagers there to question the decisions of their chief. If equality before the law is correct in Alabama, it is correct in Fiji, no matter which group got there first. And so on.

The form, therefore, of the argument, the Captain is pleased to conclude, is sound, with the following reservation. As feminists discovered in the 1970s, insisting on this Kantian principle sometimes may lead to unexpected results. Some women found themselves arguing, for example, that, like men, they should have the right to go bare-chested in public. When at the time the politically correct Captain (who was then just an ensign) heard this, he lost his bearings and wandered in a daze out of the protest march and was found unconscious with his placard by a wandering group of Picts. If, therefore, the Categorical Imperative were to force us into the position that we must include women among those people for whom we endorse the wearing of penis sheaths, some will find this unacceptable, and by *reductio ad absurdum,* find Kant's rule unacceptable as well.

Notwithstanding this twinge of reserve, having satisfied ourselves with the form, we will briskly move on to the content of our argument. We have established that it is no more wrong for person X to do A than it is for person Y to do A. It remains to be determined whether "A" is really the same in both cases and whether it is, in fact, praiseworthy to do A. The Captain believes that in the former we will find a small difference and in the latter a rather more troubling fallacy.

We will assume that the function of codpieces and penis sheaths is the same, and that function is to advertise the virility of the wearer. Apparently, however, in the case of the Ni Vanuatu, the penis sheath is a tribal advertisement, whereas the codpiece seems to be a purely personal one. Whether tribal or personal, this difference may be seen to have little effect on the substance of the issue at hand.

Moving on to the question of whether we should endorse act A: Even if we have established that it's no worse to wear a penis sheath than a codpiece, we haven't begun the difficult task of determining whether it's a good idea to wear a codpiece. And so the question is surely begged.

So, finally, to address this important matter. It is the Captain's view that any person who would denigrate another on the basis of the physical disadvantages with which nature has chosen to blemish him reveals himself to be an ill-bred boor. But just as surely, to attempt to conceal whatever shortcomings one may believe one has by the use of prosthetic devices is to play directly into this ill-bred person's hands and to confess that his assessment of one's liabilities is a sound one. Moreover, in adopting these appurtenances, whether they be penis sheaths, codpieces, elevator shoes, falsies, or toupees, the wearer inadvertently calls attention to the very inadequacy he or she wishes to conceal. Further, there is a touch of dishonesty as one represents oneself, even to one's friends, as someone other than who one is.

It is far more effective, in the Captain's view, to learn an honest trick or two to distract the intended audience from the alleged deficiency. It might be drawing funny pictures around one's belly button, wearing one of those amusing balloon hats, or becoming a drummer, songwriter, or sailor. The Captain believes it is a far better thing to be ridiculed for deeds one has accomplished through his own pluck and daring, than to be pilloried for the feckless and sometimes cruel accidents of nature.

But without question the most damning problem here is that attempting to appear more virile, or larger, or bustier, or more hirsute than one by nature is, clearly qualifies as an act of vanity. And vanity, as Pastor Riedel knows very well, is one of the seven deadly sins. The reader is referred to the *Summa Theologica*, wherein St. Thomas gives the subject the thoroughgoing treatment we would expect, for further details. (The Captain is sorry he cannot verify the exact status of vanity in the hierarchy of sins according to Aquinas, although he believes it to be number one. Alas, he had to hock his copy of the *Summa* a few years back to raise funds for hairstyling and a manicure.) Now, the Captain certainly does not presume to know more about sin than the professional, and here he is most willing to yield to the superior expertise of Reverend Riedel. But surely the pastor would admit that, if the Captain is correct and vanity is indeed the motive behind codpieces and penis sheaths alike, then right-thinking people everywhere will shun them both and seek the high ground of moral sanctity found comfortably, and at reasonable prices, in standard underwear.

Or, to take another tack entirely, if we accept, as is taught in Ecclesiastes, that "all is vanity," it follows that no particular vanity is any worse than any other insofar as its being vanity is concerned, be it sailing a wide ocean, wearing a penis sheath, or delivering the Sunday sermon. So on these grounds, the pastor's point stands. It apparently depends on what the meaning of "is" is, and there's the rub, but the Captain will save that discussion for another day.

Torres Strait, No Chaser

3:15 PM local time, Thursday, October 4 (0315 Oct. 4 UTC).
10 38 S   138 31 E
Temp. 83, Humidity 77%, Cloud Cover 05%.
In the Arafura Sea.

The Torres Strait is the name for the meeting place of the Pacific and Indian Oceans. Here, bodily fluids are exchanged as the two large masses of water commingle, with the rise and fall of the tides, in the maze of islands and reefs between them. For the sailor, it comprises a rite of passage, not perhaps in the same category as the two great capes, but in the wrong conditions just as daunting.

As we bide our time in Port Moresby, the Captain is engaged in a Byzantine analysis of hypothetical situations that might arise as we transit the Torres Strait and environs in a stiff breeze. This is one of the most dangerous parts of our voyage from a sailor's point of view, and I'm trying to do as much of my thinking ahead of time as I can. Even the most avid student of sailing and navigation would find these ruminations obsessive and tedious, so I will spare the reader the details, but here's a general idea.

What we are doing is going through a very wide part of the Great Barrier Reef of Australia. Once we get to the Bligh Entrance to the Great Northeast Passage, 200 miles from here, we will have an upwind leg of about 85 miles, and how far forward, or south in this case, the wind is, will determine whether we can sail free or will be forced to motor-sail or tack. Then we have a short dogleg and another 40 miles, some of which may be upwind, before we get to the Prince of Wales Channel. This channel can have current of up to 8 knots and there will most likely be some heavy ships going through when we do. It is essential that we not go through on an adverse current, which would produce standing waves in the face of the SE wind, and at the very least stop us in our tracks with waves breaking over the bow. There are two opportunities each day during which we can begin our sail through the channel safely, but we'd also like to be there in the daytime, so really we have one five-hour window per day. Our passage through the Torres Strait must be planned to maximize the chances of hitting this window, preferably at the beginning of it.

So the navigational problem is to do a time-speed-distance calculation on each leg to find an estimated time en route and then plan our start so that we don't have a problem when we get there. In the first three to five legs (depending on how finely you divide the route) we will also have to deal with current, not as strong as in the channel but not navigationally negligible, and will have to calculate those effects as well.

The entire game revolves around the exact direction of the wind. A southeasterly is technically from 135 degrees true, but the weathercasters can't be accurate to more than plus or minus, say, 35 degrees. If we find that the wind is a bit more east than 135, we'll be happier (reaching) than if it is a bit more south than that (requiring tacking). But the idea is to sketch out all of the possibilities assuming different wind directions and therefore points of sail and therefore speed, add in the current vectors, and get a resulting velocity made good for each leg under each assumption. The results, which have been put on a table, give a range of 18.5-57 hours between the entrance and the channel. As we approach Bramble Cay at the Bligh Entrance, the starting point, we'll see which way the wind blows, look at our table, and try to time our start accordingly. Even after all this, though, it's a bit of a crapshoot, as Robert Burns said, or words to that effect.

Ship's Intrepid Adventures Specialist Terry Shrode most probably feels that these deliberations take all the fun out of it, but if so, he is too polite to say.

As Mr. Shrode and the Captain waited fitfully through the high winds for the right weather, fishing boats came into Port Moresby complaining of heavy seas and, on Thursday, a gale. We had spoken on the HAM radio to "Pik" on *Mara*, who was hove-to inside the Great Barrier Reef in 30 knots, having survived the gale on the outside. We thought as the wind subsided Friday, we would leave, but it kept blowing until Sunday. On both Friday and Saturday, we had all but started the engine and cast off the lines before we got a last-minute "no go" from local sailors helping us watch the weather.

On Sunday our astrologer, shaman, psychotherapist, aroma therapist, and proctologist said it was time to go, and indeed even that most mysterious of auguries, the weather fax, seemed to give the same indication. With the feeling one might have getting in the barrel before going over Niagara Falls, we cast off the lines and motored out of the marina. A challenge the Captain had thought about for years was about to be met for real.

Outside the reef, for a while we encountered mild conditions. But soon the wind freshened to 30 knots and the seas built to 10-12 feet. Even so, they weren't nasty and it was just a boisterous ride. The worry with the wind, however, was that the omens were wrong after all.

Two hundred miles later, on Monday afternoon, we approached Bramble Cay and headed up to see if we could fetch our first waypoint. Turned out it was a close reach. The Captain consulted his table of obsessive calculations and picked plan 21 Charlie.

Though there are a number of navigational problems in the next 130 miles, the bottom line is that you have to get to the entrance to the Prince of Wales Channel, which spits you at last out of the area, on a west-going tide and preferably right after slack. Since we were determined not to go through in heavy weather, taking the first window after the wind abated meant that we had to go through the Strait on a spring tide, accompanied by strong currents, which would certainly not have been our first choice. This made it even more imperative that we not face an east-setting current.

We knew from HAM contacts with *Mara* that Pik was now anchored at Rennel Island inside the reef. We made a slight alteration in our plan to join him to await our weather window for the reason that we would have to anchor next to an unlit reef off an island in the middle of the night, and seeing the location of another boat might help us orient ourselves.

Although the moon was almost full, the skies were overcast when we arrived at Rennel Island and it was too dark to see a boat. We couldn't raise Pik on the radio but started slowly motoring from leeward towards the island until Lookout Terry Shrode, on the bow, thought he spotted something. Heading over there we saw it was indeed a sailboat; we tried to hail Pik but it was late and he was sound asleep. We made a guess and dropped the hook.

Pik, whose real name is Anton Willem Van Stokkum, has been cruising single-handed in his junk-rigged schooner for 17 years, all of it in the Pacific, and he and his boat are as salty as they come. He was going around the world, just like us, but on a different schedule. We caught up with him just as he was making the jump as we were to a whole new ocean.

The next morning, talking to him on the VHF, we discovered that his plan was the same as ours, and the Captain found this reassuring. Our target was to enter the channel after slack at 2109 local time, and from where we were anchored, we figured it would be about 12 hours, give or take an hour or two for current velocities we could not predict.

We weighed anchor at 0900 and began a beautiful day of sailing in about 15 knots with sunny skies and flat seas. Every leg was a reach, as we passed Arden Islet, Roberts Islet, Coconut Island, Richardson Reef, Bet Reef, Panther Shoal, Moresby Rock, Ninepin Rocks, and Beagle Rocks, and finally arrived at Alert Patches, the area right before the entrance to the channel, which was our target. We passed it at 2118, nine minutes into a favorable current, an acceptable degree of precision after sailing over 300 miles. All the planning we did was of course based on the potential for more difficult scenarios, but the conditions made it a pleasure cruise, and even shipping was light that day so there were no moments of concern as a very large ship and *Maverick* shared tight quarters with a substantial current. Going through the channel itself took almost exactly two hours. There were high fives; we had safely passed through the feared Torres Strait.

Having managed to survive this challenge, we now have completed the crossing of the largest ocean on earth, encompassing an area so vast that all of the landmasses put together would fit comfortably inside it. It feels as though we have gone through a portal to another part of the universe and a door has closed behind us, cutting us off from the waters of home. The sea is pale. There is a distant haze in every direction. The puffy trade winds clouds have thinned out, there is an austerity to the sky, and the light seems foreign. The Pacific is finished, and a siren song beckons us towards the west horizon.

Origin Of The Specious

10:30 PM local time, Monday, Oct. 15th (1430 Oct. 15th UTC)
12° 27.085'S 130° 49.420'E
Temp. 87, Humidity 77%, Cloud Cover 50%.
In a slip at the Cullen Bay Marina, Darwin, Australia.

We arrived in Darwin, Australia Tuesday morning. After the Torres Strait we headed west across the Arafura Sea and above the north coast of Australia, passing the Gulf of Carpenteria, Cape Wessel, Cape Essington, and Cape Don, and entering the Dundas Strait and Van Dieman Gulf south of Melville Island. Surrounded now by Australia, we expected to see something, but the land was low-lying and as there were no other vessels in sight, it seemed oddly desolate. We hove-to near Cape Hotham to await a favorable tide in the strong currents at the Clarence Strait between the NW Vernon and SW Vernon Islands. At about 0200 Tuesday we entered the pass between the Vernons and headed to Darwin, motoring in a stifling calm near a thunderstorm.

The spring tides in Darwin are in the neighborhood of 25 feet, that's 25 American, and therefore all the marinas are behind locks. After completing the lengthy and detailed customs requirements we were allowed to go through the lock, the first one of the voyage, and enter the Cullen Bay marina. I know you're thinking we're getting soft, staying in a marina. But the most viable alternative is anchoring off the Darwin Sailing Club at Francis Bay, and this has the disadvantage that, aside from saltwater crocodiles and box jellyfish, the sting of which is fatal, the large tide means that at low water you must pull your dinghy a mile up the beach to place it above high water.

We have heard that a large group of circumnavigating American boats are returning to Australia from Indonesia rather than continuing. Since cruisers are pretty tough folks, the fact that so many have chosen to return, because of political fears in the aftermath of 9/11, is a bit daunting. This needs some more research.

The good news is that Caroline and Theresa are braving the security concerns that now attend international flights and coming to visit us. When the Captain was on the wrestling team in high school, he was given to believe by his coach that wrestlers who spent a lot of time with their girlfriends were less masculine than those who hung around the guys and gave them the occasional pat on the ass. Manly men, it seems, should have nothing to do with women. There was some breach of logic here that troubled the young seaman, though he was not completely clear on what it was.

But now, effeminate or not, the Captain looks forward to these visits with an unalloyed anticipation that his coach would have found a distraction and an embarrassment to his sex. It's of course not easy to talk about this. But as one ages, one learns to live with one's flaws.

We paired off and toured the Northern Territory of Australia in rented cars. There was a lot to see. The wildlife is abundant, even in downtown Darwin, and exotic birds are not hard to spot. There are no koalas or kangaroos up here, but they have wallabies and saltwater crocodiles that, according to the citizens, we'll take their word, are bigger and more aggressive than our alligators. There was Aboriginal culture to investigate. It was also hot and there were flies.

In Darwin I was able to tour a replica of His Majesty's Bark *Endeavour*, Captain Cook's ship, which was by coincidence in town when we were. The replica was amazing and quite a thrill. The space shuttle named after it carried one of the pegs (*trunnels*) that hold the replica together into space and around the world for good luck before it was hammered into the ship. Making the tour more interesting was the fact that we know something about many of the officers and crew, so for instance, we can view not just the quarters in general but Joseph Banks' room. Some of the actual shells from Banks' collection were displayed in his desk. We were told the interesting fact that although the modern version is quite like the original, it sails faster than Cook said his did, and the only way this can be accounted for is that Cook must have been somewhat conservative. He said in ideal conditions, 25-30 knots aft of the beam, he made 7-8 knots, which is *Maverick* speed. The new one does 9 knots.

Darwin is the only city in the world of any size named after a major Western scientist, and ironically, Darwin was never here, having taken Australia to starboard on his westabout circumnavigation aboard the *Beagle*. It is kind of odd that other than a few minor Newtons, which may not have been named for the weird physicist and alchemist, you'll search the Atlas in vain for the towns of Aristotle, Einstein, Copernicus, and Galileo.

Faith Is The Place

6:00 PM local time, Friday, Oct. 19th (1000 Oct. 19th UTC)
12° 27.085'S   130° 49.420'E
Temp. 94, Humidity 86%, Cloud Cover 50%.
In a slip at the Cullen Bay Marina, Darwin, Australia.

Many people have written to express concern about our long-range plans in view of the recent terrorist attack, worried that we may be at risk as we head into the Muslim part of the world. Assuming we don't get on a plane, there are three ways, more or less, to get home from here. One is to turn around. This is harder than it sounds due to prevailing winds and cyclone seasons. If, therefore, we keep going west, we must decide whether to A) go directly across the Indian Ocean and around the Cape of Good Hope, thence to Brazil and up the coast of South America. We have no charts for this route but they could be obtained; it would mean missing the Mediterranean. Or B) we can continue according to plan and go up through Indonesia, Singapore, Malaysia, Thailand, etc., and eventually up the Red Sea, reaching the Med in late spring. We must make a decision by the end of October for seasonal (cyclone) reasons.

Niether the Captain nor Mr. Shrode can know what will happen between now and then. But should relatively little change, and I realize this is quite a vague phrase but I have scenarios in mind, we will continue as planned. If something unpleasant happens between the time we leave Darwin and the time we get to, say, the Maldives, we may still be able to bail or just wait somewhere if the situation is serious enough. But to be more realistic, when we leave here, we're committed to the Red Sea route, come what may.

Our decision has been based on the following. 1) We aboard *Maverick* have faith that the vast majority of Muslims, even in the relatively rare cases where they are extremists and loathe America, are unlikely to act violently no matter what that guy is trying to make you think. News teams in northern Pakistan are taping pro-Osama bin Laden demonstrations as we speak and have presumably lived to deliver the video. We're not doing anything so dangerous, by comparison. And think of it this way: Exotic-looking people (including Mr. Shrode's own daughter, Selina) and those with Middle Eastern-sounding names have been taunted and attacked in our own country in the wake of this event. Because of this, Muslim nations are no doubt warning their citizens about traveling in America, which even in peaceful times is a relatively violent country. 2) Acts of terrorism against Americans have been as a rule well planned and symbolic, not random attacks. Yachties are pretty far down the list of symbolic targets. 3) We will get updates on any hotspots over HAM radio. 4) Our arrivals and departures will—and this is a new policy—be privileged information. The press will be barred. 5) Our latitude and longitude may be encrypted. 6) We fully expect major ports and particularly the Suez Canal to be secure. A lot of valuable cargo routinely flows through these places on ships from all over the world, and many people don't want this flow to be interrupted. 7) The whole damn US Navy is going to be out here. 8) Nobody knows we're coming. (Don't you go blabbing about it!) All in all, acts of piracy remain, in the Captain's view, a more significant risk, and those are minor in comparison to of the dangers of the sea itself.

Paradise Lost

4:45 PM local time, Sunday, November 4 (1045 Nov. 4 UTC).
11 15 S 121 39E
Temp. 86, Humidity 77%, Cloud Cover 20%.
Off the southwest tip of Timor.

We left Darwin, Australia, and Beagle Gulf the morning of the 1st, having taken the womenfolk to the airport two nights previously. We have a few concerns. We're a bit late to be heading to Bali, the last boat as far as we know, and there has already been one early season cyclone in our latitude. We're bound to see gigantic thunderstorms between here and Phuket, that will have us disconnecting our radios, computer, and GPS units just in case lightning strikes, which could of course fry more than the electronics. There will be exotic weather events like incredibly heavy rain and high temperatures; last night when I woke Watch Captain Terry Shrode at 1:00 AM, it was 87 degrees with 80% humidity. There will be small fishing boats, unlit at night, and fish traps and nets we can't see. Our cruising permit for Indonesia has yet to appear, the engine is behaving in a funny way we have not been able to diagnose, and yes, there are pirates, and people who may not like Americans.

At Darwin we passed the 10,000-mile mark. That's a long way, but a longer stretch emotionally may be the one upon which we have now embarked as we leave the putative paradisiacal leg of our journey and head for what one could perhaps, taking a pessimistic view, call purgatory. Your Captain has been feeling an anxiety that is hard to account for. It could be he is a little sick at heart. The cruising life has many wonderful things to offer, but sweetness and tenderness, of the sort brought from home by Caroline and Theresa, cannot be counted among them.

We cannot know what will happen, but as they say in the NFL, that's why they play the games.

The Muslim World

BALI, HI

6:00 AM local time, Sunday, November 11 (2230 Nov. 10 UTC).
8° 44.472'S 115° 12.776'E
Temp. 79, Humidity 78%, Cloud Cover 15%.
Bali Marina, Benoa Harbor, Bali, Indonesia.

We arrived yesterday morning in Benoa after picking our way through the reef and we took a berth at the Bali Marina. The people here facilitated our acquisition, through an agent in Jakarta, of a cruising permit for Indonesia, something which to our knowledge cannot be accomplished without employing an agent who presumably uses part of your $130 fee for bribes.

The eight-day sail from Darwin, about 1000 miles, was easy after we gained our offing from Darwin and the Beagle Gulf, where we were forced to tack against light northwesterlies and unfavorable current. By about the third day, we were able to fetch our first waypoint and after that it was mostly a close reach in 10-15 knots with sunny skies, past Timor, Sumba, Sumbawa, and Lombok. We have been knocking off these thousand-mile passages without much fuss, having seen no rough seas since Fiji, and we may be a little softened up.

Benoa Harbor is notoriously dirty, smelly, crowded, and noisy, and if this were all that characterized it, it wouldn't hold many attractions. But it is in Bali, and Bali is a pretty unusual place to be. Today we took a half-hour, two-dollar cab ride into Denpasar, the largest city on the island, and toured the main temple and the bazaar in the middle of town. Throughout the Pacific we had been to the traditional markets where vendors sell produce. They consist of a large number of privately run stalls under what has now in most places become a permanent roof. Although they are a bit exotic to the person raised with Safeways, we'd gotten used to them. But this was on a completely different plane.

Downtown Denpasar is very busy and chockablock with motorbikes. And once you're inside the dark, labyrinthine market, the crowding is overwhelming. Stalls with baskets of fresh produce and cages of live poultry are so tightly packed together that the vendors may be forced to sit on their wares. The aisles are not sufficiently wide for two people to comfortably pass, particularly if one encounters, as often happens, someone carrying a 50-pound bag of lemons. The vast area, packed with chattering local people, is not paved, so one walks through mud the entire way, and the stench of decaying organic matter that has been dropped and walked on is enough for the uninitiated to quite lose any appetite for fruit or vegetables. Women approach you, pulling at your shirt and asking where you are going, to attempt to become employed as your interpreter and no doubt guide you to the produce of their relatives. Any encouragement at all will have them trailing you throughout your entire outing. Our experience there, though brief, will not soon pass from memory.

Bali is 90% Hindu and temples seem to be on every other block. Nearly every dwelling hosts a shrine in front with its daily offering to the gods, which in one's home will be primarily ancestral, a Balinese modification of the practice of India. Muslims, Christians, and Buddhists make up the remainder of the population.

Our bartender at the marina is a Muslim but says he is not a "fanatic" and doesn't mind serving alcohol, despite being prohibited from drinking it himself. Ship's Interviewer Terry Shrode managed to ask him the obvious question about The World Trade Center. He said that in his view Mr. bin Laden, or is it Mr. Laden or Mr. Osama, should go to America, turn himself in, and face the punishment. This unlikely scenario was presented matter of factly, and surely is quite a bit more than he needed to say just to appear friendly. He seemed to really think this was the appropriate and just solution. He also was proud to point out that one of his brothers is Christian and another is Hindu, and they get along fine. I suspect one of the themes in the coming weeks of these dispatches could be that Muslims may fail to fit into a stereotype.

The reader may justifiably question our use of bartenders as a source for general representations of views on important matters. But the fact is, one is not easily placed in an intimate enough setting with the local people to comfortably broach delicate subjects, though at times the Captain has been known to throw caution, and manners, aside to get his facts. Bartenders the world over are used to the talk that occurs in front of them. Like cab drivers, they are models of discretion when it is called for, and willing sounding boards and educators when asked. I recommend them to seekers of the truth everywhere.

Ain't No Bali High Enough

12 noon local time, Thursday, November 15 (0400 Nov. 15 UTC).
8° 44.472'S 115° 12.776'E
Temp. 89, Humidity 75%, Cloud Cover 15%.
Bali Marina, Benoa Harbor, Bali, Indonesia.

We hired a car and driver for two days to take us around Bali. Those who have been to Bali can profitably ignore the rest of this missive, knowing well enough that even one as erudite and knowledgeable as the Captain will not be equal to the task of describing our investigations. But as surely as *Maverick's* bow must rise to every sea, we must not shrink from the attempt.

It may seem unfair to the rest of our ports of call but is not really an exaggeration to say that any 20 minutes of our tour of Bali taken at random would have contained more exotica than the entire South Pacific put together. There are many reasons for this, and they are the people. Whether by design or culture, the Polynesians and Melanesians are a little shy about sharing themselves with outsiders. There is little of this reticence in Bali, to put it mildly. Also exotic are the prices: One night at a charming inn in Ubud with private bath, a real—not faux—bamboo and palm roof, balcony overlooking a rice paddy and forest, was $8, including breakfast. Of course, there are also prices that are exotic in the other way.

Perhaps aliens from outer space have visited here, but if not, we have to assume that the people we see around us are from the same stock of folks who designed and built the local architecture. The crafty South Pacific Islander can make a dwelling for free in a short time using found organic materials, and as a result, most traditional structures are temporary. In Asia, however, the architecture of the temple, and in Bali this is usually a Hindu temple, is highly ornate, ancient, and meant to last.

The Hindu temple is the most elaborately symbolic physical creation of the human mind, making our Gothic cathedrals seem unimaginative by comparison. The Captain hasn't the space to treat it here, but the reader is assured that his time will be well repaid by even a brief perusal of the literature on the subject. The construction of the temple is symbolic not only in space but in time. The temple is *physically* representative of animal and vegetable fertility, the makeup of the physical and spiritual structure of the human being and the world, consciousness and release therefrom, the cycle of death and rebirth of the individual and the cosmos and again, the release therefrom, and various mythological stories and other abstruse theological themes. Beyond that, the very *process* of building the temple is structured so that this activity also chronologically symbolizes most of the above.

For example, when a temple is to be built, astrologers are consulted and a year before building commences, sacred cows are put on the plot to fertilize the soil in preparation for the implantation of a seed, represented by a box containing seven little fragments that symbolize the fundamental elements of the universe. On an astrologically auspicious day, an elaborate ritual takes place and the priest, having purified himself, places the box in the fertilized ground while imagining he is having sexual intercourse, as a representative of the male half of the world, with the earth representing the female. The details of this ceremony are so complexly symbolic they can be described here only in outline. Of course, Christian architecture has the disadvantage of being much more limited by its own creed, as many of the themes considered sacred by Hindus are no-no's to the Christian, and others are not recognized as sacred. The temples are everywhere in Bali, and their design and construction, influencing the houses and workplaces, by themselves give the country a never-never-land feel.

What reaches the ears is also exotic, a strange mix of tonalities created by the gamelan orchestra. I would be willing to stipulate without bothering to carry the investigation further that this musical group creates the strangest sounds, musical or otherwise, ever heard on our planet. For starters, each orchestra is tuned only to itself, there being no objective tuning standard. Secondly, the group is split roughly in half, one part playing a scale that divides the octave into five intervals, the other dividing it into seven. Each musician plays something similar to what his neighbor is playing but the neighbor's instrument is tuned to the other odd scale, producing intervals quite peculiar to the western ear. Among these two groups are gongs, xylophones, metallophones (a xylophone-like instrument), and bonangs (which are tuned, kettle-shaped gongs), as well as bamboo flutes and a bowed string instrument called the rebab. The latter two carry a very weird melody that relates to the percussive sounds of the others in a manner that almost certainly cannot be described by science. There are also drums. The xylophone-type instruments are struck by what look like geologists' hammers, and who knows what kind of pattern they could possibly be up to, even though it's clear there is a sophisticated structure, or several at once, being followed. Things speed up and slow down, dynamics are dynamic, and the general effect is that of the Furies let loose and freaking freely in a magic forest on Venus. It makes one quite schizophrenic, if to be schizophrenic is to be separated from what is widely considered to be reality, to have these sounds enter your brain.

The gamelan band may play on its own but also accompanies the shadow puppets and the traditional dances including the Barong Dance, of which we attended two. These are performed in intensely elaborate costumes and portray simple mythological themes from a dream universe that are no doubt as familiar to the locals as old I Love Lucy reruns are to us. As part of this presentation, one sees that weird Balinese dance the women do that you may have seen on TV. They move in spectacularly strange yet graceful ways, complete with that side-to-side head movement, and then strike a really warped pose while they give out a Mona Lisa smile and do that wiggly Vulcan thing with their bent-back fingers. It is hard to convince oneself that they are not communicating with an overlord on the home planet to tell him to take the short one in the third row with the beard. (Where did the little guy go?)

The effect of the gamelan orchestra and the Barong Dance together cannot be described, so I will attempt an impression. Suppose you go to a concert and there are three pairs of musical groups playing: two bluegrass bands, two chamber orchestras, and two percussion ensembles. By some trick of subspace, a time warp allows you to hear all six simultaneously, as one of each pair plays forward and the other backward, even though they both start at the beginning, end at the end, and vary their speed independently. Meanwhile, as the lead singer starts to sing, his limbs fall off and become the Three Stooges with Dan Rather. A skill saw blade flies in from the sky like a Frisbee and cuts off the top of Curly's head, revealing a musical top inside. But as Rather listens to the top, the sound makes him turn into a red and green parrot that lays an egg that turns into a life-size replica of the Statue of Liberty, which, it turns out, only comes up to your knee. That would all seem familiar, compared to the Barong Dance.

JAVA JIVE

12 noon local time, Monday, November 19 (0400 Nov. 19 UTC).
06 36 S   114 40 E
Temp. 85, Humidity 79%, Cloud Cover 90%.
In the Java Sea.

We had returned from our little sojourn around Bali and were attending to some boat jobs. We had hired a young man named Sonny to do some detailing on *Maverick* and he yelled down to me. Emerging from the cabin, I saw another cruiser was pulling into the slip next to us so we needed to attend to fenders and lines. Something seemed familiar, and I glanced up to see...wait...who is that? OH NO!, it's Francis from *Okiva*! Unfortunately, this means we might have to party.

Not everyone here experiences the Bali we do. Sonny (pronounced Sony, like the electronics giant) solicited some work on *Maverick* when we arrived. Ship's Human Resources Manager Terry Shrode negotiated a deal where three guys would work all day in the very hot sun, cleaning, polishing, sanding, etc., for $35. This works out to $1.45 an hour, but the locals told us we were grossly overcharged and are just inflating the cost of hiring the working class, as the going daily wage for a laborer is $2.50. I expect an email from Megawati any day about our ruining Indonesia's economy.

I've always read about cruisers raving about how cheap the labor is here and there in other parts of the world, and it gives me a weird feeling. There are two sides to the story: This man will spend all day working hard in the sun for $2.50, while on the other hand, this man will spend all day working hard in the sun for $2.50. So it is with decidedly mixed feelings that Mr. Shrode and I engage in any bargaining for goods or services, and if Sonny's crew made out like bandits, we don't care, and we hired them for two more days at their inflated wages.

At age 7, Sonny was told by his parents on his native island of Java that they could no longer afford to support him. With many tears (I would think so; the mind does boggle imagining this scene), he left home to reside in the local bus station for two years where he polished shoes. By 15, he had worked his way onto a fishing boat, where he could earn $2 US per day for 21 hours of hard labor, 30 days at a time. Now 22, Sonny has not seen his family in a decade, having made his way to Bali some years ago and not having the money to make the calls or travel to locate them. But he has had the pluck to hustle up some jobs around the marina here, works very hard, and hopes to save his money and come to America. If you sail down here, you can give that argument about inflation to him personally. He's a very sweet guy, but streetwise. He'd have no trouble at all understanding just where you're coming from.

I learned about Sonny's background while spending some time with him on an extensive mission to buy teak oil, which was a sightseeing experience a bit different from our trip to the tourist centers, and equally strange. The details of his life came only after prodding, and only after our deal was said and done, for those cynics among you who may think it was a negotiating ploy. It's a bit of a trick to keep these real-world facts from invading your consciousness so that you can just cruise by, drinking beer on your big fat American yacht, and enjoy yourself. That there are poor people in the world would be such a tired, boring idea, if only it weren't true.

On our last day, we went to a temple called Uluwatu, where they tell you out front that the monkeys will steal your glasses, so you best take them off—which for me would make the experience a little like, not an experience. But if you must wear your glasses, they've got you covered, they say, and send a kid with you to keep the monkeys away, whom you have to pay of course. He does a pretty good job for a while, but he's not as smart as they are (unless it's planned that way, in which case I'm not as smart as either of them) and finally, a monkey comes out of the proverbial nowhere, where lots of stuff seems to come from, considering it's nowhere and all, and takes off my glasses like lightning. Then a couple of people show up and give the monkey peanuts and with no little effort get him to give the glasses back, and they of course want some cash. The monkey could easily have dropped my glasses over the 300-foot cliff once he got his peanuts, but whether or not this is a total scam, they're *de facto* training the monkeys that if they swipe glasses and give them back, they get peanuts. Everybody including the monkey made out a lot better than me, though, especially cuz he chewed them up for a while.

We left Bali yesterday morning and have had all kinds of conditions, but mostly no wind, or wind on the nose, or light wind on the nose, and rain, and thunder and lightning, and Terry saw a waterspout, so throw in some adverse current and we're having a pretty slow trip so far—so slow that I can almost hear the reggae music from *Okiva*, and they're still in the harbor. After sailing along the southeast coast of the island all day, through the Badung Strait and past Candi Dasa to the Lombok Strait, we were treated to a lightning show over the island as night fell. Bali sent us on our way with a magical farewell.

Gentlemen Don't Do It

6:30 PM local time, Wednesday, November 21 (1030 Nov. 21 UTC).
05 00 S 113 30 E
Temp. 85, Humidity 85%, Cloud Cover 100%.
Java Sea.

It has often been said, or maybe it hasn't, that unless you count playing the accordion, none of the doings of mankind are less natural than sailing a boat upwind. The infinite inventiveness of evolution has come up with quite a variety of means of locomotion but not this. Walking, swimming, and flying are so ordinary they've been invented scores of times. There are gliders and floaters, in air and water. There are worms that squirm, snakes that writhe; squid are jet-propelled, jellyfish do that ooching thing, and snails and slugs do whatever it is they do. Rocks and tumbleweeds roll, and tumbleweeds even bounce. Insects walk on water and By-The-Wind Sailors *(Velella velella)* sail, it's true. But nothing tattoos "MOM" on its arm, and nothing sails upwind, but the human being.

You've got your great feats of engineering. But skyscrapers were invented by termites, dams by beavers, and what is a bridge but a fallen log over a creek? Kites don't really soar that well compared to the albatross, and computers are simplified brains. Sailing upwind is an exception, and not an imitation of anything seen in nature. Men, or perhaps women, made it up out of nowhere.

Flying, an imitation of birds, seemed for centuries to be a remote possibility, and when it was finally accomplished, it was necessary to use the brute force of an engine and expend a lot of fuel in order to sustain it. But the sailboat sailing upwind performs a feat of engineering ju-jitsu: it turns the power of the wind against itself, to propel something made of wood or plastic or steel and sailcloth where the wind never planned for it to go. It doesn't make any sense, and it would not have made any sense to anyone who thought about it until someone did it. Who was that person? As Captain Ron says, nobody knows.

Gentlemen don't sail to windward, goes the old saw, but that caveat has rarely kept the crew of *Maverick* from anything. Perhaps the way gentlemen become gentlemen, however, is by avoiding doing stupid things, like sailing from Bali to Singapore in November. In our defense, neither the pilot chart, nor the cruising guides, nor any of the local folks, gave us fair warning of what we were in for. The pilot chart calls for a 15% chance of northwesterlies for the month, at force three, and zero-percent reported gales. (Force three, for you landlubbers, is characterized by 7-10 knots of wind with 2-foot seas.) But 85% of the time, the wind is supposed to be with you. I won't be the first sailor to feel that the pilot chart sold him some swampland in Florida, and I won't be the last.

Now, *Maverick* is a boat that was designed for an era of racing in which the name of the game was sailing upwind. It's narrow, with ballast almost 50 percent of displacement, so it's stiff. The hull is easily driven but there's plenty of sail, so it really will go to windward in anything from a zephyr to a gale.

Three days out of Bali, we were making little progress. We had just enough wind to move along, say 8 knots, and it was right on the nose. So far, we have no legitimate beef with the pilot chart. But the chop was out of proportion to the wind and often stopped us dead. The Captain was saying to himself that these waves were coming from somewhere, and that was right where we were heading. That morning we hit a squall of about 35 knots. The wind came from ahead and when it was done doing its thing, it shut off the breeze completely and we were left to wallow for an hour or so, going nowhere. Or really, not nowhere, because we had about 2 knots of adverse current. About noon we had another squall, a little stronger, still on the nose. But this time, it wasn't over in a half hour. The wind freshened to 40 and we learned where the seas were coming from.

So we had 40 knots of apparent wind on the nose and 1-2 knots of adverse current. We also had the genoa on the furler because we had expected light winds the whole passage. We made more leeway than we should because of the sail shape in our roller-reefed headsail, but even so, *Maverick* was sailing well. We were working hard, because the wind was not steady. It would build to 40, then back off to the high 20s, then 35, and then, oh, it's finally down to about 20 and that's the end of it…no, jeez, it's back up to 40. Too much sail meant *Maverick* was driving herself into the faces of waves, like a hound attacking a bear, or climbing up and up the face to launch herself off the other side and then fall, all 20,000 pounds of her, into the trough with a shock that made everything on the boat, including the soul of the Captain, shudder. *Maverick* is all heart and no brain. But on the other hand, too little sail and the substantial, steep waves would stop her cold, turning her bow away and putting her in danger of being helpless, beam-to the seas.

What this meant was the boat had to be sailed every minute. We hand-steered and constantly reefed and unreefed, moved jib cars, traveler up, traveler down, more outhaul, etc., with all the work that entails, hour after hour. There's no coffee break on a sailboat in these conditions. We were determined not to go backwards, and any brief lack of effort would set us back an hour of progress.

Maverick, in her racing days, would have sailed with a crew of seven, but there were only two of us. After 12 hours, we were physically beat from the motion of the boat and the constant work, and had made 4.5 miles towards our waypoint, a velocity made good of about 1/3 of a knot. We still had 800 miles to go, and at that speed, our GPS' estimated time en route read "infinite." Every hour, we would hope for conditions to abate but as it turned out, we had a long time to wait. During this passage, we came to a new understanding of just how long a day is.

So why not turn on the motor? Hey, we're not so proud...but it was quite clear after a short try that it burned a lot of fuel that we might need later, without improving anything. Our friends on *Okiva* have a nominal range under power of 1000 miles. In these conditions, by their calculations, they would be out of fuel after less than 400; and since they couldn't really go to windward at all without the engine, they had little choice but to burn it. We at least could sail and make what turned out to be about the same amount of progress.

We didn't want to turn back to Bali; the delay that entailed would mean that we'd never make it to the Red Sea in time this year. But it was time to seek some other solution, as the crew would not be able to sustain this level of effort indefinitely.

How We Ran Aground

10:00 AM local time, Tuesday, November 27 (0200 Nov. 27 UTC).
2° 44.532'S 111° 43.920'E
Temp. 84, Humidity 80%, Cloud Cover 100%.
Anchor down, Kumai, Kalimantan, Indonesia.

We had left Bali bound for the Kumai River in Kalimantan, famous for its orangutans, which we hoped to see in the wild. You geography sharks will already have figured out the colonial name for this large island and have remembered its most notorious resident. But first, we had to get there.

Four days into the passage, we decided to sail north, to the lee of Kalimantan, to seek shelter from the high winds and seas we had encountered, right on the nose, along with adverse current, that had halted our progress. Our reasoning was that in a northwesterly, the south coast of that large low island, which ran east and west, would provide flat seas, being protected from the swell raging down the Java Sea.

As happened on this passage with a regularity that was hard to convince ourselves was not diabolical, the wind had outwitted us. As it came around the southwest tip of the island, it backed to the west, as winds commonly do, so that it blew right along the coast. There was no lee. There was no shelter from the swell.

We were tired and tiring more as the hours wore on, so we made the decision to fall off slightly to a river on the coast that would take us to Banjarmasin, a town that sounded pretty interesting. There we could rest, regroup, and top off the fuel. We hadn't planned to go there, but we had reasonable charts, it seemed: a coastal chart, an electronic chart, and a navigation guide that described the approach and included a drawing of the channel. We've successfully entered harbors with less.

On the morning of the 22nd of November, which, although we were too busy to notice, was Thanksgiving, we closed the land and approached the channel, tired but in high spirits. Sailing was easier in the high winds now that we'd cracked off a bit. We would soon be there, and we had no worries about negotiating the channel, which was said to be well marked.

As we looked down the channel, we noticed that there were red and green beacons (red left returning, here), and, inside the green beacons some green buoys. But there were no corresponding red buoys marking the other side of the channel, as our charts indicated there should be, and this meant we had to guess where the middle of the channel was. The waypoints we put in the GPS put us on a track very close to the green buoys, and as the channel looked narrow in the charts, this seemed okay.

It was also pretty shallow, say eight feet, and that's also what the chart said. There was a strong current setting us to the right, making it necessary to point the boat about 25 degrees to port as we crabbed our way along. The buoys were far enough apart that they were difficult to keep in view, and a sharp watch was necessary to not drift to the right. But the second buoy, we then observed, was not in a line with the other two as the charts indicated. It stuck out in the middle of the channel. Why was this? Either it was purposely moved to indicate a shoaling of the channel, or it had been moved by storm surge or current (which might run the other way on an ebb, this being the mouth of a river) and was out of place. There was no way of knowing. We worried that if we ventured too far left to stay well clear of it, we may run out of water on that side. We stayed with the GPS track, and as we got close to that second buoy, but still within the line between the buoys, we touched bottom.

We'll discuss how dumb it was to run aground in a minute. But in any case, some stupid stuff was to follow. We, of course, tried to back off, but we were pretty well stuck. We weren't going to give up easily, so we tried some cute things like raising the main and heeling the boat, etc. We kept getting the impression we might be getting off. But Captain! Remember that current? By the time we realized we were having no success, we had drifted 100 yards from the channel. A hundred yards, as we were to find out, is a long way to move a boat that is aground, upwind against a strong current, with only the power of your arms. It was time to give up and drop the anchor, all of about six feet down.

Here I started thinking, "Maybe, after all, this is a job better left to the professional." As if on cue, a tug in the channel towing a big old barge lost power and, therefore, control of its barge, and he was just upstream from us. Aha!! Now, there's a professional for you. We were helpless, and if the tug's engine couldn't be started, *Maverick* would be destroyed. But after what seemed like a long time, we heard the engine come to life, or I wouldn't be writing this.

The radio brought no response. We hailed a passing tug, and he slowed to contemplate the situation, then realized we were too far from the channel for him to get a line to. It was time to launch the dinghy and kedge off; getting out of here was up to us alone. It's always true, but it seems a little truer when you're in a semi-civilized country where you no speaka da language, 10,000 miles from home.

We hurriedly pumped up the inflatable and Search and Rescue Squad Leader Terry Shrode got in it. We lowered the outboard into the dinghy in three feet of chop, and this is something I hope you all get to experience someday. I handed him the 25-lb. Danforth and 175 feet of rode. The Captain insisted, against protestations from the dauntless Mr. Shrode, that he wear a PFD and harness himself to the dinghy in the current and rough conditions. If he lost his balance and fell out of the dinghy, which was totally a possibility while trying to deploy the anchor, and was not connected, he surely would not have survived.

Some local fishermen in a small open boat, Muslims no doubt, tried to help by taking the line from Terry and trying to move us, but it was hopeless. That they even attempted it showed much more empathy and generosity than common sense. I couldn't figure out whether their effort was more encouraging to international relations than their failure was disappointing in our immediate circumstances.

So Mr. Shrode went back to plan A, or is it B, and dropped the anchor. When he returned with the anchor rode, we ran it over the bow roller and back to one of our primary winches. It takes about seven rotations of the winch handle, each about the equivalent of lifting a 50-pound bag of sand, to bring in one foot of line. Since we had about 300 feet to go, we had to run the anchor out twice in the dinghy. I'll do the math for you: that's 2100 reps on the winch, of which Mr. Shrode did more than his fair share. On our minds at the time was the sailor in Tonga this year, about our age, who kedged his boat off the reef but had a heart attack and died. Impressively, the Danforth had enough holding power to stay put while we dragged all ten tons of boat through the mud, as the chop frequently jerked the bar-tight rode.

Why not just wait until high tide floats you off? Well, maybe that would have been a good idea. But here's what happens when the tide rises in a decent chop: 20,000 pounds of boat is lifted up a few inches by each wave and then dropped like a piece of pie on the floor. The higher the tide gets, the farther the boat drops. This is unpleasant. A boat a football field away from a channel is going to experience a lot of those before all is said and done, and the Captain thought he could not endure the thought of this, and he was not sure the boat could endure the actuality of it. Action had to be taken.

We finally dragged the boat the whole way and got off after an afternoon of dangerous and exhausting physical work, and if we were tired on the way in to Banjarmasin, I don't know what we were by now. We motored back out of the channel, relieved but humbled.

About that time we had a radio contact with *Okiva* scheduled. The voice of Paul Moore crackled over the airwaves from out there in the welter, and he told us it was tough going and they were tired. We told them what happened to us, and that we were also very tired and not sure what we had the energy to do. We traded advice. Captain Paul told me to just anchor offshore and get some rest. Put out all your chain, says he, and the Bruce will hold, even in five feet (now) of chop and 25 knots, taking waves over the deck, near a shipping lane, on a lee shore in a bunch of current. It went against just about every rule of anchoring, but we set it anyway, using 40 feet of 5/8-inch nylon as a snubber, and it held when we challenged it. We did not want to make another mistake, so the Captain watched it for quite a while. We set the anchor alarm on the GPS (I doubt if it would have awakened me, really) and got some rest, but it was a bumpy night.

Paul was right; we didn't move an inch, although it got pretty rolly when the current put us beam-to the seas. A modern anchor is an amazing piece of technology, and both the Bruce and Danforth had proved themselves and saved *Maverick* on this day.

My advice to Paul wasn't so good, but he had little choice. I told him to head our way and seek shelter somewhere along the coast and then work his way along the shore to Kumai. Close in, the seas were a little smaller, I told him, and it would be possible to find a better anchorage, at least, than we had, up the coast. It was pretty true.

Before we went to sleep, we reviewed what had gone wrong. We at first assumed the obvious, that, exhausted and wishing to be in port, we had done some sloppy navigation. But a review of the GPS waypoints showed them exactly in the middle of the channel according to both charts and the drawing in the coastal pilot, and our track down the line between the waypoints, as recorded on the GPS and brought up for review, was spectacularly accurate. The middle of the channel had simply been moved to the left or all three sources of information were wrong.

When we woke up the next morning, chastened by this debacle, we decided to abandon the idea of getting into Banjarmasin. We would face the music and tack west along the south coast of Kalimantan, following *Okiva*. Again battling adverse current and wind, we arrived at the mouth of the Kumai River, a distance of about 160 miles, a full three days later. On the last day of our passage, we were introduced to the impressive thunderstorms for which this area of the world is well known. In another dispatch, I'll have more to say about this experience.

Okiva had made it in the previous night and was anchored in a small bay. We hired a guide named Gilang to take us through the shallows and about 10 miles upriver to the town of Kumai and the Orangutans. After we safely anchored across from town, we got together with the *Okiva* guys for dinner and sea stories. We were grateful to be on land.

KUMAI

10:00 AM local time, Wednesday, November 28, 2001.
2° 44.532'S 111° 43.920'E
Temp. 80, Humidity 83%, Cloud Cover 100%.
Kumai, Kalimantan, Indonesia.

Once at anchor near a funky fuel dock across the river from the town of Kumai, Paul and Francis of *Okiva*, First Mate Terry Shrode and the Captain were in a mood to sit in a restaurant, have a cold beer, and shake off the passage from Bali. Gilang, the guide we had hired, picked us up on the same boat we were to use on the trip to see the monkeys and orangutans, and ferried us over to the wharf where the local fishing fleet of large boats with a radical sheer was moored. Wedging the *African Queen*-style launch between the fleet and some other smaller, old-fashioned wooden boats, we clambered over the decks of a couple of them in the dark and pouring rain to a walkway consisting of loose and rotting one-by-tens between unpainted, ramshackle, clapboard buildings, and gained the main street.

The short but densely adventurous trip from the boat to the street was archaic and foreign enough, and the street made one feel as if he were in a frontier outpost in 1850. There were no streetlights. Various small wooden structures housed establishments of indeterminate function that were dimly lit by lanterns if they were lit at all. Through the heavy rain and gloom, it was possible to see that many had people sitting inside, talking and eating. These were snack bars, selling only tea and some small portions of chicken satay or whatever was the specialty. Gilang led us to believe that the main attraction of these places, beside the food, was conversation with the youngish women who would serve the customers.

The choice of restaurants for a full dinner was limited, but as we walked down the street through the mud puddles, Gilang chose what looked like it might be the biggest place in town, with a seating capacity of perhaps 15. We entered and took off our foul-weather gear that seemed like fancy city-folk attire in comparison to the dress of the locals. Choosing we knew not what from the unheated steam trays, we found the food—rice, fried chicken, vegetables, noodles—quite palatable. When we first arrived, the small room was faintly lit by the glow of a kerosene lamp, but upon our arrival, the proprietor ignited the brighter Coleman knock-off and this lent a little more cheer to the scene. Dinner and drinks for five was about $10 US.

Beer, however, was not available. This was a Muslim town in a Muslim country, and even if we had not been in the middle of Ramadan, alcohol is illegal. Gilang said its illegality had as much to do with controlling crime and rowdiness as it did religion. The prohibition applied *de facto* primarily to the poor, because rich Muslims who could afford to go to the nice restaurant in the nearby larger town of Pangkalanbun could get alcohol, although I don't remember it being on the menu. Gilang took us there on another night and it was no problem to order beer, Ramadan or no Ramadan. Bootleg whiskey could also be purchased by asking around. What was required in Kumai to break the law with impunity is not unique to Borneo: discretion and money.

Bali was strange but self-consciously so. Tourism is big business and Balinese art, dance, and music have long since established their appeal to an audience beyond the small island of their origin. But Kumai is not a tourist town. They have seen tourists, but because it is a bit difficult to get here from the outside world, the majority of these are yachties on the way from Bali to Singapore, and this is a pretty small number of people. We saw no other Westerners during the six days we were here.

There are no tourist amenities at all, except the river travel arranged by the guides, and one wilderness lodge catering to monkey seekers, up the river, closed now for the season. There are no ATMs in Kumai and only one in Pangkalanbun; and this gives only $30 at a time. The closest Internet café is 500 kilometers from here. The exotic feeling of Kumai stems from its being just what it is, an isolated town in a strange land, far from anywhere you've ever been and practicing customs you've never heard of. We saw some men playing dominoes, but they weren't gambling in the normal sense. When you lost, you had to stick a clothespin somewhere on your body. These men had them on their faces. Evidently, you play for the pleasure of seeing the other fellow's pain, and as we'll see in a later missive, this was a comparatively benign cultural practice.

On the other hand, there are satellite dishes and small stores selling lots of video CDs, which seem to be the main form of entertainment. This naturally led the Captain to ask the sophisticated Gilang about acquiring the latest album by our favorite recording artist, and I think the reader knows to whom I refer. I complained to him that in Bali we saw no Britney posters at all, and my query was really just in jest since I in fact was sure that our girl's fame could not have penetrated the primitive jungle towns of Borneo. He just lit right up, and said, "She's bloody beautiful." He regaled us with all the latest news, including Britney's new movie and tour, and something about her being set up with one of those sons of Prince Charles. I was all aflutter, you can be sure. He said I just didn't look in the right places in Bali, and before we left, Gilang presented me with a parting gift of the "Oops...I Did It Again" CD, that he bought somewhere around here. Now it turned out the CD was a bootleg and also had some tracks by that pretender to the throne, Mandy Moore. Southeast Asia is the land of bootlegs. Some nights the electricity was on in town, and though, oddly, this didn't do much to change the lighting situation, the restaurant where we had become accustomed to taking our evening meal had the video player going. On it was a karaoke Beatles video, with real Beatles music but actors playing the four Moptops. I wonder how much dough Sir Paul collects for that one.

I took a lot of pictures of Kumai, but these don't show the sounds and smell the smells and see how people relate to you and others. You can't hear the girls say, "Hey, Mistah" as you walk by. (These are not prostitutes but merely curious locals or perhaps hawkers, wishing to attract you to their eating establishment.) You can't see the traffic going one way down the street, and then later going the other way, with no signal from anywhere to notify the uninformed of the change.

At night, the muezzins in the mosques would sing the Koran from distorted loudspeakers. To become one of the singers is an honor and auditions are held. There are established ways of singing and phrasing, and it must be done properly. But at anchor across the river, we could hear the singing from four or five different mosques simultaneously and the combined effect was eerie. They began at sundown, at the same time people lit off firecrackers to celebrate the end of the day's fast. (The end of fasting for the day was announced on VHF channel 16!) The singing continued without pause until dawn.

People were friendly and a little curious but not invasively so and certainly not threatening in any way. We, like Paul of *Okiva*, have decided it feels too lame to do as some cruisers have suggested and claim to be Canadians, so we just tell them we're from America. This from time to time elicits a joke about the Captain's beard and Osama, followed by much laughter.

At a small shop (there are no large shops), a young lady of about 15 with a glowing smile, wearing the chador, asked me where we were from.

"America."

"Are you Christians?" she asked.

For an instant, the Captain considered giving his usual Kierkegaardian response, something that he will spare the reader, but be assured it is thought-provoking, moving, and profound. However, he was restrained by what the guides have told us, that there is no comprehensible answer in this part of the world that does not involve a straightforward claim for one religion or another.

"Yes," I replied.

"Then are we enemies?" she said, still smiling but in complete earnest.

When you think about it, this is heartbreaking. But the Captain did not think about it, and spontaneously laughed out loud.

"No."

She laughed, too, but asked, "Are you afraid?"

"No—should I be?"

She said, brightly, "Yes."

Gilang

10:00 AM local time, Wednesday, November 28, 2001.
2° 44.532'S 111° 43.920'E
Temp. 80, Humidity 83%, Cloud Cover 100%.
Kumai, Kalimantan, Indonesia.

Our guide up the river and around Kumai was Gilang Ramadhan Albanjari. A native of Kumai, about 30 years of age, Gilang was a thoughtful and considerate host and a very interesting person to have along. He knew about the orangutans, but it was his savvy analysis of other aspects of our experience of Borneo and Indonesia that was the more fascinating. He spoke English, Arabic, and Indonesian, though he was only educated through age 13. He'd traveled around Indonesia and was nobody's fool.

One night Paul, Francis, and I had a good time, over a bottle of bootleg whiskey on the deck of the fuel dock, trying to figure out, with Gilang, how he could corner the market on cruisers from his competitor, Harry. We argued that the key to the whole thing was moorings. If he had, say, eight moorings, which we figured he could put in for $100 each, we thought he could generate a profit of over $3000 per year, a large sum around here, without doing much work. He had a good thing going with the guy at the fuel dock, who owned the riverfront property where the moorings would be located. The moorings would lock in the cruisers for other services, such as fuel, water, ice, laundry, etc., not to mention Gilang's guide services. He could get around the alcohol laws by putting out the word to cruisers on their way here that they needed to bring their own, which Gilang could then charge to keep cold at a bar and serve, like they used to do in Oklahoma.

Francis was ready to sketch out the method for making the moorings and show how Gilang could raise them every year for inspection, since no diver would enter the crocodile-infested river, when Gilang resignedly pointed out the main flaw in our plans. In Indonesia, he said, the cost of paying off local officials, plus the army, the navy, the police, and the harbor police, made it impossible for all but the rich to set up anything this elaborate. But maybe we encouraged him to give it a go, and I hope he does.

Gilang is a Muslim in the most populous Muslim country in the world. Yet he pointed out to us that Islam is not native to Indonesia, and a more ancient, indigenous belief system is so well established that Islam has been adapted as necessary by most local practitioners to accommodate it. So the Islam of Borneo is not quite the Islam of Saudi Arabia or Iran.

I asked his views on Osama bin Laden and the Muslim activists in Jakarta and other hotspots of Indonesia. On the latter, he was rather skeptical of the purity of their motivation. He believed there was money involved, and power politics, and that recently graduated students, now unemployed, were being cynically manipulated by politicians for their own reasons. It's hard to remember this when you watch CNN and everything is seen as relating to the US, but politics is local, so that even if there is a backdrop in some quarters of international Muslim anti-Americanism, the main focus of these local groups is on their own fights, not on actions thousands of miles away.

On the subject of Osama, Gilang predicted the Taliban would cave, as it were, and Osama would flee to Kashmir. He believes Osama committed a grave crime. Gilang was sophisticated enough that he didn't blanch a bit when the Captain, in the most delicate way he could, suggested that because of his field of work, where he not only depends on Westerners for an income but also spends a lot of time with them, his views might be somewhat self-serving. What he said in response was that this was simply a case of right and wrong, and that there could be no justification for killing innocent people in an office building. (I found this attitude to be pretty common, although we remind the reader here of *Maverick's* minimalist research policy.) If America had to kill 10,000 or 20,000 Afghanis to make it clear that this wasn't acceptable, then he thought it wasn't an unnecessarily harsh way to make a point, as regrettable as it may be.

Gilang told us a story that may provide an illustration about ancient religious beliefs but also about an Indonesian sense of justice, the relationship between justice and individual rights, and in what way this idea of justice may differ from our own. This story involves ethnic, not religious, conflict, but perhaps we can see some parallels. I leave it to the reader to sort out what these relationships might be, as this would take us far beyond the Captain's mandate.

There was in Borneo a minority of people who were natives of Madura, another Indonesian island, and had migrated here. Through their behavior, which Gilang said mostly consisted of thievery, they had, over a period of time, made themselves unwelcome among the Dayak, the aboriginal people of Borneo. At one point, some Maduran teenagers raped a Dayak girl, setting off a rather severe response. The Madurans were attacked with swords and blowpipes by the Dayak, and 1,000 were killed. The Indonesian government finally brought over a ship and took the rest of the Madurans off of Borneo.

Some of the Dayak ate the hearts of the dead, believing that this would give to them the victim's power. It was also thought a good idea for those who had never killed a human before to taste the blood of the fallen enemy, to help ward off nightmares. Those who were killed were decapitated and their heads, the ones that weren't taken home as trophies, were brought to a central place. It was believed that since these people did not die naturally, their ghosts could haunt those who killed them. But by performing a rite in the presence of these heads, the souls of the dead could be freed for the afterlife, and this would eliminate the possibility that they could make trouble for the living.

It sounds like a story from Herodotus, but it happened eight months ago, about the time we left California, and Gilang, armed with sword and blowpipe, was one of the Dayak warriors. Gilang is aware that Islam does not require or condone the practice described above, but it is part of a belief system ancient and ingrained enough that the Islamic view is trumped by the aboriginal. The Captain admits that the story was foreign enough to his personal experience that he searched his mind in vain to find the appropriate social response.

The River

10:00 AM local time, Saturday, December 1, 2001.
2° 44.532'S 111° 43.920'E
Temp. 84, Humidity 80%, Cloud Cover 100%.
Kumai, Kalimantan, Indonesia.

Early in the morning of our trip up the river, Gilang arrived on our launch, the *Cayaha Purnama*, which we are told means moonlight, with its skipper and a cook. We loaded our personal gear aboard and got underway.

An aside here about traveling by sailboat. Although we have little space for personal possessions, since most of *Maverick's* volume is taken up with tanks, gear, spares, sails, tools, and provisions, we have quite a bit more stuff than you'd be able to carry in conventional travel, e.g., 100 or so books, guitar, etc. Plus, we're home all the time. No matter how exotic the place where we are may be, at night we return to a familiar and cozy, if utilitarian, living space. This was a rare trip away from *Maverick*, left anchored in the river, with a guard hired by Gilang as part of the deal.

Once aboard the *Cayaha Purnama*, Captain Paul and I found ourselves wandering instinctively to the helm to check out navigation, radio, and safety gear. What we found was a cassette deck. No compass, depthsounder, radio, or charts. We figured our skipper, Mr. Emeng, must really know what he's doing.

We chugged down the Kumai River a mile or so and took a left onto the Sekonyer, a tributary. The banks were densely lined by the Nipah Palm, a tree I'd never seen before. It's a palm but it lives right in the brackish water, where you might normally see mangroves, and is unique to my experience in that the fronds are not supported by a tall trunk but sprout directly from the waterline. The look is Mesozoic; we were entering a dreamscape, pure jungle, but not what one might have visualized.

On the right bank was Tanjung Putting National Park, home to orangutans (*Pongo pygmaeus*), proboscis monkeys, gibbons, red leaf-eating monkeys, and macaques. It's also home to a research facility established and still partly administered by Dr. Birute Galdikas, a woman in the Jane Goodall mold who's been here for 30 years. I have no idea why Diane Fossey and Jane Goodall are so famous and this name is completely unfamiliar. The park is staffed by 60 rangers and administrators, and much of their time is spent defending the reserve against timber poachers. Their budget is stressed as are organizations like this everywhere, and here eco-tourism has been hurt by the economic decline of Indonesia and bad publicity about political unrest. Orangutans are found in the wild only on two islands, both in Indonesia, one being Borneo. Their continued existence here is largely attributable to Dr. Galdikas' efforts.

On the other side of the river, and even, illegally, within the park, loggers harvest trees like ironwood, the wood of which is valuable enough, in an economically depressed area, to make the risk of breaking the law a small deterrent. If orangutans find their way across the river (they're smart enough to untie the line securing a boat to its mooring and float across), they're in a bit of danger from the loggers. But this can't be explained to them.

As we proceed on our voyage, the Nipah palms yield to trees acclimated to fresh water and the river narrows. We hear the songs of jungle birds and the whoops of gibbons. A nice lunch of local fare is prepared by the cook on a one-burner stove, and Gilang starts pointing out proboscis monkeys he spots in the trees. We at first have trouble locating them. We take a right on another, now very narrow tributary and a little while later, after a mesmerizing five-hour boat ride, we dock at Camp Leakey, named for the paleontologist and mentor of Dr. Gildakas.

We're taken by the guides at the camp on a mile-long trek into the swampy jungle, most of which is on single, springy one-by-eights nailed to small logs so that we are held a couple of inches above the water. We're warned of leeches, so we try to avoid losing our balance, and I think that I wouldn't have wanted the job of constructing this walkway. All the while, the guides whoop and call the names of the most recently released orangutans, who are alerted that it's dinnertime. Orangutan means "man of the jungle" as opposed to "man of the city." Long before Darwin, the people of Borneo recognized the primates as close relatives of humans.

The camps receive orangutans from people who try to raise them as pets without realizing what a handful they will become. They also get them from loggers. The mother will become aggressive trying to defend her offspring, and the loggers kill her so they can do their work, as they don't have the skill necessary to capture her—although those that do will poach orangutans to sell. Sometimes they take the orphans to one of the camps, where the staff will train them to live in the wild and release them. They then become part of the larger community of wild orangutans living in the area. But unlike the social chimpanzees and gorillas, the orangutan will live life alone.

The feeding stations, set up near the camps to act as sort of a halfway house for the newly released orphans, are where you are taken by the staff to observe the orangutans as they come to get bananas and milk. We reach a small clearing with a platform and a couple of benches—only the crews of *Okiva* and *Maverick* are there today—and we wait and slap mosquitoes while the guides put out food and continue to call. Then, before we notice anything, the guides sense that a primate is approaching, often guessing who it is. Soon, we see the trees shaking as they swing towards us. The guides can tell whether monkeys or orangutans are coming, and they know all the orangutans by name.

Then they appear, emerging from the deep jungle around and beyond us. One at a time, they warily swoop down to slurp some milk and grab a bunch of bananas, and then retreat to a tree branch to feast. Most are females, but we also see a big male in each camp, only one. The males don't tolerate one another, so if a dominant male is around, the others will not approach. They keep their distance, but at one point a male heads over towards us, and the guides gently persuade him to retreat. If he got a notion to become aggressive, he could easily tear us limb from limb. Most of these animals have been released into the preserve, but there are wild orangutans that come for the food, too, and we see one large male who was born in the wild.

We stay on the boat that night, moored near another camp, and listen to the sounds of the jungle. The next day we visit two other camps, see more orangutans, and meet "Barry," a tame gibbon who lives with the guides and jumps on the boat as soon as we arrive. The gibbons in the jungle are shy and are difficult to observe, but Barry was raised as a pet and given to the park, and has the run of the camp. He immediately made friends with Ship's Primatologist Terry Shrode. You've seen gibbons in zoos, but there can't be many things quicker or more uncivilized than a gibbon on the loose. We were incapacitated with laughter.

On the trip back down river, we'd become pretty good at spotting the proboscis monkeys in the trees along the riverbank, and in the waning afternoon, there were hundreds of them. The river widened and finally we entered the Kumai.

It was bittersweet to come back to see *Maverick* and *Okiva* peacefully at anchor. We had ventured into the jungle. The Captain had taken the measure of the Wild Man of Borneo, and vice versa. But the beautiful trip to visit him, his courtiers, and his mysterious realm, the true forest primeval, had come to an end, never to be experienced again.

1000 Miles to Windward

10:00 AM local time, Tuesday, December 11 (0200 Dec. 11 UTC).
1° 11.776'N 104° 5.785'E
Temp. 86, Humidity 80%, Cloud Cover 100%.
At a slip, Nongsa Point Marina, Batam, Indonesia. (Across the Singapore Strait from Singapore)

When we returned from the river expedition and prepared once again to go out and wage war, which is how we conceived of it, we decided to change down to our 90% from the genoa we had unfortunately had up until Kumai. When we went to do this, we discovered that the part of the furler extrusion that connects to the drum, and therefore takes the strain of turning the entire extrusion, had become a tangled mess of aluminum. (For you non-sailors, the furler is a mechanism that allows us to wind up the headsail like a window shade.) This was due to the failure of a bearing inside the extrusion holding it straight and off the forestay, which was not an issue until the whole rig had been put under so much tension during the passage from Bali. Even Master Bosun Terry Shrode, who always describes gear failure in relaxed terms, was a bit worried about this one. It was a complete mess, seeming not to allow room for a fix. If we couldn't jury rig something, it would comprise a dire situation. With 600 heavy upwind miles to go, we would have to raise and lower the sail on the extrusion slot every time we needed to douse or hoist. This would be a daunting prospect even for both of us when a thunderstorm headed our way.

Mr. Shrode managed a genius repair using more bearings, many hose clamps, and some J. B. Weld. The latter didn't do much, but with it and the hose clamps, we hoped that we could use the furler, if we never used it to reef. This meant keeping too much sail or not enough sail up at times, but we couldn't risk the strain on that section that reefing would entail. We knew how important it was to have just the right amount of power at all times. Facing that mess out there with questionable gear was weighing heavily on the Captain's mind.

I mentioned that the day before we entered the Kumai River, we experienced the first of many thunderstorms we were to encounter on this trip. We had seen squalls all the way from California, but they aren't all the same. Sometimes they don't do anything to the wind, sometimes they shut it off and there's heavy rain. Then, other times, the breeze builds as the cold wind, dropping down from 30,000 feet or more, rushes out below the thunderhead.

Borneo is among the areas in the world with most severe and frequent thunderstorms on record. They appear on the horizon as a black and sinister band of clouds. They don't mess around but attack you within minutes, and when they hit, they mean business, featuring lightning, rain, and winds in excess of 50 knots.

The first couple of these were pretty exciting because we prepared ourselves for our usual 35-knot breeze and that's a little too much sail to have up in 55 knots. (On one of these, Paul's anemometer read 60 knots. Ours is broken.) Not a few boats on this passage shredded their headsails by not dealing with them in time. We fell off to just above a beam reach, where we could control the amount of wind in the sails by luffing up just a little, and took off at 10-11 knots. We suffered no harm other than that necessitating a change of underwear.

Soon enough, we learned to roll up the headsail completely and put a double reef in the main. The Captain decided our policy would be that if a thunderstorm developed when one of us was asleep, the off-watch person would be awakened before it hit. One of us could handle things if nothing went wrong, but if something happened, by the time the other person was awake and had his harness on, we could lose a sail. Losing a little sleep was preferable.

One night, both jib sheets went overboard in one of these storms because we had changed to some different jib cars that were larger and allowed our normal figure-8 to escape. As the wind raged, the Captain crawled up to the foredeck to retrieve the violently flailing lines and thought that by comparison to slogging to windward day after day, it was quite a bit of fun.

Excitement is one thing, but the last thing we wanted was to be robbed of our hard-earned miles by yet another obstacle to add to headwinds, chop, and current. In one 36-hour period, we experienced four of these Borneo specials, and since they left dead air in their wake and blew us off course, each one may have set us back as much as four hours. Doesn't sound like much, I guess.

Now as we prepared to leave we knew we'd have these monsters to deal with, with the crippled furler in the back of our minds. Nonetheless, there was nothing for it but to do it, so right after *Okiva*, we weighed anchor and turned to face the sea.

After departing the Kumai River, we again set ourselves out into the westerlies blowing along the coast, and tacked up to the southwest tip of Kalimantan. Here we hoped that, if the wind was really a westerly, when we cleared the light at Fox Bank and headed northwest, we'd be able to fetch our waypoint on port tack.

First, we had to get around the corner. At 0730 the morning of the second day, we had covered 70 miles from the river mouth, were 20 miles from the light, and were satisfied with our progress. Fifteen hours later, we were 42 miles from it. (The adverse current around this corner was about 3 knots.) At about 0800 the next morning we finally cleared the bank, had advanced our position a little over 40 miles in 24 hours, and were beat from tacking, sail handling, and hand-steering. We changed our course to northwest. So did the wind, and there would be no fetching the mark.

A few nights later, *Okiva* had pulled up behind the island of Serutu, at the last point before entering the South China Sea, and anchored to effect some repairs. Not long after, during our radio contact, we realized we were very close so they shined their beacon into the night and we could see its loom aboard *Maverick*, perhaps four miles away. We hadn't been following each other, so it seemed weird and wonderful to be out there and just hook up like that at the end of the Java Sea. But we sailed on, not wishing to waste any time.

Soon afterwards, following another thunderstorm, the sky cleared and I saw some stars and the moon over the island. Since we had almost never seen anything but clouds from the time we left Bali, this was a beautiful, serene vision, a good omen, I thought. As we rounded the island, the wind veered to the north, and I could make our course! I headed up to 310 true and was even able to crack off a little. It looked as though we were finally going to be able to sail free the rest of the way to Singapore.

Not more than five minutes of euphoria had passed before a small squall came through and the wind stopped. After an hour or so, it came back up, and blew 25. From 310 degrees, right on the nose.

This Charlie Brown kind of experience, where we convinced ourselves that around this island, or that cape, or when we finally crossed into the South China Sea from the Java Sea, Lucy would not pull the football away and we would finally, at last, be able to sail free, was to be with us for the entire passage. We had to keep telling ourselves things would change, and when they didn't, the disappointment could be bitter. All the boats on the same track had seen worse weather and endured prolonged high winds, but agreed there was something relentlessly unmerciful about this passage. Here, it seemed that the sea had turned its will against us and was methodically and apathetically grinding us down, just waiting us out until something blew.

Every skipper and crew had to press on day after day, with two particularly troubling worries. One was there might be a major gear failure, or failure in judgment, as the boats and crews were being pressed very hard; in fact, much gear did fail. If the wrong thing broke—if the wrong sail blew out, for example—progress to windward, we all knew, might become impossible. This led to the other concern, which may be hard for the reader to appreciate and was not openly voiced among us, and that was that it really seemed possible we might not make it. Until the moment we finally were released from the trap that we were in, the question remained undecided. On *Maverick,* we'd never felt that way before on a passage. Usually, when progress is slow, it is because there is not any wind, and therefore little strain on anything, or anyone...only waiting. But here, the slow progress was matched with day after day of rough conditions and grueling work, and it wore down your will and your confidence.

On *Okiva,* even Paul Moore's confidence began to fade, and that's saying something. Not that he ever whined, or anything of the sort. They had multiple mechanical and electrical problems, all of which they managed to find some way to deal with but could not properly fix. They were also very concerned about fuel, and tired. *Okiva,* according to Paul, can't really make any progress to windward in a breeze without the engine. It was not at all out of the question that if the wind continued to blow hard, they would run out of fuel in the middle of the South China Sea. I have no doubt Paul would have figured out something, but it would have to have involved going backwards. He'd never run into this problem before, because of *Okiva's* long range, the low chance of encountering an upwind passage of this length, and the large distance between ports on this run. But the main weakness of the motor-sailer is that when you find yourself in a situation where you must go upwind without the motor, you've got a problem. Usually it's mentioned in the context of having to claw off a lee shore (which can happen in low wind as well as high wind). But this was another example of potential vulnerability and it had Paul worried, with good reason.

The boys of *Maverick* attempted to cheer the *Okiva* crew, and ourselves as well, with some success, by the heartfelt singing over the VHF radio of that old masterpiece by the Fugs, "Wide, Wide River."

For those wishing to follow along at home, this is sung in gospel harmony in ¾ time, at a stately adagio, with prayerful conviction:

Verse One
River of shit (I)
River of shit (IV)
Flow on (I), Flow on (V)
River of shit (I)
Verse Two
Right from my toes (I)
Up to my nose (IV)
Flow on (I), Flow on (V)
River of shit (I)

The Captain and Mr. Shrode

As we got within 100 miles of the Singapore Strait, the wind went light but did not change direction. *Maverick* motor-sailed the last one and a half days it took for this distance because in the adverse current and light air on the nose, we could otherwise make no progress. But the height of the seas was diminished, and for the first time since the third day out of Bali, *Maverick* was not taking waves over the foredeck. The stress level was down as well. Almost as a footnote, we had passed over to the northern hemisphere, crossing the equator for the second and last time.

Finally, on the 9th of December, long after we had accepted beating to windward as central to the life we would live forevermore, we rounded the northeast corner of the Indonesian island of Bintan, headed into the Singapore Strait, and eased the sheets for the first time in 1,000 miles. To make good that distance from Bali, we had sailed 1,700 miles over the ground, not counting the side trip to Kalimantan. If you add in 25%, which I believe is conservative, for adverse current, *Maverick* had sailed more than 2,100 miles through those waves. But Mr. Shrode's genius repair of the roller furling gear had stood the test of the South China Sea, and we'd made it.

So imagine how we felt when, having arrived at the Nongsa Point Marina on Batam Island, Indonesia, tired and relieved to be at a dock, we and *Okiva* were told that our papers were not in order and we would have to leave immediately. (Paul and Francis of *Okiva* were 15 minutes behind, and that gives you your comparison of the upwind performance of race boat *Maverick* vs. motor-sailer *Okiva*. They had stopped in a small village and traded for diesel, and in the lighter conditions at the end of the trip, they were able to use less fuel and arrived on fumes.) Your Captain pointed out to the gentleman that we needed to check out of the country at this port and could not do so if we could not check in. We were not going to turn around and go back to Kumai to straighten this out, and that was a certainty. Well, it turned out that this was a very tedious, lengthy, and ham-fisted, yet successful attempt at soliciting a bribe. They got $30 US from each of us.

There were other troubles with other boats, but by far the biggest horror story of this passage was that of *Oceans Free*. They had left a week or two before us. We had thought we were late, but it turned out that the winds were a full six weeks early this year, and even the more prudent boats had been slammed.

Oceans Free is a 71-foot Oyster yacht and as Bristol as they come. It had just had a complete refit in Cairns and was easily worth a million bucks. We had met the very affable Peter and his pretty wife, Lynn, in Australia and they are headed for the Red Sea on the same schedule we are.

A few days out of Bali, their fuel filters began to clog in the rough seas, perhaps from bad fuel or an ineffective tank cleaning in Cairns. They had plenty of primary filters but less of the secondary and eventually ran through all their spares and could not run the engine. So they sailed the entire way and described the trip in the same terms we did. When they finally reached the entrance to the Nongsa Marina, they were tired, and as it was dark they decided to anchor under sail outside the channel. Peter had Admiralty charts and an electronic chart, both of which improperly located the surrounding reef. (This is not just his excuse. We know it is true, having seen the reef.) They hit it, and without an engine, could not back off. They called for help on the radio, and in ten minutes a tug from Singapore showed up to get them off. *Oceans Free* would be saved.

The local Indonesian officials intervened and told the tug it could not operate in Indonesian waters and forced it to leave. On the other hand, they couldn't or wouldn't provide any assistance themselves. Peter kept issuing a "pan-pan" on the radio, and after a day or so the Indonesian Navy showed up. They instructed him and his crew to leave the boat, and told him they would send their men aboard to get it off the reef. Even in America, I would be extremely reluctant to follow such instructions on *Maverick*. But in Indonesia, Peter had little doubt that this was an attempt to get him to abandon his vessel so they could strip it of its equipment. He refused, and they left, rendering no assistance and calling no other vessel to assist. Finally, after three and a half days, Peter was able to arrange for an Indonesian tug to pull him off. He still had no engine, and although he didn't know it at the time, *Oceans Free* had only half a keel and half a rudder left.

But Peter's no sissy, and he managed to get the boat into the harbor under sail and tie up. He noticed she was handling strangely. A few days later, he had her hauled in Singapore and saw the damage. The repairs will cost $150,000.

Merry Christmas from Phuket

4:40 PM local time, Tuesday, December 25. 7° 48.701'N 98° 23.528'E
Temp. 88, Humidity 60%, Cloud Cover 0%.
At anchor, Chalong Bay, Phuket Island, Thailand.

The passage from Singapore to Phuket, up the Strait of Malacca and along the west coast of Malaysia, was completely free of its advertised horrors. We saw some impressive lightning but hazards from humans were not to be found. Most of the sail was a close reach with some current help. We made the trip, a little less than 600 miles, in exactly four days, and this includes dodging the shipping traffic around Singapore.

It's a pretty Christmas day here in Phuket. Mr. Shrode has left for home to visit his ailing mother, and the Captain is alone on the boat. Neither of us had thought of returning to the Bay Area before *Maverick* does, and we talked about his abrupt departure. Even though he'll be home for Christmas, because of the circumstances of his mother's illness, it will not be with unalloyed happiness that he returns to see his family.

My Christmas festivities will consist of writing to you all, as this is really the most pleasant thing I can think of doing in the way of celebration. We have not really been here long enough to meet many of the other cruisers in our anchorage and the ones we know from other boats are not nearby, so I'll not be joining any of them, which is a bit of a shame. But don't cry for me, America. I'd rather be with the raven-haired Theresa today, but I'm sure this is a Christmas I'll remember.

The subject of this report is all the bad things that didn't happen to us in Indonesia and the South China Sea. It's most probably just luck, but it is more pleasing to think that others' warnings about the sinister behavior of people around here were based on fears and rumors, and not observation of the true nature of the folks who populate this area of the world. We still have to go through the Red Sea, where some of these concerns will again surface, but we'll give the report up till now.

The five things we were repeatedly warned about were lots of dangerous debris in the water, big ships that will run you down, fishermen carrying inappropriate lights or none at all and not knowing the rules of the road, pirates, and Muslims. Other than the last, these have long been thought of as the dangers of the South China Sea and the Strait of Malacca.

1. Debris in the water. A bit more than usual, but not so bad.

2. Large ships that will run you down. A big deal is made out of the fact that in the Strait of Malacca, you have a choice of either being in the shipping lanes or running into fish traps along the shore. But this gives you a fairly safe zone that is rarely less than three miles wide! Unless you're a single-hander and asleep, that should be well within your capabilities in terms of navigational accuracy. Another supposed nightmare is that you have to cross the "highway" of heavy ships approaching and departing Singapore. Well, they are huge and going fast, but there are usually at least a couple of miles between them. If you feel this is too much traffic for you, I wouldn't be comfortable on your boat on any given weekend on San Francisco Bay where numerous regattas are being held among the shipping lanes, ferries, and tour boats.

3. Local fishing boats without lights, or with the wrong lights, whose skippers don't observe the rules of the road. It is to a certain extent true that one may see boats with creative navigational lights. One night I even saw one without lights, but he stayed well clear. Mostly what you see are small boats fishing through the night with an all-around white light, and I believe most of these were anchored but some may have been drifting. The lights in some cases may not be technically correct, but they're certainly visible and you'd have to be a pretty big fool to run into boats displaying them.

Now, there might be a little bit of yacht-club fussiness here. I mean, most of these boats don't just have the wrong lights. They have no charts, no radio, no compass, no pfd's, no fire extinguisher, no visible or audible signaling device, no throwable cushions, not to mention no EPIRB, no life raft, no flares, etc. In fact, many of these boats have no packing gland, so the boat is effectively sinking at all times, making it necessary to constantly bail. The crews of these boats, large or small, are poor folks. They survive out here not because they have all the right safety equipment, but in spite of the fact that they don't. They have been at sea since they were 5, their fathers were fishermen, their grandfathers were fishermen, and their uncles and brothers and everyone they know is a fisherman. They are lifetime professionals who know more about this area of the sea than any 20 average cruisers laid end to end, and if they didn't have sense enough to either be visible or get out of the way when they aren't, not even one generation of them would have survived. Often, after we'd shaken off the effects of one of those 50-knot squalls, we'd see some guy in an open, 20-foot boat, with no protection from the elements but a threadbare cotton shirt, placidly putting along, far out of sight of land. We are humbled; we don't presume to question this man's seamanship.

4. Pirates. Well, *Maverick* sashayed her way through the dreaded South China Sea and Strait of Malacca, hiked up her skirt, and with a wink and a nudge, cooed, "Hey, Sailor," and nobody answered the call. We got desperate enough that we'd sail over to some likely prospect and yell, "Hey, are you guys pirates?" But usually, they'd wave and smile and hold up a bonito. Maybe this was some kind of code for "give me your money and your women," but if so they were disappointed and somehow allowed us to escape.

There were over 400 reported acts of piracy in the year 2000 in this area, so someone is getting hit. I have no idea how many were reported by cruisers, but I can't believe it's a large number. Many people have reported being very frightened by boats acting strangely or seeming to follow them or trap them.

A woman we met, Jay of the boat *Joy*, had an interesting experience that is relevant here. She said that at Kumai she had to hire two Indonesians as crew because some romance or something stole her other crew away. She said the Indonesians didn't know how to sail but were very nice and stood their watches diligently. At one point, they were apparently being hassled by a couple of Indonesian fishing boats. Here her crew was quite an asset and talked to them on the radio but couldn't get them to go away. The reason? Not piracy, but superstition. They didn't want her to cross their bow, because if she did so, she would leave her bad luck with them. But since they had nets between the two boats, they couldn't let her go behind, either. Now one who has a suspicious mind might surmise that this is a complete misinterpretation or worse, misrepresentation on the part of her crew; but on the other hand, they at no time showed any concern that the boat might be piratized, and since they wouldn't get paid if this happened, you'd think they'd have an issue with that. So there you go. Sometimes you gotta know the territory.

5. Muslims. Aside from the story about the mysterious answer from the girl in Kumai, the worst experience we had with Muslims was the following: The day before we were to leave Nongsa in Batam, a man in the marina office begged me, with some emotion, to delay our departure for a day so that we could experience *'id al-fitr*, the festivities commemorating the end of Ramadan. This seemed to Ship's Ecumenical Studies Expert Terry Shrode and the Captain to be a splendid idea, so we elected to leave a day later to observe the occasion. We hired a car for the following day to take us wherever the celebrations were. But when the driver arrived, he said that there were no such festivities in the immediate vicinity. We didn't believe him and asked him to take us to the largest mosque in the nearby city. When we arrived, it was deserted. There were

no festivals in the streets, nor any crowds, nor any sign of celebration. A little Muslim humor? We'll never know.

WHAT TERRY MISSED

7:00 PM local time, Saturday, January 5 (1200 Jan. UTC)
8° 10.225'N 98° 20.484'E
Temp. 87, Humidity 66%, Cloud Cover 0%.
In a slip at Yacht Haven, Phuket Island, Thailand.

Mary Shrode, Terry's mother, departed this life early on the morning of the 29th of December. I didn't know her well, but one among her many accomplishments was raising, with her devoted Allen, our stalwart first mate, than whom a more steadfast, decent person would be hard to find; and for this alone, she has our gratitude. Terry was able to make it home in time to visit with her before she passed away.

Mr. Shrode has returned from the United States and we have moved the boat to a marina at the top end of Phuket Island, from where we plan to visit the much-photographed Phang Nga (pronounced Pang-ah) Bay, where two of the James Bond movies were filmed. It would be reasonable to think that after so much time spending 24 hours a day together, it would be a welcome respite for the Captain to have the boat to himself, but this is far from the case. Mr. Shrode is as much a part of the voyage as *Maverick* is, and those things not made more difficult by his absence were made less enjoyable. Nevertheless, it is our solemn duty to report on our adventures, whether they include Mr. Shrode or not.

The Captain has long been fond of travel, for the reason that it does quite a good job of providing one with the rather pleasant illusion that he is going somewhere. In my time alone here, when I wasn't employed in the maintenance and repair of *Maverick*, I undertook to avail myself, incognito, of just the type of tourist excursions a person might indulge in, were he not a distinguished sea captain.

One of these was the popular elephant ride/whitewater rafting adventure. The two go together like a horse and carriage and were both accomplished in one fun-packed day. The elephant ride had almost all the excitement that you felt when at age 6, your father took you to a pony ride at a nearby amusement park. Half-way through the excursion, the mahout gets off the elephant and makes the Captain, er, drive. So I sit on the substantial head, or neck, of this fella, and he's got a lot of very course hair sticking into my uncovered legs like ice picks. But that's not his fault. There's a little bit of the mule in him, as he's reluctant to move once the mahout, with his sharp stick, is not aboard. There is little doubt that the elephant could recognize the Captain's rather limited expertise in elephantmanship, and it seemed to me that, if he should get in a frisky mood and try to, like, kill me or something, the mahout would be too far away for timely remedial action.

I also booked a boat to James Bond island, toured a rubber plantation, and waded through a limestone cave. All of these little trips were fun but suffered in comparison to the greater mission Mr. Shrode and I had undertaken.

There are, no doubt, those among our readers who hope for a salacious account of the famous fleshpots of Phuket and Bangkok. Nothing pains me more than to give an inadequate report in this vital area, yet the Captain will have to demur. Oddly enough for a man of his worldly years and macho accomplishments, he has never visited a brothel. To this I owe no debt to morality. Indeed, I am persuaded by the arguments of Kant, who is followed in his own fetching, blowhard way by Nietzsche, that a person deserves no moral credit whatever for refraining from things he had no inclination to do in the first place. Given a moment's reflection, it seems this dictum would rule out 95% of all moralizing, which is generally the effort to clothe one's predilections in more imposing garments than those of personal taste, to the disadvantage of the victim. No, my reticence in this regard has to do with not being able to rid myself of two thoughts: (1) "Does your mother know where you are, young lady?" And, as commanded by my grandmother: (2) "Put that down. You don't know where it's been." Plus, the Captain is still not perfectly comfortable with the level of intimacy required for a haircut and protests like a 3-year old whenever it becomes necessary to visit a professional. This is not even to mention, unless that's what I'm about to do, a visit to the doctor. I'm in therapy about this and other seamanlike problems.

Anyway, that about covers the fun stuff. I did manage to leave the dinghy in a place where it suffered some damage from the surf. I had been working on a dreadful job of grinding fiberglass. The reason being, one of *Maverick's* bulkheads was becoming more and more detached from the hull, and as some finicky sailors feel their boats are better prepared for the sea if this is not so, I thought I'd just touch up the tabbing a bit. In any case, after a day of inhaling fiberglass and rubbing it into my skin, I felt I had earned a night off from working on my new translation of Virgil, so I plunked myself down at a local establishment with a TV to watch a sophisticated comedy entitled *Ace Ventura, Pet Detective*. I found the "talking ass" sequence to be quite thought-provoking, although many of its subtle nuances surely must be lost on the common man. Anyway, I was so enthralled I didn't check the dinghy as the tide rose and later found it full of water, taking a beating in the waves. Certain things were damaged or lost. I haven't told Mr. Shrode, so don't you.

Ceylon

9:00 AM local time, Tuesday, January 22 (0300 Jan. 22 UTC).
6° 2.064'N 80° 13.831'E
Temp. 83, Humidity 76%, Cloud Cover 0%.
At a dock in Galle Harbor, Sri Lanka (Ceylon).

As planned, we departed our marina in Phuket at dawn on Tuesday January 8 and headed for Phang Nga Bay, a three-hour journey. We set our anchor near a hong, which is an island with a hole in the middle, where lots of tourist boats were unloading their charges for a paddling adventure. We launched the dinghy to head in after them and enjoyed that flush of superiority with which a person who has sailed his boat across an ocean gets to entertain himself, at the expense of whoever is in range. The tourists were herded around on a schedule, while we beached the dinghy and strutted provocatively about the hong's interior in our wanton guidelessness. We drove wherever we wished, whenever we wished, and commandeered a deserted beach, to the disgruntlement of resident crustaceans. After the tourist boats left, we had Phang Nga Bay, which ranks right up there with the most beautiful places of the voyage, all to ourselves. We sautéed some prawns and steamed a lobster bought from local fishermen, and in general amused ourselves by ruling all that we surveyed.

The next day we had a pleasant sail down the east coast of Phuket, and when we were abeam of the island of Hi, we turned our bow west toward the open sea. We crossed the Andaman Sea in about two days and left Pygmalion Point on Great Nicobar Island to starboard. The passage was notable primarily for two things. One was its speed. We made the 1132 miles from Phuket to our waypoint off of Sri Lanka in 164 hours, an average of 6.9 knots. We broke the 200-mile barrier in one particularly quick 24-hour run.

The second was that we lost the use of our computer. A large wave broke over the deck one night, and as the main hatch was just cracked open to give us a little air in the cabin, a couple of bucketfuls found their way below. Most of it fell harmlessly on the sleeping Mr. Shrode. Had his howls and yelps been amplified by the Grateful Dead's sound system, however, they would not have been heard by the Captain, who was staring at a wet computer and a blank screen.

The job of replacing this and recovering the data on the hard drive here in Sri Lanka has been odious. Hiring a car and driver, I have so far made the trip to Columbo, three scary hours each way, four times. While the data has been saved, the new, quite expensive computer will still not communicate with the radio or GPS. I have been able to see almost none of this country, which superficially at least seems nearly as beautiful and unusual as Bali. The road from Galle to Columbo holds some interest in itself, as drivers stop at Buddhist temples to quickly give prayers and an offering, a sort of supernatural toll, which they certainly need on this road. Among the travelers they dodge at terrifying speed are pedestrians, bicycle riders, tuk-tuks, buses, trucks, dogs, goats, cows, and the occasional elephant.

One thing I did see, while dining at a fancy beachside resort, was a local mother carrying her child, about 12 years of age, along the beach so he could hear the surf and see the birds dive in the blue water. His atrophied limbs hung uselessly from his torso, but although he was grown nearly as big as she was, she carried him with an ease that gave evidence that she probably has carried him in the same way since she arose from the birthing bed, and one imagines she will continue to do so until she can no longer walk.

So the Captain's whining about the problems with his laptop were interrupted by this image, changing his mood quite dramatically to one of gratitude for existing on the same planet with this woman, and her son.

Hell on Wheels

10:00 PM local time, Thursday, January 24 (1600 Jan. 24 UTC).
6° 2.064'N 80° 13.831'E
Temp. 84, Humidity 82%, Cloud Cover 100%.
At a dock in Galle Harbor, Sri Lanka (Ceylon).

Sri Lanka, as the reader may know, is the home of the Tamil Tigers, who are not a baseball team. They are descendants of former slaves located mainly in the northern part of the island who now are fighting to subdivide Sri Lanka, which one would think is small enough already, into two states. In the recent past, the harbor at Galle, where *Maverick* is now rafted up to a large steel yacht, has been the target of attacks by the Tigers. They put a frogman in the water with explosives, who swims into the harbor underwater and blows boats to smithereens (remember that band?).

The government of Sri Lanka has taken the following defensive measures: (1) There are guard towers at the shipping entrance to the harbor and around the perimeter. (2) There are guards armed with machine guns and a checkpoint for IDs at the road into the harbor and more armed guards patrolling the area. (3) At night, fishing nets are strung across the harbor entrance and at other potential attack points. (4) All through the night, the Sri Lankan Navy drops small depth charges into the water at random intervals but more or less about every 10 to 15 minutes, and at random places within the harbor. Sometimes these sound as if they are within feet of *Maverick's* hull, which is a bit disconcerting. Usually one to three are fired off at a time, and they are not huge explosions but are more like very big cherry bombs.

On our way here, we had the incident with the "pirates" recounted in the Prologue, which I shan't repeat. We had heard about the counter-terrorist measures before we got here, and we were also warned about the Windsors, who are yacht agents that take care of many of the labyrinthine and arbitrary formalities for a supposedly exorbitant fee. So we didn't have a really good feeling about the place when we were stopped and searched by a patrol boat before entering the harbor.

The Windsors have been compared to mafia thugs. We had no trouble with them whatsoever. Their fees were little higher than those of the last several countries we've visited, but they were quite straightforward and timely, which was a positive change from Thailand and Indonesia. As far as the mafia comparison goes, the Captain, in one of his former careers, had occasion to meet with members of the mafia, primarily in nightclubs in the northeastern US, to discuss matters of mutual interest like whether drinks were free for the band. He will confirm that they shared two traits with the Windsors, and those are courtesy and efficiency. In dealings with either group, there have not been any misunderstandings, and this may account for the Captain's lack of experience with whatever negative aspects there may in some cases be.

Ship's Motorcycle Enthusiast Terry Shrode and the Captain spent the day riding around southern Sri Lanka on rented 250cc dirt bikes in the rain. We finally got to see some of the tea plantations and rice paddies we've heard about, and some small villages. Not many large buildings have been built in the countryside since the Sri Lankans gained independence from the British in 1948. This, and the tendency of women to carry parasols against the heat of the sun, gives the country a 19th century look. (As everywhere we've been since the Marquesas has been hot, one would have thought that this charming custom would be more widely observed.) The cultivation of rice and tea makes for a different look from the rural areas of many of the tropical places we've visited, although here it seems the countryside is referred to as jungle anyway. We didn't actually make it up to the highlands but what we saw was very beautiful.

The reader may by now be tired of the apparently uncritical eye of the Captain, who seems ready to give a thumbs up wherever he may wander. But of course we have sought, as the reader would have done, to travel when possible to the most beautiful and interesting destinations along our route. Since the world is not an undiscovered place any longer, these are all too well known. You'll be notified when something sucks.

A Measured Response

6:00 PM local time, Thursday, January 31 (1200 Jan. 31 UTC).
7° 4.729'N   72° 55.191'E
Temp. 84, Humidity 76%, Cloud Cover 20%.
At anchor, Uligan, The Maldives.

Since we left America, I have occasionally posted distances in kilometers or meters on our website. I am in receipt of the following admonition from the redoubtable Jim Mead, who is senior staff at our Internet offices on the mainland:

Dear Captain,

As webmaster for the USS MAVERICK website, and an executive branch employee of the United States Government, it is my responsibility to ensure that our site complies with all regulatory orders, directives, and treaties, issued by, or entered into, by our officials in Washington. In that regard, I have checked with the National Institute of Standards and Technology's Office of Weights and Measures (an agency of the Commerce Department), and they have informed me that we in the United States are still on the English system of measurement, and that the so-called "metric system" has no legal standing here.

In light of the above, I am requesting that you discontinue using units such as kilograms and kilometers when describing weight and distance.

I here make public my response to Mr. Mead, the pertinence of which to the reader is the promise contained therein, extending to himself as well:

Dear Mr. Mead,

While it never fails to be an occasion of great joy to receive word from you, you can well imagine how thunderstruck I was with your implication that, having not seen any sign or notice of distances expressed in units other than the metric system since departing our dear country, I had innocently enough been herded down the road towards internationalism in measurement, which is, as I now realize thanks to your vigilance, one of the greatest threats to our freedom and way of life. Your straightforward and honest patriotism evidenced in the bold championing of this cause, together with your tender concern that the common American not be burdened with hard arithmetic problems, shames the rest of us and has had a bracing effect on my attention to this all-too-oft-neglected issue.

When the Captain was still a lad in school, he was informed by his betters that the United States would soon be converting to the morally subversive system referred to in your letter. As the reaction of the public remained pococurante, the government seemed to recognize the potential evil of this policy and gave it to various of their agencies for burial. But, Sir, the beast was not so easily slain, and I now urge you not to be content with a scolding of the Captain but take your protest to the highest levels. For I have in my hands this moment a document issued by our very own government, and this makes typing quite difficult. It bears the imprimatur of the Defense Mapping Agency of the United States of America, the arm of the US government that publishes this sort of thing for mariners, and, by the by, for the US Navy. It is chart number INT 71, Indian Ocean, but I could give many other equally egregious examples, wherein soundings are given in METERS. It would appear that a teetering of resolve to protect the American Way has infected the deepest levels of our military defense system.

Alas, it must be confessed that there is no recognized system of measurement that can trace its origins to American soil. All measurements besides the day, the month, and the year (which are themselves replete with fallacious assumptions born of man's *hubris*), and perhaps God's own unit, the cubit, are arbitrary, foreign, and uncanonical. The day may as well be divided into ten hours, a circle into 100 degrees, etc. There are, of course, many practical advantages of adhering to a standard of measurement understood in all lands, however weak its theological or astronomical foundation, yet these need not concern men like ourselves for whom the tawdry din of commerce is but a faint hum.

But since above all, Mr. Mead, no man exists who more fervently than the Captain wishes to remain within the halo of your high esteem, and notwithstanding the absence of an American provenance for the measurements you propose, he is proud to give his solemn word herewith that in the composition of whatsoever missives be delivered of his pen from this day forth, he shall forswear the use of the insidious metric system of his beloved, yet alien, France.

Until the happy day I can learn of your approval of this sincere plan, I carry the hope that good fortune will gratify my ambition to have the honor of remaining,

Dear sir,
Your most humble servant and admirer,
The Captain

Uligan

6:00 PM local time, Thursday, January 31 (1200 Jan. 31 UTC).
7° 4.729'N   72° 55.191'E
Temp. 84, Humidity 76%, Cloud Cover 20%.
At anchor, Uligan, The Maldives.

We left Galle, Sri Lanka, as planned on Friday, January 25, and arrived at the island of Uligan, the Maldives, on the morning of Tuesday, 29th. The spelling of Uligan differs widely on the charts and pilots, so I am using the spelling employed by the natives on their welcome sign. The three and one-half day passage was a short one, about 147 leagues, and was mostly upwind in moderate conditions.

Many cruisers choose to call here en route from Sri Lanka to Oman. It provides a convenient and lovely rest stop where fuel and water are available. The Maldives is an independent country southwest of India comprised of many small island groups that have the geological structure of atolls. Uligan, which is the second most northerly island in the Maldives, is about 52 leagues north of the capital, Male, and therefore is not far out of the way from a direct line between Sri Lanka and Oman.

The coral atoll is an interesting geological structure that is born as coral grows along the shores of, most commonly, an island volcano like those of the South Pacific. It is now believed that in the Maldives, however, the atolls have grown along what were once continental shores. In the more common volcanic form, as the relatively new weight of a volcano presses down on the seafloor on which it is perched, it sinks beneath the waves. The process is slow enough that the coral can keep building itself up so that it remains near the surface as the volcano sinks. The same process can occur as the result of a slow rise in sea level, such as with the melting of the great ice sheets 10,000 years or so ago, at the end of the Pleistocene. It can also occur, and perhaps did here in the Maldives, as a result of continental subsidence.

The result is that, at the first stage, we have a reef just on the beach, followed by a stage where we have a fringing reef that rings the land or volcano at some distance and creates a lagoon, as in Bora Bora. The final stage is what we saw in the Rangiroa, where the volcano has slipped completely below the surface and the coral reef is a ring enclosing a lagoon, in the middle of the ocean. Charles Darwin is the man who first understood the formation of coral atolls, on which subject he published *The Structure and Distribution of Coral Reefs* in 1842. Had he not written his *Origin of the Species*, his place in the history of science would have been secured by this comparatively minor work, which is nonetheless an impressive bit of speculation. Darwin had no access to the tools of the modern geologist, yet his theory remains for the most part unchallenged.

We hadn't given the destination much thought as it would be a brief stop and we had seen enough beautiful tropical islands that we didn't expect much novelty. But it has turned out to be a memorable waypoint in our approach towards the Red Sea. The two significant factors have been the nature of the island's village, and the nature of the cruisers who are anchored here.

The Maldives is a Muslim country of a little over a quarter of a million people. The customs, immigration, and other officials who came out to the boat to complete formalities before we could disembark were the most professional and courteous we have encountered since Australia. They were very warm and extended their condolences for the events of September 11. They said that "terrorism is a very bad thing." This declaration, as I found later, was not to be taken as a sign that they agree with the way America has dealt with the World Trade Center event, but simply to extend their sympathies. Interestingly enough, they had an experience in the late 1980s that involved the Tamil Tigers, a group with which the crew of *Maverick* had recently become familiar. The Tamil Tigers took over Male for a day and attempted to capture the president. According to the version I heard from local residents, the two countries that were most involved in helping the Maldivians repel the attack were India and the United States, under the orders of the elder Bush. So they don't have a bad impression of the US. However, some of them feel, and there is certainly a point here, that if the French, for instance, had refused to turn over to the US a person suspected of a terrorist act, their country would not have been bombed. These opinions were stated in the gentlest, most reasonable tones, as a thoughtful person speaks to another he respects, and included no sloganeering or hint of underlying hostility.

The village on the island is home to 420 people. There are no cars and there is no municipal electricity, although some houses have generators. There are no bars or restaurants and it is impossible to buy alcohol and not that easy to buy food. The village has a biblical look. Houses are made of bricks cut from coral and of mortar, although some buildings are made of thatched palm leaves. The streets where the only vehicles are bicycles and wheelbarrows are hard sand. Every day the area around each house is raked and swept by its owner, and each week the beaches and public spaces are cleaned by everyone. The result is that it would be hard to find a tidier island in all of the tropics that wasn't a resort kept that way for tourists. The residents say all the islands of the Maldives are similar in this respect.

Aside from the cruisers, there are no tourists here and no tourist facilities. To get here you would have to fly to Male and then perhaps take a ferry to an island to the north, where you would have to hire a fisherman to take you the rest of the way. Since *Maverick's* crew has neglected the outlying islands of Fiji and Vanuatu in our rush to meet our itinerary, this is the most remote place we've been.

Most anchorages are a little more enclosed than this one and it's normally necessary to douse one's sails before entering them. But here we are merely anchored in the lee of an island, and the passes between the islands are large enough that it's possible to sail in and out of the anchorage. This lends a touch of romance to the arrivals and departures of the boats as we see them fade into the horizon.

The sailors who crew the 20 or so boats that are sheltered here are all long-distance voyagers. There are no local cruisers, no regional cruisers, and no charter boats. Every boat here is going around the world, and there is a crescendo of intensity and concern, not to say paranoia, about what we face in the near future in the Red Sea. I don't know if this makes for a special camaraderie or not. It's interesting to see who these folks are. The majority of the boats are from five countries: Great Britain, New Zealand, Australia, France, and the US. Germany, Holland, Switzerland, Canada, and the Scandinavian countries are also represented, but the former seafaring powers of Greece, Italy, and Spain together make a meager showing. You'd wait a long time before seeing a flag from Brazil, Mexico, India, or Egypt.

It's possible now to get a rough sense of how many people are doing this. There is no official record of circumnavigations. It's a difficult number to come up with because the voyages start from different parts of the world and are on completely different schedules. Some boats, like Pik's *Mara* from the Torres strait, have only gotten a quarter of the way around in 17 years, while *Maverick* is on a pretty fast pace. But the Red Sea is a choke point. Unless they are doing non-stop circumnavigations, which is exceedingly rare, all boats must either go through here or around the Cape of Good Hope, and a guess is that 80% or more go up the Red Sea.

The number going up the Red Sea is about 80-120 a year. If we add 20-30 boats going around Africa, we get a total of 100-150 boats a year. I'm going to say the number of crew averages 2.2, so this means that somewhere between 220 and 330 people a year pass through this stage of the voyage, less than the population of this small island. (Unless the crew are a nuclear family, it is unusual for more than two people per boat to make the entire voyage. Additional crew will more often do just a leg or two.) Perhaps a fifth of them are American, so each year, say, 44-66 of your fellow citizens could be returning to the US after sailing around the world, and that's probably a little on the high side. But these averages don't go back more than a couple of decades, because a lot fewer folks tried it before GPS.

The west coast sailing magazine *Latitude 38* has compiled a list of boats that have circumnavigated beginning last century. It's less than 350 boats. If we assume that, despite their sincere efforts, they've missed half of them, which neither they nor I believe is likely, we'd have 700 boats. Doubling this for the East Coast, we'd have 1400. If we use 2.2 crew as an estimate, that gives us 3080 Americans. Given that we're randomly doubling our list, I'd figure that the actual number is less than 2000 folks and not more than 1000 skippers. By comparison, about 2500 players own World Series rings, about 2600 Americans have won Olympic gold medals, and about 2000 have won academy awards.

We'll probably spend a couple of days more here. We plan to tune the rig and perhaps switch some halyards end for end. There are a couple of minor repairs and winch maintenance, but nothing big. Then we will head for Oman, about 377 leagues distant. There, cruisers will make the possibly crucial decision about whether to travel with a group of boats when running the gauntlet of pirates between the coasts of Yemen and Somalia and, if so, will try to settle into convoys of boats that travel at similar speeds. Or they may decide to go it alone. We haven't made up our minds yet.

HIGH WIND, HEAVY SEAS

1:00 PM local time, Thursday, February 7 (0800 Feb. 7 UTC).
12 52 N   062 35 E
Temp. 81, Humidity 75%, Cloud Cover 20%.
Arabian Sea, 175 leagues from Oman.

If you take a pencil and draw a line on a map between the northernmost Maldives and Salalah, Oman, you will have the location of a string of about 30 boats who are at present getting their brains beat out by the seas created by several days of sustained 25-30 knot winds, with lengthy 2-3 hour squalls to 45, as they are on a tight reach for the harbor. *Maverick* is among them. The motion of the boat would be hard to convey to one not accustomed to being in car wrecks. Standing is impossible and crawling treacherous as *Maverick* rolls her lee rail under. One boat has lost its backstay and another has lost its upper leeward mizzen shroud, although both, through a combination of luck and good seamanship, kept their rigs up. Earlier, though unrelated to the conditions, *Maverick* lost the use of its engine, which sprang a leak in the oil cooler. Master Shade Tree Fix-It Man Terry Shrode improvised a repair with bubblegum and rubber bands, and with our repaired email facility and Theresa's help, we were able to arrange for parts to be shipped to Oman, where if things go right, they will await us.

To write this, I'm sitting under a tent fabricated of garbage bags and tape to protect the computer in case we get a splash. It's wet below, as the deck, constantly awash, is leaking at the partners and the water has collected in a marsh-type environment in the carpet on *Maverick's* cabin sole. We have the cabin buttoned up as best we can so things are festering a bit in the hot and moist conditions, creating a special ambiance.

Adding to the adventure, in this area we have Iranian drift net fishermen. This type of fishing has earned the animadversion of nature lovers worldwide as it catches and kills everything it traps in nets strung out over a league or two of ocean, including sailboats. Four boats have been captured in the nets, which are impossible to see as they are set at night and unlit, and in three cases this necessitated crew diving into the raging seas in the middle of the night to free them. This is a bit of a nightmare. Since the boat is helpless, should the person in the water become separated from it, recovering him or her would be impossible. *Maverick* is in the middle of the fleet of fishing boats, and tonight, like last night, we'll run the gauntlet.

Pirate Plotting

10:00 PM local time, Wednesday, February 13 (1800 Feb. 13 UTC).
16° 56.238'N 54° 0.365'E
Temp. 79, Humidity 61%, Cloud Cover 20%.
Rafted up to Stitches Explorer, at a dock in Raysut, the port of Salalah, Oman.

We arrived in Oman yesterday. After the rough stuff on the way, things mellowed out and the last two days we had a beam reach in comfortable seas and sunshine. On the way, we passed the 58th meridian, meaning we have sailed one half of the way around the world, in longitude, from San Francisco and now are on our way home, although we've been saying that since the first day. To get here we have sailed 16,326 nautical miles or 5,442 nautical leagues. (There are statute leagues, just as there are statute miles.) Of the 335 days since we left, we've spent 135 underway, at sea, about four out of ten days. Some short day sails can be added to this total.

The harbor here is crowded with about 25 yachts, which is causing some stress for the local harbormaster. It's a commercial and military port, and the cruisers are really just in the way. The Omanis, nevertheless, have been friendly. We have to check in and out of a security gate and guardhouse, and get day passes to go to the nearby city of Salalah. Some Americans were told by the officers who issue the passes to "tell your American friends we are not a bunch of crazy Arabs and we wish them no harm. Muslims are peaceful people." Our driver, Saheed, explained that Islam teaches one to help, not to kill. And it just occurred to me yesterday that in all our travels, the only people who have not been the least bit shy about expressing hostile criticism of the US are Europeans. Muslims have been very sweet.

Yesterday there was a model boat regatta in the harbor. The rules were that the hulls were to be constructed out of no more than six beer cans. I questioned the organizers about other technical design rules, not wishing to risk disqualification, but that was it. We immediately repaired to a semi-distant bar that, in this Muslim country, is one of the few places that serves alcohol, and we consumed the necessary quantity of beer to meet our construction requirements, making sure to order the larger cans of Foster's to maximize our waterline. Ship's Naval Architect Terry Shrode and the Captain produced a trimaran with four beer cans for a hull and one beer can each side for amas attached to the hull with tongue depressors from the epoxy kit. We understood that since the race was to be downwind, the main design issues for a successful campaign were sail area, initial stability, and directional stability. We used tongue depressors, taped together with duct tape, for a two-masted rig, each mast mounted with duct tape on the outboard side of the amas, and spinnaker cloth from the sail repair kit for a square sail, which flew between the two masts. On the aft end of the hull, we attached two fin keels cut from a plastic plate and secured with duct tape. Standing rigging consisted of marline backstays and a marline forestay attached to a bowsprit made of yet another tongue depressor.

We partially filled the aft beer can with a clever water ballast system, as we found in sea trials that our prodigious sail area tended to make the vessel pitch-pole. This problem solved, we dominated the first two races, and were ahead in the third when a very angry port captain demanded we quit, as we were creating a hazard to navigation in his harbor. We claimed our prize, Mr. Shrode exulting. The Captain was a little more reserved than his companion, given the realization that none of our competitors had passed his or her tenth birthday. But hey, we won fair and square. If their parents didn't like it, they should get a life.

Convoys are being organized to run the Yemeni and Somali coast where cruisers have been attacked by pirates. The threat here is a bit more serious than in the South China Sea and Strait of Malacca. People who have given it the most thought feel the best idea is for about five boats of similar speed to stay quite close together and if one is approached, the others will converge, but probably not do anything confrontational, and stand by to help after the incident. The fact that these people have given it a lot of thought means nothing, I'm afraid. There's really not much you can do, and by approaching, you may increase your chances of being the next victim. As you may imagine, there are lots of thoughts and opinions on the subject, as everyone's dream is at stake. Ship's Chief of Intelligence Terry Shrode and the Captain are weighing their defensive options, but there is some prudence in the convoy and it is likely we will participate, if we can get our engine fixed in time to match up with a group.

OMAN

9:00 PM local time, Thursday, February 16.
16° 56.238'N 54° 0.365'E
Temp. 76, Humidity 67%, Cloud Cover 30%.
Rafted up to Stitches Explorer, at a dock in Raysut, the port of Salalah, Oman.

Oman has exactly the look you would imagine, like Arizona but next to the sea. Men wear a sort of dress that goes to the ankles called a *dishdasha* and a hat. I found it odd that in this dusty country, their white garments were immaculate. The women wear the full *chador*, black, with only hands, feet, and eyes showing. It's interesting to see how they meet the challenge of creating an allure with just these areas, to which they obviously devote much attention. Whether these efforts break the spirit of the law is a question far wide of the Captain's mandate.

The people are not particularly poor. The Omanis have oil money and much of the work is done by Pakistani and Indian labor. It was odd to see the fishermen down at the beach using $40,000 SUVs to tow the boats they use to fish with nets in the traditional fashion. A day's catch would probably not buy their gas. In addition, the influx of oil money has enabled Omanis to afford big water pumps, which has led to wasteful and extravagant water use. In the not too distant future, they may have less water than oil.

Cell phones are common, and only slightly less common are logos of western commerce. KFC, Holiday Inn, Hilton, and Pizza Hut are noticed in the sprawling town of Salalah, of which Raysut, where we are anchored, is the port. Camels and goats roam, apparently without supervision, on the outskirts of town. Many citizens speak a bit of English, which is taught in the schools. Not a few are at pains to separate themselves from other Arabs or Muslims with anti-western feelings, and in general all are as warm as could be, if I may say so in this climate, which has turned surprisingly cold at night.

But although we were able to take a day trip to the mountains where we were shown what we were told was the tomb of Job, much too much of our time was spent on boat jobs and endless meetings concerning security en route to the Red Sea. These were not a bit more enchanting than the ones you may attend at your profession. The background of fear, stronger in some than others but felt by all, made the tone of the meetings severe, and the feeling in the anchorage was not the relaxed, warm camaraderie you usually find among voyagers. At times, tempers flared, although not those of your boys, the crew of *Maverick*. Secrecy and the whole spy-vs.-spy deliberations came quite unnaturally to us. One other cruiser at a tense moment declared loudly that the Captain couldn't have cut it in the CIA, something I gather was meant as an insult.

However, in addition to the regatta previously described, some lightening of the mood was accomplished on a British tanker that made the strategic mistake of inviting the entire anchorage of cruisers for cocktails. They didn't realize that among drinkers, sailors fall into a group not known for their moderation. Considering they themselves are sailors they should have been able to figure this out. Apparently, the assembled drank up most of the ship's alcohol reserves, and disciplinary action may have been taken against the junior officers who issued the invitation.

A Fissiparous Fleet

10:00 AM local time, Saturday, March 2 (0700 March 2 UTC).
15° 36.655'N 39° 27.704'E
Temp. 84, Humidity 73%, Cloud Cover 100%.
At anchor in Massawa, Eritrea. (We've sailed 17,404 miles, but a flight of 7456 miles would get us home.)

We left the harbor at Raysut, Oman, about midday on February 18[th,] in the company of four other boats, having joined up for the safety of numbers for the duration of the pirate zone.

The passage we faced to get from Oman through the Suez Canal is the part of sailing around the world that has the most unpleasant reputation, unless you count going around Cape Horn. The first part, through the Gulf of Aden and between Yemen and Somalia, is renowned for pirates. During the week we were getting ready in Oman, there were three pirate attacks against merchant ships that were right on our route. Then the Red Sea itself is characterized by anywhere from 500 to 900 miles of strong headwinds, with short, choppy seas and dust storms. If world cruising just involved a nice motor-sail to the next anchorage and cocktails with Hubert and Henrietta, we probably would have stayed home. But Mr. Shrode and the Captain had, back on the safe waters of San Francisco Bay, decided that these challenges were just the things that, for us, would make the adventure, and now we were anxious to get on with it.

It didn't exactly help our confidence that, about five miles out, *Maverick's* engine burst an oil hose. This meant that we had to sail back into the anchorage without using the engine, and our companions also had to return. We called the port captain, who was generous enough to allow us to come back without going through formalities in order to complete the necessary repair. Although the Captain considers himself a reasonable mechanic, Mr. Shrode has, I'm not proud to report, the better of him in this regard. Within two or three hours he had us on our way again.

The trip started benignly enough, in light air. It quickly became apparent that *Maverick* would have to be reefed down, in 8 to 10 knots, to not get too far in front of the rest. In fact, *Maverick*, since it was never the slowest and rarely not the fastest boat in the fleet, was sailing slower than normal 100% of the time.

About three or four days out, the wind built to 25 knots and the seas picked up to 10-12 feet. In these conditions, one of the skippers needed to reduce speed because his boat, the smallest boat in our group with a full keel and barn door rudder, was beginning to broach and jibe out of control.

[For the following account we will provide new names for the individuals involved, so that the character of one of them can be sullied with abandon, for the amusement of our readers.] The skipper of a larger boat, Colonel Mustard, became, as the conditions continued, increasingly frustrated with the slower boat and started to berate its owner, Mr. Green, as his boat was stable and he didn't want to slow down. (*Maverick*, need I say, had slowed down as well.) Mr. Green, trying to be accommodating, attempted to sail as directed by Colonel Mustard, and said he'd do his best to keep up. Colonel Mustard had no shortage of ideas about how Mr. Green could speed up by using some different sail combinations, except he kept leaving out the correct one, and that was to reduce sail. A boat that is sailed out of control is a very slow boat, even if safety is not considered.

An attempt was made by Colonel Mustard to enlist your Captain as an ally. I politely declined, because, as I said, no one but the skipper should be involved in making any determinations about how his boat should be most safely sailed. The problem, I said, was not the skipper but the conditions, and what we needed was a little patience until the seas quieted down a bit, when we could all comfortably be on our way. I did not mention the facts that others had had to slow down for Colonel Mustard in different conditions that he had now apparently forgotten, that he had been the most forceful in our meetings in expressing the opinion that the slowest boat sets the pace, and the much more important point that he was helping to create a danger to Mr. Green's boat and by extension to all of us who would have to assist if something bad happened to his boat through a bad jibe in the heavy seas.

Colonel Mustard seemed not to notice that the slower boat was sailed mainly by one person, while his wife stood watches and called him when something happened, not an uncommon arrangement among cruisers. So, in effect, Mr. Green was having to sail the boat 24 hours a day to satisfy Colonel Mustard. Later that night, Mr. Green reported, in a matter-of-fact tone, no whining, that they were taking waves in the cockpit (Colonel Mustard's response to this was that "that's what scuppers are for"), he had gotten no rest, and he couldn't get the boat under control at those speeds. *Maverick's* skipper, to the irritation of Colonel Mustard, immediately returned Mr. Green's call and said to slow the boat down until he was safe and we'd come over and stand by at whatever speed he set. When we had taken up a position on his hip, your Captain retired.

Come morning, I awakened to the news, reported by Mr. Shrode (his real name), that Colonel Mustard's ketch and another boat, a catamaran, had left the fleet, right in the middle of the worst pirate area. Although she was sailing fast now, the catamaran was another boat we had slowed for, since she wouldn't sail for beans in light air. Colonel Mustard had told Mr. Shrode it had been a "nightmare" slowing down for Mr. Green, and he had again tried to enlist Mr. Shrode in his effort to get Mr. Green to speed up. Mr. Shrode declined, but gently suggested, after many forceful "hints" by Colonel Mustard, that if he felt he must go ahead with the other Judas, then he could do whatever he thought best but that the two of them should discuss this with Mr. Green. Colonel Mustard agreed, and he used this opportunity to further berate Mr. Green and tell him that he, Mr. Green, had been a danger to the fleet and he hoped this had been an "educational experience" for him. Mr. Green remained cool. A boat sailed by a wonderful Dutch couple had already peeled off for Djibouti as planned, so this departure left just *Maverick* and Mr. Green's boat as a convoy of two. By the way, Mr. Green has still never spoken ill of Colonel Mustard, expressing instead the sentiment, "life's too short." Fortunately for our readers, the Captain feels his life is going to be long, so he will not forbear.

Colonel Mustard and the skipper of the catamaran had reneged on a serious agreement, forged not for convenience but for mutual safety, and had put impatience above seamanship. In another fleet, faced with exactly the same situation, *First Light*, a J-44 (which for cruise boats is a rocket ship) from the Richmond Yacht Club, doused their headsail, double reefed their main, and sheeted it amidships, sailing back and forth along the course to maintain a slow enough speed to accommodate boats that were having problems. While *Maverick* definitely had slowed way down to stay with Mr. Green's boat, the experience hardly qualifies as a "nightmare."

Mr. Green and *Maverick* arrived in Massawa, Eritrea, on February 27th; the catamaran and Colonel Mustard's boat took four and two days longer, respectively, despite their frustration with Mr. Green's pace. After the other two boats went off on their own, we encountered wind in the high 30's with the consequent seas, and Mr. Green had no problem keeping his boat under control, sailing at pretty good speed, with no coaching from anyone.

Unfortunately, Colonel Mustard and his wife, self-described humanists, are people I like. The Colonel himself had in fact helped us with our diesel in Oman. It's going to be awkward seeing them again.

THE BAB EL MANDEB

10:00 AM local time, Saturday, March 3.
15° 36.655'N 39° 27.704'E
Temp. 82, Humidity 70%, Cloud Cover 100%.
At anchor in Massawa, Eritrea.

The skipper of *Maverick* had often opined that our best protection against pirates would be 30 knots and 12-foot seas. The theory was that Mrs. Pirate would have nothing to do with her man going out in weather like that in a small, open boat, even if the kids were crying for computers to play games on. In real life, so the Captain surmised, pirates are weenies. He has little to base this on.

In any case we got pretty lucky in this regard. As previously described, conditions got suitably rough the day or two before we passed Aden. Besides the protection of the elements, some folks in other groups ran without lights in an area full of big ships (creating, in your Captain's opinion, a greater risk to themselves than the pirates), maintained radio silence on VHF, and gave their whereabouts on SSB relative to waypoints identified by name only, so that someone listening on the radio, if they could even find them on the high frequency bands, wouldn't be able to figure out where they were.

I guess none of the cruisers remembered that surveillance planes and ships will often hail on VHF 16 as follows: "sailboat at position --- (giving our lat and long), on course ---, at --- knots, this is container ship *India Princess* on your starboard bow." This of course announced their carefully encrypted position to anyone listening within a diameter of forty miles. The French navy flew over us and identified us thusly, causing Colonel Mustard of the previous missive to give them an earful about their "mistake" as if they knew what our precautions had been and as if his complaint would change military procedures. Whether or not his attitude was a factor, they never came back. We were hailed a few times by ships in this fashion though, and apparently the pirates didn't have their ears on because we were never approached. Maybe they forgot to steal the instruction book with that GPS they got last time.

After we passed Aden, the weather calmed down, but lo and behold, warships of several nations became plentiful and the day we went through the strait at the bottom of the Red Sea, the Bab El Mandeb, we were scarcely ever very far from someone with very large guns. Then, after we got through the strait and the warships thinned out, the wind and seas came back up. There seemed to never be a good opportunity for pirates to make their move. Or maybe there weren't any pirates, who knows? They hung some guys last year for piracy against yachts, and for all we know they were doing the lion's share of the robberies.

According to Tristan Jones, whose Arabic is better than the Captain's, Bab El Mandeb means "Gate of Tears." I'm not sure which direction makes you cry, though. We were happy to get through the strait, about 10 miles wide, with Yemen on our right and Djibouti on our left. Even though we weren't technically out of the danger zone for pirates, we were past the area of most attacks and finally in the Red Sea proper. We hoisted a beer to celebrate, as we watched the sun set over Africa.

The wind blew a solid 35 that night, with gusts to 40, but it was behind us and the seas not too rough. After a day and a half, the wind was down to a pleasant 15 knots, and then it died and turned around, coming from the north. In the Red Sea in this season, you hope for southerlies for as far as 400 or 500 miles, but it seemed that 200 might be all we'd get. In addition, this meant we wouldn't make it to Massawa that night and would have to anchor 10 leagues away at Shumma Island in four fathoms, a cable from shore.

We arrived in Massawa before almost all the boats in the two fleets ahead of us, as they had made rest stops along the way. Once they passed through the strait, they had proclaimed themselves in "cruiser mode," and presumably out of danger. Massawa is a dusty, Third World port, with lots of bomb damage and bullet holes from their war with Ethiopia. We'll get some fuel, water, and provisions, do a few repairs, and change down to our smaller headsail. If we have time, we'll make a trip to the more metropolitan capital city of Asmara. Then we'll set sail up the Red Sea.

The Road to Asmara

3:30 PM local time, Thursday, March 7 (1230 March 7 UTC).
15° 36.655'N 39° 27.704'E
Temp. 86, Humidity 72%, Cloud Cover 100%.
At anchor in Massawa, Eritrea.

In Eritrea, there are plenty of brand-new $40,000 white SUVs driving around, but they're from the United Nations. Eritrea is one of the poorest countries in the world, and this is where some of your tax dollars are being spent. Seems like a good investment.

The country is recovering from a 10-year battle with Ethiopia that they call "The Struggle," and from more than 30 years of instability. Wounded veterans are plentiful and the economy is a mess. Yet the people don't seem desperate, nor have social mores collapsed. There are no muggings and no looting, and there are no parentless, starving children wandering the unpaved streets. People smile easily, a big smile if you're American, and welcome you to their country. A couple of them want to leave, though, if they can do it aboard *Maverick*. It didn't hurt our first impression that, surprise surprise, Americans were given a discount on their visas. Citizens not holding US passports were charged $40, your guys $25.

The fact that the people are nice here in Eritrea doesn't mean it's a good place for everything, and when Mr. Shrode's temperature rose to 103 degrees a few days after we arrived, it made the Captain fret a bit. You never know what kind of disease may be floating around in Africa, and medical care might be difficult to come by. I emailed Dr. Frank, but as it turned out, Terry started showing improvement within 24 hours and his fever passed.

Nevertheless, he didn't feel well enough for the trip we had planned to the capital city of Asmara, a three-hour, 70-cent bus drive into the mountains near the coast. The Captain, satisfied Mr. Shrode was on the mend, headed out for the inland adventure in the company of Spencer, of New York, and Nana, of Columbia, the crew of *Adverse Conditions*.

As the small, crowded bus headed out of Massawa, we climbed, slowly at first, and then steeply, on dusty switchbacks and hairpin turns, up the hot and dry gullies dotted with miserly and thorny vegetation. The temperature is in the high 80s, though it's still winter; Eritrea has one of the highest average temperatures on earth. About midway we paused at the African equivalent of a truck stop near a town in the mountains, where taxis, in the form of donkey carts, awaited the disembarking travelers. Goats and camels wandered around the many small restaurants where cold Sprites and Cokes were sold.

We paid with local money, *nakfa*, we had gotten on the black market in Massawa. Banks offered 13 to the dollar, if they were open, but if you wandered into almost any store at any hour other than the break from 1:00 to 4:00, they would give 18 to the dollar or 19 for a C-note. We wouldn't have sought this out, but it was the normal way to get money in Massawa. Sometimes someone was called in, and the whole transaction had the atmosphere of a drug deal. Not that the Captain has ever been witness to one of those.

As we jammed ourselves back into our cramped seats, the little bus climbed farther into the mountains. The road cuts revealed upturned and broken layers of sandstone, evidence of the shallow marine origin of the rock. The area has been uplifted and distorted by tectonic forces, as they divide Africa from Asia at a rate similar to the growing of a fingernail. The result of this divergence is the three-armed fissure consisting of the Great African Rift Valley, the Gulf of Aden, and the Red Sea, although some consider the Red Sea an extension of the Great Rift Valley. The divergence itself does not tend towards mountain building, rather a widening valley, but the region has also been lifted and stretched due to volcanic activity associated with the continuing dismemberment of Pangaea that began approximately at the beginning of the Cretaceous. In addition to the moderately high mountains we were climbing, this activity produced the Ethiopian Plateau, on which Asmara, our destination, was situated.

It is, to say the least, an inconvenience that the railroad built during the Italian colonization of this area is no longer functional, as almost everything necessary for the maintenance of life in Asmara now must be trucked from Massawa up the same narrow road we traveled, along which the old tracks looked in pretty good shape. I asked the locals why Asmara was located so far from any river or sea, one of its many unusual aspects. They didn't know, but one might surmise that the high plateau has the most fertile land and, as a result, was the center of Eritrea's agriculturally based economy. On the slopes along our way, we saw the terraces typical of mountain farming in Asia, but they were overgrown; on the lee side of the mountains, they were dry and barren. Again I asked my neighbors on the bus why the terraces were no longer cultivated but could not find an answer.

We came to a village situated on a high mountain pass which looked, through the haze, like the end of the world. But instead of continuing over the saddle as I expected, we turned and drove precariously along the shoulder of the adjoining range, still gaining altitude, and gazed down at a precipitous drop. At the pass I noted prickly pear cactus (*genus Opuntia;*

the native name is *Beles*), which was strange to see at this altitude, but even odder was the presence, cheek-by-jowl with the cactus, of Eucalyptus (native name *Kelamintos*). In this environment the tree did not grow to the size we are used to seeing in California where, like here, it has been introduced by humans.

We had passed several guarded checkpoints along the way, where papers were inspected and the Captain presented his $25 visa that worked just as well as Nana's $40 one. But when we arrived at the city, there was no feeling of siege and no more military guards than you'd see in California. In fact, here, we saw none of the bomb damage and bullet holes we witnessed in Massawa. Maybe it was too long of a drive for the enemy soldiers.

The city doesn't fit your idea of east Africa, whatever that may be. It has paved streets and is large, home to half a million people, perhaps two-thirds in western dress. It is pleasantly quiet, even in the midst of a bustling day on the main street, Independence Avenue. The air is a bit dusty, but it has the crispness one would associate with a mountain valley on a beautiful day. There are European style hotels, and the Captain sprang for one to have a private bath, hot and cold running water, and CNN. It was worth the investment, because along with the BBC and CNN I was able to watch Saudi Arabian TV news, printed on the screen in English while the Koran was sung, and I found the content not as different from CNN as one might have thought. I noticed they also broadcast *Sesame Street* and *Candid Camera*, programs evidently thought to be not too lascivious for the Saudi audience.

Returning to the boat the next day, I found Mr. Shrode almost completely recovered. *Maverick* is covered in dust and salt, the former from Massawa, the latter still not rinsed off from the wet trip from the Maldives to Oman. The halyards and sheets are a dirty brown and stiff as wire from the salt. The topsides are stained with oil from the harbor and marred from rubbing against the various craft that carry officials to check us in the countries we visit. These will need some work. But hey, she floats.

THE NIGHT THE SEA TURNED WHITE

9:00 PM local time, Wednesday, March 13 (1800 March 13 UTC).
22 55 N   036 54 E
Temp. 86, Humidity 73%, Cloud Cover 0%.
Off the coast of Sudan, Red Sea.

We left Massawa on the afternoon of March 8, and we're now 460 miles farther up the Red Sea. We have about 270 more to go before we reach our next port of call, Safaga, Egypt. Progress has been slow for us—we've averaged about 90 miles a day—and we've had some problems. I'll go into those next time, but right now I think I'll give some impressions of standing watch at night.

Soon after dinner, off-watch Terry Shrode took to his bunk. The night is split into two six-hour watches, starting a bit after dark at 7. This is the schedule we've used since we left home and we're comfortable with it. Unlike many other crews, we're rarely exhausted when we arrive at a port.

As his watch begins, the Captain arms himself with the tools of the solitary sailor after dark, including a harness and tether to keep himself connected to the boat at all times he is out of the cabin, as going overboard at night, with no one else awake, would mean certain, but not immediate, death. He has a flashlight, a Leatherman, and a kitchen timer on a lanyard. This is set to sound its alarm to correspond with the radar, which wakes up every 20 minutes, less if we're in a neighborhood with traffic, and looks around for things we don't want to hit. Binoculars and a night vision scope are ready to hand. Navigation and instrument lights are turned on, and he's now solely responsible for the safety of the boat and the sleeping crew.

If the sky is clear, the moonlight, or even starlight, beats a path to the boat. This path is yours alone and if another boat were to pass nearby, your path would be completely invisible to her crew, although they'd have one of their own, which would be invisible to you. If you were an infinite being, or a very large one with a million eyes in a million places, you could see that the moonlight is, in fact, reflected everywhere it touches, so you might say that the specificity of your moonlight path to you is evidence and at the same time a metaphor for both your finitude and your separation from all other souls. If you're into that kind of thing.

If the night is as black as a bat under a witch's hat, on the other hand, being on a boat in the middle of the ocean can be unsettling. This is particularly true in two circumstances: when the boat is moving, and when the boat is not moving.

Most of the time, under wind or engine power, the boat will be sailing through the night. The reader might think that this is similar to driving a car after dark, but it isn't. The main reason is that a car has headlights, and a boat, no matter how large or modern, has none. Effectively, you and 20,000 pounds of sailboat are going just as fast as you can, rumbling your way through the black water, blind. You wouldn't do that in a car, but in a boat, the idea is that there's nothing out there to hit, and you can't run off the road. Unfortunately, neither of these assumptions is completely true.

Other boats at sea and obstructions are supposed to be lit at night, but if they aren't, you won't see them until it's too late. And in any ocean there may be debris—logs or 55-gallon drums or containers or whatnot, awaiting you in the dark. Then there are reefs, of course, and rocks and islands and headlands, and you like to have some confidence both that these are properly on the chart, and that you know for sure where you are on the chart. Not seeing them at all in the dark means that being in close proximity to them requires faith in your navigation and the skill of the cartographer. The explorers, like Columbus, had no charts or GPS or radar or, actually, brains. That's why Columbus is no longer alive. But we, like they, try as best we can to put all the unpleasant scenarios out of our mind.

Of course, there may be times on a long passage when the boat is not moving at all, like last night, here, in the Red Sea. In a high or in the Doldrums, the wind may entirely die away and the water may become glassy. If you need to conserve your fuel, you just sit there, you and the water and the sky, in the middle of the dark. The darkness is at the same time vast and claustrophobic, and since you have no reference, you have no idea how far you can see. If you get the notion to escape, the only refuge is in your little cabin. Unless the power goes out, the darkness can't get in there.

Officer of the Watch Terry Shrode was sitting alone in the dead of a black night in the cockpit of *Maverick*, becalmed and nearly motionless in the Pacific High a thousand miles from anywhere, and he heard a sound. It came from, say 15 feet out into the murky dark, almost close enough to touch with the boat hook, but on the other hand, beyond the glow of the cabin lights on the water and a world beyond his safe little cosmos. There was no boat within miles of us, but the sound he heard was a cough. Great googahmoogah.

Throughout the oceans of the world, at night you'll also be visited by the microscopic bioluminescent dinoflagellate *Noctiluca miliaris*. Known by sailors of old as "sea stars," they get excited by the turbulence of the boat's passage and light up in her wake. Seems dumb to me, cuz now I can see 'em and eat 'em if I'm that kind of boat. As though they were fireflies of the deep, they emit a blue-green light, near the point in the visible light spectrum of maximum transmission for seawater. Sometimes they get splashed onto the deck or pumped into the head and little sparkly guys swirl around the toilet bowl. In daylight, in a glass of seawater, they're too small to see, but at night, when they light up, their glow makes them appear to be a quarter inch in diameter.

I came up out of the cabin to take a look around a couple of nights before making landfall in Oman, and the whole sea was a luminescent white, from horizon to horizon. It was a dark night and it was hard to tell what you were looking at, but it seemed as though the boat was flying gently on the top of a cloud. So I went down below to shake it off. Came back up, still there. It was so surreal that I woke the off-watch crew, Mr. Terry Shrode, to confirm that I hadn't lost either my mind or my sight. He saw it too, but he's a loony old coot. He also made out dark shadows moving in the water, which he figured were fish. I believe this effect was caused by billions of microscopic guys, at some convention or another, all lit up, not quite as brilliantly as usual. Usually they flash brightly for a couple of seconds, but apparently all of them were set on "dim" because the light wasn't enough to make the ocean light up or even glow, just appear white. This way, I surmise, they could stay illuminated for quite a while.

But two skippers reported something stranger, that I would not have believed, had not I and several other cruisers seen the ocean turn white. They had been surrounded by the same weird whiteness, and then all of a sudden, the water around their boat, perhaps twice the beam and twice the length, lit up incredibly brightly. They compared it to the water in a lit swimming pool at night. Evidently the boat, or perhaps the lights on the boat, had stimulated this group of guys to shift simultaneously to the bright setting for a few moments, the way fish in a school all turn together. Then it faded, leaving the ocean once again uniformly white.

I'd read a lot of books about the sea but never heard either of these phenomena mentioned before. Although studies are ongoing, because of their infrequency and tendency to appear ephemerally in remote areas, no authority in the world of marine biology is certain how they are caused. Even if they eventually find out, it will not change the fact that I don't expect to see anything to the end of my days that will be as strange as what I saw that night.

THE FULL RED SEA MONTY

9:00 PM local time, Tuesday, March 26 (1900 March 26 UTC).
27° 24.447'N 33° 40.541'E
Temp. 69, Humidity 31%, Cloud Cover 0%.
Abu Tig Marina, El Gouna Resort, near Hurghada, Egypt.

As mentioned earlier, we left the harbor at Massawa on March 8, well within the time window favored by the bible of sailors in this area, the *Red Sea Pilot*. For quite a long time, we had light wind, never exceeding 10 knots, from several directions, just as predicted by our stateside weatherman and webmaster, Jim Mead. Off and on we ran the motor but at very low rpm to save our ailing engine. We had left ourselves enough time for the passage and had no need to push it, so we intended to keep the motor use to a minimum and sail.

The route we had chosen was right up the middle. We had talked to a small number of veterans of the Red Sea before the passage, and they assured us that "no one does it that way anymore." I guess they were right, because aside from two very large motor-sailers that could power the whole way, the rest of our colleagues chose the more common route of short hops up the western shore, stopping to anchor, rest, and check out the wonderful diving and snorkeling along the way. If the wind blew hard from the wrong direction, they could hide away until it changed and thus limit their sailing, or more often, motoring, to peaceful conditions. We're not divers, and we wanted to leave time for the repairs that needed attending to before the womenfolk showed up, so again following Admiral Nelson, we said, "Damn the maneuvers, just go straight at 'em."

Five days out of Massawa, we finally had a nice little breeze. It was right on the nose, NNW, but as it was blowing in the high teens, we could forget the light air sails and get on up the road. It was actually great sailing. So nice was it that on March 17th, nine days out of Massawa, the Captain became a little frustrated. We had sailed half-way around the world to challenge the Red Sea, and now it was just a pussycat. Some folks apparently don't consider sailing upwind in 15 to 20 knots much fun at all, and on the radio we would hear people saying they would stay anchored until conditions improved. These people are dauntless cruising sailors, but some of their boats are not very weatherly and the Captain would never, ever, think of calling them *weenies*. However, *pantywaists*, now there's another word. But jeez, for San Francisco sailors to cower in those conditions would be embarrassing. So the Captain, about whom it may not be correct to say, "Mama didn't raise no fool," declared, to no one in particular, "Enough of this stuff. LET'S GET IT ON!"

The Captain, as a rule, has few supernatural powers. But in this instance, within a few hours during his watch that night, the wind freshened to about 30, still on the nose. He had reefed early and there was not much cause for concern, but the wind was still building as Mr. Shrode came on duty at 0100. An hour or two later, the skipper was awakened by the stalwart Mr. Shrode, who wanted him to have a look at the conditions. *Maverick* was overpowered with the double reef and having trouble making headway. I stuck my head out of the companionway and said, "Dude, it's blowing forty." (Our anemometer is being repaired, but nearby on the catamaran *Liberator*, theirs peaked at 48 knots.) Mr. Shrode went forward to tuck in the third reef and even with that, we couldn't do much in the way of sailing upwind, so we decided to forereach. We sailed a bit above a beam reach with only a small amount of jib out and this way we kept our speed to about 3 knots, there was little strain on the rig, and the boat was riding pretty comfortably and had her head well up so she did not wallow in the troughs.

It was blowing a full gale. What's this like? Well, with these fairly regular seas, it's not that much of a problem. You don't like it, because even though you're reefed and the rig isn't likely to fail, the sheets are hard as rebar and the strain on what's left of the sails is worrisome, particularly when a wave changes the boat's angle to the wind and some flogging results. The seas get pretty big and once in a while will break aboard, though that night not more than 10 gallons ever occupied the cockpit.

One particularly high wave caught the foot of the jib and caused the furling line to part. Mr. Shrode and I strapped onto the jacklines and made our way to the foredeck. In these seas, which were in the 15-20 foot range, when you're on the crest of a wave you're looking down from the bow about two stories to the bottom of the trough. Then *Maverick* plunges into the abyss, and seconds later you're submerged knee-deep into the face of the next wave. In these conditions it's a bit dicey to attend to repairs, but it needed to be done or we'd lose the sail.

You'd stare in awe when one of the steep, bigger guys came rolling your way like a wall 15 feet high, looking quite deadly, but then *Maverick* would just magically levitate herself right over the top of it, *no problema* except for a bit of water over the deck. The violence of the scene and the sound is a bit viscerally stressful, but intellectually you know that you're pretty certain to be okay.

We heard a faint call on 16 to any vessel in the vicinity. It was the above-mentioned *Liberator* looking for some assistance. They were about 20 miles closer to the coast and had broken a backstay and lost the use of their engine. They replaced the backstay with a couple of halyards and saved the rig, but although they were in no immediate danger, they had no idea how they were going to get into the harbor at Safaga, Egypt, the nearest refuge, without a tow. We responded and said we were of little help, other than offering to do a radio relay. We could not have done much in the way of towing them, nor could anyone else, until conditions were quite a bit calmer. We told them we'd stand by on 16 and that we were slowly heading their way. By working through the night, they managed to get the engine running and the following day they were reported safely at anchor in Safaga.

Although we had planned to call at Safaga to do our official check-in to Egypt, morning found us, a bit surprisingly, in the position of having to backtrack some distance downwind to approach the harbor. We elected to carry on to Hurghada, another port of entry. But that afternoon it was clear we wouldn't make Hurghada until dusk, so we decided to anchor about 15 miles south at a protected cove. By then the wind had abated to 15, and we sailed between a reef and the mainland and anchored in five fathoms.

About dinnertime the wind turned around and blew from the south. The anchorage we were in was very well protected, from every direction *except* the south, and now we were on a lee shore. As the night wore on, the wind built up to the 20s and made it pretty bumpy, so we continued our regular watch schedule instead of just going to sleep, but the Bruce held. By morning the wind was again from the north and light, but as the southerly had blown 30 offshore, there was a pretty big swell behind us as we tacked up to Hurghada. It was cool to be hard on the wind, but surfing down the swells anyway.

Still not wanting to use the engine, we were under sail and in among the reefs that surround the harbor at Hurghada when a squall hit us from the northwest. I was below doing navigation and calling the tacks, redundantly by computer and by paper chart because of the close proximity of the reefs not visible to the driver. Mr. Shrode was manning the helm and sheets. Another squall came through, again blowing, say, 25, and he began to complain of the dryness of the air and the lack of visibility.

In a few moments it was apparent we were in the middle of one of the dust storms for which the Red Sea is famous. We were surrounded by reefs, had a six-foot swell behind us, seas building from the wind in the 20s in front of us, dust accumulating everywhere including our mouths, noses, and eyes, and visibility was down to about 200 yards. We didn't want to start the engine, so tacking required pretty precise navigation. It was a great day at sea.

The most difficult and stressful part of sailing around the world, so far, that is, has not been moments like this. We felt we knew what we were doing. I had confidence in Mr. Shrode's boat handling, and he had to have faith in my navigation, as he couldn't see a thing. These are things that feel familiar. The stressful bit is the stuff over which you have little control, like finding a part or fixing an essential piece of gear in a weird part of the world. And paying for it.

The gloom had still not lifted as we attempted to call Hurghada port control for instructions on how to proceed to the customs dock. They never answered, but our wonderful Dutch friends Jan and Susanne from *Adrena-line*, a boat we had sailed with in our convoy from Oman, hailed us back and advised us to come anchor near them, close to the Sheraton Hotel.

"You should see the Sheraton, Mr. Shrode, bearing 310 at a range of one mile."

"I see nothing."

"Range is now one half mile."

"Nada."

"Quarter mile at 290. You must see it now."

"Oh, yeah…no never mind, that's a cloud shadow or something."

"Let's douse and motor over there…it's a bit close for comfort."

We finally saw *Adrena-line* through the dust and lowered the hook.

We checked in on the casual net on high frequency radio as we were sailing up here and talked to the guys in the anchorages. One said we were an inspiration to him, about what *not* to do. So far, we don't think anyone we know got quite the beating we did from the Red Sea. People are reporting remarkably benign trips this year, with no pirates, certainly no sign of unpleasantness from Muslims, and no strong headwinds, except in the case of *Liberator*, and ourselves. But even our trip was a walk in the park compared to what we had in the Java and South China Seas.

And now we're in a peachy marina where we have hot showers for the first time since Australia—with the exception of the Captain's night in Asmara—and we're surrounded by all the folks we've become familiar with ever since Sri Lanka. Although tonight, ramen is on the menu, if we wanted we could get a decent steak or a gin and tonic. There are fresh croissants and lattes, workable Internet cafés, and even a go-cart track. I don't know what the human rights record is or whether individual liberties are suffering under Egyptian law, but like other travelers, for better or worse the Captain identifies the former list of things as markers of civilization and is very happy to see them.

Celebration at the top of the Red Sea. The dust storm is beginning to clear so that the shore is visible. Taken by our friends on *Adrena-line* from their boat.

Send Your Camel to Bed

8:00 AM local time, Wednesday, April 17 (0600 April 17 UTC).
27° 24.447'N 33° 40.541'E
Temp. 80, Humidity 74%, Cloud Cover 0%.
Abu Tig Marina, El-Gouna Resort, near Hurghada, Egypt.

We're in the very nice harbor here in El-Gouna, a completely new resort town where they've blasted a hole through the reef on the shore of the Red Sea and dug a maze of canals you can buzz through in your dinghy. The developers plan to make this the Egyptian St. Tropez, so they're trying to attract some celebrities to add a splash of cachet and the crew of *Maverick* has deigned to oblige them.

Caroline and Theresa came to visit, bringing a lot of stuff we need and, way more importantly, their wonderful selves. Caroline and Terry took off for Luxor and Cairo, but Theresa and I delayed our departure for a couple of days so that we could relax here by ourselves before the sightseeing frenzy we knew we were about to face.

One afternoon we hired a car to take us out to the nearby oasis that, unlike the brand new artificial resort town, has been occupied since time beyond memory. We had not come with an organized event, during which the inhabitants of the oasis, real Bedouins, step aside for the chefs and entertainers brought in by the resort hotels for their guests. We just showed up, uninvited, having established that this was permitted. But we had no idea what to expect and really thought we'd just go walk around and if possible talk to a couple of people. The oasis looked like your fantasy of one. The surrounding area had the feel of the Mohave desert in California, and the oasis, at the foot of a small mountain range, was lush with date palms.

A handsome man of about 40 came out from somewhere, dressed in Bedouin robes, and welcomed us. He showed us the tower where they keep doves, as Mohammed did. He showed us the well, which is of course the *raison d'être* of the community. We were then taken to a structure that was tent-like in feel but semi-permanent as it was constructed of reeds and palm fronds. We were invited to sit on the rugs and cushions placed on the dirt floor and asked if we'd like some tea. This we accepted, and as we drank from small glasses, we were regaled by our host with stories of Bedouin life.

For example, we were told that they used to fish and swim where the current resort town of El-Gouna has been raised out of the desert, as is happening all along the Red Sea coast of Egypt. Now, he says, they take their camels and ride 15 miles north, because, he said without a trace of bitterness or sarcasm, they are too "shy" to be around the western women from the resorts who swim in skimpy beachwear or even topless. The Bedouin women, when they go to the beach, immerse themselves in the sea clothed head to foot.

Then our host asked if we'd like to try the *sheesha*, something you readers of a certain age will remember as a hookah. We were quite aware that this was not an invitation to smoke hashish or the like, but rather tobacco flavored with molasses and sometimes also with apple or strawberry. At an Egyptian restaurant, the *sheesha* can be ordered from the menu and the pipe will be filled with the mixture of your choosing and lit, then brought to the table for you to smoke. Theresa and I are non-smokers, and we at first begged off, but we were reassured that it wasn't harsh and we should give it a try. I had crossed several seas, endured gales, drunk kava, ridden an elephant, dived into an underwater cave, held a baby alligator back in Darwin, and drunk homebrew with some guys from Tonga. Why should I be intimidated by a water pipe? We were given the apple-flavored version, and, it's true, I inhaled. The smoke didn't cause much of any feeling going down, the taste was sweet, and the sensation of exhaling was very pleasant. Theresa tried it and as she was saying she didn't think she got anything, smoke came out of her mouth, which gives an idea of how mellow it was.

Next, we were shown green coffee beans from Ethiopia, which were roasted for us in a frying pan over coals, ground in a mortar and pestle with cardamom, mint, and other spices, and then brewed in an earthenware pot. We were each given a little in thimble-sized cups with quite a bit of sugar, and this also was good. As we drank the coffee, the sheik of the oasis entered and we were introduced, and told that the man we'd been talking to was his son. Throughout, our host and his assistants were as sweet and gentle as could be.

As we rose to leave, we asked if we could give him something and handed over, if I remember, 20 Egyptian pounds, or about five dollars. I haven't the faintest idea whether this was too much, too little, or just right, because he gave no indication whatever and had asked for nothing. We walked by some camels on the way out, and when Theresa wanted a picture, they insisted she sit on one. They had the camel kneel but it was still a big step to get up so she needed a boost. However, their customs prohibited them from touching her, and they indicated that I should help her up onto the camel, which I did. After the photo we said many warm goodbyes and then left them to the night.

INTO THE VALLEY OF THE NILE

8:00 AM local time, Thursday, April 18 (0600 April 18 UTC).
27° 24.447'N 33° 40.541'E
Temp. 77, Humidity 39%, Cloud Cover 0%. Stiff breeze.
Abu Tig Marina, El-Gouna Resort, near Hurghada, Egypt.

To get to Luxor from El-Gouna, one travels overland, first south to Safaga along the Red Sea coast and then west through the mountains to the Eastern Desert and the Nile. In Safaga, your vehicle, in this case a large, comfortable Mercedes van, joins up with a group of others to make up a convoy. The convoys run several times a day and the idea is to protect tourists from whatever terrors may lurk along the road. Security is tough everywhere in Egypt. There are airport-type metal detectors and bags are checked at the entrances to all major hotels and theatres and many stores, and in the Egyptian Museum in Cairo you go through two of them. The convoy is a peculiar idea, as it makes a much better target for whomever we're worried about. Public transportation would be seemingly less attractive for the bad guys since the majority of passengers are locals. Mr. Shrode and Caroline traveled this way. Technically, tourists are supposed to be restricted to a convoy, but no one at the bus station suggested to them that there was any problem and it's much less expensive. Anyway, the convoy is headed by a pickup truck full of armed soldiers, and there's another similar one bringing up the rear. We scream down the road dangerously tailgating the truck ahead of us.

Dusk fell as we entered the mountains to the west, which I think were basalt but my request to stop the convoy so I could take a sample with the geologist's hammer I always carry for such purposes was denied. As we emerged from the mountains and approached the floodplain of the Nile, I began to notice numerous strange towers befetished with bright green lights on strings, like Christmas tree lights. Only they weren't, because the towers they were on, as I could see the next morning, were the minarets of mosques.

Luxor is the current name of the ancient city of Thebes, once the center of Egypt's power and situated directly on the Nile. It is home to the ruins of the temples of Karnak and Luxor among others, the Valley of the Kings and Valley of the Queens, and innumerable other antiquities.

I won't bother to further elaborate on the ruins of Luxor and vicinity, which are among the world's best-known destinations and have been described thousands of times. Herodotus was one of the earlier tourists, and the Captain, one of the most recent, has nothing new to add.

Our hotel in Luxor was not a budget accommodation but was still pretty cheap by American standards. When we checked in, we noticed on the form that breakfast was "compulsory," and though we think they meant complimentary, we showed up every day just in case. The Movenpick Resort stands on a large island in the Nile, and walking its grounds was one of our favorite experiences in Egypt. There was abundant bird life, including the cartoon-like hoopoes (*Upupa epops*), wheatears, pied kingfishers, white storks, white wagtails, bulbuls, and numerous other species. A farmer living in a mud-brick hut next to the hotel, so commonly seen everywhere in Egypt, toiled in his field using only a water buffalo and his own strength for power.

The island had its own small dock, where feluccas were available for a sail on the Nile, something Theresa and the Captain could not resist. This is a common tourist outing but that doesn't detract from its charm. Unlike the atmosphere at the temples and tombs, where one is unremittingly fending off touts, the boat is, like all watercraft, a world of its own, separate from the cares of land-bound folks. A lateen-rigged sloop, the felucca is a latter-day version of the traditional vessel. It's made of steel, not wood, and has a swing keel where the traditional boat had the disadvantage of a short keel, which was deep enough so that it was vulnerable to grounding but on the other hand shoal enough that sailing upwind was frustrating. But still, the newer version is no race boat. It's heavy, beamy, and flat-bottomed, and my best guess, although no compass was aboard, is that it tacks through about 120 degrees. The sailors who sail them have to be good, since without an auxiliary engine they must be skilled enough to not leave the tourists stranded when the wind dies and they head for the Mediterranean on the swift current of the Nile.

Our captain, Abdul, a funny guy, poled us out into the river and then unfurled his sail, set the boom, and immediately had us reaching along in a nice breeze. When dousing, he merely raises the boom up against the mast using a tackle, but to furl the sail at night he must shinny up the mast and then up the long yard that holds the luff of the sail at about a 60-degree angle to the mast. The felucca is an ancient type of sailboat, and its yard gave birth, we believe, to the square rig. It isn't known whether the Egyptians or Arabs invented it, but in both civilizations, sailing predates recorded history.

Our own sail was very romantic and got us back to the dock in time to enjoy the most civilized event I have seen since I attended a concert by the London Fire Brigade Orchestra at Hyde Park 30 years ago. Perhaps the Captain's use of the word "civilized" could use some updating. The hotel set up stereo speakers, for what it called an evening concert, in front of a small amphitheatre on the banks of the Nile, facing west towards the river. There, as one nursed a gin and tonic and observed the "silence please" admonition, he could watch the sun set over the Nile while feluccas glided dreamily by. Once in a while a tired barge would morosely motor up the river, but this did not affect the peaceful ambiance as we listened to violin concertos by various composers. Withal, the scene was a 19th century tableau, one that Monet would have been pleased to capture.

Night Train to Cairo

8:00 AM local time, Thursday, April 18 (0600 April 18 UTC).
27° 24.447'N   33° 40.541'E
Temp. 77, Humidity 39%, Cloud Cover 0%. Stiff breeze.
Abu Tig Marina, El-Gouna Resort, near Hurghada, Egypt.

Theresa and I departed Luxor at 9:30 in the evening and boarded the train taking us north, which on the Nile is downstream. We had booked our own sleeping cabin and the rather steep price included dinner, so I had naively envisioned something like the Orient Express. Instead we got airplane meals that we took in our compartment. Although the trip didn't live up to my fantasy, it was nonetheless memorable. The next morning we were awakened to tea and soon thereafter arrived at the Giza station, where we hailed a cab to our hotel. James Brown doesn't mention Cairo in his litany of cities, but for us it would be the home of the blues, because after a visit to the pyramids, Theresa would end her brief stay and fly home.

The pyramids at Giza are big and old and hard to lift. Little has changed since Mark Twain said over 100 years ago that you have to do your meditating on their impressive age and size either before you get here or after you leave, because while you're there, you are constantly importuned by guides, postcard dealers, and people trying to get you, that is, me, to ride a camel or a horse or a carriage, as if I looked like I was too old to walk, which I do.

Since even with a strong recommendation from as highly respected a man of letters as the Captain, the reader, let's face it, is too lazy to find and read *Innocents Abroad*, I'll relate, with apologies to the author, one of Twain's stories about his experience here. He was approached by a local who told him he could run up and down, or was it down and up, the great pyramid of Cheops, in less than nine minutes, for a dollar. Twain thought this was an interesting bet and took him up on it, only to find that the man did it with 20 seconds to spare. So, feeling he had the best of him as he was now winded, Twain made the same bet again. And again, and again. But dollar after dollar, the man prevailed. Then Twain decided to up the ante and offered $100 if the man would jump off the pyramid. While this was being contemplated and negotiated, the athlete's mother appeared, and, discovering the nature of the bet, began to cry. Twain, admitting that like most men he turns to mush at the sight of a woman crying, quit trying to persuade her son to try the jump. He offered *her* the $100 to do it.

The baksheesh, the haggling, and the scams visited upon the tourist to Egypt are no less annoying just because one has been prepared for them. Actually, the baksheesh and the haggling can be gotten used to as part of local custom, at least if you stay long enough, which of course you can't. But a scam is a scam and a false pretense of warm friendship when one has nothing but cold cash in mind is a corruption of human intercourse. The average Egyptian has a tendency towards sweetness that is irresistible, and when the counterfeit of this is proffered, it constitutes a corrosive perversion of the currency of understanding. The unfortunate result is that when the honest man offers his hospitality, one is immediately put on his guard, and it is this, rather than the money one might lose, that is the essence of the crime.

I cannot think about the pyramids without thinking of the great steel guitar player, Bobby "Blue" Black. Bobby actually backed up Hank Williams when he was a teenager and has played with many of the greats. He's also an incredibly nice guy, but the pertinent point here is that he has mastered hieroglyphics. If anyone else knows of another country and western musician, or any kind of musician, who can make the same claim, I'd be most interested, and he probably would be too. Bobby bribed a guard when he was in Egypt a while back and was able to spend a night inside the great pyramid, like Napoleon.

While at the pyramids I visited the museum of the so-called "solar boat," a sleek wooden boat that was interred next to the great pyramid and perhaps carried the pharaoh's mummy to its resting place. The claim is that this is the oldest boat in the world, although, typically for an Egyptian museum, no dates are given. Apparently, the Egyptians also made ships on this same general plan from papyrus and/or reeds, and Thor Heyerdahl made an Atlantic crossing in 1970 attempting to prove that an Egyptian voyage to the new world would have been possible.

It is very likely that boats are among the very oldest of human technologies, along with stone tools. The reader may remember that when we were in Kumai, we found that orangutans were able to visualize the utility of boats, as they would untie a painter on local craft to float across the river. There is no reason to believe that *Homo habilis*, the first of our genus according to current theory and the original "Handy Man," whose *floruit* was 2.5 million years ago, was less clever than an orangutan. Perhaps even *Australopithecus afarensis*, a still earlier species predating the genus *Homo*, could float his own boat; all it took was jumping on a log. It really doesn't seem necessary that the idea had to await the evolution of our species about 125,000 years ago, and so boating is very likely more ancient than what we know as human beings and was practiced by proto-humans.* It's interesting to note that neither ancient Egyptians nor native North Americans had the wheel, but both had developed sophisticated watercraft. Since, until the middle of the 19th century, all barges, canoes, and ships were made out of cellulose, no ancient remains survive. The Egyptian claim on this one is therefore impressive, if true.

In Cairo we bid our wistful farewells to Theresa and Caroline and arranged for a bus trip back to Hurghada. On the ride there, we observed sedimentary layers of limestone, which is calcium carbonate usually formed on a shallow seabed as the result of millions of years of raining down of the remains of shelled marine life, and microorganisms like foraminifera, that become compacted and ossified. These guys, living beings far older than the ancient Egyptians, are also immortalized in the pyramids, the stone for which was quarried near where the monuments now attract the tourists. The earth is an old, old place, and for the geologist, the pyramids' age is barely worth measuring. Their forms will still tower above the desert, however, long after the great dam at Aswan, a modern engineering feat, has silted up and disappeared.

Soon our bus came to the shores of the Red Sea, where a fresh northeasterly whipped up whitecaps beyond the sand, and we turned south towards the marina, and poor *Maverick*.

---

*The 2003 discovery of *Homo floresiensis* on Flores Island in Indonesia, unreachable by land, lends credence to this idea. The most interesting interpretation makes this species part of *Homo erectus*, which may push the date back to a million years ago or more.

Condo Made of Stona: The Sequel

8:00 PM local time, Saturday, April 20 (1800 April 20 UTC).
27° 24.447'N 33° 40.541'E
Temp. 73, Humidity 38%, Cloud Cover 0%.
Abu Tig Marina, El-Gouna Resort, near Hurghada, Egypt.

We're back here in Abu Tig marina, where we've been stuck for quite a while now. We were one of the first boats here, and three waves of cruisers have come, done their inland travel, and then sailed off while we've stood on the wharf and smiled and shouted our best wishes for a safe passage.

We've got a few hurdles to get over. The one that's keeping us here is the problem we've had with our Perkins 4-107 ever since we lost oil pressure on the way to Oman by reason of the bracket on the oil cooler chafing through the unit. The noise we've been hearing since then, and the reason we babied the engine all through the Gulf of Aden and particularly up the Red Sea, was not a sticky valve as Chief Engineer Terry Shrode and the Captain had thought, but a much more serious spun big-end bearing on the number one cylinder. The engine is disassembled down to the crank, and the head and other assorted parts are stowed on the ice box and here and there throughout the boat.

Meanwhile, there are other areas of concern. The rigging, only three years old, is showing signs of fatigue. Of the eleven 1x19 wires that hold up the rig, counting the detachable inner forestay, four including the headstay were found, upon the Captain's regular inspection of the rig, to have one broken strand. The breakages have occurred at the tops of the wires, where they enter the professionally done swage.

Another problem has been the Martec folding prop that since the Tahiti incident with the reef has been slightly out of balance, though the shop back in the United States did the best they could to straighten it. As the vibration had started to concern him, the Captain finally bit the bullet and coughed up nearly $900 for a new one which Theresa had brought to us.

Other things that required repair were the windlass, the furling line, the anemometer, the dinghy, and the autopilot. In addition, fuel filters were replaced, diesel and gasoline were obtained, the winches and batteries were serviced, the SSB ground and antenna connections were renewed, the backstay insulators were cleaned, topsides were scrubbed, a passerelle was constructed, blocks were hosed down to try to clean out the grit from sandstorms, running rigging was soaked in fresh water, new docklines were purchased and whipped, and so on. The reader may feel that this old boat is just falling apart, but the reality is that all the things that have failed were quite new before we left. The engine had 800 hours on it and the rest of the above were new and of very good reputation.

The mechanical problems we've been faced with have kept us pinned in Egypt, and this has had a dampening effect on the Skipper's morale of late, as he sits in the marina peevishly growing his beard. Although the majority of boats have made it through the Suez Canal by now with only modest difficulty, the following gives some examples of what has happened to other boats in the Red Sea in the last couple of months, putting things in perspective.

The Kiwi boat *Achates* was struck by lightning in a thunderstorm early in March as they headed up the Red Sea. Their VHF and autopilot were destroyed.

Oceans Free, the beautiful British-flagged Oyster 71 some of you will remember as having lost half its rudder and keel as a result of a grounding across from Singapore in Batam, Indonesia, is finally through the Suez Canal but at a price. The boat had to be hauled a second time in Malaysia after the packing gland failed at sea causing a serious condition of flooding that required hacking out some furniture to get at the source of the influx. The boat made it to the harbor after some scary hours, but Captain Peter and his wife, Lynn, decided they'd had enough. They abandoned their dream of completing the circumnavigation themselves, and hired a delivery crew to await repairs and take the boat to the Med. Once through the Suez Canal, however, the boat suffered another problem when the engine failed during a gale on the way to Malta. When last heard from, *Oceans Free* was becalmed and without power.

The engine of *Grace,* flag unknown by this correspondent, has malfunctioned and cannot be repaired. They have considered putting the boat in a container at Safaga, Egypt, and having it shipped to the Med for repairs, and another possibility is sailing to Jeddah in Saudi Arabia to install a new engine. Saudi Arabia can only be visited in an emergency and this may be stretching the definition.

The vessel *Northstar* has found diesel entering the oil in the engine at the rate of about a liter an hour, indicating broken rings perhaps, and is attempting to sail to Safaga for major engine repairs.

Chamois, a French or French-Canadian boat, hit the reef attempting to enter an anchorage after dark with two other boats that made it. She couldn't be kedged off and had to be abandoned by her owner and crew. At last report she is still on the reef and salvage attempts have not been successful.

A steel French boat of indeterminate name has gone on the reef between here and Suez, presumably as a result of its anchor dragging, and cannot be salvaged.

The Kiwi-flagged *Cariad* fetched up on a reef while trying to enter an anchorage, was holed and sank as it was being towed to a harbor after being pulled off. Attempts are being made to refloat her. A beautifully finished wooden sailboat, she was the life's work and sole possession of her owner.

The owner of the large catamaran *Bohay* was killed in an accident that occurred when he was attempting to remove the rig from his boat in Phuket, Thailand. He was detaching the rigging wires at the masthead when the pivoting spar, which had not been adequately supported, fell to the ground. He died a few hours later at the hospital. The boat was sold by his widow to a German couple, who made it to the Bab Al Mandeb at the bottom of the Red Sea, where they suffered a dismasting in 50 knots and rough seas. Although there were no serious injuries, they decided to issue a mayday, abandoned the boat, and were rescued by German navy helicopter. The boat was taken in tow by a Chinese freighter and a rendezvous was scheduled with a tug that would take it into a Yemenese port. When the freighter arrived at the rendezvous, the tug was not there, and the owners of the shipping company instructed the captain to cut the boat loose to maintain his schedule. About a week later the boat was found, but all gear had been stripped.

Forward Progress

9:00 PM local time, Sunday, May 12 (1800 May 8 UTC).
29° 34.538'N 32° 41.268'E
Temp. 84, Humidity 35%, Cloud Cover 0%.
At anchor at Ras Sudr, about 26 miles south of Suez.

We got the predicted low we had been anticipating, left at dawn on Friday, and had an easy sail through the reefs and out to the Gulf of Suez. We used the engine, which seems to be finally running well after extensive repairs, in light air for half a day since we needed to make as many miles as possible before the weather turned on us. By midnight, however, the low had passed, the barometer had been rising steeply, and as a high had followed the low through, we found ourselves in a squash zone. Winds built to the 30s, on the nose, and by dawn Saturday we were trying to make it to Marsa Thelemet, an anchorage in a horseshoe bay surrounded by coral. As we approached the entrance, we compared our computerized chart with the waypoints given in the *Red Sea Pilot* and also the aids to navigation on shore, and we found that no two agreed. To make things worse, there were two sets of range marks ashore indicating the safe route into the bay, and they were not in alignment with one another. Our paper chart was up-to-date but was at too small a scale to be of much use in entering the pass, and because of the rough conditions, we couldn't see the reef itself. All the boats that have been lost in the Red Sea of late, and also our grounding back in Borneo, weighed heavily on our minds as we contemplated the discrepancies in the information at hand. After some fidgeting and circling, we determined to follow one of the two pairs of range marks on the land, though they were very hard to see. After a few moments of high anxiety, we found our way safely into the anchorage. The computer would have put us on the reef.

Later in the day the wind rose to forty and they closed the Suez Canal for a period, so we had made the right choice in seeking shelter. Just a mile away, under the jagged peaks of raw limestone, we could see the highway from Suez to Hurghada, along which our bus had brought us from Cairo a few weeks back. Aboard that bus, people were sitting in air-conditioned comfort watching bad movies (we saw an Arabic remake of "Some Like It Hot"), completely oblivious to the chaos and violence just beyond the beach.

On Sunday morning we headed out and had a pleasant sail up to our present location, talking along the way on the radio with Alan, the skipper of *Karma*. He had lost forward gear in his transmission and as the wind had died, he was contemplating driving to Suez backwards. A veteran of the British infantry, he considered it all just a good challenge, and when we last spoke, the wind had come back up and he was trying to make Suez by sail tonight. As I write this, though, there's no wind, and Alan is out there somewhere, among the big ships. They may find it confusing when he backs up to dodge them.

On the Hook in the Suez Canal

9:00 PM local time, Thursday, May 16 (1800 May 16 UTC).
31° 15.162'N 32° 18.783'E .
Temp. 73, Humidity 65%, Cloud Cover 0%.
Tied bows-to the Port Fouad Yacht Club, Port Fouad.

This afternoon we reached the northern end of the Suez Canal at the twin cities of Port Said and Port Fouad, situated respectively on the western and eastern banks of the entrance. We had begun our transit Tuesday morning and sailed the first half, up to the city of Ismailia, that day. There we had a celebration at a local bar with the crews of some boats we'd been with since Sri Lanka, then continued here the following day.

For a yacht coming north, transit is arranged at Port Suez by an agent, through whom fees are paid based on a formula that determines your Suez Canal tonnage after an official admeasurer comes aboard. On the day of departure, in our case the next day, a pilot is delivered to your boat who guides you up the first leg of the transit. All boats in the canal must have a pilot aboard at all times. It was the first time since we'd left California that another person was aboard *Maverick* while we were underway. Pilots have a bad reputation for being very demanding of baksheesh in the form of money, cigarettes, beer, food, etc., but most are nice and we were lucky to come up with good ones both days.

The Suez is a sea-level canal, meaning there are no locks, and though it is a conduit for a lot of tonnage, it is far surpassed in this regard by the much less famous Kiel Canal of Germany. The traffic for big ships is one-way and convoys are organized at Port Suez in the south and Port Said in the north, where each ship picks up a pilot and joins together with others to form a group that proceeds in single file through the canal. Although there are a couple of bypasses, the southbound traffic is allowed to finish before the northbound traffic begins, and there are two convoys of each every day.

You depart Suez at the end of the morning's northbound convoy of big ships. As you come north in the canal, the Sinai remains desert all the way, but the west bank becomes more verdant as you near the Nile Delta. For the most part, it is like a river cruise absent recreational facilities, towns, and vacation homes. We had a pretty good time until, on the second day of our transit, *Maverick's* engine, which had been running fine since we left El Gouna, sputtered and died in the middle of the Canal. It was necessary to hastily lower the anchor in 60 feet, change fuel filters, and bleed the diesel before getting underway, only to have the same thing happen a couple of hours later. We think we may have traced the problem to a stripped screw on one of our fuel filters, but in the meantime, we have the distinction of not only having sailed the Suez Canal but having anchored in it as well.

Sailing on the Canal, we thought of its opening in 1869. (There was actually a canal here in ancient times used by the Pharaohs, which silted up in the 8th century.) The Canal's completion brought an end to the era of the Tea Clippers, boats originally designed and built by Americans, then copied by others, that plied the China tea trade in the middle of the 19th century. In their day, these were incredibly powerful ships that could deliver fresh tea far more rapidly than their competitors from Britain, and along with the first-ever America's Cup, they established American sailormen as second to none. Because the Canal was too narrow to permit efficient navigation using wind power, its opening, more than any other event, signaled the end of the days of sail and ushered in the new era of the steamship.

Now that we've finally managed to reach this watershed, it's time to review the experiences of the last six months or so, and compare them with our expectations. When we left Australia at the beginning of November, I confessed to having misgivings about the upcoming segment of our voyage through Indonesia, Thailand, Sri Lanka, the Maldives, Oman, Eritrea, and up the Red Sea, encompassing as it did countries less familiar and perhaps less friendly than those of the South Pacific. I said that, having passed through "paradise," we perhaps were now about to enter "purgatory." If good fortune prevailed through these trials, it seemed we might be spit out at last, departing Port Said, from these ethereal realms back onto the terra firma of Western Civilization. Adding to our concerns and those of our friends and loved ones back home were the events of September 11, then fresh in our minds, after which many advice-givers, including our insurance company, cautioned us to abort, modify, or at least postpone our voyage.

At the time my response to this was: "We aboard *Maverick* have faith that the vast majority of Muslims...even in the relatively rare cases where they are extremists and loathe America, are unlikely to act violently no matter what that guy is trying to make you think." Admittedly, this was easy for us to say, as we were a long way from Ground Zero, both geographically and psychologically, and weren't exposed to the nightly doses of fear you heard back home. In any event, by now you know that no boats or crews were treated with hostility as they traversed this area of the world and even the pirates stayed at home. The worst misunderstandings had nothing to do with religion or politics, but rather that equally old source of conflict, money. Every American boat had family and friends at home who advised them not to continue, but 26 US-flagged yachts came up the Red Sea this year anyway, four from the San Francisco Bay Area, five if you include Santa Cruz. As of the end of April, 87 boats had come through the Suez Canal, and by the end of the season, this total will be about 110, a little down from other years.

The worst troubles in the Red Sea this year were groundings and engine failures. The Muslims have been very nice to us, seeming to want to put a lot of distance between themselves and acts of violence but also because it seems to be natural for them. We do, however, look forward to being in Christian countries where it is no problem to find a gin and tonic. "A Christian," says Mr. Shrode, "is the next best thing to a proper heathen."

We therefore bid the very nice purgatory section of the world farewell and set forth with our hopes high. The only sad note is our concomitant adieu to all the other crews who have become so very close to us in the part of the world's oceans between Thailand and Port Said, reserved as it is for voyagers who undertake to sail around the world. We will greatly miss these fellow seafarers and kindred spirits, with whom we shared our fears and consequent triumphs.

The Med

I Can See Clearly Now

9:00 AM local time, Saturday, May 25 (0600 May 25 UTC).
36° 17.619'N   30° 9.067'E
Temp. 73, Humidity 67%, Cloud Cover 0%.
At a marina in Finike, Turkey.

The dust is gone, and I wish I could see all obstacles in my way, but I know I can't. After we departed Port Said and cleared ourselves from the heavy traffic approaching the Suez Canal, the wind was at first calm but soon freshened and allowed us to sail with Finike, our destination, broad on the starboard bow. After a few hours of coasting along the shores of northern Egypt and dodging more shipping, the wind shifted and port tack became favored. We steered *Maverick* through the eye of the wind and sheeted in smartly, close-hauled at first. But as the day wore on, we got lifted and were able sail free to the harbor, which we reached in about three days.

Last night in our marina here in Finike, I took note of the fact that the Big Dipper is once again high in the sky, the lip of its cup pointing to Polaris. We're finally in the Mediterranean Sea, the sea where Xerxes launched his ships en route to his ill-fated attack on Greece and where St. Paul sailed as prisoner on a Roman galley. It's the wine-dark sea of Odysseus' wanderings, illuminated by the rosy fingers of dawn.

Across the Pacific, our voyage took us over waters where every event up to about 200 years ago occurred before written language. The ancient Near Eastern texts and the Bible give us bits of history of some of the lands of the Arabian Peninsula and Egypt, but of course Australia, Asia, and Indonesia were not part of this. In the parts of the world we've visited to this point, untold centuries of human activity remain sheathed in silence. But here every stone seems ready to tell an ancient and stirring tale.

Nature has not been ungenerous to Finike in either beauty or fertility. It sits at the head of a bay formed by a pocket in a spur of the Taurus Mountains, which have shed a bit of their cover to provide the alluvium that's farmed by the tiny humans below. We can see snow-capped peaks from the marina, yet the temperature is very pleasant and spring is in the air, and in the air as well is the sound of birdsong. The crew of *Maverick* has not seen a spring since we left home because by the time it arrived in the northern hemisphere, we were in the southern; and by the time it had reached the southern, we were back in the northern.

As for its debut in history, this part of Turkey was settled (i.e., the indigenous peoples were conquered), by Ionian Greeks who had just visited their ten-year vengeance on those naughty Trojans for Paris' making away with that strumpet, Helen. The Greeks continued to humiliate the poor Trojans well into the 20th century, when they became a school mascot and a prophylactic.

But southern Turkey is also Alexander the Great country. He came through here in 334 BC, kicking some serious ass. There are not a few respectable scholars who believe that Alexander, student of Aristotle, who was a student of Plato, who was a student of Socrates, who was a student of life, was bisexual, although I doubt that his sexual preference made much of a difference to the people he sliced and diced along his merry way. General George Patton, who was a passionate admirer of Alexander, was probably not a subscriber to the bisexual hypothesis. Alexander was 33 when he fell victim to a lethal level of ennui, since he had no more worlds to conquer and nothing left to do, poor dear. He became the first young person of note to actually die of boredom, though it's the rare teenager that doesn't make the threat.

As the *Maverick* boys pillage and plunder our way through the world of Alexander, using our looks and charm to conquer instead of those dangerous weapons our mothers warned us about, we hum a threnody to the man and his dreams. One dream he did not see through to fruition was the defeat of Termessos, a mountain fortress not far from *Maverick's* berth. Legend has it that it was the only stronghold Alexander could not destroy. We visited Termessos, inhabited in Alexander's time by the Termessosaurians, a name you won't find in *The Illiad* because I just made it up. The warriors called *Solymians* were spoken highly of therein, though, and they are the same folks. Alexander took a look at their fortifications, found them impregnable, and decided discretion was the better part, etc. Yet the crew of *Maverick* assaulted the summit unopposed. Shows what a little charm will do. You catch more flies with honey than you do with vinegar, Alexander.

The lair of the Termessosaurians is a mountain aerie at about 3,000 feet. It feels like something a commune of hippies would have made for a hideout far from the Establishment, except that no hippies I ever knew would have undertaken the insane amount of physical labor required to quarry the limestone for their buildings, hew it into huge, precise blocks, and then haul these by heaven knows what means to awkward and dangerous precipices to be emplaced. The amphitheaters that we've seen in this region, from the late Hellenic and early Roman periods, are all dramatically situated, none more so than the one at Termessos, where the audience looks over the performers to a spectacular view of a steep gorge. It's pretty magical up there.

We also visited Perge, which has another amphitheater and a lot of columns. St. Paul is supposed to have given his first sermon here, but I'm not any more convinced of that than I am that the actual Job is buried at the "Job's Tomb" they took us to in Oman. We saw ruins at Aspendos, where the theater is remarkably well preserved and still hosts performances, and also Limyra and Arykanda. This area is in the vicinity of ancient Lycia and is considerably more hospitable than I had visualized it. At the ruins, we were left totally on our own to contemplate the sweep of history, unharassed by the touts we came to dread in Egypt.

To see all this, we had rented a car in Finike and driven through the mountains along the beautiful southern coast, through a mixed conifer forest that was reminiscent of Colorado yet goes right down to the shores of the Mediterranean. It is as pleasant a place as you'll ever see. We drove to Antalya, the capital of the "Turkish Riviera" and a city of half a million with a thoroughly modern infrastructure but a center with a medieval feel. The whole area supports a standard of living not significantly lower than our own, which came as a surprise to me. I reveled at being in Europe. I realize that because we are southeast of the Bosporus, we're technically in Asia, but that's not how it seems. The food, the architecture, the roads, and the freedom to travel were liberating. Yet the music and language are Turkish, and we did see an ancient goatherd with her flock standing right by the ATM in downtown Finike. In so many ways, nevertheless, it felt like we were getting close to home.

CAN YOU HEAR THOSE CHURCH BELLS RINGIN'?

8:00 PM local time, Friday, June 7 (1700 June 7 UTC).
36° 36.984'N 27° 50.189'E
Temp. 79, Humidity 54%, Cloud Cover 5%.
Med-tied stern-to at Symi harbor on Symi, the Greek Islands.

We're now in Symi. At least that's the official t-shirt spelling, whereas the pilot and the chart say "Simi," which agrees with the baseball cap spelling. It's in Greece, which is to say it belongs to Greece. We had to sail 30 miles from Marmaris to get here but it's only about four miles from the closest part of Turkey.

I don't know if there is any important way in which Symi would not live up to your fantasy of the perfect Greek Island. Rugged and rocky mountains under a crystalline sky, a cute little harbor with white and yellow and blue and buff houses climbing the steep hills that you have to climb too, if you want to get up them. There is one road that goes over the hill to the next, smaller bay, but the houses that overlook the main harbor, below the church at the top of the hill that stands on the site of the old acropolis, are connected by stairs. Cars and motor scooters do not operate efficiently on stairs. This means there is a relatively insignificant amount of automobile traffic on the hillsides and that means that there is little of that commotion that until about 100 years ago was never heard on earth. Rome, London, and all the great cities of history didn't whine and roar like ours do. For all the long centuries up until the twentieth, every city, even the biggest ones, sounded different from nowadays. What you hear here is like that. It's the sound you can't put in a museum, of ordinary life revealed. It's not just like being out in the country, where you hear chainsaws and coyotes and front loaders. It's the sound of a village going about its business, without being masked by the internal combustion engine. It's as though someone took a shroud away or removed some earplugs. Conversation, donkeys braying, children at play, dogs, goats, birds, and roosters are nakedly audible. Not that a rooster isn't a bird.

And bells. We're back to the Christian world, even though it's the kinky one with the guys in beards and black robes and hats. No more calls to prayer by the muezzin five times a day. It's nothing more than hearing what you grew up with, I know, but I do prefer the bells. They're non-verbal, for one thing, and for another, if there are notes involved in the ringing, they all come from a scale with which I have some familiarity, so they're, you know, comforting. Call me parochial. Or call me provincial, which I believe is the same thing. I've been called much worse, at times with admirable accuracy. I can deal.

Reunited

8:20 PM local time, Thursday, June 13 (1720 June 13 UTC).
36° 32.567'N 26° 20.674'E
Temp. 79, Humidity 55%, Cloud Cover 0%.
Anchored at Skala harbor on the island of Astipalaia, Greece.

We had heard a rumor on the nets that *Okiva* had planned to be in Rhodes on June 4. We got to Symi, which is close to Rhodes, on the 5th and thought we'd take a ferry over there to see if we could find them and to see Rhodes. We hadn't seen them since Nongsa Point across from Singapore back in December, and we'd both been through quite a bit since then. We moved from a small bay to the main harbor at Symi on the 6th and planned to take the ferry on the 7th to see what we could see. But we missed it. We ended up taking the one on the 8th, and sure enough, when we got to the harbor, there was no *Okiva*. We knew they were trying to get to Athens by the 11th so we figured they'd left a day or two before, making it especially painful that we'd missed the ferry the previous day.

We were disappointed but thought we'd use the day sightseeing on Rhodes. We called on the Colossus but were told he was unavailable, as he was busy not existing. We took a bus to Lindos, a journey of about 175 stadia, and found a Byzantine castle, constructed over Greek ruins, swarming with tourists and surrounded by shops. Returning to the city of Rhodes, we headed towards the ancient walled city that makes up the center of town. On the way, we walked by the harbor and Ship's Lookout Terry Shrode thought he spotted a ketch where there was another boat earlier in the day, so we walked over and were just blown away to find *Okiva*. Francis was aboard and soon Paula, who had joined them in Cypress, and Paul returned. There were hugs...we'd found out in the Muslim world that was okay for men. As usual, Paul and Francis were at work on the electrical system but gave us some of the details of their adventures while they worked. And also as usual, their stories were better than ours.

When their engine blew up in Malaysia, they didn't have the luxury, as *Maverick* did, to get into a (reasonably) suitable port. They found a small harbor and then managed to contact a local mechanic for help. He told them they'd have to take the engine out themselves, which, he said, would require sawing a big hole in the cockpit sole. The engine is right underneath the sole in Paul's Freeport 41, but there is no hatch. I don't know what the deal is with that design. Anyway, Paul and Francis had a beer and thought it over. They sure didn't want to tear up the cockpit, so they figured they could detach the cockpit scupper hoses from the drains on the cockpit sole, which were located at each corner, and run lines through them from the engine to various winches. They got a couple of local guys to help and after undoing the shaft and the mounts, managed to lift the engine, an inch this way on one winch, an inch that way on another, high enough that they could get it out the engine room door and then muscle it up to the companionway, so they could use the boom to lift it off the boat. You love stuff like this, if you don't have to do it yourself.

That accomplished, the engine was repaired and then reinstalled using the same method. As the mechanics were driving away, at the beginning of a 10-day holiday, Paul tried to start the engine but there was nothing but sparks and smoke. Realizing that if they got away he would sit there for ten days, Paul ran after the guys and after much pleading they finally returned and got him going. He and Francis had heard through the grapevine that the crew of *Maverick* had doubted whether *Okiva* would make it to the Med this year, and claimed that it was mainly this challenge that made them determined to go for it. So they left that same night without sea trials.

They sailed non-stop from Malaysia to Sri Lanka and on the way discovered a very bad oil leak, a gift from their mechanic, requiring about one quart every six hours. When they got there, the people in Sri Lanka said, "Oh, yeah, *Maverick*, they left a week ago. They went that-a-way." So they bought a lot of oil and headed for the Red Sea, but somewhere in Eritrea, they ran out. And they had also run out of cash. Without proper entry papers or money, they stopped in an obscure harbor where the locals had never seen their like and were none too happy about their uninvited guests. Our voyagers asked to trade for oil, but their request was met at first by blank stares. The crew couldn't think of anything much they had to trade, and then Francis remembered two "Rolex" watches he'd bought on the street somewhere for $25. When these were produced, the local folks came up with dusty and ancient, but unopened, oil containers, and *Okiva* was ready to sail.

They headed on up the Red Sea but still ran short of oil, so they began collecting it in two frying pans they strategically located under the sump. Every couple of hours, whatever the sea conditions, whoever was on watch would reach past the whirring alternator belt and carefully pull out the frying pans, decant them with a funnel into a container, and, after replacing the frying pans, pour them back into the engine. Using this method they made it past *Maverick* in Egypt to Suez and eventually to Cypress, where an attempt, unfortunately unsuccessful, was made to remedy the leak, using the method described above to once again raise the engine from its mounts to gain access to the pan. So as we write this, they are heading for Athens, putting in a quart every six hours.

They were forced to conserve power because of their ailing electrical system, so before they went through the Suez Canal, they had little opportunity to use their radio and therefore had no news of other boats. They had assumed we had long since made it to the Mediterranean. But in Ismailia they partied with a boat named *Altair*, that both *Maverick* and *Okiva* had met back in Nongsa, and the crew of *Altair* was none the better for it the day after. *Altair* mentioned the party on the SSB net on their way to Cypress, and we heard them and told them about our situation and that we were amazed and very happy that *Okiva* had made it. When next they saw them, *Altair* told *Okiva* we were still stuck in Egypt with our own engine problems. They are gentlemen and would never have celebrated in our presence, but I know them well enough to assume that they did a bit of a victory dance when they heard that. They had beaten *Maverick* to the Med.

And a Bad Go-Getter

9:00 PM local time, Sunday, June 16 (1800 June 16 UTC).
36° 49.679'N 25° 51.872'E.
Temp. 72, Humidity 50%, Cloud Cover 20%.
Anchored at Katapola harbor on the island of Amorgos, Greece.

We've called at quite a few islands so far here in the Aegean Sea. Rhodes, of course, we reached by ferry, but the rest, including Symi, Nisiros, Kos, Astipalaia, and now Amorgos, we visited with *Maverick*. We're approximately halfway across the Aegean, in the part of the islands known as the Cyclades. They are all different, but share a family resemblance, and the one thing they all have in common is motor scooters, the jet-skis of the roadway.

Fortunately, Ship's Chief Engineer Terry Shrode at one time was a fellow at Trinity College, Cambridge, where he concentrated on studies in terrestrial vehicle velocity. This gives him a special insight into the operation of road-racing machines of all types, which he often uses to put the Captain at a disadvantage when we are ashore. Back in Egypt, we patronized the local go-cart track. No money was placed on the outcome, of course, as we are above that sort of thing.

The Captain, being less experienced than Mr. Shrode in land-based racing, compensated for this handicap by applying his rich trove of nautical knowledge to the challenge of piloting a go-cart. Having studied the weather that morning in preparation for the race, he arrived at the asphalt harbor where the go-carts were berthed and, like any responsible mariner, took a serious look at his vessel with regard to safety. He checked for audible and visual distress signals, a fire extinguisher, etc., and noticed the absence of a life jacket. The proprietor was clearly not trained in these matters and seemed more than a little put upon by this last request, which I must confess I pressed rather forcefully, as safety is number one with me. I finally accepted his child's inflatable toy as a workable facsimile. I was willing to forego the type-IV throwable PFD, which is irrelevant for a single-hander, but otherwise I was determined not to leave the dock until I was "safe to go," as the literature is filled with voyages coming to a bad end because of an overly hasty and ill-prepared departure.

Mr. Shrode, who, I'm sorry to report, cast off the lines without taking the above precautions, smiled rather unreservedly, I should have thought, as he screamed by me failing to yield to the starboard cart, which was the stand-on vessel in this situation. Fortunately, I was alert enough to avoid a collision. I navigated cautiously and in a seamanlike fashion, somewhat below hull speed, as I gained my offing, keeping a sharp lookout for shoals, wrecks, reefs, and headlands as Mr. Shrode drove by me, lapping me yet again. The reader may be forgiven for assuming that after the fifth, tenth, or fifteenth such encounter, the insane gleam in Mr. Shrode's eye would have dimmed a bit, but if so, he or she undoubtedly has not had the privilege of his acquaintance.

So it goes with most of our adventures on land, and yet there are times when I prevail. Mr. Shrode is the better of the Captain in every manly virtue save one, and that is shortness, and its attendant lack of bulk, if I may say so without impropriety. As a direct result, when climbing hills on underpowered motor scooters, it is Mr. Shrode who is at a disadvantage and the Captain who emerges victorious. There, I've said it, flinging modesty aside. The truth is out. Let the chips fall where they may.

Scooters are lots of fun but we have also our serious work to do as we visit these islands. Part of our mission, under the heading of archaeological and cultural findings, is to contribute what we can to the search for the actual geographical locations of the adventures of that sailor of legend, Odysseus, in whose wine-dark sea *Maverick* now finds herself. This problem has fascinated scholars since the times of Homer himself. Even then, it was believed by some that Homer's tales were pure fiction. Eratosthenes, the old windbag who figured out that the earth was round and came up with a pretty good estimate of its circumference, said that the actual places of Odysseus' wanderings would be discovered when the "cobbler who sewed up Aeolus' bag of winds was found." The best work on this subject in your correspondent's opinion is *The Ulysses Voyage* by Tim Severin. Severin, a Cambridge man like our Mr. Shrode, oversees the reconstruction of a Bronze Age galley and sets out to sail it along the logical route for a mariner returning from Troy to Ithaca. It's a great tale, to which, if the reader is fortunate, we may return at a later date.

For now, however, it will suffice to describe our own careful methodology as we search for the home of Polyphemus, the Cyclops who eats some of Odysseus' crew and then is maimed and taunted by our hero in the most famous story of the Odyssey. We are sorry to report that although our knowledge of ancient Greek is sufficient, the modern version does not come easily to our ear, so we have devised the following stratagem for communicating our main question to the locals, the question being, of course, where is the Cyclops? Using Mr. Shrode's skills as a graphic artist, we have drawn a large and bold question mark on a yellow legal pad.

Thus equipped, we set out on our travels. When we have secured our anchor at a likely island, we take the dinghy ashore with our question mark and look for a man or woman who, though advanced in years, seems to possess that certain *pomme de terre* that signifies obscure and ancient knowledge. We approach politely and then proceed with the following pantomime to signal our inquiry: The Captain places the forefinger of his left hand to the forefinger of his right hand, then he places the thumb of his right hand to the thumb of his left hand. Having completed this maneuver, he meticulously and subtly forms the four digits into a circle. This he places flatly against the middle of his forehead, with the junction of the two thumbs resting on the bridge of his nose and the lateral remainder of the thumbs covering his two eyes, now plainly representing a one-eyed monster. He accompanies this likeness with frightening grimaces and gruesome grunts and howls, stomping around heavily as he does so. Mr. Shrode holds our carefully prepared question mark next to the monster's head, pointing to him urgently as he shrugs his shoulders and raises his eyebrows. Even though we do not share a common verbal language with the person we are addressing, we have little doubt that our intentions are made crystal clear to even the dullest mind.

    We didn't undertake these, or for that matter, any of our studies, just to satisfy our own vain curiosity; we have humanity's larger interests at stake. And we never thought it would be easy. We've got a lot more islands to visit, so the fact that our efforts have thus far met with few positive responses, and some which were, frankly, puzzling, does not discourage us. Homer lovers, we are finding, are a rarer breed than we had heretofore supposed. For the sake of those at home who depend on us to seek out the facts, however, we intend to soldier on undaunted until we find the true home of that unfortunate giant of olden times, Polyphemus, son of the earth-shaker Poseidon.

Meltemi

9:00 PM local time, Saturday, June 22 (1800 June 22 UTC).
37° 6.310'N   25° 22.464'E
Temp. 78, Humidity 67%, Cloud Cover 0%.
Med-tied stern-to at the dock at Naxos Harbor, the island of Naxos, Greece.

We're hunkered down here in Naxos, the largest of the Cyclades, because it's been blowing outside. Back when we were in Nisiros, on the 9th of June, we heard that the wind was going to strengthen to force 5 to 6 and that the harbor there may become untenable, so we made a run for the lee side of Kos. Weather services and sailors here all use the Beaufort scale, which was devised by a man who was coincidentally himself named Beaufort back in the 19th century. But Beaufort called for sea states to go along with wind speeds, and these seem to not coincide with what we get in the Med. For example, he says force 6 gives you 10-foot waves or so, but in the Med, we've yet to see anything over about half of that. However, the seas we do get are uncomfortable to a degree that is far out of proportion to their size.

So we get up to Kos and get anchored. The sails we take from island to island or along the coast here are often navigated as the sailors of the Bronze Age did it, by line of sight. It is not unusual to be able to see the day's destination as soon as you clear the harbor. We set waypoints and study the chart anyway, in case we encounter bad visibility but also just because that is ship's SOP.

We are meticulous about setting our anchor, as we notice few others are. The main step we rarely observe others taking is backing down on the anchor and then challenging it with full power. Now in some anchorages, full power will pull your anchor out and it must be reset, and perhaps this process must be carried out several times. We are probably regarded as fools, setting our anchor and then backing down on it so hard we pull it out, only to set it again and pull it out. But if the anchor will just not hold when challenged, you have some information that those who did not challenge it do not. Knowing how good the holding is having tested it, you can move to another anchorage with better holding or stay where you are with some extra precautions depending on how settled the weather is.

Later that day in Kos the wind shifted about 120 degrees and rose to about 25 knots. Out of six boats in the anchorage, three immediately dragged. Luckily someone was aboard each boat, and they managed to reset, although one was well out to sea before the problem was noticed.

Maverick didn't budge, but we took the precaution of starting the engine and challenging the anchor again anyway, and it held satisfactorily. Or so we thought. But we had taken the wrong lesson from the other boats' dragging. We should have noted that the holding was particularly bad because anchors, no matter how poorly set, usually do not drag. But since we held, we only smugly considered our superior technique. This particular anchorage was also rather steep, meaning that whereas you're anchored in about 20 feet, within 100 yards to seaward the depth is 50 and soon after that, over 100. So if you have five to one out at 20 feet and drag and it's downwind to a deeper bottom, pretty soon you find yourself adrift at sea with a hundred feet of chain and an anchor hanging off the bow.

Mr. Shrode's knee was bothering him a little, so I took the dinghy ashore for the hour-long bus ride to check out the main harbor at Kos on the other side of the island. I returned in the afternoon, and Mr. Shrode reported that just as he was dozing off earlier in the day, he noticed something didn't feel right, and when he reached the deck, he realized we had drug about 30 feet towards another, smaller boat. Had Mr. Shrode been less alert, or worse, if his knee wasn't bothering him and he had done the more usual thing of accompanying me, *Maverick* would have bounced off of the other boat, then off some rocks, and headed for the next island to leeward, about six miles, where she would have foundered. As it was, he was able to get the anchor properly reset in a timely fashion. It is the first time our anchor has dragged, ruining a perfect record, and will mean we will be even more cautious in the future. It's not like we can stop using the anchor or anything.

We believed that the wind we saw that day was what's known around here as a *meltemi*. According to the pilot, it blows sporadically in June and then strengthens in July and August, starting at about force 4 and working up to 7 or 8, which is about 40 knots, more or less northerly. So we figured that what we had, which was say force 5, and then gusting to 6 on the lee side of the island, was our first experience of the *meltemi* and typical for its strength at this time of year. The seas got choppy, but nevertheless we headed off next for Astipalaia and then Amorgos and Dhenousa, upwind and bumpy every inch of the way. Each time we arose when it was still dark and were underway as soon as there was enough light to see, since the wind and seas pick up in the afternoon and this way we could make our destination before then.

But in Dhenousa, we heard another forecast and it reminded me of that scene in the movie *Crocodile Dundee*, where he's accosted by muggers who produce a knife and he says, "That's not a knife. This is a knife." Then he pulls out something with a 12-inch blade. The new forecast called for force 7 to 8, gusting to 9, meaning up there close to 50 knots, so the conditions we had seen so far weren't the real *meltemi*. The seas at 20 knots hadn't been pleasant, so we didn't like the prospect of more wind. We were in a safe enough anchorage on Dhenousa, but there was absolutely nothing around and it was gusty and pretty rolly considering what the expected wind speed might do. If we stayed there, it would make for an uncomfortable and boring few days. We decided to make a run for Naxos before the strong winds hit and got here, to a very secure harbor. The wind came up that afternoon, a few hours after we arrived, and it looked pretty lumpy out to sea.

In Naxos, the ferries have been on strike so what you have is a bunch of travelers who are stranded here and looking for rides. As a result, there's an endless parade of young German and Scandinavian girls that come down to the dock and ask, or actually, plead with the crew of *Maverick*, to take them to Ios, which is where they are heading to amuse themselves. We could easily get a full boat to go there, and it's only about 25 miles, all downwind. Ios is where young adults from all nations take their clothes off and cavort on the beach, or so we've heard. Needless to say, we have absolutely no interest in such behavior, unless we may profit from its observation in our sedulous sociological researches. But, if you will, "a boatload of young girls desperate to get naked and party." It is a phrase with a certain charm, is it not? Scarcely a word out of place, one might be tempted to say.

Delos

10:30 PM local time, Tuesday, June 25 (1930 June 25 UTC).
37° 25.204'N 25° 19.421'E
Temp. 81, Humidity 65%, Cloud Cover 0%.
Anchored at Ornos Bay on the island of Mikonos, Greece.

As dawn spread her rosy fingers across the Aegean one spring morning in the year 399 BC, the captain of a Greek galley stood at the harbor at Delos contemplating the sky and sea, and decided the winds had finally turned fair for the return trip to Athens. He and his crew had come here to transport the priests and dignitaries who had traveled to Delos on their yearly trip to pay tribute to the god Apollo at the site of his birth, to repay an old debt. Although Phaedo, who tells the story in Plato's account, doesn't give us a season, I'm thinking it was in the spring because they certainly wouldn't sail in winter and summer breezes are either too strong and contrary or nonexistent. And fall doesn't seem right for a trip of this sort. Besides, Apollo's birthday is in the spring.

After the sacrifices had been made, the prayers offered, and the libations poured, they had waited for a couple of weeks or more for the wind. This we know, because it wouldn't have taken more than two or three days to make the voyage from Athens and Xenophon tells us that the round trip took a month. A galley from that period could not sail upwind at all, and they couldn't row against more than 8 or so knots and make any progress, and that at the price of some very tired oarsmen. So they waited until the wind was favorable. Getting to Delos would not have been much of a problem since the winds are northwesterly about three days out of four that time of year and Delos lies to the southeast of Athens. But returning means waiting for two or three days together of fair wind, using your best weather forecaster or soothsayer, so there could be delays. And in that time of year, there was still the danger of storms, which were not infrequently disastrous for vessels in this era.

It's only about 90 miles as the crow flies to Piraeus, the port of Athens, from Delos and they could probably do 5 knots with a good following breeze, so you would think it would be less than a day's sail. But they wouldn't have done it that way, because they couldn't see the landmarks they needed to navigate by at night so they had to be in a safe harbor by dusk. Ancient Greek sailors didn't like overnight passages and avoided them, not only because of navigation but because they didn't have decent sea berths and lee cloths like *Maverick* does, or a gimbaled stove, or even a deck, and couldn't comfortably sleep or cook. So if they left Delos at dawn with a fresh breeze aft of the beam, by mid-afternoon they'd have made it halfway there, to a safe anchorage on Kithnos or Kea, islands off the peninsula southeast of Athens. If the next day gave favorable conditions, they may have made Athens in a total of two days, but if not, it may have taken a week to return.

There might have been other reasons, too, for delay that caused the round trip to take a month. There may have been people on board of some influence who were not anxious to return to home, since the same day they returned, a man would die. By tradition, there could be no executions while the sacred ship to Delos was on its yearly mission, so if a death sentence were handed down after the priest of Apollo at Athens had consecrated the ship for the journey, anyone on death row would benefit from a reprieve until her return. At most times, the executions were of common criminals of no great reputation. But this year, it was different. Awaiting death until the day they made landfall was someone everyone on board knew, or at least knew about, and undoubtedly had an opinion of, whether they thought he was a great man, or a fool. It was Socrates.

I had to go to the island of Delos and see for myself the place where they made their decision to sail. Perhaps it was just business as usual for them but this seems unlikely. The captain without question would have put the safety of the boat and crew above any other consideration when he made his call. Yet even among Socrates' worst enemies, there appears to have been more annoyance with him than hatred, and there were many others who admired and loved him deeply. So I would think that the gravity of the galley's arrival in Attica would have been an unwelcome burden for a skipper to bear.

Today the ancient harbor was before me, now silted up next to the new mole to the south where the ferries dock. It was quiet except for the wind and the harbor seemed tiny, relative to both its role in history and its reputation as a great port. There wasn't much to see but I know that this is just where that captain stood and I'll have it in my memory, when I think of that voyage, for the rest of my life.

CITY-STATES

12:30 PM local time, Friday, June 28 (0930 June 28 UTC).
37° 25.204'N 25° 19.421'E
Temp. 77, Humidity 67%, Cloud Cover 05%. Wind 30, gusting to 45.
Anchored at Ornos Bay on the island of Mikonos, Greece.

When the Captain was in the fourth grade and had as yet no military rank, his battle-axe of a teacher, whose name he has finally purged from his hard drive, taught us that the ancient Greeks lived in "city-states." Oh, they started you young. Then no doubt in junior high school and in high school and so on, city-states, city-states, city-states. To my shame I forgot most of what they taught, but that stuck in my mind because they gave no reason, at least that I absorbed, for why the Greeks would organize their society so much differently from the Egyptians, the Romans, the Persians, and everyone else. You never hear of Chinese "city-states."

We're here in Mikonos waiting out a blow. Another *meltemi* got up a day earlier than predicted so although we had planned our departure for the morning after we visited Delos, the wind came up at about 0300 and we're still here. It's been blowing a steady thirty since then and sometimes it gets in a mood and picks it up to the mid-forties. When he's feeling cranky, it wouldn't be much of a challenge to get the Captain to say that the he has seen enough of forty knots for this lifetime, whether at sea or in the harbor. Delos is right next door and it's a mystery to me how an important port would be located in this area, the worst in the Aegean for the *meltemi*. *Cyclades* comes from the Greek word for circle, and the Cyclades are the islands in a circle around Delos. I'd move if I were they.

The *meltemi* is the result of a very large squash zone, a meteorological phenomenon we have had occasion to be squished by before. To review, it occurs when a high, which in the northern hemisphere pushes the wind away from itself in a clockwise spiral, is next to a low, which pulls the wind towards itself in a counter-clockwise spiral. Where they commingle, the winds are amplified. In this case, the high is over the Azores in the Atlantic Ocean while the low is over Pakistan, and we're in the squishy place between. Your barometer doesn't do you any good because the pressure where you are stays about the same, as the low and high each weaken or strengthen way the hell and gone out there and make your timbers shiver.

We've been on the boat, standing our regular 24-hour watch in case we or someone else happens to drag, for well over 48 hours now. Except for the howling of the wind that works on the mind, we're pretty comfortable but we don't feel like it's safe to leave the boat to go ashore so it's a bit on the dull side. Making matters a little worse, somehow the knob on the barbeque got jammed under a support rod for the solar panel and leaked two months' worth of butane out into space where we can't retrieve it, and since the other tank is empty, we've got no stove.

Our arrival at Mikonos was a bit of a circus. We tried our faithful Bruce anchor half a dozen times but after backing down on it, it would drag in a rather dramatic way. Finally, we wrestled the 45-lb. CQR out of the starboard lazarette and lugged it up to the bow to give it a try. It dragged even worse; and on the second attempt, as it dragged, it snagged the anchor at the bottom of someone's mooring. Ship's Frogman Terry Shrode dove in to see what he could see, as the Captain has to douse his glasses to don his mask and can't see 10 feet. The bottom was 30 feet down, and Mr. Shrode couldn't quite make out the tangle but could get the general idea. We made a loop of chain and put it around our anchor chain, and jiggled it down to the bottom. The idea is to try to work the loop all the way down the shank of the anchor to the crown and then, pulling laterally on the new chain and easing the old one, pull the anchor free. It was a great idea but didn't work, and the new chain also got fouled. Did I mention it was blowing 25?

Eventually we managed to raise the whole mess using our windlass, after popping the circuit breaker a few times, and this revealed that the mooring anchor was attached by a cable to something else on the bottom. We passed 30 feet of 5/8 nylon rope under the cable, cleated it off to the bow, and then eased off on our windlass. This took the strain off our anchor and Mr. Shrode was able to release it. Then we eased away the nylon and we were free. Took about two and a half hours.

When you go through stuff like this, you attract an audience of folks who are interested in not being too close to you when you set your anchor, the assumption being you're idiots. And you open yourself up to receiving some unsolicited advice from other boaters who really are trying to help—and, again, are making the assumption that you're idiots. Since it's already been a bit of a frustrating day, the Captain has gotten a bit testy and there's a temptation to say, "My good man, it is apparently the case that you are unaware of whom you have the honor of addressing." But he thanks them kindly for their advice, even if it is wacko, as it was.

We finally got the plow to bite and set it real well, but overall, our view of the holding in this bay was tinged with not a little skepticism. Aside from our personal experience, it didn't help that one of the other boats said he had dragged twice and that we witnessed several others dragging. So when the *meltemi* hit a day early, we were sitting in an anchorage that was not to our liking. We were glad to have made the extra effort to be positive that the anchor was well set even if it did take all day and cause us some humiliation. Because when the *meltemi* hit, *Maverick* was among the few boats that didn't drag.

The truth is that if we had to, we could sail to another island. It would be a pain because where we need to go is dead upwind so with these conditions and the short chop you have to power into, you need all available sail plus the engine unless you want to do 1-2 knots or sometimes zero. The seas would be lousy but we've seen lousy seas before. However, we really don't have to leave if the anchor sticks, and we've kept a good watch and it has held. The guy next to us made a run for it but came back, saying the sea state was "a bit grim."

But the Greeks could not have sailed at all in these conditions, which brings me back to city-states. Mainland Greece (and for that matter, we can also include the coast of Turkey, which was in ancient times part of Greece) is made up of plains and peninsulas cut off from one another by rugged and sometimes impassable mountains, and islands that are separated much of the time by some nasty seas and formidable winds. Although from the top of the peaks on most islands, they could see at least one other island inhabited by people who shared their language and culture, they couldn't sail there for a large number of days a year and if they could, they wouldn't be able to return.

The Greek sailors were tough guys. You could strip all the electronics, the entire electrical system, the engine, the dodger, the winches, even the deck (replace that with some ribs to stiffen the hull) off of *Maverick*. You could remove the autopilot and the self-steering vane, the compass and charts and binoculars, the stove, sink, head, and berths. Toss the fire extinguishers, life raft, bilge pumps, dinghy, strobe, EPIRB, flares, and life jackets. There was certainly no calling a mayday on the radio. Forget that night-vision scope for sure. Replace the Bruce, CQR, and Danforth with a rock with a stick lashed to it, and disconnect the steering wheel so you're just using the emergency tiller. You'd still have a craft that was way more seaworthy than a Greek galley, but they went out in them anyway.

The Greeks would not have sailed intentionally in the conditions we have now, but they certainly would have been caught out in them. When they were, they could do nothing except go where the wind took them, and if that's not where they planned to go, the best they could do was reduce sail and hold on. If there was a lee shore nearby, they were dead men, and this is not just a figure of speech. If the wind lasted long enough, the whole sea was on a lee shore.

So now I understand why the Greeks had city-states. There were other reasons; they were independent-minded, contentious, and vainglorious. But the main thing was, they couldn't get there from here.

The Odyssey

7:53 AM local time, Monday, July 1 (0453 July 1 UTC).
37 37 N   024 01 E
Temp. 83, Humidity 64%, Cloud Cover 5%.
Underway off Cape Sounion, Greece, en route from Kea to Salamis.

You've got your Connor, Turner, Taberly, Knox-Johnston, Moitessier, Chichester, and Slocum. There's Magellan, Columbus, Nelson, Drake, Jones, and Cook. Don't neglect Noah. But mirror, mirror, on the wall, who's the greatest sailor of all? No, silly, not your Captain. You're making me blush. It's our man, Odysseus.

The ancient temple of Poseidon was clearly visible a moment ago as we came abeam of Cape Sounion at the tip of the Attic Peninsula and crossed the course of Odysseus when he sailed homeward from Troy for Ithaca lo these 3200 years past. The seas are flat calm, a relief from the *meltemi* that finally abated after 72 hours, and we are motoring instead of rowing, as his crew would have done in the same conditions. But Odysseus, Agamemnon, Nestor, and Menalaus had to carry on from here and find their way around the Peloponnesus, so harsh challenges still lay ahead.

Now, many of our readers may think that Odysseus was a mythical character made up by Homer, and this was the common view until the last part of the 19th century, when, to everyone's astonishment, a man named Schliemann discovered the ruins of Troy. By the end of the following century, few scholars doubted that as well as Troy, the locations of Agamemnon's Mycenae, Menelaus' Sparta, Nestor's Pylos, and Odysseus' Ithaca had been identified. The sense now is that the *Iliad* and the *Odyssey* relate real historic events about real historic people, enhanced for the telling, just like Hollywood. Some parts of Odysseus' story, the tale that interests us most, are more myth than fact, but some researchers feel they can separate the skeleton of reality from the layers of legend and locate the general path of Odysseus' actual voyage.

Even though we think of classical Greece as the birthplace of Western culture, the Greek gods and heroes were so different from our own that it is hard for us to resonate with them, perhaps to our disadvantage. Almost all of our familiar American heroes are chaste to the point of being mythical non-humans themselves. Superman had a Platonic relationship with Lois. Della Street took notes for Perry Mason, but that's all she did. Bogie scrapes off Ingrid at the end of Casablanca, Clint Eastwood's Stranger is a loner, and Spiderman wasn't allowed to get next to that girl. This is not to mention, unless that's just what I'm about to do, the more exotic cases of Batman and Robin, and the Lone Ranger and Tonto. You're hard-pressed to find a real macho hero in American mythology who has what one would call an intimate relationship with an important woman in his life. We're used to it being this way, and we think it's normal.

But Odysseus had his Penelope, along with the domineering Calypso and Circe, and he needed Athena's help to kill the bad guys. Agamemnon had Clytemnestra, although that didn't work out too well, and Menelaus had that trollop, Helen. The whole Trojan War was fought over Helen, but Homer doesn't portray Helen as the type of unambiguously pure, helpless victim we like in our damsels in distress. Achilles has a hissy-fit over little Briseis and spends most of the war sitting out the fighting and pouting about her while his friends are getting killed. Would Rambo do that? Even the big man, Zeus, has a woman to answer to, an idea not remotely conceivable in the Judeo-Christian tradition.

The Greek heroes and gods are characters who are well known for being fickle, lusty, mercurial, and vicious, not like our prim good guys. Homer's Gods are playboys and the folks on Olympus don't see eye to eye on much of anything. The humans are no worse, but on the other hand, American culture would have a hard time making them look heroic, as a TV movie of the *Odyssey* once proved. Menelaus is history's most famous cuckold. Agamemnon did what Abraham would not and stuck the knife in his daughter but unlike Abraham, who wasn't offered a reward, he expected to get a good sailing breeze in the bargain. Among modern sailors, one can think of only two or three who would make the same deal. The *Iliad* is filled with ceaseless, repetitious, graphic violence that is the paradigm of gratuitous, and Odysseus' revenge consists of gruesomely slaughtering over 100 men whose most violent act was throwing a footstool at someone they took for a beggar.

Homer almost never refers to Odysseus without us learning that he's wily, clever, cunning, or a smooth talker. He did come up with the Trojan horse thing and was tough enough to be one of those inside it. As a sea captain and hero, however, he leaves a bit to be desired. It took him 10 years to get home from Troy. A remote-controlled 30-inch model sailboat could make it a lot quicker than that. I suppose that wouldn't be so bad if all hands had returned safely, but the captain himself was the only one to make it home alive. Shackleton, he's not. He wasn't such a hero to his men either, if Homer is to be believed; otherwise, why do they have so little respect for his orders? Disaster follows disaster as he fails to control them.

And about that cleverness. If you were away from your home and family for approximately 40 times as long as you should have been, would it be a good excuse to tell everyone that you were captured by a goddess who made you have sex with her for seven years? Nice try, O wily one.

However, that's our hero, and his being heroic requires that we subsume his flaws in his glory and place him in the empyrean, beyond the reach of the Captain's impertinent remarks. I'm down with that.

Now, as I've mentioned before, Tim Severin sailed his way around the Aegean in a replica of a Bronze Age galley looking for Odysseus' trail and wrote about it in *The Ulysses Voyage*. His general thesis is that many of the places mentioned, like the homes of the Cyclops, the lotus-eaters, and Scylla and Charybdis, correspond to landfalls, capes, islands, and bays that would naturally fall along the logical sailing route from Troy to Ithaca, and that these locations are moreover corroborated by local place-names and folklore that have grown up around hazardous sections of the journey. He believes that, departing Troy, Odysseus coast-hopped westward along the northern Aegean, then worked his way south, rarely out of sight of land. When he reached Cape Malea on the southern coast of the Peloponnesus, which to this day the *Sailing Directions* instruct us to treat with great respect, Odysseus could not double it (as we mariners still say following Homer) and so was blown southward past Crete to Africa. This is where his problems got worse and the weird stories began, but from a sailing point of view, the scenario to this point is entirely credible. As time went on, local legends were added to the story, according to Severin's theory, until it was given its final shape by Homer. Severin gives little credence to many of the more traditional attempts at locating our hero's adventures, for instance placing Scylla and Charybdis at the Straits of Messina, declaring it is unlikely that Odysseus would have been a poor enough navigator to have found himself lost so far to windward of his destination. These are a sailor's arguments, and if the tale is to have any basis in history, it must have been a sailor's yarn to begin with.

Since *Maverick* sailed from southern Turkey and not from Troy, and since we will not go around the Peloponnesus but through the Corinth canal, we'll only cross his path in two places, one of which we've just passed. The other will be at his legendary home with Penelope, Ithaca.

THE BATTLE OF SALAMIS

7:00 PM local time, Tuesday, July 9 (1600 July 9 UTC).
37° 56.786'N 23° 32.611'E
Temp. 89, Humidity 38%, Cloud Cover 5%.
On the hard at Theo Bekris and Co. shipyard, island of Salamis, Greece.

Having assisted with the haul-out of *Maverick*, Mr. Shrode returned to America a couple of days ago to remind Caroline of his existence. Theresa feels her email contacts with the Captain are quite sufficient for her needs, if not providing a bothersome surplus. And so it is that I can selflessly absent myself from contact with those closest to me to the satisfaction of all concerned, with the exception, that is, of myself.

The Captain, when he is not arranging repairs or scraping bottom paint or grinding fiberglass or smashing his toe quite impressively with the airline-type ladder used to climb up to *Maverick's* cockpit, causing a dramatic flow of his life's blood, lounges about his modestly commodious bachelor pad—*Maverick's* cabin—and reads books that he flatters himself may have the effect of improving his mind if not his toe. Currently, he's making his way through Herodotus' *Histories*. Some minds are more easily improved than others, I fear. There are those who feel that the accumulation of new thoughts is a vain and unwarranted extravagance when the same threadbare but comfortable concepts they've entertained since youth have faithfully kept them ticking along without incident. I would like to believe that this is not the wisest course to take, but it beats me how evidence could be provided to the contrary. So perhaps it is the illusion of improving a mind so in need of improvement, and not the actuality of it, that serves the day.

From my quarters, which are only 10 yards or so from a bay given over to industrial use and ship repair, I have access by ferry to Piraeus, the commercial and historical port of Athens, and from there to Athens itself by bus or train. Unlike the harbor at Delos, which has not been developed in centuries, this area is a congested pool of cranes, fuel tanks, wrecks, and pollution. After the workers leave in the afternoon, on the other hand, it is very quiet here. I've made friends with the pack of large junkyard, or rather, boatyard dogs that have the run of the place and at first were a bit intimidating. They take little notice of me now when I cross the yard to visit the head and cold shower, where one might have hoped for just a tiny bit more luxury.

Most yachts never come to this area because the harbor at Piraeus is not available to them and there's little other reason to sail here, as Salamis is no tourist island. There's an anchorage on the west side but to get there, you'd go south of the island and miss the nearby strait between the mainland and Salamis, where an important sea battle once took place.

My apartment in the shipyard has a view of a distinguished venue. It was to Salamis that the Athenians fled the Persians under the leadership of Themistocles, one of the most important and, fortunately for us, duplicitous characters in western history. After Darius of Persia failed earlier, amazingly, in his attempt to conquer the outnumbered Greeks, the Athenians felt that they had nothing to fear from another attack. Like Californians thinking about an earthquake, they found the idea too disconcerting to contemplate and so convinced themselves it wouldn't happen, and opposed taking measures to improve their defenses. Themistocles could not persuade them to raise a navy against the Persians, so he focused their attention on the hated Aegineans from an island close by. Whipping up fears of invasion from a nearer and more beatable foe, Themistocles got the Athenians to triple the size of their navy for the real enemy he was wise enough to see was coming. That was his first duplicity, against his own people.

When the Persians under Xerxes, son of Darius, advanced just as Themistocles had predicted, their fleet was diminished in a battle on the coast northeast of Athens. But it became clear that it would be impossible to defend Athens from Xerxes' ground forces. Themistocles knew, however, that the ground troops could not succeed without supplies from the navy, and he had built his own navy specifically to fight theirs. The Greek ships were smaller and more maneuverable and this proved decisive.

As Xerxes approached, the Athenians abandoned their city and fled to the island of Salamis, giving Xerxes the impression that they were terrified and had retreated in complete chaos. Actually, this was pretty much the case, but there was method in it. Themistocles sent, in his second major duplicity, a double agent claiming to be a representative of a treasonous Greek general who was willing to desert. He told Xerxes that the Athenians had escaped to Salamis, that they were divided and demoralized, and that many would join him and fight the others. The Greek fleet was bottled up and helpless in the mile-wide strait between the mainland and the island, and Xerxes' advisors realized that if he blocked the escape routes at each end of the strait, the Greeks would be fatally trapped.

Relying on this information, Xerxes commanded his navy to attack. With, according to Herodotus, a westerly blowing, the Persians sailed against the Greeks but soon found that they, and not their foes, were the ones who could not escape. Although the Persians had 800 galleys to the Greeks' 380, the audacity and viciousness of the counterattack, together with the fact that as Themistocles had hoped, his ships were able to outflank and outmaneuver the larger, slower Persian fleet in the constricted trap he had lured them to, led to the sinking of 300 Persian galleys to the Greeks' 40 and the disabling of many more. Xerxes watched the whole thing from a silver throne set up at an excellent vantage point on a hillside on the mainland. With his navy decimated and retreating in disorder and his ground troops dependent on naval support, he realized he had to retire. It was the earliest recorded naval battle and is still considered one of the most brilliant in history. It essentially ended the Persian invasion.

Had Themistocles not succeeded in either of his two duplicities, it's hard to say what would have happened. The battle took place in 480 BC and in the next 100 years or so Greece, but largely Athens, produced Pericles, Demosthenes, Sophocles, Aristophanes, Euripides, Aeschylus, Democritus, Anaxagoras, Hippocrates, Protagoras, Socrates, Plato, Aristotle, Herodotus, Xenophon, and Thucydides, and that's just the A-list. During the same period, the Athenians invented drama and democracy, firmly set the foundation of western civilization, and still had time to be almost constantly at war. But never again against Persia.

Agoraphobia

5:40 PM local time, Saturday, July 13 (1440 July 13 UTC).
37° 56.786'N 23° 32.611'E
Temp. 96, Humidity 30%, Cloud Cover 5%.
On the hard at Theo Bekris and Co. shipyard, island of Salamis, Greece.

Since my last visit to Athens, I had obtained a small book called *Socrates In The Agora*, published by the American School of Classical Studies that has something to do with restoration projects and, I believe, runs the museum and bookstore at the ruins of the agora, the downtown of ancient Athens. This book describes an archaeological excavation in the agora that matches exactly the description that Socrates' friend Phaedo gives, in the Platonic dialogue of the same name, of the prison in which Socrates was kept and spent his last days. Somehow, this had escaped my attention on previous visits to Athens. The prison doesn't show up on the map of the agora in the book, nor in other maps I've seen, but I meant to find it. Besides Delos and Ithaca, it was the only place in our voyage around the world I felt I absolutely had to see.

On a second visit after the first one was aborted by a thunderstorm, I went into the small bookstore in the museum where there was an information booth. There was a young lady behind the counter and I asked her where the site of the prison was, where Socrates drank the hemlock the day the boat returned from Delos.

She shrugged and rolled her eyes, tossing her head back just a little, and said, "Nobody knows."

To which I returned, "Miss, your skepticism gives you away. I see you have the natural reserve that follows on, and is the fruit of, years of careful study, and the caution of the born and bred scholar. Of course I realize that you and I are not CERTAIN," giving her a knowing wink, "where the prison is. We have neither fingerprints nor DNA samples, no videotape, no graffiti Socrates may have carved in the stone that could well be a later forgery, nothing that would withstand two minutes of cross-examination by even the least qualified of legal minds, among whom I count some of my oldest acquaintances. After all, it is tradition and not science that, for example, locates St. Peter's remains in the Vatican, and many sites of historical and cultural significance are accepted without the sort of rigor that I so admire in your approach. I applaud your honest forthrightness, Miss, and beg your pardon, as I did not have the honor of appreciating the subtlety of the intellect to which I addressed myself. What I should have asked, but didn't in my haste, was the location of the ruins that SOME scholars have proposed MAY have been the location of the state prison where Socrates was held."

As the line behind me grew, there was some mumbling but it was in a language I did not comprehend so it could be ignored. More to the point, the young lady's response to this restated inquiry was another and now helpless shrug, more rolling of the eyes, a tossing of the head that seemed amplified from the first time, and she repeated, with a little of what I should have thought was unwarranted impatience, "Nobody knows!"

At this, I drew her attention to a copy of the book I mentioned above, for sale less than an arm's length away, which, I repeat, was published by the institute of which she was an employee. I opened it to a page on which there was a photograph of the ruins in question taken, according to the authors, at the very agora where she and I currently conversed much as did the philosophers of old. I mentioned that the photograph is also displayed, along with some artifacts found at the site, in the same museum where she was a provider of information.

"Now, Miss," I said, "perhaps we have misunderstood one another. How are we to account for the fact of the existence of a photograph of the ruins I wish to view and the baffling mystery of the location where the photograph was taken, which according to the authors is within easy sight of the place where we now stand? It's a puzzle, is it not? There's a very famous place within 200 yards of here that we have a photograph of, yet no one on earth knows where it is. Why, it almost has the quality of being a miracle. Perhaps it's an enchantment, one that the Knight of the Doleful Countenance would understand. And in fact if either a miracle or an enchantment has occurred here, Miss, it is an occasion that would make an impression on my memory even more significant than that which was the original object of my visit."

Another helpless and exasperated shrug. "Nobody knows."

More grumbling. I depart to the satisfaction of all those assembled.

At another area of the agora, I found a distinguished and official-looking gentleman with a guide's badge, whom I approached.

"Sir," I said, still a little steamed, "I have just been speaking with the flibbertigibbet in your information booth and she cannot tell me the location, on the grounds here, of Socrates' imprisonment. Perhaps you could be of assistance. I've traveled a long way to see it."

And, with a helpless shrug of the shoulders and a roll of the eyes, he said, "Nobody knows." Yet another scholar. They work for peanuts.

Not relenting, I said, "Well, sir, where do some people say it is?"

"Over there, about 30 yards. You'll see the iron bars on the cell where it is said the jail was."

Oh, for sure. Oh, yes indeedy. There are some 2400-year-old iron bars left from Socrates' cell, still nice and square. Aside from their philosophical, dramatic, mathematical, and political skills, I suppose the ancient Greeks were regular masters of rust-proofing. Well, actually they were but that was not germane to our present case.

I found no fewer than three more employees who gave me more or less the same answer, and the enchantment idea had begun to be my prime hypothesis. Undeterred, I wandered past the iron bars that didn't look more than about 50 years old and kept looking at my book and kept walking and looking at ruins, and after awhile I saw something that looked like it might be the very thing. There was no marble sign like you'll find on the Eponymous Heroes and it looked a little different from the photograph. But the dig occurred more than 25 years ago and perhaps it had filled in over that period of time. It wasn't, like, carefully maintained or anything. There were no fresh flowers or other offerings like those we had seen at the resting place of Gauguin in the Marquesas. There was no one there besides me.

And as I carefully looked back and forth between the photograph and the jumble of rocks, studying it from different angles, it finally became clear that these were, unmistakably, the ruins I sought.

Socrates had been in prison a month while the sacred boat from Delos was awaited. During this time, Crito had come to offer to bribe the guards, organize an escape, and pay the expenses for Socrates' relocation with his family to another country. It could all be so easily arranged, and, as Crito argues in the Platonic dialogue that bears his name, it was Socrates' moral obligation, to his family and friends and his calling, to escape the consequences of a wrongful verdict. Socrates' argument against taking advantage of this offer is not only persuasive, it is the paradigm, if that is not too weak a term, of disinterested reasoning.

The arguments of the archaeologists who made the claim of these rocks being the foundation of the prison are a little on the thin side, but certainly no more so than Socrates' arguments for eternal life in the dialogue, the *Phaedo*, where they find their evidence. In the *Phaedo*, the boat has returned and Socrates' friends convene at the prison to spend his last day with him, as he must drink the hemlock at sunset. In the conversation Plato recounts, Socrates uncharacteristically is placed in the role of one proposing a thesis with which others find fault, and the thesis is that Socrates' soul will survive his death. He insists that they objectively discuss the merits of the arguments to pass his last hours on earth, and he encourages his friends to find the errors in his logic even if it means his accepting his own mortality. Plato's rendering of Socrates' belief in this process and his calm practice of it until the last minutes of his life, along with the serenity with which he accepts the poison, paints the noblest scene of one of the most noble lives in history. It would be a famous story, even if it were fiction.

But it is Phaedo's clear description of Socrates' retiring, at one point, into another room of his cell to bathe, thereby sparing those who will care for his dead body that task, that convinced the archaeologists that this was the location of his death. For at the ruins I viewed, which are not like a house or a temple or any other known type of characteristic building of ancient Greece, there is a row of several small rooms opening on a narrow courtyard and what must have been a sort of tower, perhaps a guard tower. Only the end room has an adjoining chamber that has no exit to the courtyard, and in it are a washbasin and a sunken bath like those Phaedo described. It was the cell of final honor, for the man condemned to die.

CORINTH

10:50 PM local time, Wednesday, July 24 (1950 July 24 UTC).
38° 22.555'N   22° 23.231'E
Temp. 87, Humidity 45%, Cloud Cover 0%.
On the quay at Galaxidi, Greece.

We are currently bows-to in the beautifully serene little harbor of Galaxidi on the north shores of the Gulf of Corinth, about 40 miles west of the Corinth Canal. The Italianate architecture is a welcome change from the tacky buildings of Salamis and Athens, and to tell the truth, much of the eastern Mediterranean. This area of the world had the misfortune of suffering numerous devastating earthquakes in the 1950s, with the result that most of the rebuilding was done at the 5000-year nadir of western architectural design. But there are few new buildings in this town, and it retains the picturesque Mediterranean look that we all wish for when we travel here. From Galaxidi, a great science fiction name, we will travel to the Temple of Apollo at Delphi on nearby Mount Parnassus, and consult the Oracle concerning our prospects for a safe return home.

After two and one half weeks on the hard, during which time the Captain had only two afternoons free for the visits to the Athens agora previously reported, *Maverick* was relaunched in Salamis at Theo Bekris' shipyard on Wednesday July 17. The Captain had completed a long list of repairs and painted the bottom, but the rest had to wait until Mr. Shrode returned from the US bearing a heavy load of parts for the Perkins diesel, among other things. Our Chief of Engineering soon had the engine running and we were ready to go.

By Friday we were in a private marina on the mainland near Athens picking up supplies from a chandlery along with some Greek charts and collecting our mainsail from the sailmaker, who had done some minor repairs. We had accomplished a lot but as is not unusual when there are so many things to do, there were a few glitches. For example, there was a little misunderstanding about a small fiberglass job I should have done myself. Because of the language problem, the yard's guy apparently thought I told him to use cocaine instead of the normal white powder we use for thickening epoxy. At least, that's the only way I can account for the price I was charged.

Departing Athens, we sailed to the west side of Salamis to put more finishing touches on some repairs and wait for a Monday departure for the Corinth Canal. They charge a premium for weekend transits so it made more sense to delay a day. On Monday we sailed for Isthmia, the canal's eastern entrance, arriving midday, and forked over €132 to the canal authority. After a short wait, we motored through the deep, narrow ditch that links the Aegean Sea to the Ionian and cuts the mainland off from the Peloponnesus. It was a beautiful day. The cicadas were boisterous. The slice in the limestone that holds the canal was a lot more dramatic than it looks in the pictures, and the 40-minute trip was one of the coolest experiences of the voyage.

Once through the canal, you're in the Gulf of Corinth and the harbor of the modern city of Corinth is only a mile away. We tied stern-to and the next day took a bus to the nearby ruins of ancient Corinth, the place St. Paul sent those letters to. He was quite the ramblin' guy, old Paul. Though he was a rabbi from Tarsus, near Syria, he was a Roman citizen and spoke and wrote Greek fluently, and these together made travel less of a struggle than it might otherwise have been, at least on a practical level. He visited Corinth three times, probably under sail, calling most likely at the ancient port of Cenchreae on the eastern shore of the isthmus at Corinth, the ruins of which are now visible underwater. However, I believe the last time he had to leave by road to avoid a plot against him. Paul managed to get himself in a peck of trouble wherever he went, which isn't so much as a bushel, in fact, it's only a quarter of a bushel. He might have gotten into several bushels of trouble in Rome, maybe a kilderkin or even a hogshead full. We'll never know for sure.

When Paul visited Corinth, he probably took the hike up to the Acrocorinth, which, unless I missed my tack, means high Corinth, just like *acropolis* means high city. When you get up there, you find the climb's been hot enough and steep enough that you've left most everyone behind. From the top, you have a perfect view of the narrow isthmus that connects the Peloponnesus with the rest of mainland Greece, which was a true crossroads in that all land traffic had to come through here, for instance the Spartans on their way to die to the last man at Thermopylae. But in addition, ancient sea traffic came to the east end of the Gulf of Corinth and could be transported by wheeled carts overland across the isthmus to the Saronic Gulf, thereby avoiding the long and dangerous voyage around the Peloponnesian peninsula. The Corinthians collected a lot of money for this service, and the old roadway is still visible down to the ruts worn by the carts over two thousand years ago. The Romans tried building a canal to replace this labor-intensive method of portage, but even those masters of public works couldn't pull it off and it had to wait until the end of the 19th century.

The canal is only 28 stadia or 23 cables or 256 chains or 9/10 of a league or 2816 orguia, if it's easier for you to think in those, or 16,896 feet or 1,024 rods or 25.6 furlongs or 9,300 cubits (in biblical cubits; but of course in classical Greece, it would have been 11,140 cubits, due to inflation) or for you sailors, 2.7826086965217391304347826086957 nautical miles long. The cut is 250 feet deep to the waterline and holds about 23 feet of water. It's 81 feet wide but looks narrower when you're driving a boat through it.

I would give these figures in the metric system were this not prohibited under rule number F-435a section M.0001 paragraph S4 of my agreement with webmaster Jim Mead. As some of you will remember, Mr. Mead's patriotism prompted him to write protesting the Captain's slip-sliding in his use of foreign measurement systems, thereby heading his crew down the road to world domination by the Trilateral Commission. I made this agreement on January 31 of this year in the Maldives but have since received further enlightenment from one of our readers. Pirates, Muslims, our engine, and sloth have contributed to delaying our reporting of this but now's the time, I think, for you lucky readers to get another view.

Jim Turner, who is a very old friend of the Captain and there are less and less of the other kind, is certainly the most gentle person ever to be admitted to the bar in these United States. Frankly, for this reason I'm sorry to say I wouldn't be able to recommend hiring him to support your cause in a vicious divorce or to preserve your corporate hegemony, but despite this professional handicap, he's managed to make a go of it. Since graduating from law school back in the last century, he has spent all but three years working for the US House of Representatives and its Committee on Science. For ten years he was the Committee's Technology Staff Director, but in 1994, when certain political events changed the lay of the land in Washington, he became Chief Democratic Counsel for the Committee on Science. All this would be neither here nor there but we need to establish his credentials before wading into this very emotional arena again.

Mr. Turner, in his various capacities at the House of Representatives, had occasion to write several of the provisions of the US Code pertaining to the metric system. In a word, Mr. Turner was among those who wrote the book on measurement in the United States. The US, according to Turner, was well on its way to converting to the metric system until the Reagan administration abolished the US Metric Board during its watch. One of the groups lobbying against the metric system was the Cowboy Hall of Fame—I'm not making this up, folks—which we can all agree is a fine institution but one does have the feeling that in that majestic hall where the greatest of cowboys are honored, there just might be a statue of Ronald Reagan. Ergo: bye-bye metric system.

Mr. Turner also reports that, as some of you may remember, the Mars Climate Orbiter crashed because of the failure of someone to remember he needed to convert from (or was it to) metric. Aside from commercial considerations, like for instance that the entire rest of the world uses another system of measurement, Mr. Turner is concerned about the safety of travel, since even your Captain and Ship's Navigation Officer Terry Shrode are put in the position of having to make lots of conversions to or from the metric system in order to do *Maverick's* navigation. It is not likely that people flying airplanes are less able navigators than your correspondent, but it's not impossible.

Now Mr. Mead, who works for the Executive Branch of the Government, may have a different mandate from that of Mr. Turner, who works for the Legislative Branch, and this may speak to the issues that separate them in the great dialogue concerning the fundamentals of the American Way. They are each collecting a salary to thwart one another's efforts in steering the American ship of state towards the safe harbor that is a certain distance away but may have to be converted to another distance. It's the system of checks and balances working for you, the taxpayer.

Your reporter out here in the field can confirm that in addition to our different measuring system and our habit of calling a sport "soccer" that the rest of the world calls "football," a couple of other things display our cavalier propensity towards doing the mashed potato to the beat of a different drummer. First, only in North and South America and a bit of Asia do aids to navigation follow the "Red, Right, Returning" rule. Everywhere else, red is on the left and green on the right as you return to port, matching your side lights, and it's hard to believe that this contrariness contributes to safety on the water. But second, and perhaps an even more troubling and dangerous result of the lack of unanimity and cooperation among the many nations and cultures of the world, is the fact that in most places in the world but the United States, the rear brake on a bicycle is on your left hand, not on your right.

Ithaka

4:00 PM local time, Friday, August 2 (1300 August 2 UTC).
38° 11.153'N 20° 29.078'E
Temp. 86, Humidity 64%, Cloud Cover 0%.
Stern-to on the quay in Argostoli, island of Cephalonia, Greece.

I got up at 2:30 last night and took a walk. Things were bothering me. The Italians in a large crewed charter next to us were still partying, and they bore the thought that their activities may incommode their neighbors with wonderful equanimity. But that wasn't what was keeping me awake.

The *Maverick* crew had left Salamis about a week earlier feeling sanguine about the future. The boat had been hauled, extensive repairs made, and all troubling issues resolved, leaving just a few minor jobs waiting for parts from the US. But our sense of well-being was short-lived.

The dirty weather that I had experienced back in the agora of Athens, during which, I learned later, several people were killed in flooding incidents, was not finished. The unseasonable skies, with tremendous thundershowers and lightning, are unusual for Greece in the summer when scarcely is there ever a drop of rain. On our way from the island of Trizonia to Mesolongion in the Gulf of Patras, the squally weather reappeared. That night, after we had tied to a secure wharf, there was a violent thunderstorm. We felt a deafening explosion, and the boat next to *Maverick* suffered a direct lightning strike that turned its electrical distribution panel to soup. We checked our electronic instruments, most of which had been unplugged out of concern for the weather, and everything seemed to work. When we got underway a day later, however, we discovered that some things were amiss. Our radar, tachometer, autopilot, and oil and water gauges were fried. The high-frequency radio would not transmit. So some effects of the lightning came our way.

We can get by for the nonce without radar and the tachometer. We've got a backup autopilot or had one—now it's in service. But not being able to transmit means we have no onboard email, cannot talk with other boats, and can't call for emergency assistance at a distance beyond about 20 miles. Making the repairs will have to take priority over seeing some of the places we intended to visit. People get by without HF radio but we'd rather not, and it's a good idea to have the radar to help gauge the range, heading, and speed of ships at night, or more importantly, in fog.

So the episodes of finding parts or service for complicated equipment in odd places will continue, and this is what was keeping the Captain up. Perhaps the reader has had the experience of navigating through a voicemail system in a foreign language.

As I walked through the town, still rocking at this hour, I thought about my fears, and I realized that when we're at sea in rough weather and it's *Maverick's* job to take care of us, I'm not really afraid. She'd go over Niagara Falls if we asked her to. It's when it's my job to take care of her, to guide her into a harbor, to see she's safely moored, to watch out for dangerous weather that might compromise the shelter there, to make sure all her systems are maintained and her contingency gear is ready for use, these are the things that bring me worries.

On we sailed, in the continuing squally weather with yet more lightning, to Ithaca, fabled home of Odysseus, who it pleases me to believe was a real person. It's a very beautiful island, really, prettier than all those ones in the Aegean. Hard to find a vista that offends the eye. There are groves of olives and the ever-present cicadas but also beautiful stands of cypress, as this side of Greece gets a bit more rainfall than the eastern islands. I saw lots of goats, particularly in the vicinity of an ancient stone cottage on a high ridge, and wondered if they may not be descendants of Odysseus' own herd. Unless they were eliminated from the island sometime in the past, it's hard to believe that they aren't. Goats are notoriously bad record-keepers, though.

We stayed at a rolly and picturesque little harbor named Frikes, not the bigger southern harbor of Vathi. The entire island is only 13 miles long, but apparently Odysseus' kingdom extended to the neighboring, much larger island of Cephalonia, where *Maverick* is now berthed. As kingdoms go, Ithaca wasn't so big, I suppose, and this of course accounts for Odysseus' lower status in the war than Agamemnon, for example. There is no agreement on where Odysseus' palace may have been, or where the Cave of the Nymphs was, or where Odysseus may have kept his fleet, but many Bronze Age finds establish that the island was inhabited well before the time of our hero. The earliest piece they have with Odysseus' name on it, in the archaeological museum on the mountain above Frikes, is, however, only 2nd century BC, one thousand years after the Trojan War.

Now that we have seen Ithaca, it is easy to believe how much Odysseus must have thought it worth returning to, just as your reporter dreams about Theresa and the fragrance of the California bay laurels on a walk above Phoenix Lake. Soon we will sail through the Strait of Messina, by tradition the place of the feared Scylla and Charybdis of the Odyssey and to this day a hazardous bit of water, and the Captain will do his best to see that Mr. Shrode is not eaten.

BEEN SUCH A LONG WAY HOME

11:00 PM local time, Friday, August 9 (2000 August 9 UTC).
37° 30.009'N 15° 5.884'E
Temp. 82, Humidity 55%, Cloud Cover 0%.
At a marina in Catania on the island of Sicily, Italy.

There may have been those among our readership who were disappointed with our treatment of Ithaca last time. They were hoping for one of the Captain's nonpareil ventures into the world of literary criticism, but they got instead some simple geographical information. After all, our mission is not merely to report our physical whereabouts and the price of beer at local stores, but also to savor and celebrate with our readers the reveries that attend our endeavors.

Our adventure is an epic of grand proportions. There is no reason to soften this with a false humility, as our goals are, in the course of otherwise unexceptional lives, heroic, or at least that's what the guy who sold me the boat said. Note that I do not claim that *we* are heroic or, for that matter, even competent. I merely point out that the voyage has a mythical resonance with many such adventures in literature, whether fictional or fact, and whether from Homer or from modern cruisers writing to *Latitude 38*. We all follow a mythology in our daily lives that may be described as heroic if we like, and we usually do. This, in part, was the message of Joyce's other *Ulysses*. The legends and stories we read inform our mundane trials and help us fill them with significance beyond the prosaic. Without them the crew of *Maverick* would never have, once upon a time, set sail on a mysterious voyage to unknown lands, battling sea monsters and pirates, searching for treasure, defending liberty and justice, and rescuing various damsels as we were taught to do by the Courageous and Woeful Knight of long ago and far, far away.

The *Odyssey* formed the pattern for the numberless tales of homecoming that have followed in western literature. The Captain's pick is a song by Garnett Mimms and the Enchanters, speaking of Don Quixote, called "Been Such a Long Way Home." In the song, there has been a departure, an absence, and now there is a coming home. Here literature and the performing arts are able to represent what is more difficult in painting, sculpture, and architecture, and that is the passage of time together with a dénouement, a moment of closure and victory after a struggle. Music has the power to make the listener feel the separation and long for the return, leaving us spent at the moment of homecoming. Perhaps the greatest ending in music occurs at the finale of

Shostakovich's Symphony #5, but Jerry Ragavoy, Billy Sherrill, and Phil Spector were able to create great drama in their three-minute songs. These often included a coda, which, after the iterations of verse and chorus, used the repetition of a phrase to build tension and then finally release it, just like what happens in Homer's *Odyssey*.

There was a bass player in San Diego named Pat Fitzpatrick, and he and I were insane about a particular guitar "chink," or actually a double chink, that occurs just after the climax of "Been Such a Long Way Home," which was produced by Ragavoy. Towards the end of the tune, the band lingers on the five-chord, building the suspense that is the musical correlative of an anguished absence, and during this time, the singer repeats in a call-and-response mantra "been such a long way." When the song finally resolves to the tonic, which is the one-chord, or "home" in harmony, Garnet Mimms sings the word "home." The release is so intense that the music seems to pause and take a breath, as if the song's own heart skips a beat, and in this space, there's a "chink" from an otherwise unheard rhythm guitar player. Pat and I would listen to it over and over, convulsed in rapture, unless there's a hipper way to describe that.

When we meet Odysseus in the *Iliad*, he is already a wily and toughened warrior; we don't learn of his young days at his home on Ithaca until the very end of the *Odyssey*. He is a relatively minor player in the first poem. Why didn't Homer choose to relate Agamemnon's trip home, or that of Achilles, or Menalaus, or Nestor? Some of their return voyages were not so easy, either. My theory is that it is because Odysseus' return really was the worst, his separation from hearth and home the longest, and it became legendary.

The heroic thing about Odysseus is that he never doubts that it is worth it all to return. He is threatened not only by storms and disaster but also by a dialectically counterbalanced temptation, the offer of eternal life and the protection, not to mention affection, of a goddess. He continually resists the drugs and spells of sleep and death that affect his crew, along with the song of the sirens and the lure of eternal bliss. What is it that makes it seem so clear to Odysseus that Penelope and home are worth more than Calypso and life everlasting? It is of a piece with the Greek culture that visualized the gods as inhabiting a different, though intertwined, part of the world from the mortals. *Moira* in Greek means "fate" but in the sense of "portion" or "place." The gods' place was on Olympus, and a man's was on earth. It was *hubris* for a mortal to aspire to the life of a god or to escape the death that is the fate of man, and though many were tempted, Odysseus would not yield. He was never lost in this sense: He was certain where he wanted to go.

It is the belief that there is a home that can be struggled for and won that the existentialists ridiculed. Under the thrall of Nietzsche and Kierkegaard, and wounded by two world wars, Heidegger and Sartre and Camus among others decided that the fate of humans was to never have a home on earth, and unlike the Christians, they disdained the one in heaven. Their views, in this reporter's opinion, provided a needed corrective but ignored the heroic in Nietzsche and Kierkegaard. A simple-minded version became widely fashionable among the *beau monde*.

Philosopher G. E. M. Anscombe, however, called the chic existentialists "wet behind the ears," which world-weary types would certainly not want made public. Perhaps this charge recalls an ancient suspicion that their sort of freewheeling anguish is based on vanity. Just what is the ultimate source of the intensity of emotion we can all feel at the resolution of the *Odyssey*, the Garnet Mimms song, or any other such story? If there is no home for humans, then why do we all feel so good when we get there?

Odysseus wasn't troubled by ennui or angst, nor was Socrates. Somehow war and deprivation didn't shatter them. Who could say what the difference is between them and the intellectuals of the 20th century? Odysseus never doubts there's a home to get to, and Socrates knows that somewhere there is a truth. Even if they doubted themselves, they would never have been persuaded that their quests were naive.

Throughout the *Odyssey*, Homer is building the tension, vamping on the dominant seventh chord, stretching the bow tighter and tighter. We want Odysseus to return. Even after he arrives at Ithaca, Homer presents still more twists and turns before his hero is finally brought, with the reader, all the way back. And when, after his 20-year absence and all of his battles with ships, armies, gods, and storms, he at last strings the bow of his youth and in a heartbeat sends the arrow home, straight and true, the most macho reader can be forgiven if he bursts into tears.

The Wandering Rocks

11:00 AM local time, Thursday, August 29 (0900 August 29 UTC).
39° 8.840'N 8° 18.906'E
Temp. 79, Humidity 65%, Cloud Cover 80%.
At anchor in the harbour of Carloforte on Isola di San Pietro (The Island of St. Peter), Italy.

Since our last dispatch, we have sailed to Sicily, calling at Catania at the foot of Mt. Etna, at the Aeolian Islands that the ancients called the "Wandering Rocks," and then on to Sardinia.

Our choice to call at Catania on Sicily was based on two needs. One, we wanted to consult electronic technicians to see if our radio, radar, and autopilot, among other pieces of equipment, could be repaired. Two, we were to meet with Fred Feller and family, who were bringing some parts from the US. It was really great to see friendly faces from home. They are the only people, aside from Theresa and Caroline, who have travelled abroad to meet us. The Fellers had studied some Italian but didn't remember anything other than *ciao*, so we gave them some of our language advice. The first thing to do when you're not understood is to speak slowly and shout. The other person will soon switch into the same mode. If this doesn't accomplish what you need, the next thing is to loudly yell, "Speak English! What're you, stupid or somethin'?" This simple trick has gotten us more than half-way around the world.

What we determined from the technicians, at some expense, was that although they could make the repairs, they 1) would charge us more than the original cost of the equipment, 2) could not guarantee their work would render the instruments usable, and 3) couldn't complete the repairs until the end of August as all of Italy is on vacation. So we are ordering new stuff from the US and are looking into having it shipped to Spain.

But not completely satisfied with this outcome, the Captain—who, if you weren't able to deduce this from our dispatches, is a licensed HAM—assisted by Chief Junior High-Frequency Gizmo Specialist Terry Shrode, determined that they could make a jury-rigged antenna with parts already on the boat. The problem with our radio was that the antenna tuner, which was not disconnected from the antenna during the lightning strike, had a bunch of fried thingamajigs inside. What needs to happen with the kind of antenna we use is that the length of the antenna has to have a certain mathematical relationship to the frequency on which we transmit. Since we use the backstay as our antenna, its length is impossible to adjust. What the antenna tuner does is fool the watchamacallits in the radio into thinking that the antenna wire is the length it should be, even though it isn't. Sadly, we must live our lives in a world where even radio equipment is dishonest in its dealings with other radio equipment. Anyway, it's a simple matter to bypass this deceitful box, figure the math, and construct an honest antenna for a certain frequency, the downside being that you need a different length wire for each frequency. So we made up two, one for our email contact in Brussels, and one for our morning weather net in the Med. We hoisted the wires up the mast with a halyard, and, bingo, we now have email. Slap me five, Radio Man.

After Sicily, we sailed to the harbor at Cagliari on the southern end of Sardinia. From there, Chief Engineer (in the choo-choo sense) Mr. Terry Shrode and the Captain took a train ride all the way up to the top of the island and back, and it was mostly boring but the Captain stood staring out the window like a child, so much does he love trains. The railroad is, after all, quite a fine invention. Never have I puked my guts out from a rough crossing on a train. Nor have I looked up while riding a train at the wonderful, wondrous, mysterious, and motherly blue sky, and all its clouds and majesty, with dread and apprehension. I have never had to change the oil on a train. They clickety-clack along. They've got rhythm.

The night before our early morning departure from Cagliari, en route to the Balearics, we checked weather on the Internet, and did so again shortly after getting underway through our morning high-frequency report. All was benign. We left with a very nice southeasterly right behind us and were going fast. We were *sailing*, a very unusual experience of late. Six hours later, we heard a report on VHF from Italian weather personnel who weren't on vacation that in our area, there was an "unstable air mass" flanked by a low to the west and a high to the east. "Unstable air mass" is a phrase a sailor would just as soon not hear. They also called for gale-force winds at our destination, Menorca. We decided that, since we were not yet clear of the vicinity of Sardinia, it would be a good idea to look to see if we could find a safe harbor to wait out the blow. Mind you, the force 6 they predicted in the area where we were now wouldn't be bad, as it would be behind us, but we didn't relish the idea of arriving at a strange port during a gale, particularly since with the extra wind we'd be going faster than anticipated and therefore arriving in the middle of the night. After a little chart study, several harbors became candidates, two of which could be reached before dark, and these were on islands near the southwestern coast of Sardinia.

We chose Casaletta on Isola di Sant' Antioco, which appeared to offer the best protection from southeasterlies, the predicted direction of strong winds. We arrived there in the late afternoon and got a spot on the quay for 25 Euros a night, which is a bit expensive for us, but it did turn out to give us perfect protection. The following evening the wind gusted into the 40s and that night there was a ferocious thunderstorm, with flashes of lightning firing off like strobe lights, 10 a second or so, for an hour. I feared for our newly refurbished wind instruments at the masthead, which had survived the previous lightning strike that had left all that other equipment fried, but all appears to be fine.

The next morning we made the shortest passage of our voyage, three nautical miles, to Carloforte, a harbor on the neighboring Isola di San Pietro where we can anchor for free. St. Peter was shipwrecked here according to the locals, but not according to the Captain's reading of *Acts*. Before we even got our anchor set, two dinghies buzzed over to greet us, and we were very surprised and pleased to recognize the crews of the Canadian Cal-39 *Delphis* and the steel Spanish boat *Vulcano*, neither of which we had seen since the Red Sea. They gave us news of some of our other friends from that passage, like those on the California boats *Voyager*, who are in San Tropez, and *Warrior*, who are going to be wintering in Italy.

The weather in our area and in the Balearics has remained unsettled (it's blowing 30 as I write this), with almost daily gale warnings from different quadrants. We can stay here in Carloforte until things improve, and it's a very pleasant town. When it blows, though, even in a protected anchorage, things can happen. Today a French boat anchored upwind began to drag down on us. They were quickly on top of it (as was I!), but they motored up and ran right over the float for our anchor trip line, which we used because of evidence that the bottom was foul. I thought for sure they would get the trip line in their prop, which would have been a doozy. They would have simultaneously pulled out our anchor, which would now be hanging from their boat, and fouled their prop. Two boats, linked by chain, would have started to drift towards several more boats at anchor, in 30 knots, with only one capable of using its motor, and that at the risk of fouling its prop on the chain. The carnage that would have resulted is terrible to contemplate. I took a deep breath when I saw the fender we used as a float bob up on the other side of their boat.

I took a bus yesterday to the opposite, windward side of the island, a 15-minute ride, to have a look at the *mistral* that was blowing. They have lots of names for winds in the Mediterranean, and among them in addition to *mistral* are not Mariah but *meltemi, lips, zephyr, bora, sirocco, firtina, levanter, vendeval,* and a couple of dozen more. Why, by the way, do San Franciscans have no name for their summer westerlies or the warm offshore breeze we sometimes get in September and October? At least those Southern Californians have the poetry to name a wind a *Santa Ana*. For the modern mariner, who associates wind with highs, lows, isobars, Boyle's Law, and dry and wet adiabatic rates, these names seem quaint and imprecise; but of course our methods, although scientifically based, have made little improvement on the prediction of actual weather in the Med.

When the bus dropped me at Capo Sandalo on the western shore, the *mistral* was not particularly fierce, but as the day wore on, whitecaps appeared and soon the sea did not look very inviting. I observed a mighty peregrine falcon, the fastest animal in existence, riding the updrafts that result where the *mistral* meets the beetling cliffs of the Cape. I watched him swoop and dive for a long time, there being no human traffic to distract me, until, reading my thoughts, he flew away and, without a backward glance, disappeared into the sky.

Dismasted

4:00 PM local time, Thursday, September 26 (1400 September 26 UTC).
37 08 N 001 20 W
Temp. 76, Humidity 79%, Cloud Cover 100%.
Underway in the western Med.

I have felt in the last month or six weeks like someone who signed up to ride the bull but instead has been relegated to shaving the poodle, as our adventures have been limited to kicking the computer and doing battle with electronic repair people—stuff you can do without leaving the comfort of your home town. And you, dear readers, who look to the Captain for tales of derring-do at sea, have been patiently awaiting the real thing. But this can't continue, so in the absence of a real-time story, I have taken the liberty of composing one about an incident that happened before we left San Francisco. This I do in the immodest hope that it may serve the same lofty purpose as those heart-stopping magazine stories in the dentist's waiting room.

In 1999 I entered *Maverick* in the Double-handed Farallones Race, which takes place in March of each year off the Pacific Coast near San Francisco. The race starts at the city front, continues under the Golden Gate Bridge, and then takes us 25.5 miles offshore, to the southeast Farallon island and back, for a total of about 53 miles. The course out is 255 degrees true, and the prevailing wind is northwest at about 300 degrees, meaning that under perfect conditions a sailboat can fetch the island, and it's a broad reach all the way back. This race has a reputation for carnage, as it often is held in rough weather, and in some years it has been deadly.

This was to be one of those years. By the end of the day, one skipper would drown, two sailors on a capsized trimaran would be rescued by the amazingly brave actions of other competitors, four boats would be dismasted, and there would be lots of damaged gear, ripped sails, minor injuries, and seasickness. Among the dismasted boats was none other than our trusty friend, *Maverick*.

I had warily been watching the buoy reports on the Internet along with the weather forecasts, in the days preceding the race. At the San Francisco buoy, which is almost half-way to the island, weather instruments had, on the morning of the race, reported a steep swell of 15 feet, topped by 3-5-ft. wind waves. The wind was in the high 20s, gusting to 33. We would never have chosen to sail in conditions like this, unless, of course, there was a race.

My redoubtable crew, Ship's Tactician Mr. Terry Shrode, and I had given some thought to our strategy. Having been in the Gulf of the Farallones in similar conditions before, we knew that there would be little enthusiasm for reefing and sail changes, particularly as we would be fresh out of the harbor and would have had no time to gain our sea legs. Perhaps our competition were men of steel, but we surmised that changing down from a number one on a 40-footer, in 15-ft. seas with only two people aboard, would take a long time and make almost anyone sick. So we decided that, no matter what the conditions at the start, we'd put up the amount of sail we thought would be appropriate for what we'd see outside the Gate.

As a result, we were the weenies of the start, and we were perhaps the only boat to cross the line with a reef in the main and a 90% headsail. Problem was, inside the Bay we had light wind, no more than 10 knots, so we ate it big time until we got past Point Bonita. By that time, almost every boat had passed us. But it was all part of the master plan.

After we passed Point Bonita, the wind and seas picked up as expected, and by the time we were half-way to the island, we were pretty happy with our strategy. A majority of the boats who had been in front of us were now well to leeward either because they were completely over-canvassed and trying to sail with what they had or because changing to a smaller headsail turned into a major hassle. In either case, they couldn't point. Mr. Shrode also noticed that a couple of Coast Guard cutters were in the vicinity, maybe just by chance on maneuvers but perhaps alerted to stand by in case they were needed, like ambulances at a bullfight.

As we neared the southeast Farallon, we saw the first sign that the day might not end without some serious problems. Over the island, on the seaward side out of our vision, someone launched one, then another, parachute flare. We had heard nothing on the VHF radio, and that was alarming since it meant that, whatever the trouble was, it included the loss of radio communications, which would have been the first choice in calling for help. At the time we thought someone might have been dismasted, since that would have brought down the masthead VHF antenna. We knew there were boats closer than us, and in any case, we were getting there as fast as we could, so there was nothing else we could do to help but sail.

We hadn't quite laid the mark without a tack, as few if any boats could in these conditions, so we threw in a couple of tacks to approach the island. We didn't want to get too close to it, since we had sailed near the island once before in heavy weather and knew that the seas steepened up in an intimidating way as they approached it. We tacked onto port and when we thought we could fetch it safely, we tacked back to starboard.

As we began to sheet in, there was a loud noise and the rig fell to leeward. The top two-thirds of the mast buckled in half, leaving the part above the upper spreaders in the water with the heads of the sails. The middle third was still attached to both the top part, now in the water, and the section from the deck up to the first spreaders, which was still standing. The intermediate windward shroud had failed at the deck, but the rest of the rigging was still attached. It was impressive to see all that stuff come tumbling out of the sky. I'd read about getting dismasted in heavy seas and it had sounded like something awfully difficult to handle. But here it was.

Mr. Shrode and I were, to use a sailing phrase, taken aback. The deck was all ahoo with sails and rigging wires flailing wildly. But my instant concern was that we were close enough to fetching the island that a combination of wind, waves, and current might put us in intimate contact with it, in a very unpleasant way. I ran to the bow with the idea of deploying the anchor. It was only about 60 feet deep just to windward of the island, and I had been at sea and listened on the radio when, in another Farallones race, a skipper had been able to set his anchor while he cleaned up the mess of a dismasting. The conditions were worse today though. In any event, it soon became apparent that we would miss the island and begin to drift towards Half Moon Bay.

As we tried to gather our wits, a very surprising thing happened. In all the chaos we had forgotten that we were still on a sailboat and that it was still under sail. The triangle of sail between the first spreaders and the boom was still up and drawing, and because of the new sail configuration, as it were, the boom was a foot or two lower than normal. The boat was pitching, rolling, and yawing madly in the seas and all of a sudden we had an uncontrolled (to say the least) jibe. The boom of a 39-ft. boat coming across the deck in 30 knots of wind is a mighty thing. It grazed the top of Mr. Shrode's head, and the Captain felt the wind rush by as the end of the boom missed his ear by a couple of inches. Had either one of us been hit, it is a tossup whether the survivor would have had the wherewithal to deal with a dead body on top of everything else. If both of us had been hit, no problem.

While all this was occurring, on the windward side of the island an amazing rescue was taking place. The trimaran *Boogieman*, a Corsair F-31R, had flipped because, as the crew admitted later, they had gotten too close to shore in the heavy, steep seas. They were holding on to the upturned hull in 50-degree water but had somehow managed to get to their flares and shoot off the ones we'd seen. Ryle Radke and Jonathan Yelda on *Friday Harbour*, a J/35, and Bay Area rigger and veteran sailor Bruce Schwab, with Joakim Jonsson on *Azzura*, a 31-ft. ultralight, came to the rescue. Since the capsize, the trimaran had of course drifted closer to the rocks, which meant that the rescuers would have to put their boats in worse conditions than the ones that caused the trimaran to flip in the first place. The stakes were high, because no other vessels could have gotten there before the stranded crew had met a very bad end, driven into the rocks by huge waves. So they went in, and somehow each boat picked up one survivor and managed to escape the surf. The crews of *Azzura* and *Friday Harbour* downplayed it later, but the conditions were suicidal.

Meanwhile, back on *Maverick*, we had turned on the autopilot. Since we were making about 3 knots under "reduced" sail, we had steerage and the autopilot kept us on a broad reach, making another jibe unlikely. I had been looking at the mass of heavy metal that was violently flailing against the boat in the heavy seas, and worrying that if we didn't either cut it away or get it under control, it might punch a hole in the hull and sink us. We couldn't really cut it away, since we had no access to the places where the mast was broken without either going overboard or up to the lower spreaders, and neither alternative seemed to promise much entertainment value.

I was surveying the situation and noticed that the masthead was within about eight feet of the hull, and attached to it there was a wire flipping around that I recognized to be the topping lift. Grabbing a boat hook, I snagged it and brought it to a cockpit winch. I thought it would break, but it held, and voilà! I winched the masthead close to the boat. From there, it was a matter of getting more lashings around it and securing it wherever we could.

Both Mr. Shrode and I had started puking almost from the moment the mast came down. The motion of the boat became very violent without the dampening effects of the rig and sails. Some people think there is a stress factor in nausea, and that can't be ruled out of course. In any case, we had to continually take breaks in the work for a bout of the dry heaves and then get back to it. We moved to the foredeck, where another hour or two of wrestling got the jib out of the water and the furler drum disconnected and aboard. Now, it was a matter of policing up the lines and making sure there was nothing in the water to foul the prop. Satisfied, we started up the Perkins and put it in gear. The prop was fine. We set a course for home and felt a big wave of relief.

At this point, we had no radio because the VHF antenna was underwater. A couple of boats had sailed by to offer assistance, and though there was little they could do, it was brave of them and made us feel better. We just asked them to radio the race committee to let them know what had happened. We did, however, have a cell phone aboard, and thought it would be prudent to alert the Coast Guard so we called "911." The woman answering the call could not be made to understand that we couldn't provide her with a street address, as we were at sea. No doubt it was part of her procedure, but it took some doing to get her to patch us through to Group San Francisco. When they answered, we gave them our position, boat name, number and condition of crew, etc. We made it clear that we were not requesting any assistance but wanted to apprise them of our situation.

And our situation was that we were both wet, hypothermic, and exhausted. I felt alert, however, and Mr. Shrode went below to get some rest. We had drifted quite a few miles towards Half Moon Bay and the sun was starting to think about setting. I considered heading for Half Moon Bay, which was downwind, but determined to try to make it back home and use that alternative as a backup. It would feel a lot better to make it safely back to our slip.

We had about 15 miles upwind to get to the San Francisco shipping channel, and then about another eight to the Golden Gate, and it was tough going in the heavy seas. The conditions had not abated, and as I sat in the companionway and pondered the whole scenario there were two more concerns. One was that the mast was apparently being held up by the coax for the VHF and the wires for the masthead lights. This scarcely gave me confidence in the strength of our new "rig," which still supported a lot of aluminum and Dacron. Secondly, in big seas it's not at all out of the question that debris in the fuel tanks could be stirred up, clogging the filters and stopping the engine. These jolly thoughts occupied my mind through the next four hours or so it took to make it back to the channel.

As it got dark, I was glad to have the autopilot, since standing at the wheel in the breeze was freezing and I was already wet all over. And I was glad to have a GPS, since at night in those conditions, it was hard to find the channel, and trying to take multiple bearings from a pitching deck would have been arduous. But everything went okay, and by about 8:00 PM we gained the channel. The channel itself, being a window through the "Potato Patch," a dangerous shoal, was treacherous in those seas with our unwieldy rig, but we could turn downwind and it now seemed like we were definitely going to make it. Even though he probably would have been happier dreaming, I couldn't resist waking Mr. Shrode and telling him that I thought we'd be safe. A little more than an hour later, we were under the Golden Gate Bridge in the protected waters of San Francisco Bay.

Upon trying the VHF once more, we found that we could make tenuous contact with the race committee. To our dismay, they asked us if we had seen another boat, which was unaccounted for. They sent their condolences and were sensitive enough to leave it at that, knowing that we'd soon enough find out about the real bad news of the day.

We made it back to our slip late that night and just left the mess there and went home to get some rest. The next day I had to teach a sailing class and when I came down to the boat late that afternoon, I found that earlier that day a friend of ours, the well-known Bay Area sailor Mike Jefferson of *Foxxfire*, had come over to look at the wreckage, as Mr. Shrode was beginning to try to make sense of the situation.

Mike, who had also been in the race, says, "It looks like you could use a hand."

By the time I arrived, Mike and Terry had pretty much disassembled the whole mess, and Mike's girlfriend and Caroline had gotten the cabin under control. I get the Tom Sawyer award. It was a big emotional lift to get moving that quickly on the damage, and I'll always remember the favor they all did.

That same day we heard the story of the rescue of the *Boogieman* crew, of the other dismastings, and of Harvey Shiasky on the J/29 *White Lightning*. On the downwind leg, his boat had broached in a big sea and capsized, throwing skipper Shiasky and his crew overboard. They were both tethered to the boat, but Shiasky's tether was connected on the low side and he was being dragged some distance from the cockpit. The crew, tethered on the high side, got himself back aboard with great effort to find the boom and other gear broken. With the boat back on its feet, because of the chaos and wrecked gear, he was not able to stop it and Shiasky was being dragged underwater at speed. The crew decided the only option was to cut the tether so Shiasky could get to the surface and then hope that he or another boat could recover him. As it turned out, there was a Coast Guard cutter near them that had come to the assistance of another race boat, and they managed to get him aboard. But he could not be revived.

Rock This Way

8:00 PM local time, Tuesday, October 8 (1800 Oct. 8 UTC).
36° 8.972'N 5° 21.267'W
Temp. 74, Humidity 77%, Cloud Cover 100%. Rain.
At a berth in Gibraltar.

When we last gave a report of our whereabouts, we were in Carloforte, near the island of Sardinia. We and some other boats watched for the perfect window to sail to the Balearics. This was interesting because we had access to weather forecasts from four countries. They rarely came close to agreeing, which in itself is a notable fact, but one day they did and called for force 4 and dying but on the nose. This was as good as we could expect so we all left and in about four hours were in force 6 gusting to 7. What a job, being a weatherman!

On that passage of a couple of hundred miles, we got the biggest seas we'd seen since the Red Sea and the Captain was thinking about puking and wondering whether he still had it in him. He decided he didn't, but Mr. Shrode, who by now must be tired of taking care of things the Captain doesn't find within his jurisdiction, had him covered when he took over for his watch. Nevertheless, we had some reasonably good sailing and only motored about a third of the way.

We were rather fond of the Balearics. Mahon on Menorca was about as pleasant a harbor as we've seen anywhere in the world, and we were treated to some kind of horsey event there, a big festival lasting several days in the crowded town square. The main deal seemed to be to get your horse to prance on his hind legs while brave young men pressed in upon him to touch him and help him stand up. There just seemed to be no end to this. A little girl near me was crying because she thought she might get trampled, either by the horses or by the men trying to get to the horses. Her father tenderly reassured her, but I don't see why, as her assessment of the situation was bang on. An ambulance stood by for casualties, of which there were a few.

From Mahon we sailed to Mallorca and then to Ibiza. Ibiza was just fine, but it was not the den of iniquity we had been led to believe. There is a robust bar scene at the harbor, and some women do go topless at the beaches. It is no doubt ungallant of the Captain to propose that appearing topless in public areas is not the wisest fashion choice for every woman. Or man, for that matter. But there it is. There also may be some strip joints in Ibiza. I don't know, we rarely stay up that late. As Mr. Shrode says, "Hey, I'm not 50 anymore, ya know."

I took a ferry trip over to Formentera, which is a small island next to Ibiza. This island had been highly recommended, albeit 30 years ago, by my friend Lowell Turner. Mr. Turner was, at the time I first knew him, the co-host of a radio program called "The Jack and Harriet Show" with another friend, Kip Sullivan. When last I heard, Mr. Turner had been forced to take a professor's chair at Cornell to earn his keep, and Kip was a lawyer. Alack-a-day, how the mighty have fallen.

Should I have the good fortune to see my old friend's face again, I would have to report that Formentera now has the highest number of motor scooter rentals per square inch of anywhere in the world. They also have a hippie market, which is highly touted, so Ship's Purchasing Agent Terry Shrode made me go to see what a decent hippie costs nowadays. It seems like yesterday when they were a dime a dozen, but I imagine that as the supply has diminished, so has the demand. The hippie market was a bit sad, I'm afraid, compared to its forebears. Only a trace of patchouli in the air brought a frisson of past glory to the Captain's heart.

Departing Ibiza, we motored every inch of the way to Gibraltar, stopping to anchor overnight at Motril, an unpleasantly fragrant town on the south coast of Spain. When we approached Gibraltar, about 100 miles farther along, we knew it only by the GPS, since we encountered very thick fog. We would certainly have preferred to see that famous landmark from afar and reflect on the symbolism of our proximity to it, but it was not to be. So thick was the fog that the Captain perched himself on the bow to watch and listen for traffic. We slowed down and sounded our horn at the prescribed intervals, because, as the reader may remember, we had no radar, which was a victim of the lightning in Greece. I heard an engine and shouted back to Mr. Shrode at the helm that there was a boat at two o'clock, broad on the starboard bow. I peered through the mist and could make out a dark shape, perhaps an eighth of a mile away. About 10 seconds later, a giant supertanker appeared that took up the whole horizon. The dark shape had been its rudder; we were about 75 feet from it.

"Hard to port!" I shouted, and by the time I did, I realized it was at anchor. It was a little unsettling to know just how far we could, or rather, couldn't see. We slowed down even more and headed farther inshore, thinking we'd avoid any heavy traffic, and we felt our way around Europa Point and into the Bay of Gibraltar.

We were lucky to find a berth at one of the three marinas here. We are situated about five hundred feet from the runway of the airport, but there aren't that many flights so it doesn't bother our repose. Apparently, there are several plane wrecks off the end of the runway, right in the anchorage, that are popular dive sites. Here with us are Red Sea compadres *Delphis*, *L'Oasis*, *Stitches Explorer*, *Karma*, *Otter*, and

Francis on *Okiva*. (Paul and Paula are in the US.) The Rock itself is only a half mile from us, but it is so foggy we can't see it at all.

The city of Gibraltar, along with the Rock, is one of the most interesting places we've been in the Mediterranean. For one thing, it is part Britain, part Spain. They have a language of their own, but many people, of quite diverse origin, are bilingual as well. There are several proper pubs in town with pub food and Newcastle Brown on tap. There are British ceremonies, and the Queen's likeness appears on the twenty-pound note, although the money is slightly different from the English sort. The entire area is chock-a-block with historical sites and places of interest to the geologist. Perhaps we'll visit some of them after a Newcastle Brown or two.

IN A LITTLE SPANISH TOWN

8:00 PM local time, Monday, October 14 (1800 October 14 UTC).
36° 8.972'N 5° 21.267'W
Temp. 75, Humidity 68%, Cloud Cover 0%.
At a berth in Gibraltar.

As the train in Spain rolled gamely through the rain, which, as a matter of fact, does not fall mainly on the plain, I reflected that I had never been to Spain, but I have been to Oklahoma, and arguably have spent somewhat more of my life than was strictly prudent, living on Tulsa time. Now I had left *Maverick* in Mr. Shrode's care and I had set out to visit Granada and Seville by rail.

Granada was about five hours away. For the first couple of hours, the landscape was little different from our oak woodlands in California. Out the window familiar trees rushed by, including eucalyptus, live oak, alder, cottonwood, cypress, poplar, acacia, and what could have been tan oak. There was also agave, prickly pear cactus, sword fern, and perhaps some sage. But there were some less familiar plants. I observed the cork oak, (*Quercus suber*), like we saw in Sardinia. Cork is obtained by stripping the bark from the lowest 12 feet or so of the trunk, which can be done repeatedly without killing the tree. I also saw a curious palm shrub, consisting of numerous fronds growing in a clump no more than 4 feet high but up to 15 feet in diameter, and thousands of acres of olive trees.

As the journey continued, we passed into some topography much like the more arable parts of northern Utah and headed into the mountains. Granada is located in a setting similar to that of Auburn, California, in the foothills of mountains someone had the nerve to name the Sierra Nevada. I took a big liking to this place, which has endless cobblestone streets and feels somewhat less modern than other European cities its size although it really isn't. There's a bazaar that is much more like a hippie market than that place in Formentera. Noticing a strong smell of incense, I glimpsed mysterious, furtive characters, dark tea-houses, and exotic and elaborately ornate bags, lamps, clothes, and jewelry, inspired by Arabic designs. The main tourist attraction is an Arabic palace, which is located in a complex of fortifications and buildings called the Alhambra. The palace has a lot of intricate carvings, doodads, and thing-a-ma-jigs.

After a day and a half, I took another train on to Seville. It's a larger city, less quaint, and located in a less picturesque setting. The first night I was there, I found myself at a flamenco performance. I hadn't planned on going to one. All that stomping and clomping, those severe looks and knitted brows. But there was a show right around the corner from the cheap *pensione* where I was installed.

Is it better when we know nothing of the art we experience? It's been 20 years at least since I could watch a band play without picking it to pieces, whereas when I was a kid, almost any band was a source of fascination and wonder. If it were just hormones, I suppose I would expect to have a reduced emotional response to anything sensual, like the narrator of Wordsworth's "Ode to the Intimations of Immortality," but I don't think this is the case, exactly. Perhaps something's lost but something's gained, or perhaps something's not lost or something's not gained, or perhaps things are about the same or maybe they're different. How should I know?

The performance was held in the courtyard of a traditional Spanish house, and it was sold out. The troupe consisted of just a guitar player and a singer, both male, and a female dancer. The guitarist looked about 25 and was an astonishing virtuoso. There were solo guitar pieces, songs by the vocalist with guitar accompaniment, and dances. Unaccountably, and more or less uncontrollably, almost from the moment they began until the end of the hour, I wept.

The next afternoon I attended a bullfight. I wasn't going to go, as the idea has always struck me as abhorrent. Theresa had seen one in Mexico City and reported that the only thing that made sense was seeing the matador get gored. Yet there was the Plaza de Toros, one of the oldest such arenas in the world, and there was I. I inquired about seats and found they weren't cheap, with the most expensive about $94. I bought one for $25.

The bull enters the ring ready to rumble. I don't know what they do to him just before they let him in there, but he isn't doing zen meditation or getting a nice massage. The *subalternos*, who are sort of assistant matadors without all the caping privileges granted to the matador, taunt him and get him to run across the entire ring, giving him a bit of aerobic exercise. Then the fight progresses in three stages, as 1. a man (the *picador*) on the back of a blindfolded and padded horse goads the bull into attacking the poor horse and then repeatedly sinks a lance into the fleshy base of his neck, further weakening him; the matador then briefly capes the bull to gauge his charge, strength and fighting spirit; 2. another man (the *bandillero*) sticks three pairs of *banderillas* in the bull's back; and then 3. the matador makes a series of elaborate passes with the cape, and finally kills the bull by sticking a sword between his shoulder blades up to the hilt.

I'll say this for it, there are no special effects, not even an announcer, just that familiar sound of the bullring music. The bull really is trying to kill someone, the men are really in danger (one was gored in the leg on the day I was there), and they have a practiced and steady courage in the face of it, which is the point.

After only two or three minutes of the bullfight, the bull shows signs of tiring and is probably dimly aware that all of his might and ferocity are having little effect on his opponents. By the time the *banderillas* are in his back, he is in a lot of pain, is spent, panting, and confused. What he cannot know is that the man he now faces is a professional, exquisitely skilled killer who has dispatched hundreds like him. He has spent most of the days of his life since childhood learning and rehearsing the subtle moves necessary to make a fool of the bull while he poses gracefully and ever so slightly out of range of the deadly horns, in a ballet costume.

It is easier to cry than to laugh at the bull's inability to see that it is the man he must fight, not the cape. After a particularly impotent set of charges by the bull, the matador will flick the sword in his direction in an arrogant dismissal, turn his back on him and strut away in an outrageously disdainful manner that for some reason no one in the arena, including the bull, finds laughable. By contrast, even in all of his agony, the bull is unbowed and dignified. He never turns his back on the fight, never seems to consider running away, and pretends to no coy displays with which to charm an audience.

The moment before the matador attempts to pierce the bull with his sword, he holds it towards him as if aiming, but perhaps it is a salute, or a prayer. The man, aided by his assistants, has used an ancient cunning to trump the bull's power and speed, and yet the bull remains unafraid. A perfect thrust will kill the bull immediately. If it doesn't, even now, when the sword is plunged home, the bull strikes out with what's left of his strength, enraged. The *subalternos* immediately run out with their pink capes and engage him, turning him from one attack to the other. The apparent reason for this is to make sure that his proud but lacerated heart will pump its last blood at a high enough rate that his blood pressure will quickly drop, and he will faint. We don't want to keep the customers waiting. Down on his belly, he still holds his head up and offers his horns to anyone who steps near. Finally, if the sword thrust has failed, someone does, and with a deft move as the animal's consciousness dims, he takes a small knife and severs his spinal cord.

Two guys woke up the other day, looked up at the blue sky, felt the sun on their backs, maybe had something to eat. They both made their way to the arena, where one was tortured mentally and physically, and then ritually killed, never losing his courage; the other paid a price to relax on a stone bench and sip a cold beverage while he observed the whole scene as if it were an entertainment. Honestly, I'd just as soon have been neither of those guys.

The Pillars Of Hercules

Same time and date and conditions. At a berth in Gibraltar.

As Africa and Europe form two opposing pincers at the end of the Mediterranean Sea, it would appear on a typical world map that they face each other from sharp points of land, with Gibraltar on the north side and the mountains of Morocco on the south. But a larger-scale map will show that the Strait of Gibraltar is an asymmetrical slot about 30 miles long, which narrows to eight miles in width between Point Marroquí (Spain) and Point Cires (Morocco). On the northeast corner of the slot is a bay shaped like a horseshoe on a wall, the west side of which is glued to the land, leaving the eastern side to form a peninsula about three-quarters of a mile wide. The southern three miles of this peninsula is occupied by the British colony of Gibraltar. The Rock itself extends for about two of these three miles, and on its western flank is the city and port of Gibraltar. On most approaches, it would not be visible from the open sea.

We took a cable car to the top of the Rock. It's solid limestone, and hosts a cave that rivals any I've seen for stalactites and stalagmites. There are 32 miles of tunnels made by armed forces of various eras up to WWII, which is a lot of tunnels in a two-mile rock. There are so-called Barbary apes, really a tailless, terrestrial macaque, that have free run of the place, à la Bali. At the southern tip of the rock is a 9.2-inch gun that can fire a 380-lb. shell all the way past the shore of Morocco, which from there is about 13 miles.

But all this is of small consequence compared to the view. Looking out on the vista brings one of the rare moments in this voyage where there is some sense of the weight of the whole undertaking. In Tahiti, you must pinch yourself. You sailed all the way to the South Pacific. The Torres Strait. The South China Sea. Borneo. Ceylon. The Red Sea. The Suez Canal. The recounting of it suggests drama, but like life at home, this often gets lost in concerns over the everyday.

Now you look south and can see the mountains of Morocco across the Strait. To the east is the Mediterranean Sea you've just traversed, to the west, the large Bay of Gibraltar, full of ships from all over the world. And to the southwest, there is an ominous yet seductive haze reaching through the throat of the Strait out into the void, the beginning of the same great Atlantic Ocean that heaves itself onto the shores of Cape Kennedy, and Myrtle Beach, and Kitty Hawk, and Asbury Park, and Coney Island, and New Bedford, in *America*.

THE ATLANTIC

The Marrakesh Express

8:15 PM local time, Friday, October 25 (2015 October 25 UTC).
31° 30.544'N 9° 46.434'W
Temp. 72, Humidity 73%, Cloud Cover 0%.
Rafted up to the pontoon with a French boat in Essaouira, Morocco.

We departed Gibraltar about two hours before first light on Wednesday October 16. Hardworking order clerks, forklift drivers, bookkeepers, truck drivers, pilots, and deliverymen in America, who had *not* been on vacation, had delivered our needed electronic parts to Gibraltar right on time. So now we had our HF radio and radar and autopilot back, and we were all set to break something else.

It's a bit of a puzzle getting through the Strait of Gibraltar, because you're looking for a weather window to take you down the coast of northern Africa, but it's 40 miles of weird current, strong winds, and shipping traffic to get to the Atlantic from Gibraltar and they don't organize it so the right conditions out to sea coincide with the right conditions to get through the Strait. It's hellishly inconvenient.

Before six million years ago, the Mediterranean was cut off from the Atlantic Ocean. Since the evaporation rate in the Med is more than twice the rate of influx from the rivers and rain that flow into it, it dried up. Perhaps it didn't completely dry up and perhaps it dried up many times and the details are sketchy, but at times there were a few basins with deep and very salty lakes. It would have been a desert-like environment much more severe, and much deeper, than our Death Valley, as some parts were well over a mile below sea level. And then sometime around five million years ago, the dam broke at Gibraltar and the Atlantic ran into the Med full blast, with a flow that has been estimated by geologist K. J. Hsu at a thousand times greater than Niagara Falls, far more spectacular than any on earth today. Even so, it would have taken more than 100 years to fill up the Mediterranean basin like a big bathtub.

Because of that evaporation rate, even today there is a net flow of water from the Atlantic through the Strait of Gibraltar into the Med, keeping it full, and it was against this current that *Maverick* had to sail.

Yet defying most of the rules for the passage through the Strait so that we could avoid a gale at sea, the crew of *Maverick* managed with one little glitch to sort it out and pick our way through unscathed. The glitch occurred when the top swivel on the furler jammed. This gave us an excuse to sail into Tangier and have a look, at least from the anchorage, at the city. There, Mr. Shrode hauled the Captain up the mast, and with the use of some of the old blatherskite's best billingsgate, our end was achieved. By late afternoon we had doubled Cape Spartel and were in the Atlantic Ocean proper.

We feel liberated to be at sea at last. Even though we covered 2,000 miles this season, Mr. Shrode and the Captain do a lot more sailing in a normal summer at home than we did in the Med, if you define sailing as operating a boat under wind power.

We arrived at El-Jadida on the northwest coast of Morocco on the morning of October 18. We had come in about a day or so ahead of the bad weather that was predicted to hit the coast of Africa, connected, by the typical comma shape of a cold front, to a ferocious low of 966 millibars off to the northwest. On the passage down, we experienced the waves created by the storm center, but as it was a few hundred miles away, by the time the swell had reached us it was down to about 6-8 feet at 10 seconds. It was a long time since we'd seen a real ocean swell and we were just as glad it was a benign one. The passage consisted of wind from all directions, relatively light, although the first night was squally and blowing in the 20s with gusts to 30 on Mr. Shrode's watch. But it was an easy two-day trip from Gibraltar.

El-Jadida takes us back to the Third World, and we re-enter the realm of Islam. The small fishing port of El-Jadida is next to a city with teeming multitudes and a bazaar of tiny shops selling odd assortments of things, and it is more reminiscent of Asia than of Egypt or Oman. We hear the call to prayer from the mosque near the harbor, but this one sounds a little like one of those cow toys that moo when you turn them upside down. The harbor is ancient and crammed with fishing boats. There's a fortress on the shore directly by the anchorage, and inside it is the ancient town, a remnant of Portuguese rule.

There was no direct train from El-Jadida to Marrakesh, so, leaving *Maverick* in the harbor, we boarded a bus instead and I'm afraid it wasn't much of an express. The ride took us through increasingly sparse vegetation until the last things standing were eucalyptus trees and two types of cactus, prickly pear and cholla.

In the afternoon we arrived in Marrakesh at the base of the Atlas Mountains, which run southwest to northeast, parallel to the coast. If you were to keep going east through the mountains, you'd meet the Sahara on the other side. Marrakesh was a bit tidier and held considerably more tourists than El-Jadida, which itself is a sort of beach resort for Moroccans. We checked into a cheap hotel ($10) and went out to have a look at the famous market in Place Jema al-Fna. Lots of food stalls and street musicians, and about 50 stands selling fresh orange juice. It really wasn't that exotic, but it amused me to imagine that it was.

While in the vicinity, the Captain appears to have been offered sex. A prim-looking young Moroccan lady followed your reporter out of an

Internet café and in French explained that she wanted to "take a walk" with him, if I followed her in my limited command of the language. I affected to not understand. She seemed to insist on it, and then, unless my ears misled me, she mentioned, in English, the word "sex." There was no talk of money, so she had apparently simply been smitten by the Captain, who, truth be told, does present a particularly striking image as he effortlessly plies the keyboard, his face an inch from the screen to adjust his vision. Again, I said I didn't understand what she was talking about, and she received this with quite a show of disbelief. Of the statistically insignificant number of our readers who actually have any knowledge or interest in the Captain's understanding of sex, surely none would have had the least difficulty taking his claim at face value, so her skepticism was unexpected. What is it, exactly, anyway?

As I seemed to be under the obligation of providing the young lady with some reason for my lack of interest in her proposal that she could accept without injury to her self-esteem, the sort of thing to which we must all be sensitive these days, I avowed that I was exhausted from traveling and must rest. Having said this, I felt the need, for the sake of my own personal integrity, to repair to my modest lodgings and read myself to sleep under a bare light bulb, on pain of making myself a liar, liar, pants on fire. This concludes the "sex" portion of our adventure.

Earlier in the day, an enterprising young man or two offered to provide kif or hash for the Captain's enjoyment. Not being a fan of Nancy Reagan but rather the son of a mother who, unlike Mrs. Reagan, had some manners, I did not "Just say no." I just said, "No THANK YOU." So I scraped these young entrepreneurs off and got an ice cream. This concludes the "drugs" portion of our story.

The next day we took the train, quite a fast one so I suppose it was an express, to Casablanca. On the outskirts of town, we saw a crowded neighborhood of dwellings consisting of rusty tin shacks, their roofs held down with rocks. Almost every one of them sported a satellite dish.

When we disembarked at our destination, the first thing we did was ask a cab driver to take us to Rick's Café Americain.

"You got an address?" he asked.

"You know, where Bogie hangs with Ingrid. We don't need no stinking address."

So he gives us the big RCA dog look. He seemed to have no association whatsoever with these names. We looked for another cabbie. We went through at least ten. The RCA dog is quite a fashion here. We finally headed for the Hyatt, thinking the concierge could help us out. We couldn't find the concierge, but the hotel had a bar called the "Casablanca Bar" that had lots of photos of Bogie and Ingrid. We asked the bartender where Rick's was, and he said "This is it!" I mean, he said it straight as a board. We asked him, if it's Rick's, why is it called the "Casablanca Bar?" The real Rick's has a sign out front that says "Rick's Café Americain." Don't tell me it doesn't. Yeah, and instead of Sam, they had Kenny Rogers on the sound system. We reckoned that it was good for a drink anyway, so I popped for a $9 Bombay and tonic and Mr. Shrode had a $9 shot of tequila, which was almost twice as much as our hotel room in Marrakesh.

Bogie was a sailor, you know, and his boat, *Santana*, has been painstakingly restored and lives in San Francisco. He would have been cool and stood us the drinks, I reckon, even at this fake bar. We thought of him when we left El-Jadida to sail 120 miles down the coast of Morocco to Essaouira. We left at dawn to get out before low tide and planned to reach our destination on a rising tide the next day. The tides are big here at springs, and the entrances to the harbors shallow and exposed to the swell from the north Atlantic, so it's prudent to time your arrivals and departures. It was pretty cold and we had on full fleece and foul weather jackets for most of the trip. I bought a new foulie jacket before we left and it's still new; since about a week out of San Francisco, we have rarely had to do more than put on a t-shirt if we were cold.

In the morning we started out motoring, but by evening the wind was in the high 20s, gusting to 35, and the seas got up pretty good during the night. Rock and roll, *Maverick*-style.

The Master

9:30 PM local time, Saturday, November 2 (2130 Nov. 2 UTC).
28° 27.986'N 16° 14.647'W
Temp. 77, Humidity 67%, Cloud Cover 0%.
At a slip at the Marina del Atlantico, Santa Cruz, Tenerife, Islas Canarias (Canary Islands), Spain (Espana)

We sailed into Essaouira with the tide, as planned. This was our favorite city in Morocco, with a very busy fishing harbor where we could observe traditional boatbuilding as well as the activities of the fishermen. I say "traditional" but it's not as though there's some kind of school here of interest to the nautical historian. It's how they still do it, using a template or two but mainly just fastening planks by eye to the frames.

Tourists and locals are encouraged to come into the port and deal directly with the fishermen for the huge variety of their catch, and there are a dozen or so booths that will cook the fish to order on the spot. I wish I didn't have to bring this up, but people here were friendly to the crew of *Maverick*, as they have been throughout the Muslim world. We flew the stars and stripes just like we do in every port we come to, in accordance with the traditions of flag etiquette.

As we did in El-Jadida, we visited a local *hammam* in Essaouira, a public bath in the Greek and Roman tradition. The ones we went to were a bit dingy and dimly lit, with heated walls of ceramic tile. You change into a bathing suit at the entry and are given a bucket or two. You go through a door and then into a series of rooms, each one hotter than the one before. Taking water in your bucket from the very hot and cold taps, you mix to your preference, and sit on the tile floor and bathe. For an extra fee someone will bathe and massage you. I passed on that. The total experience was more pleasant than it sounds.

From Essaouira, we made the two-day crossing to the Canaries, making landfall on the small island of Graciosa on the northeast corner of Lanzarote. The Canaries are volcanic islands at about the latitude of Baja California and have the dramatically barren look of, say, Death Valley, with an ocean view. Once you leave the sandy lanes in the town of La Sociedad near our anchorage, the rest of the island of Graciosa is unencumbered by fences or any other sign of land ownership, so you can wander to your heart's content. Although the island has a remote look and feel, it has sophisticated markets and restaurants, and a fast Internet café.

After Graciosa, we had a 150-mile sail to Tenerife, another one of the Canary Islands. We left in a hurry to beat some big seas and strong winds that were forecast, and the whole way we had 15-25 knots slightly aft of the beam with 3-8-ft. seas. It was the best sail we've had since leaving the Red Sea. We'll stay here for a few weeks, and the Captain looks forward to a visit from Theresa who will fly across the Atlantic, looking down at the two or three boats already attempting the passage.

Some of our readers, particularly those whose plans include a cruise of their own in the future, may be interested in the formalities with which a voyager must comply as he or she travels from port to port. You've heard about Byzantine regulations, bribes, and dishonest officials who have absolute authority over the yachtsman. In most countries, in addition to being held accountable for any damage the boat itself may cause in the harbor as a result of dragging anchor or a mistake at the helm, the captain of a boat is responsible for the behavior of his crew when ashore. In New Guinea, a yacht was seized when a new crew member whom the captain barely knew tried to buy pot from an undercover agent at a bar in town. The crew was arrested, and the captain ended up shelling out about $5,000 in legal fees to obtain the release of his boat.

In general, here's what happens: As you approach the new port, you try to raise the authorities on VHF 16 or another channel specified in the pilot. If they answer, which happens about 25% of the time, you follow their instructions. If they don't, you head into the harbor and start looking for the customs dock or simply anchor until you get some more info, often from fellow cruisers already there.

Sometimes, as in Sri Lanka, where there are security concerns at the port, the yacht's movements are controlled until you've checked in, usually by armed personnel who come alongside in a launch and then come aboard for the preliminary paperwork before you're allowed to proceed into the harbor. In Australia, they patrol their waters with overflights and the officials aboard the plane contact you on VHF radio while you're under sail and ask for some details. Usually precautions are a little less uptight, and you come alongside where instructed or anchor and wait for the authorities to come to you, or go into their office.

You've hoisted your "Q" flag, which is solid yellow, on the flag halyard beneath the starboard spreaders prior to entering the port. (The American flag is flown from a flagstaff at the stern or from the backstay.) The Q stands for quarantine, and technically the yacht is quarantined until customs, immigration, the port captain, and sometimes other authorities are satisfied, so either you can't go ashore or can't go any farther than the officials' offices. When formalities are completed, you replace the Q flag on the flag halyard with a courtesy flag, which is a miniature flag of the country you're visiting, and leave it there for the duration of your visit. In most places, you can get away without this (they're expensive, about $15-$30 US), but we carry them for every country and the vast majority of yachts do, particularly world cruisers. It's a traditional sign of respect for the host country, and in some places they demand it.

The formalities consist of presenting a clearance from your last port of call, the boat document, a crew list, passports, and very rarely, proof of insurance, and filling out long forms for various officials. About one time out of ten, there is a search of the boat, usually cursory, but in Australia rather thorough. Rarely, this is an excuse to confiscate cigarettes or alcohol for the official's own use. In some countries, for example, Sri Lanka, Indonesia, and Egypt, you can't get away without having an agent do all the paperwork for you for a non-trivial fee, which includes bribes for officials although this is not stated. You may be able to do it yourself without the agent, but it will be a major hassle that may take days. Though I've heard of it, I've never personally known anyone who attempted to get around the agents in countries where it's the normal practice.

So there are now ledgers by the dozens gathering dust in the offices of port officials across the globe that contain *Maverick's* vital statistics and those of her crew. Yet the process is less odious than you might think and not a major issue, in my opinion. I wouldn't let it worry you, if you're heading out. It's your first contact in the new country, and most officials are as pleasant and efficient as can be, given their circumstances.

It is true that in some countries there have been major issues of compliance, like Australia, where we had to haul out because of a tiny bit of growth on the hull. And in some we have been hit up for bribes, like the time on the island of Batam, Indonesia, when we ended up in a bathroom handing over $30 in US bills to an "agent." Egypt is a special case because every port is its own fiefdom controlled by authorities who not only do not comply with any written information, or even copies of laws that you may have, they change the regulations from day to day depending on what they think they can get away with. The problems we've had along these lines were all between Australia and the Med, and they were more of an annoyance than anything else. To put it in perspective, on the whole trip we've paid less for bribes, even including agents' fees, than it would cost to replace a small self-tailing winch, say $700. So as far as expenses are concerned, boat repairs are a much larger part of the budget. Some people just can't accept bribery, and every once in a while, it rubs you the wrong way. But it's a little easier to handle if you know what to expect in advance, as you will, since you'll be in touch with other cruisers. You could always stay home, you know.

In dealing with officials, you're called the captain, or sometimes, the master, of the vessel. The first time someone addressed me as the master, it was rather a pleasant surprise.

"And you are the master?" asked the customs agent.

Hmmm. "The Master," I thought. That has a damn fine ring to it. "The Master." I paused to contemplate it. Contemplating turned to meditating, and the meditating turned into a kind of mantra, as I repeated silently, "I am the MASTER. I am THE master. I AM the master."

The official was drumming his fingers on his desk.

"Sir? Are you the master?"

I stood up and bowed from the waist, dusting the floor with my cap.

"I am he, sir, the very same," I proclaimed grandly.

The official rolled his eyes, which I thought was quite unseemly, considering he was speaking with the Master.

I left the office in a reverie, contemplating my newfound self. I resolved to immediately email Theresa, informing her of my new title and advising her that hereafter, I was to be addressed as "Master," in a manner not unlike that seen in the old sitcom, *I Dream of Jeannie*.

From the salutation of her response, which was sent back quite promptly, I could tell that there was some feeling for the issue and that she was quite happy to negotiate. "Listen to me, you miserable, festering little wart," she began. You see! A counter-offer. The rest of the letter was admittedly somewhat less conciliatory, but one must take an opening when it's given. We're mature adults and we always can work things out reasonably. It was finally determined that she would excise the word "little" from her proposal, as she was persuaded by the powerful reasoning that I so often can bring to bear, that my stature was a given and that pointing it out was a needless redundancy. The poor dear. She is so enamored of me that I almost always prevail in disagreements of this sort. I have very little reason to doubt that down deep, when she's all alone, she always thinks of me as the Master.

But I digress. Departure from a country is, as a rule, the reverse of arrival and is less difficult, although there are exceptions, particularly in Egypt, where officials may withhold your papers as a bargaining chip until you pony up various creative fees they feel like requesting, that differ from boat to boat depending on what their astrologer says or how expensive your haircut looks. They held up the departure of some friends of ours on weird whims, until some boats missed a weather window to continue up the Red Sea. This meant, after the papers were finally complete, that the crew would have to extend their stay, which meant they would have to check back in, which meant they would have to pay the agent's fees and all other fees all over again—the alternative being, heading directly out into 35 knots on the nose. They took the 35 knots.

Here in the Canaries, they don't give a groat about your papers. It's become so much a part of our rituals that now I almost miss it. Nobody even cares enough about our arrival to put us through a few hoops just to make sure we're the actual heroes of the legendary *Maverick* that they've heard so much about, and not some phonies. Perhaps I'll phone the US embassy and demand to be hassled by some local bureaucrats, just to make sure I'm really me.

And Your Bird Can Sing

8:00 PM local time, Thursday, November 21 (2000 Nov. 21 UTC).
28° 27.986'N 16° 14.647'W
Temp. 75, Humidity 63%, Cloud Cover 20%.
At a slip at the Marina del Atlantico, Santa Cruz, Tenerife, Islas Canarias (Canary Islands), Spain (Espana)

We arrived at the harbor in Santa Cruz, Tenerife, on November 2. Your reporter spent a day or two grinding fiberglass and doing glass work, and soon thereafter, Theresa showed up and she and the Captain rented a car and buzzed off, leaving Mr. Shrode to deal with some problems on *Maverick*. In our absence, he rebuilt the top swivel on the furler, re-fueled, rebuilt the foot-operated water pump under the galley sink, rebuilt the traveller blocks, rebuilt the carburetor on the outboard, installed a new tach to replace the one damaged by lightning, and replaced the key in the prop shaft that connects it to the transmission. This last was not only a difficult job that must be performed in a cramped and uncomfortable position, it's pretty important. The key had been improperly installed by the yard in Athens and had worked loose. If it had gone unnoticed and uncorrected, one day, when we put the transmission into reverse, the prop would have pulled the shaft right out of the boat, sinking to the bottom and leaving a big hole in the hull. It happens.

The bird called the canary (*Serinus canaria*) is named after the islands, not the reverse. They're native to these islands, as are the Canary Palms (*Phoenix canariensis*) that San Franciscans have imported to festoon the Embarcadero. No one knows for sure where the islands, and therefore the palms and the birds, got their name. A species not native to the islands is the human being, but therein lies a tale.

In the great days of exploration, the Spanish and Portuguese sailed to the Canaries and about the same time discovered the Azores, Madeira, and the Cape Verde Islands, the other volcanic islands in the eastern Atlantic. Only the Canaries were inhabited. Aside from speculation that the islands were mentioned in Hesiod or Homer, and legends that the Phoenicians or Carthaginians may have found them, the first actual report of them is by Pliny the Elder, who recounted an expedition here by a North African king in 40 BC. Although it is clear that the islands were inhabited during the first, if not the second or third millennium BC, no one knows where the people came from. There is circumstantial evidence that the first settlers arrived before the Bronze Age, which started between 1900 and 3000 BC in various parts of the world. This is based on the facts that no metal implements have been found in archaeological digs, and that the people discovered living here in the 1300s had none, either. There is no Clovis-type site to absolutely prove inhabitation before about 200 BC, but there is every possibility that people were here in the Neolithic Period. An odd thing about the people the Portuguese discovered in the middle of the 14th century was that they were tall, blue-eyed, and fair-haired. No one has any evidence of who they were or where they originated. But how did they get there?

You can't see the Canaries from mainland Africa. The highest point on Fuerteventura, which is the island nearest the coast, is 2372 feet, and this peak is 64 nautical miles from the mainland. To find how far, in nautical miles, the peak can be seen from a small boat before it drops below the horizon, we multiply the square root of the height in feet times 1.17, which in this case gives us about 56 miles. So if a stone-age sailor was about 56 miles from the mountain, or 8 miles off the shore of Africa on a perfectly clear day, and he sailed northwest, he'd begin to see something pop up above the waves once in a while. Since the peak is 12 miles inland, he'd then have to sail 56 minus 12, or 44 miles farther, to make landfall. He would have hoped all the way that the mountain didn't disappear into the haze, which would have been all too likely. To complete the voyage, unless he could make more than about 4 knots, he would have to continue his navigation by the stars.

Now, it might be argued that no navigation was necessary, and all that was needed for discovery was that a fisherman got caught out in an offshore breeze, made landfall on an unknown island, and then waited until the wind turned around to take him home. The problem is that in this scenario just one man gets here or at best a few. If you want to start a community, you need women, and supplies, and tools. You have to make a few trips, so you have to be able to find the place. Even in the Stone Age when men and women were outdoorsy sorts, I'm sure there were plenty of women around, who, like Theresa and Caroline, would have said, "No way I'm getting in that thing, even if you do have a GPS." Or maybe it was men saying that to the explorers, who were women.

So what we have is evidence that at a bare minimum of 2200 years ago, and very possibly as long as 5000 years ago or more, sailors in Africa had navigation skills and seaworthy vessels that could manage a crossing of 52 miles. This doesn't match up to the great voyages of the early Polynesians, of course, but it happened at about the same time and is nothing to sneeze at, as Bay Area sailors who have sailed to the Farallones, which is only half as far, can testify. Strangely enough, the people discovered by the Portuguese in the Canaries had lost the ability to sail anything but rudimentary dugout canoes and had no knowledge of navigation. They rarely traveled between islands.

The real champions of early exploration by boat remain, however, the Aborigines of Australia, who were there by at least 40,000 BC. There's no way to explain their arrival, no matter how much you speculate on sea levels, except to assume that they were blue-water sailors. I've already argued, back when I saw the "oldest boat" in Egypt, that there is a strong possibility that hominids earlier than *Homo sapiens* had watercraft. I see no reason not to believe that sailing is one of the oldest technologies on earth.

In a day or two, we'll put ourselves out there once again for a short trip to La Gomera, about 65 miles, just slightly longer than our Stone-Age counterparts who first came to these islands. We'll be using a boat and techniques that have the benefit of over 40,000 years of development and trial and error, so we've got a lot of help.

CHRISTOPHER COLUMBUS

8:30 AM local time, Monday, November 25 (0830 Nov. 25 UTC).
28° 5.353'N 17° 6.536'W
Temp. 75, Humidity 77%, Cloud Cover 100%. Rain.
At a slip at the Marina La Gomera, San Sebastian, La Gomera, Canary Islands, Spain.

Mr. Shrode and I had an easy sail overnight from Tenerife to La Gomera the night of November 22. We came here to see the harbor from which Columbus set sail to discover the New World. According to local lore, there are places on this island where Columbus lingered, but for the sailor the main thing is seeing the harbor itself, where we know the *Niña,* the *Pinta,* and the *Santa Maria* were anchored. Today, there's a modern seawall and good protection from any direction, but in Columbus' day it was pretty much an open roadstead with no protection from the southeast. The captains of the three boats, that had no motors and couldn't reliably sail to windward to accomplish an escape, were fortunate that at the time of year they were there, wind from that quadrant is unusual.

Today we have some dirty weather associated with a low of 964 millibars off to the north. Columbus may have had to sit out something like this, and without a seawall it would have made for a rolly anchorage, but we're pretty snug.

We've got some problems needing serious attention. The prop shaft repair completed in Tenerife didn't hold so Mr. Shrode is trying another fix today. Then your reporter will be diving under the boat to look for the cause of some vibration in the prop, and grinding fiberglass to repair a broken cockpit scupper. We wanted to leave tomorrow (Tuesday 26th) but I don't think that will happen.

We're not very nervous about the crossing, but that could be a bad sign. You never know what could happen out there, and a late-season hurricane is not metaphysically impossible. Any sailor would consider an Atlantic crossing a big feather in his cap, and we hope soon to be putting that feather in ours. Our preparations are nothing out of the ordinary as we do the same checks before every passage of more than a couple of days. But we do find it exhilarating to be attempting the same route as Christopher and his fleet, 500 years ago.

No longer politically correct, is poor old Columbus. I suppose it's possible that the indigenous peoples of North and South America would have been left alone forever had he never lived or that the next guy would have been as selfless as Mother Theresa. Columbus was an autocratic leader who often made decisions based on superstition, biblical passages, or just plain wishful thinking. Does that put him beyond the pale when compared to other historical figures? He was ridiculously wrong about a lot of things, but the same could be said of Newton, Jefferson, and Plato.

The great explorers went to places that were unknown in a way it's hard to imagine things being unknown today. Columbus sailed across an ocean and back with primitive navigational instruments and without any charts. This is a stunt that is so scary to contemplate that we could forget all the rest of the things he did that were neurotic or despotic, and we could still classify him as a certified nutcase based on his guts alone. Even with modern charts, few sailors today would dare to attempt the same voyage with the technology Columbus used. There was no ground support team, no emergency radio contact with the outside world. As soon as he cast off the docklines, Columbus was utterly on his own.

Having sailed from Spain, Columbus left San Sebastian on La Gomera in the Canary Islands on September 6, 1492. Previously that same year he had been in Granada at the Alhambra and witnessed the fall of the last Moor bastion in Spain. Despite the Muslims' loss of Spain, the Ottomans' power was peaking not far to the east. The overland trade routes from Europe to China and India were now essentially unusable, and the sea routes problematic. A new way to trade with the East was needed.

The Portuguese had found the way around the Cape of Good Hope, but Columbus thought he had an idea for a more direct route. The political and economic threat of the Islamic world to Europe at the time was, in a manner not unlike what we see in our day, clothed in the garments of religion, and Columbus occasionally, possibly disingenuously, used the cause of spreading the Gospel to justify actions that the motives of power and greed could not.

Whatever his personal shortcomings, Columbus is rarely criticized as a navigator and sailor, nor is his courage questioned. He was so canny, or lucky, in his judgment of the best route westward from Europe by sail that in the subsequent 500 years no one has discovered a better way to cross the Atlantic. Just as he did, every cruiser heading to the Caribbean this year, including *Maverick,* will go south and either stop at the Canaries, or continue to sail until they get to the southeast trade winds that will carry them across. The only thing different about today's passages from the Canaries is that we tend to leave a little later to avoid the late-season hurricanes along the way, something Columbus had no knowledge of, because no known ship had ever encountered an Atlantic hurricane before. He was fortunate and didn't experience one. Even more improbably, since no one had sailed east from America, he also found the westerlies to take him home.

Today we have what are called *pilot charts* of the oceans of the world. *Maverick* carries a set aboard. These charts are really books of 12 charts for each ocean, one for every month of the year. The oceans they portray are divided into small sections in which the average direction and velocity of winds are graphically represented, along with the frequency of gales and calms for the month. These types of guides were the idea of Matthew Maury, a lieutenant in the US Navy, who published his first maps of the winds of the earth in 1848, more than three centuries too late for Columbus.

Yet what Columbus missed from Maury's charts was redeemed by good fortune, which is often a mysterious talent of those who do great things. Columbus set a course based not on meteorology, but on a route that he thought would take him directly to Japan. Yet it took him to the trade winds, the highway ships have used since then, which had been previously unknown. Moreover, the trades were blowing at a higher than average latitude the year he sailed. If they had been in their more normal position, he would have been becalmed in the horse latitudes, and the delay might, at best, have put his discoveries off for a long time.

Columbus' little fleet, as is well known, consisted of the *Santa Maria*, a boat about 100 feet long on deck, and the *Niña* and *Pinta*, both about 60 feet. Columbus had the big one. There were about 30 men on each boat, a few less on the small ones and more on the *Santa Maria*. In Redwood City, California, about 10 years ago, Theresa and I visited a replica of the *Niña* constructed with traditional methods and materials. The replica was based on an accumulation of information and guesswork, but still, it was close enough to the original to learn some surprising things.

The shear was fairly radical and amidships, at the lowest point of the deck, freeboard was less than two feet, not as much as *Maverick*'s. In paintings, this is disguised by the large gunwales, perhaps three feet high, which make the height of the deck above the water appear greater than it is. The scuppers were large, however, and since water can drain either in or out of them, this meant that the deck of the 100-ton ship was awash in any reasonably large seas. That wouldn't be so bad if there were quarters for the crew belowdecks, but there weren't. That space was reserved for provisions and gear, and at least these items had better lodgings than the supplies carried by the sailors in the Greek galleys. The crew did not, however, so in all weather, they were exposed to the elements. The luxury berth for the senior seamen consisted of sleeping on a coil of rope rather than directly on the deck itself. For modern cruisers, who live in a reasonably dry cabin and who are protected by a dodger and Bimini when out in the cockpit, it's hard to imagine enduring a month or more at sea with absolutely no shelter. It can get plenty uncomfortable out here even with our advantages.

Belowdecks on Columbus' ships was no pleasure palace either. In addition to salted meat and other not particularly savory foodstuffs, they carried live cows, chickens, and pigs. The cows and pigs were suspended in slings, which is pretty tough duty, but if they were loose in pens, they would break their legs with the boat's motion. Of course, they had to be fed and cleaned up after.

Columbus' sailors are customarily portrayed in popular culture as fearful, ignorant fools who were afraid they were going to fall off the edge of the earth. In fact, most men aboard including the officers knew the world was round, but they had every reason to feel fear on other grounds. I don't think we have any records that tell us what the mortality rate among seamen was at the time of Columbus, but going to sea was undoubtedly one of the most dangerous professions in the world, as it remains in our day, even with infinitely improved navigation and safety precautions. It's not unreasonable to estimate that per man-hour at sea in Columbus' time, the death rate was a hundred times what it is today.

Even in their home waters, experienced captains could make fatal mistakes in navigation, since they had no way of establishing longitude, how far west or east they were on the planet measured from the Prime Meridian. The British Navy was so concerned about accidents caused by navigational error that the government of England finally offered a prize in the early 18th century, amounting to what would now be millions of dollars, to anyone who could figure out a reliable way to find one's longitude at sea. John Harrison's clock was the result, as without a timepiece, there is no way of determining longitude. But it was no help to Columbus, sailing 250 years earlier.

In Columbus' day the sextant had not been invented. He had only a clumsy quadrant, from which he could judge the angle of the stars and so obtain a workable approximation of latitude from Polaris. Though crude, compasses were familiar instruments, and of course Columbus used this instrument to find direction. However, it wasn't well understood why the needle didn't consistently point to Polaris. We know now that this is because the magnetic north pole isn't in the same place as the geographic north pole, and what's more, it moves.

So Columbus, using the best equipment of his day, could not determine where on earth he was. But he had an even more serious navigational problem. He believed, despite ample evidence to the contrary, that the earth was only about 3/4 of the size it is. He also thought it was farther to Asia from Europe by land than many of his contemporaries did, and as a result he thought Japan was far to the east of where it actually is. So when he found land, he had a completely erroneous idea of where he was, which he never revised. He died thinking he had sailed to Asia.

The ironic thing is that if Columbus had used the correct measurements of the earth, the length of the voyage—leaving the unknown continent of America out of the picture—would have most likely prevented him from trying it. It would have been a much longer voyage than anyone could have believed was achievable, and therefore it would have been impossible to enlist crew or secure financing. Usually, we think of visionaries as those who are proven right when doubters think something can't be done. Yet in this case, it was absolutely necessary that Columbus' assessment of the undertaking be very, very wrong, just so he could get underway.

Even if he had been able to figure his latitude and longitude and knew how big the earth was, he would have had no idea how close to land he was as he had no chart of these heretofore completely unknown shores. The books say there are certain signs of land, but in my opinion, they're overrated. Birds are a clue, that is, if the island supports birds other than the kind you see at sea, and not all do. Columbus thought that seeing a Booby was an indication of land, because this bird never ventures far away from its roost on solid earth. I knew this was wrong as we've seen Boobies a thousand miles from land, and I was surprised that an experienced mariner wouldn't know this. But when I looked up the Booby's range in *Sea Birds of the World,* I learned that the range of the Booby in the Atlantic goes no farther north than the Canaries, which is the only place Columbus could have seen them. And the ones on the Canaries don't venture far offshore. Score one for the old navigator.

He continually reports seeing weed floating in the water, a good sign of land, if it weren't for the fact that since both wind and current were going in the same direction he was, they could never be an indication that land was anything but behind him. But this is explained by the fact that Columbus had no way of comparing his progress through the water with his progress over the ground, which we do today by comparing the knotmeter to the GPS, giving us set and drift. He believed he had current against him and so if he did see weed in the water, it made sense for him to believe the land it came from was in front of him.

You can't smell land from upwind, which is the direction from which Columbus was approaching. A reflection of green on the underside of clouds? I've never been able to make it out with certainty, that is, in the absence of knowledge that an island is there, which of course I have, since I'm a 21st century guy. But maybe the seamen of olden times could. And of course, there were no city lights or lighthouses.

A good watch at the crow's nest would see land, you'd think, but that didn't stop the *Titanic* from hitting an iceberg. Columbus had even less of a chance of spotting San Salvador at night, as it's not white and it's very low, probably no more than 50 feet above sea level at any point. This reporter has sailed to San Salvador and been on watch at night when we were five miles from the island. The only reason we knew we were five miles from the island is that we had a good chart and GPS. Otherwise, it was completely invisible. It gave me the willies to imagine Columbus sailing in these waters with no way of seeing the land in the dark.

In the great days of sail, it was not unusual for a ship to carry a lead line, which is a long line with a lead weight on the end, over a mile long. They could "sound," or lower the line to the bottom, either underway or after heaving-to, and when the weight hit the bottom, they could judge their depth by marks on the line at the surface. Tallow was placed in a hollow on the bottom of the weight, so when it was brought back aboard some of the bottom was stuck to the tallow, and they could see whether they were over sand or mud or gravel. Today, we say a boat is "off soundings" when it passes the continental shelf, or when it's in water deeper than 100 fathoms, but we read the depth off a screen of an electronic depth-sounder. In Columbus' day, both the physical handling of the lead line and the reading of it were highly skilled arts.

Now, you'd think the lead line would be of service, as you could be warned you were in shallower water and start looking for land. But according to the chart of San Salvador that I have in my possession, the seabed rises from the abyssal plain of the Atlantic Ocean to the east, where the bottom is 3 miles down, to the surface of the island, in a distance of less than 7 miles. Less than 4.5 miles from shore, it's still 5,000 feet down. Columbus could have been sending his crew out with the lead line all the way across the Atlantic. If he had been sounding with 500 feet of line, he would have found the bottom, depending on where he was along the shore, about half a mile from the reef. It would be about four minutes to impact at this point, and the grounding, on a lee shore of the trade winds, would have been catastrophic. If all the ships had been lost, there would be no record of the voyage. He would have been just another captain who had disappeared at sea.

Suppose it was a nice, bright, sunny day with 10 knots of wind and calm seas when they approached the land, like in the movies. Sure they'd see it, no problem. On the other hand, suppose it wasn't. Suppose it was night, in fog or rain, or 35 knots and 12-foot seas. Only clairvoyance would have prevented their hitting the reef and sinking, thousands of miles from home. In fact, land was sighted by the light of a moon that was just past full at 0200 on October 12. But from a very few days out of the Canaries, now in unknown waters and heading for a landfall only existing in Columbus' visionary mind, the voyagers must have had a constant concern of running aground. In fact, the *Santa Maria* foundered on a reef later on the voyage, so only two ships returned to Europe.

Perhaps we could say these men were ignorant; every explorer is ignorant of what he's going to see, and that's why we call them *explorers*. If a painter or a teacher or a storyteller wishes to portray Columbus' men as weak, ignorant cowards, let him climb aloft in a gale to furl a sail and then perhaps reassess the courage of these old seamen. Sure they were afraid to go where Columbus was attempting to sail, but for a perfectly good reason: It was dangerous as hell.

We plan to make landfall somewhere south of where Columbus did, on the islands that are known in the Caribbean as The Windwards. We won't be nearly as nervous about hitting the rocks. We'll have charts, GPS, a depth sounder, radar, and we'll know we're close to land long before we get there. If it's night, we'll slow down until dawn so we can find our way into a harbor in the daytime, guided by navigation aids that those who have gone before have put in place to mark our way. Piece of cake.

Head Out on the Highway

1:30 PM local time, Wednesday, November 27 (0130 Nov. 27 UTC).
28 04 N 017 07 W
Temp. 75, Humidity 72%, Cloud Cover 100%.
Underway.

We just departed La Gomera for the passage across the Atlantic. A high has begun to settle in and should soon provide strong northeasterlies for our trip southwest to a waypoint Mr. Shrode has named "wind" for the trades we expect to follow to the Caribbean. When we get to our waypoint, after about 650 miles, we'll turn right and head just south of due west for Grenada, our planned landfall, which will then be about 2100 miles away.

We won't be able to use the engine, as we have not been able to resolve the problem with the prop shaft, so we'll have to sail all the way. Columbus did it without an engine, too. The Captain has some butterflies, and that's what we're here for, thrill-seekers. We haven't had what we would call an adventure since we left the Red Sea six months ago, and now there's a little excitement in the air.

Wish us luck.

Looking for Adventure

1:30 PM local time, Monday, December 2 (1330 Dec. 2 UTC).
21 35 N 027 22 W
Temp. 78, Humidity 70%, Cloud Cover 70%.
Sixth day at sea.

As the song goes "...or whatever comes our way." We got you covered on the whatever. I'm back in my old familiar seat, strapped with a kind of seat-belt arrangement into the nav station at the computer. This must be the first missive I've written at sea since the Red Sea. It's almost cheating to send the other ones out, since they were written from a stable platform. It's rolly out here, but quite a bit nicer than the last few days, and we're doing about 7.5 knots under triple-reefed main and a poled-out genoa in 25 to 30 knots of wind and 6- to 8-ft. seas. We're south of 23 27 north, so we're technically in the tropics, and it is beginning to feel like it.

Our boys are not in such bad shape, but we haven't gotten off to a very good start, either. As you will remember, we can't use our engine for propulsion, so when the weather looked good for strong northeasterlies to get us down to the trades, it was a good time to go. The first day the wind hadn't settled in and we found ourselves jibing between Tenerife and La Gomera, looking for some breeze. The next day, however, we got the wind, and along with the wind, the seas. For four days we had 25-30 all day, picking up to 30-35 with gusts to 40 at night. The seas soon built to 12 and then 15 feet, with occasional 20 footers. The problem was that there was already a 12-foot swell from the northwest, so the ocean got a bit ugly. All the forecasts called for rough to very rough seas, and that's a pretty fair assessment.

I was happy to talk to a British skipper who allowed as how it was "bloody miserable," the reason being I've heard just about enough from Brits and Aussies and especially Kiwis who delight in calling 45 knots a "nice sailing breeze." I don't think the crew of *Maverick* was miserable, but it wasn't really a cakewalk out here. Soon the cockpit cushions, which we had given up trying to keep on the seats, began soaking up water from the frequent waves we got in the cockpit and became 50-lb. sponges. Cooking was pretty much abandoned and it was a little hard to stay in the bunk. We made our way from head to galley with nimble gibbon-type movements, using handholds. Francis on *Okiva* was near Italy when he fell after missing a handhold, requiring a helicopter to take him to the hospital for about 20 stitches in his head. But we're not close to anywhere and can't afford an injury.

All in a day's work, of course, but yesterday things went a bit catawampus. A control line on the vane broke. No big deal at all. Then later, Ship's Chief of Wind Vane Engineering Terry Shrode noticed the vane acting a little funny. Taking a closer look, he discovered that the setscrews on the shaft that the paddle is hung on had worked loose and the shaft was connected only at one end. Before long, this would have worked loose and there are not enough spares aboard to replace the parts that would have gone missing, with the result that we'd be hand-steering across the Atlantic.

While Mr. Shrode hung himself over the transom to deal with the situation, which he did with his normal aplomb, the Captain steered. Steering at sea is something we rarely do and I'd forgotten that it's pretty cool. We were surfing down the faces of these huge waves and then one big guy came along and woohoo! I looked at the GPS and found we had hit 17.7 knots, which isn't bad for an old boat. Mr. Shrode's enthusiasm for this speed record was dampened by his precarious position at the stern.

Later we tried to start the engine, but it just went thunk. Now we don't need the engine for propulsion, but we do need it to charge the batteries so we can have running lights, cabin lights, talk on the radio, and use the computer. The idea of crossing another 2200 miles of Atlantic without power was not attractive, so the Captain immediately looked at the alternative, which would have been a close reach to Cape Verdes in 30 knots and 12-foot seas. Yuck.

After some head-scratching, we started disassembling things, and it became apparent that we had seawater in the combustion chambers, which had come in through the exhaust system, not the raw water pump. The raw water system, exhaust system, and injectors were pulled apart, although in 12-foot seas this wasn't quite as easy as it would be at home in a calm harbor. We cleared out the water from the cylinders and got the engine started. But today we had the same problem, requiring the same repair. We've sailed a lot of miles with the same exhaust system, in big following seas, and can't see how anything's changed. Every part of the system is by the book (Calder) and seems normal. We don't have a valve to shut off the exhaust as he suggests, but it's never been an issue and these aren't the biggest seas we've seen.

The problems haven't slowed us down too much, although we did reduce sail while we were fixing things. We've averaged about 140 miles a day, even counting the first one, which was very slow, and yesterday and today, when we've had to slow down to work on the engine. The GPS tells us we have about 1990 to go.

The Bung

10:00 PM local time, Tuesday, December 3 (2200 Dec. 3 UTC).
19 38 N   029 52 W
Temp. 79, Humidity 69%, Cloud Cover 60%.
Seventh day at sea.

"Bung." It is a fine word, my friends, exceptionally fine. Verb or noun, as you will. Has an onomatopoeic feeling, does it not, although I'm not clear on the correlative. The Captain will brook no disparagement of this word. The crafty wordsmith who first uttered it was a man who was top drawer and at the peak of his powers. Rhymes with rung, sung, tongue, lung, stung, and dung, as devil-may-care a group as you please. The onboard *American Heritage Dictionary* traces it from Latin to the Middle English "bunge"; and when we think Middle English, we think Chaucer, that most scatological of bards. The first word we think of when we think of *The Canterbury Tales*, unless we're a weirdo, is "arse." Now, "bunge" and "arse" go together like a horse and carriage but may be considered coarse by some of our readers in whose hearts there dwells no poetry.

But if the word is an excellent one, how much more excellent the actual object to which it refers. Each well-found vessel will carry many aboard, for the reason that a Bung is used to Bung things that we don't favor on boats, although elsewhere they are fine, and that is holes. Boats do have holes in them, for the influx of things we want in and discharge of things we want out. Holes below the waterline are guarded by sea cocks, valves that can be opened or closed at the Captain's discretion, or at that of Mr. Shrode, acting as Executive Officer, letting in or out the substances alluded to above. When the valves are in the closed position, we may say, if we wish, that the areas that were formerly holes are now "non-holes," as we have changed them into their opposites, à la Hegel or the Tao Te Ching. When a valve fails, we must resort to another solution to accomplish our yin-yang magic. We use the Bung.

It so happens that a recent problem on *Maverick* was solved, at least for the nonce, by use of the mellifluously named yet humble item under discussion. The reader may remember that saltwater was flowing in an inappropriate manner into the combustion chamber of our diesel engine. At our present stage of technology, engines will not run on seawater, although there are those who will dispute this. The water was coming from the exhaust pipe through the muffler into the engine, and damned if this isn't exactly backwards. Since nothing has visibly changed in the exhaust system and the influx is occurring even though the seas are down, our theory is that a baffle inside the muffler has failed. It's an unsubstantiated theory for which we have no evidence in a field in which we have no knowledge, and our lives depend on it, ha ha! We dare not try to take it apart, for the simple reason that we might not be able to put it back together. So it's a little black box of mystery. But the solution is as follows: When the engine is not in use, we disconnect the exhaust from the muffler and Bung a Bung into it. Carefully Bunged thusly, *Maverick* wends her way homeward. The Mighty Bung has saved the day! May It reign forever in Its enchanted kingdom across the sea.

At dawn this morning, the crew of *Maverick* poked their heads out of the companionway like groundhogs, and, with little more in the way of intelligent awareness, blinked in the sun. The seas had subsided a little, the wind was down, and puffy trade winds clouds had appeared. For six days we had barely left the cabin except to trim sails, adjust the vane, and check the horizon for traffic. Any time spent in the cockpit would sooner rather than later be repaid by a cold bath from a wave that tripped into the boat, so it was just not worth the hassle to be outdoors.

We were at about 21 degrees north, just on the border of the trades, and as the day progressed, the wind got fluky and veered to the southeast. The rule of thumb crossing the Atlantic is not to get greedy but to head southwest from the Canaries, perhaps more south than west, until you reach the 20th parallel, and then turn right. A month of studying wind patterns on the Internet had done nothing to make the Captain doubt the wisdom of this rule. The most direct route across the globe is of course a great circle route, which can be defined as the line where a plane intersecting the beginning and end of your route and the center of the earth meets its circumference. But this route would take you too far north, into the no-wind zone of the Azores High. Some optimistic sailors sail the rhumb line, which is a line that looks straight on a Mercator projection but is actually longer than and to the south of the great circle route. But the safest route, in terms of having the most reliable wind—essential as *Maverick* will not be motoring—is to head even farther to the south, for the 20th parallel.

Hunkered down in the cabin, we had been moving fast with the strong winds of the high to our north and with one more day, we would have been there, but the change in winds was a harbinger of the weakening of the high, and so we determined to steer a course more directly south to get to about latitude 19, and hoped thereby to be in the trade winds drawn by the low of the ITCZ rather than the dying winds pushed by the high pressure. At that point we would make our course change towards the Caribbean. Our heading is currently about 200 degrees true, but by tomorrow, unless our wind completely disappears, we should be able to set a great circle course of about 260. We have gnomonic paper charts to figure it, but the GPS will give it to us automatically.

Tonight, Ship's Chef Terry Shrode prepared an excellent curry complete with papadums, and as the sun set, we put on our favorite sailing tape, Van Morrison's album with the Chieftains. The first stars appeared in the dying twilight, and to the tune of the fiddle and the bones and the pennywhistle, *Maverick* leapt through the waves of the great Atlantic Ocean.

The Dolphin's Rings

9:30 PM local time, Friday, December 6 (2130 Dec. 6 UTC).
18 01 N 033 55 W
Temp. 80, Humidity 67%, Cloud Cover 20%.
Tenth day at sea.

As planned, we turned right to 264 true at about 1100 on December 4 at 18 30N and 30 30W. Even though the wind's been pretty light because of a low-pressure trough that is shutting down the trades, it's been peachy out here. There are days at sea when you just hold on, like the first few of this passage, but this isn't one of them. Right now we're reaching at about 6 knots in 10 knots on the beam. Twilight tonight was pure Maxfield Parrish, with a silvery crescent moon in Sagittarius illuminating fleecy tradewind clouds in a field of stars. In the last couple of days, we've had to get out the poles and remember where all the strings went, and today we had Luigi flying and were doing 7 knots on a mellow sea.

Yesterday we saw our first dolphins in the Atlantic, but they wouldn't come and play. We were becalmed and just sitting there so they had about as much interest in us as Britney does. We've seen dolphins ever since a week or two out of San Francisco. We saw them in the Pacific and the Indian Oceans, the Red Sea and the Mediterranean, and even in the Suez Canal. Their arrival still is the occasion for calling the off-watch up if he is not asleep, and it cannot help but lift one's spirits.

Sometime in the 1990s, *Scientific American* ran an article on dolphin behavior. What had been observed was that at times they would blow a string of bubbles and then somehow create a circle by capturing the bubbles in a vortex. Over a period of time, it became clear to the scientists that while novices would produce irregular and unstable rings, much like someone who blows his first smoke rings, as they became more experienced, they could reliably create almost perfect circles. The researchers were occupied with the question of how this behavior related to other known dolphin activities like mating, the establishment of territory, and hunting. Having exhausted the possibilities after much observation, they were forced to conclude the dolphins were just goofing off. Big deal, I do it all the time, like right now. But there was another issue that seemed much more peculiar to me, which is: How does a dolphin know what a circle is?

Of course, nobody knows, but the more interesting thing is that we don't even know how humans know what a circle is. The question is the same one raised by Plato in his superficially unassuming dialogue, *Meno*.

In the *Meno*, Plato gives a demonstration of the question's mystery, in a scene unlike any other in the history of philosophy. We meet Meno's slave boy, who has, like the dolphins, no previous education in mathematics or geometry. To illustrate a point, Socrates presents him with a geometric puzzle, one with a solution that probably would not occur immediately to any of you reading this, even those who stayed awake in geometry class in high school. The problem is: given a certain square, construct a square with twice the area. With a little prodding and questioning the slave boy arrives at the correct solution. This seems to indicate that even though he had never heard of the solution before, he had the knowledge somewhere in his mind and just needed to remember it.

Every geometry teacher prods his students to do the same sort of thing every day. But at some time in history, some person had to be the first person to figure it out from scratch, so obviously he wasn't taught by anyone. How, or where, did he come by the solution? This, along with the related question of whether the relationship between the two squares represents something real in the universe or is just a projection of our minds, is a fundamental issue of western philosophy. But it's the same as the puzzle of the dolphin's rings, or at least close enough for this publication. How did the first dolphin come to understand what a circle is?

The two traditional schools of thought are *empiricism*, that we know circles and the like through our senses, and *rationalism*, that somehow either God or the universe or evolution has put the patterns in our heads and we know them *a priori*, that is, before we ever look at anything, and this latter one is what Socrates is trying to show. To save you the trouble of reading all those boring books, the Captain will spill the beans and tell you that after 2500 years, it would not be going too far to say that both theories have failed to settle the matter. We don't know how we know mathematics, and we don't know if mathematics represents the world. Even Einstein saw this as a mystery. String theory, according to the physicists, consists of beautiful mathematics and resolves the troubling incongruity between quantum mechanics and relativity. But as yet they can't say if it describes the real world, and no one can say out of what ether the mathematics for it magically appeared in our consciousness

Our understanding of mathematics is kind of like clairvoyance, or foreknowledge, sometimes of events but more often of principles or mathematical objects, things that we represent by little squiggles we thought up to count sheep and bushels, yet seem to govern the universe. This knowledge is so familiar to us that we don't think it borders on the supernatural, but the Pythagoreans who first discovered it understood that it does. You could train a dog or a parrot or a dolphin to recognize certain shapes. But it's something different when a dolphin, like Meno's slave, comes up with a mathematically perfect structure on his own, like some humans did a long time ago.

So when I see a dolphin dive under the bow, I know we share a little secret. We each know something that seems completely clear and obvious, and yet we don't know how we know it.

If It's Going to Happen, It'll Happen Out There

10:30 PM local time, Sunday, December 8 (2230 Dec. 8 UTC).
17 38 N   038 42 W
Temp. 79, Humidity 73%, Cloud Cover 20%.
Twelfth day at sea.

The last couple of days we've had great sailing in a slightly lumpy cross swell coming from a low up north. We've got 12-20 knots and beautiful weather. In the mornings we participate in a couple of SSB nets, the first an informal one with three other circumnavigator friends we met along the way, plus, occasionally, *Okiva*. Paul and Francis, when last heard, still had a major oil leak. They put a huge amount aboard and are heading for a brief stop in the Canaries before attempting the crossing. The other net consists of about 50 boats not involved in the Atlantic Rally for Cruisers who do daily check-ins to report their positions and conditions.

Even though the sailing is pretty pleasant, there are some clouds on the horizon, both literally and figuratively. The real clouds are puffy cumulus, typical tradewind clouds indicative of good weather. Among them are some cumulus that get pretty big and become squalls, and some of the cruisers have been complaining about them on the net. The crew of *Maverick* has survived the squalls in the Java Sea and is unlikely to be intimidated by these. I know I shouldn't say that.

The figurative clouds are referenced in the title of our piece, a quote from Captain Ron in the movie of the same name. We've had a few more problems, for the reason that the old ones have been solved. When we had light air for a couple of days, lots of people passed us, as we could not use our engine for propulsion, but we don't mind sitting around in the middle of the sea. We're not in a hurry to be someplace. In the harbor, we're just tourists or boat mechanics, but at sea, we're sailors. This is what we've paid the price, in many ways, to do, so we don't feel in a rush to get it over with.

We're happy with the bung solution. Every day, Ship's Chief Diesel Proctologist Terry Shrode shows up for work in his white lab coat, with his briefcase full of bungs of all sizes and materials, and his collection of bung mallets. He carefully emplaces *Maverick's* bung and sends it home with a satisfying "thwack." So that's taken care of for now.

But another issue has arisen. The very next day after speaking in praise of the Monitor vane that does our steering at sea, of the four boats on our little circumnavigator net, all of whom use Monitors, three had reported broken vanes. *Otter* and *Delphis* were able to make satisfactory jury-rigs that will get them across, but on *Maverick,* the break in a weld on the water vane pivot shaft that holds the vane's rudder on will not allow of any simple solution. We've thought of one, but it would be difficult and the repair would be considerably weaker that the original, probably uselessly so. This is a part of the Monitor that experiences the highest loads.

The result is that, with about 1400 miles to go, we'll have to rely on our two Navico wheelpilots to get us there. Navico completely lied to your correspondent about certain aspects of their product on several occasions. It was clear when we left that it would steer the boat in heavy conditions. But when I tried to buy spare belts, the company assured us that they were Kevlar and would never break. Yet the first one broke on the way out of the Golden Gate in 30 knots in the shipping lane and in the process made the boat unsteerable. They actually will do the job of getting us across, if we can avoid using up all our spare belts. This will require a combination of going slow, hand-steering, and, if the wind is in the right direction, setting up the double headsail rig, which can help the boat better steer itself. Once the belts are gone, we steer by hand.

There is an additional serious consequence from the failure of the vane. The emergency rudder *Maverick* carries depends on using the Monitor as a frame. Now, this important backup is lost.

Correspondent Chris Harry, a knowledgeable sailor whom I've never met, warned of the possibility of "one thing leading to another." Let's hope he's not a particularly prescient guy.

HAND JIVE

9:30 PM local time, Monday, December 9 (2130 Dec. 9 UTC).
17 01 N 041 00 W
Temp. 80, Humidity 71%, Cloud Cover 30%.
Thirteenth day at sea.

Yesterday's concern about our backup rudder now has a somewhat more urgent feel. We just sailed by the place where, about 3:00 this afternoon, the 45-ft. Hunter *F-2* was abandoned by its owners and sent to the bottom of the sea. It's about two miles deep here, and it occurs to me to wonder whether it's hit bottom yet. Its rudder actually fell out of the boat. An emergency rudder was fashioned by a nearby square-rigger with an onboard machine shop, but after trying for several days to get the backup to function properly, it also broke away. The owners, a couple, were exhausted, and another boat took them and some of their possessions aboard and will deliver them to the Caribbean.

We've had another problem on *Maverick*, but I don't think we're at the abandoning stage yet. We discovered that the main water tank has some yucky growth in it. We may have enough other water to get to Grenada, and maybe we can filter this stuff. Ship's Nutritionist Terry Shrode tells me water is one of the main food groups. We've drunk the water in Eritrea and Thailand and Borneo, and we had to go to a ritzy marina in the Canaries to get a tank full of bad water. There seems to be no fresh water available out here in the Atlantic.

We're doing a bit more hand-steering to help out the fragile autopilots. Cruisers almost never hand-steer on passages, and it's kind of weird to be on a sailboat you are used to tacking and jibing and maneuvering all the time and yet never touch the wheel except getting in and out of harbors.

But give me the helm of a 30-year-old race boat with 20 knots of wind behind me and turn the stereo up to "stun." We'll be surfing at 8 or 9 knots. There goes a sunset, and a moonrise, and, as our friend Dave Tolmie would say, I'm "all the way live."

Houston, We've Had a Problem

9:00 PM local time, Friday, December 20 (2100 Dec. 20 UTC).
12° 27.159'N 61° 29.256'W
Temp. 84, Humidity 66%, Cloud Cover 00%.
On the hard at Tyrrel Bay Yacht Haulout, Carriacou Island, Grenada.

At about 4:00 AM after three hours of sleep, I was awakened by Mr. Shrode, a highly unusual occurrence. We had a lot of water in the bilge, he said, almost up to the floorboards, and we needed to find where it was coming from. It took about one minute to check all the usual suspects: the through-hulls, packing gland, and rudder tube. The exhaust pipe, as the reader will remember, was bunged, so that wasn't it.

I quickly started pulling up hatches in the cabin sole and just as quickly spotted a group of ten or so little fountains at the forward end of the keel, each about a pencil lead in diameter. The ocean was coming into the boat, right through the hull. I informed Mr. Shrode and we assumed our customary chores in dodgy situations, a product both of our different roles and our different personalities. We cover for each other pretty well.

Mr. Shrode attacked the direct problem with alacrity. He cut some pieces of plywood to use as pads, wedged in by other pieces of plywood. Under these he compressed a combination of rags and modeling clay. This did appear to slow down the flow.

Meanwhile the Captain started to think about the worst possible scenario. A leak has opened up in the hull, without our having hit anything, at least as far as we know. I say as far as we know because, in the violence of the heavy cross-seas of the first week of the passage, the boat took so many ferocious hits from waves that one of them could possibly have been something else, like a whale. Who knows? But the force of the waves was serious enough.

Anyway, the problem has finally shown itself, and since we didn't know the nature of the breach in the outside of the hull, we didn't know whether it was likely to get larger. *Maverick's* hull was originally glassed together lengthwise from two halves because of its tumblehome. If the seam joining the two halves had started to separate, the hull could, with any particular roll of the boat, come apart swiftly, and the influx would be unstoppable. An unlikely and terrifying scenario, and as it turned out, not correct, but it could have theoretically happened.

I took a quick fix on the chart, noting that we were about 30 miles away from our intended landfall, seven hours at our current speed. I got the abandon ship gear ready. The crash bag is always kept packed with flares, a handheld VHF, a handheld GPS, water, and a variety of other emergency stuff, so attending to this only amounted to adding our essential papers and zipping it up. I ascertained that our life vests were ready-to-hand and made sure we both had knives to cut away the life raft.

With Mr. Shrode hard at work at the stoppage, we needed to gauge whether the leak was getting worse, so we set a timer at ten minutes and noted how high the water would get in the bilge in that time. I then began calling a "pan-pan" on the radio, first on VHF 16 and then on all the SSB emergency frequencies. Although we were only about 20 miles from the closest land at the time, we got no response for the first couple of hours. By 5:00 AM, local time, one of the morning high-frequency nets had come on, the early one with our circumnavigator buddies, all knowledgeable sailors. They volunteered to stand by on a 6-meg frequency and call every half hour to check on our situation. They also had some good ideas. When we got in the lee of the island we could heave-to and dive under the boat to try to spot the leak and then perhaps apply some underwater epoxy, which we carry aboard. We could launch the dinghy and tow the boat in with the outboard if the shaft failed, etc. They didn't tell us anything we hadn't thought of but their concern gave us a big morale boost. Plus, sometimes you aren't thinking straight when things get weird, and a reminder is never a bad idea.

Finally, a man named Bob on *Figment*, at anchor at a nearby island, responded to the "pan-pan" on VHF 16. We gave him our position and a description of the situation. We knew there was a travel-lift at Tyrrel Bay on Carriacou, and that would be our first opportunity to get *Maverick* out of the water. Bob was on the job in a hot second, attempting to relay our information to Tyrrel Bay Yacht Haulout, who were out of our VHF range on the other side of Carriacou. He kept calling until they showed up at the office about 7:30 and gave them the story. He came back to us with the reassuring news that they'd be there waiting for us and we should just give them a call on 16 when we were in range. I told Bob we owed him a six-pack, but I haven't been able to reach him since.

When we next checked our timing on the water in the bilge, we discovered it was now coming up to our mark in five minutes, so the hole was opening up and the water was flowing in twice as fast as when we first measured it. Mr. Shrode redoubled his efforts and I concentrated on sailing the boat. I'm really not much of a racer, notwithstanding my wish that the reader might think I am, but nevertheless those hours on the race course are invaluable training when you really have to get somewhere. How's the sail trim? Will the wind accelerate between the islands? When will we be in the lee and lose our wind? Should we sail a wider arc around the island to avoid sailing into a hole? Where's the current and what is it doing? And of course there was navigation to be done. I wanted to minimize the prop shaft use so we continued to sail, and in the back of my mind was reader Chris Harry's warning that things could pile up on us.

Checking the rate of influx again, we noted that it had increased another 30% or so. We began to run the bilge pump more often and for longer periods. We tried to calculate how long we could keep going before the pump was overwhelmed, but the fact is, as mentioned above, this really could happen in an instant so far as we knew. It was now only another hour or so to get to the boatyard at our present pace. Since the wind held, the decision was to keep sailing and not heave-to and go overboard to check the leak, and knowing what we know now, that was the right call. First off, it would have been pretty unnerving to see what the damage really was. Second, the underwater epoxy would have been no help. It could not have prevented the crack in the hull from opening further. Finally, all these options take time, and we needed every moment to get to the lift.

We again hailed Tyrrel Bay Yacht Haulout and as promised they were standing right by the radio. They talked us through finding the marks to follow through the reef to their dock. As we rounded the point just north of the bay, we could not yet see any of the marks, but we headed up and sheeted in and were moving well. Soon the marks came into view in the binoculars, and we called the yard guys to ask which side to put the docklines and fenders on. Mr. Shrode was down below tending to his water control project, so I engaged the autopilot and set up the fenders and docklines. What I didn't know at the time was that there was now a river coming into the boat, and the pump was barely able to keep up with the flow. Heading up and sheeting in had put additional stress on the hull, and opened up the hole.

When we got closer in, we doused the sails and started the engine. As we approached the dock, Terry was preoccupied with the pump so I tossed lines to the four or five guys ready to help. We were still running the pump as the travel lift hoisted *Maverick* out of the water.

When we got off the boat and could take a look, what we saw was a pretty bad piece of business. There was a lateral tear, rising athwartships 12-18 inches on both port and starboard just forward of the keel, right through the boat, about 3/8-inch wide. There wasn't just a hole in the boat. *Maverick* had been literally breaking in two.

We became the focus of attention around the yard, as no one had seen anything quite like it. Many folks said we were very lucky to have made it alive and to have gotten the boat out of the water before she sank. I wasn't feeling very lucky. We'd had a lot of tough breaks on this trip, but this one made the rest look minor. And this time, it wasn't clear that *Maverick* could be saved.

It is most likely that, whatever the cause, *Maverick* suffered a catastrophic stress of some kind back in the heavy weather the first week out, as none of the seas since then would have much bothered a Catalina 25. Had the hull opened up in those seas, which got up to 20 feet, it would have opened up real fast. It's unlikely we would have been able to stop it. Had we been able to launch the raft and get in it, we would have been rolled and flipped and tossed about in the huge seas. It would have been close to a perfect impossibility for another cruiser to find us, and Search And Rescue from the Canaries might have not had the range. If they did, a rescue would have been dodgy, to say the least, even if they could have located us.

There were a couple of other scenarios less pleasant than what happened. Had we been even one hour further away, not to mention a thousand miles, with the flow of water increasing seemingly every second, and the hole opening up, I don't think we would have made it. Or, had we been one day later, when the wind finally died after bringing us all the way across, we would have had that prop shaft issue. We had sailed a little yellow brick road of wind to a safe harbor.

Maverick, as wounded and crippled as if her back had been broken, had held herself together and carried on. She sailed as fast as we know she can, and got her crew, who were unaware of her miseries, across 2,000 miles of ocean. Not until it was clear we would make it safely to land did she design to give us an indication of her condition and say, "Guys, you need to get me to the hospital."

Now it's our turn to see if we can save her.

Parrot Talk

1:45 PM local time, Tuesday, December 24 (1745 Dec. 24 UTC).
12° 27.159'N 61° 29.256'W
Temp. 86, Humidity 67%, Cloud Cover 50%.
On the hard at Tyrrel Bay Yacht Haulout, Carriacou Island, Grenada.

Mr. Shrode has taken a ferry to Grenada to await the arrival of Caroline and the Captain is alone on *Maverick*. We have no news yet about *Maverick's* prognosis, but in the meantime on this Christmas Eve, we send our holiday greetings and something to peck at:

In the neck of the woods, if I may use this nautically inappropriate phrase, where we now find ourselves, many who sail boats feel that an activity essential to establishing their bona fides is listening to, and paradoxically, enjoying the music of Jimmy Buffet. A man can gather quite a few fans if he names himself after a manner of serving food, and he might be even more successful with the first name, "Free." In any case, he's doing quite well enough, and such is his success that his fans have adopted a special sobriquet all their own, and it's a reasonable bet that they didn't have to wrestle anybody to get it; they call themselves *Parrotheads*.

The etymology of this word is not without interest, derived as it is from the conjoining of the word *parrot*, meaning a bird of the order *Psittaciformes* with a hooked bill and bright plumage, with *head*, a word meaning an appendage of the body some have found useful, although not the Parrotheads. Further, we can trace the origins of this word to the precedent, "Deadheads" which was derived from "potheads" and "acidheads," which were modified from still earlier appellations, "meathead," "pinhead," "blockhead," and "poo-poo head." It's a shame to see the way the language has degenerated.

In their quaint way, the Parrotheads probably intended a little joke with their name. They may have meant to suggest, "See how we, like the birds, enjoy being manipulated to robotically repeat things we do not comprehend, ha ha." Or they might mean, "See how we, arrayed in our fine, bright, Hawaiian shirts and our hooked beaks, resemble our betters, the parrots!" Or "You couldn't tell it by looking at me, but my brain is the size of a parrot's!"

But my hypothesis is that each one actually has a real parrot inside his head, and in the event of the untimely death of a Parrothead (although how could such a thing be untimely?), an autopsy would reveal, inside an otherwise vacant cranium, a dead parrot. Unless, that is, there exists among Parrotheads a transmigration of the parrot, so that upon the death of the body, the parrot flies out the ear and is reborn in another receptacle, in which case the head of the deceased would be quite uninhabited. In any event, this hypothesis, called the *Actual Parrots inside the Heads of the Parrotheads* hypothesis and here published for the first time for peer review, has been found to be, after the rejection of many others, the best way of accounting for the behavior of an ordinary looking but non-human creature, who will, upon drinking a copious amount of alcohol, and hearing a secret provocation from the bird in his head, start singing "Wasted away again, in Margaritaville..." and laughing or crying in a most ignoble and bothersome way. It turns out that you at home can contribute to the march of science by helping to empirically verify our thesis, by simply chopping open the head of any Jimmy Buffet fan you see, and emailing us your conclusions.

Now, it can't be said that Mr. Buffet has no talent, unless the five words immediately preceding the comma preceding the word "unless" in this sentence actually do the very thing that it started off by saying couldn't be done, in which case we must set it aside to be examined at a later time with a view to analyzing its logical structure.

It's true he has a flat voice, but his apologists will say that Bob Dylan can't sing, either. This is a canard, and to refute it, compare anyone else's rendering of, say, "Don't Think Twice, It's Alright" with Dylan's own. Dylan's voice communicates defeat, resignation, bitterness, tenderness, love, courage, anguish, forgiveness, and hope. A lesser singer will be doing well to achieve a mawkish suggestion of self-pity, but I'm sorry to say even this is beyond the emotional range of Mr. Buffet's instrument.

It's also true that Buffet's sense of irony rarely rises to the level of the sophomoric but in fairness to him, this is above average for an entertainer. It's way below Bugs and Daffy, though.

One day back in the mid-60s, I was driving on the freeway and "Shotgun" came on the radio. The sound of the saxophone on this record so enraptured me, unexpected and fresh as it was and yet at the same time comforting and familiar, that I found it necessary to pull the car over to the side of the road so that every cell of my body could be focused on perceiving and absorbing what was being played. A few years later, through a series of coincidences, some groveling, and the deep and unaccountable generosity of the universe, I had the honor of being retained by Mr. Junior Walker in the percussion chair of his ensemble, the "All-Stars."

Junior Walker was one of the most lyrical musicians of my generation. His tone is big and powerful but silky and erotic; no saxophonist has matched it. Often, players would talk their way backstage to ask Junior about his horn. They learned that it was a good Selmer with a metal mouthpiece and a reed that was neither hard nor soft—nothing out of the ordinary for a professional. They were looking for the secret to his tone, but they'd never find it there, because that's not where it was. It was in his heart.

His phrasing, so fluid, technically precise, and possessed of a subtlety its directness belies, depends on force, exuberance, and commitment rather than complexity. It has been imitated with effete results by many others, few of whom would ever admit his influence. The genre is simply born too much of the chitlin' circuit to possess either the faux gravitas or the facile cynicism the *beau monde* prefers. In Mr. Walker's oeuvre, there is little of the pseudo-intellectual adventurism that the critics of the day celebrated, peppered as it is with such songs as "Shake and Fingerpop" and "Pucker Up, Buttercup." He was a real limited guy. He didn't know about anything except joy.

Generally, Junior would count off every song by tapping his foot, but as one of my duties, it fell to me to cue the beginning of "Shotgun" by playing the syncopated snare drum figure at the top of the song. This was the finale, the flagship, the climax of the show, and the recollection of Junior pointing to me and with a smile calling, "Shotgun," and the thrill of laying down those familiar, famous, first strokes, to this day makes me feel like jumping up and down in glee. Okay, so I really do.

We were playing in Myrtle Beach, South Carolina, one hot and humid summer night. The venue, a dance hall, held perhaps 3,000 and was packed. When Junior stepped onto the stage, he transformed, like a sorcerer, every musician in the band into something he could not otherwise be. He was never a disappointment, but that night his playing was on some higher level. At one point in the performance, if memory serves it was the vamp out of "Sweet Soul," Junior began playing such great stuff that I felt faint, right there on the stage. It was the same feeling I had back on the freeway in San Diego, that I just did not want to do anything but listen to what he was playing. Performing my part seemed so far away, and listening to him so mesmerizing, that I felt disassociated from my hands and feet, and out of breath. I wanted to stop time and go up to him and say, "Hey, Junior, if you want me to do my job, you're just going to have to cool it."

I made it through the tune but it was one of those nights when the audience too seemed aware of some extra energy in the room. We got off the stage, did an encore or two, and then repaired to the dressing room. But the crowd was hysterical. The place had to close, but everyone was screaming for us to come back and no one would leave. They sang "How Sweet It Is to Be Loved by You" over and over. We were trapped in an 8x8 room for what seemed like an hour, I remember cuz I needed to pee, while the police kept the crowd from backstage and calmly cleared everyone out of the building. That was nothing compared to what Junior played, though.

As of the time of the present holiday, I suppose I haven't completely given up aspiring to eternal life, or escaping the cycle of death and rebirth, or achieving nirvana. But those are paths that I seldom find myself looking down these days. It's not so much that I have a problem with the evidence for any of them; every day at sea, we make decisions with serious consequences, based on our best guess. It's just that after a respectable number of years of effort, I find I don't have the faintest idea what they are.

What I do hope for is to, from time to time, feel the authority, and taste the knee-weakening kiss, of the things on earth that are beautiful. Every musician devotes thousands of tedious hours of his life practicing in anticipation of those rare and magical days that Beauty will deign to use him as her voice. But who's to say that an evening at a local tavern with a few cocktails, some convivial friends, and Jimmy Buffet on the jukebox doesn't satisfy the same human aspiration for perfection?

Who indeed, if not the Captain.

Mr. Walker was lecturing me one night, as occasionally was his wont.

"You know when I go to blowin', and the people can't hep theyselves and they commence to dancin' and shoutin' and carryin' on? Some folks say, 'They partyin'.' But that ain't what they doin'. Naaaaahhh. That ain't it at all. You know what they doin'?"

He looked at me in earnest, with a paradoxical pride that was more that of a monk humble before a mysterious secret he was anxious to communicate than that of a swaggering rhythm and blues star. There was a twinkle in his eye.

He said, "They rejoicin'."

Junior Walker, nee Autry DeWalt Mixon, departed this life November 23, 1995, in Battle Creek, Michigan.

Fixing a Hole

9:45 AM local time, Tuesday, January 15 (1345 Jan. 15 UTC).
12° 27.159'N 61° 29.256'W
Temp. 79, Humidity 72%, Cloud Cover 50%.
On the hard at Tyrrel Bay Yacht Haulout, Carriacou Island, Grenada.

I arose early today and was greeted by a torrent of rain from a passing squall just before dawn. It lent the bay a romantic ambiance as the anchor lights of the boats twinkled through the twilight mist and gently swayed in the swell. The crew of *Maverick* has removed itself from the boat to get out of the way of the work being done and to avoid the clouds of fiberglass dust in the cabin, and we have sealed up the lockers in the hope of keeping the dust confined to an area that can be cleaned. We have taken lodgings in a cottage on the hill above the boatyard that, although utilitarian and lacking hot water, has a veranda with a beautiful view of the anchorage, and what's more, cable with HBO. For the first time since March of 2001, I'm able to watch programming that is 100% American. I saw the 49ers get thumped in the playoffs instead of the non-stop soccer the rest of the world calls *football*, and I watched Tom Brokaw giving the news rather than CNN. And although I'm way behind because of all the episodes I've missed, I'm starting to catch up on the Teletubbies.

Ship's Jet-Setter Terry Shrode has flown home to visit Caroline, whose planned Christmas rendezvous with him in Carriacou was aborted when she was not able to get a flight out of San Francisco. It's the third time since we've left that he's been to America and been able to see the changes that have taken place in our absence. I have made a vow to stay with *Maverick* until she is able to return, although this policy is subject to review pending the outcome of the present repairs.

There are times when world history hangs in the balance, and this is one of them. What if the boat can't be made seaworthy, but we are convinced it is, and then we sink and die, and as a result I fail to discover the secret to cheap fusion power? It's ultimately my decision whether we are ready for sea or not, not that of the experts repairing the boat, and this is where the Captain feels the full burden of command. The guys at the yard will not be aboard in the teeth of a gale when and if the hull decides it's not quite fixed yet. But that's why they pay me the big bucks.

Maverick has a big hole in its hull where the local glass man, George, has cut out the affected area in preparation for repairs. These unfortunately await the return of Uwe, whose specialty is engineering.

Uwe was committed to another large job that couldn't be dropped simply because the legendary *Maverick* showed up with a big boo-boo.

The damage has been assessed by George, Uwe, Roy (who manages the yard), and a surveyor named Alan Hooper. All of these men inspire confidence and all maintain that the hull can be made seaworthy, which is the reassuring news. The not-so-reassuring news is that no one has any certainty about why it happened, and this includes the boat's designer, Bruce King, who was reluctant to venture an opinion on the phone. All claim to have never seen anything like it except on boats at the highest end of competitive racing, e.g., the America's Cup. There are two possible explanations of its rarity, and one is that it never has happened. The other is a little more sinister, which is that although it has happened before, the boats it happened to sank, and never made it to a yard where the damage could be scrutinized.

In all sailboats, the mast is trying to push through the bottom of the boat and the weight of the keel is pulling in the same direction, while the two ends of the boat are buoyant and pushing up, and the stays are trying to pull them up towards the masthead. So theoretically, all sailboats could break in half just where *Maverick* did. But they don't, and *Maverick* did, and beyond that actuality lies speculation. It's not too comforting that the fact that all these boat experts have never seen anything like this before means they have never fixed anything like this before.

Right now, as the Captain channel-surfs in his bungalow, he is biting his nails hoping the repairs can be done in time to get to Panama in time to get through the Canal in time to get to San Diego in time to miss the hurricane season off the Mexican coast. The rest of our planned cruise through the lovely islands of this area of the world is out the window, in a manner similar to a large chunk of the Captain's savings. Assuming the repairs are done in time, the next worry is whether they will hold through the big following seas of the western Caribbean and the thousands of miles of head seas on the way towards home.

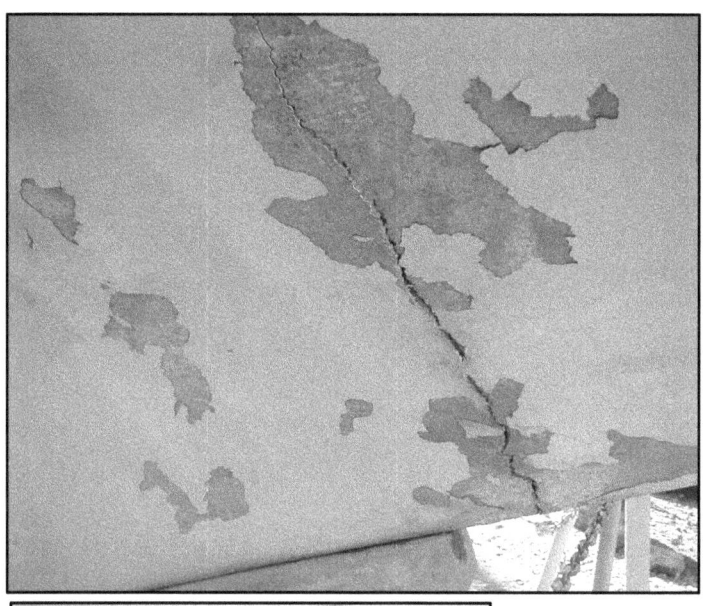

SEA TRIALS

8:30 PM local time, Wednesday, February 19 (0030 Feb. 20 UTC).
12° 29.597'N   70° 0.783'W
Temp. 84, Humidity 67%, Cloud Cover 30%.
At anchor in Paarden Baai, Aruba.

There were a lot of tasks to accomplish in Carriacou. In addition to the hull repair, we re-tuned the rig, installed a new knotmeter and transducer, added an alarm to the bilge, disassembled the Monitor vane and installed a new part to replace the one that failed in the Atlantic crossing, replaced the prop shaft coupling to deal with the vibration that had prevented us from using the engine, put on another coat of bottom paint, installed a check valve in the exhaust to prevent seawater from following seas entering the engine, replaced the transmission cable, and disassembled the steering system in the binnacle, a job that took Mr. Shrode two days just to get to a set screw that needed tightening. And now we were afloat again.

It was a dark and stormy night, the night we launched. But being warm and dry in the cozy cabin of a small boat anchored in a protected harbor on a stormy night, as long as it's not too stormy, is one of the snuggest feelings in the world. Theresa had come to visit and returned home, but she had left with us a tape of Dorothy Love Coates and the Gospel Harmonettes, which, now having access to *Maverick's* stereo, we played for the first time as we hoisted a couple of beverages in celebration of being back on the water. Had I not the company of Ms. Fisher to look forward to at another distant time, in comparison to which all other pleasures are but weak tea, I could have considered our situation heaven on earth.

The next day we made the rounds and said our goodbyes to all the good people we'd come to know in Carriacou. George and Uwe, who'd fixed the boat, were busy on a new project but stopped long enough to hear a brief word of gratitude from the skipper. Jerry and Roy, the owner and manager, respectively, of Tyrrel Bay Yacht Haulout, and their assistant Kisha had been uncommonly generous and helpful in arranging odd things for us, like a place to stay, which normally wouldn't fall under the heading of boatyard responsibilities. And we will never forget that when we first met Jerry and Roy, they were at the dock with the Travel Lift ready to go as the ailing *Maverick* limped her way to the slings, and it was their quick action that saved the boat.

We bid farewells to Luciana, Daniella, and Benton at the Turtle Dove, a pizza place near the boatyard, and to John Smith, a real salt who's been cruising Central America and the Caribbean since 1968 in engineless, wooden boats. I think Trevor, who runs the Carriacou Yacht Club, and Harold of the powerboat *Hallelujah* were disappointed to see us go because they believed that they may have had a chance to convert the Captain to creationism, given just another couple of days. I told them that one small act of fellowship was worth a thousand pages of theology, and since they freely gave the former, the failure to make dents in the thoughts of the Captain on the latter was of little account. Harold still sent me off with a piece of freshly baked cake.

In a couple of days, we sailed to Grenada where Alan Hooper, the surveyor, had a final look at the repairs and determined they were top-drawer. The concept of "six degrees of separation" was at work for us. It turns out that one of our favorite correspondents, WWII and '79 Fastnet vet Hank Strauss, whose character is beyond reproach, solidly vouched for Alan, who had the highest regard for Roy of the boatyard, who had nothing but praise for Uwe and George, not that we needed anything like that string of recommendations to know that Uwe and George were good guys.

The Captain, ignoring warnings that the water in the lagoon at St. George where we anchored in Grenada might not meet the high standards of the EPA, dove overboard and when he got close enough, he could see through the muck that there were no new cracks around the repair, which would have been a bad sign. Although this may seem like an unnecessary precaution, we had a heavy trip in front of us and I wanted to see if the boisterous 30-mile sail from Carriacou had given any indication of movement in the hull.

After having a couple of meals at the Grenada Yacht Club, and reprovisioning and checking out, on Saturday February 15th we sailed with the intention of going straight to the San Blas Islands of Panama, about 1100 miles. But the going was a bit on the heavy side. After sailing over 25,000 miles with little or no damage to the whisker poles, we broke both of them in two days. The wind wasn't all that strong, say 25-30 knots, and the seas weren't all that big, say 10-12 feet. But they were steep and square and very rough. This piece of water begins a somewhat treacherous patch.

We have four main known challenges between here and San Francisco, although many others may present themselves. One is Point Conception, off of Santa Barbara. Another is the Gulf of Tehuantapec in Mexico. The third is the Panama Canal, where things can go awry in the locks. The fourth is the passage from here to Panama, where the seas and currents of the northeast trades come up against a stone wall as they dead end at Central America. Our friends on the Canadian Cal-39 *Delphis*, who are now a little ahead of us and who have raved about all the islands

The Captain and Mr. Shrode

we will miss visiting because of the repair, reported heavy, steep seas in this area that they described as "scary." These guys are on the last legs of a five-year circumnavigation, so for them to have called the seas scary made one pause. They were repeatedly pooped, took water down the companionway, and lost a solar panel when it was ripped off its mount by a wave.

So when we heard on a weather net, after three days of heavy going, that we could expect even heavier weather around the top of Columbia in the next few days, we elected to divert to Aruba to await better conditions. When we rounded the northwest end of the island to get into the lee, the wind that accelerated around the landmass hit 35, then 40, 45, and finally gusted to 50 knots. We had a bit of a job close-reaching in that wind to get to our present anchorage. Even in here, it's blowing like stink but there's a sand bottom with good holding.

Mr. Shrode and the Captain spent the day kluging together one good pole from the remains of the two broken ones. It'll do fine, particularly as the 500-600 miles we will sail from here to Panama will probably be the last downwind sailing of the circumnavigation. If we don't make a mistake with the pole, there's no reason it won't last that long.

Meanwhile, Ship's Chef Terry Shrode, who is required by regulations to wear one of those silly puffy hats when making deserts, has taken inspiration from Harold back on Carriacou and baked a cake tonight.

We put on the Gospel Harmonettes again. I once saw Dorothy Love Coates at the Cow Palace in San Francisco. She was, in her prime, an imposing figure. She looked like she could have played in the NFL, and if I were a lineman on the opposing side and she looked at me with that, "Son, you might as well step aside 'cause I'm COMING THROUGH" look of hers, by God I'd get out of the way. She did for the street what Mahalia did for the concert hall and as long as she sang, you were a Christian. She's singing, "There's No Hiding Place Down Here." No sailor is going to argue with that.

A Different Drummer

8:30 AM local time, Friday, February 28 (1330 Feb. 28 UTC.)
9 30N 79 1W
Temp. 83, Humidity 80%, Cloud Cover 100%.
At anchor behind Carti Tupile, an island in the San Blas Archipelago, on the north coast of Panama.

Our last report had us anchored off of Aruba, where we had decided to await better weather conditions before heading around the top of Columbia. But after three days of waiting for the wind to subside, our best information was that it would be another week before we could expect milder conditions, and as we weren't willing to hold off that long, we'd just have to go out there and take our medicine.

A couple of days later, I was a little cranky since I had not slept much in the last two days at sea, during which time my total diet had consisted of a cup of soup and about seven saltines. I had a splitting headache, my back was cramped from holding myself from falling out of the nav station, and my left foot was throbbing. I had apparently broken some bone in it the day before we left Grenada, a bone so small that a real man wouldn't admit to having one in his body, much less breaking it. As *Maverick*'s x-ray machine is broken, Ship's Orthopedic Surgeon Terry Shrode put a stethoscope on my foot, hit the area of the swelling and discoloration a couple of times with a ball peen hammer, and announced that "it sounds like a fractured phalange to me."

Maverick, just out of the convalescent hospital herself, was taking a pounding. About every two minutes we were getting hit by solid waves that seemed to come from everywhere. It felt like we were inside a big bass drum being played by a very large, but not particularly talented, drummer. One particularly bad one sounded like an explosion or an automobile wreck. I ran, or rather, limped, up on deck expecting to see bent stanchions and gear ripped off the foredeck, but the only thing that seemed strange was how clean it looked.

Maybe now's the time to try to describe how the motion feels in a small boat in a big sea during heavy weather. Imagine a carousel that instead of horses has platforms that go up and down about 12 feet every eight seconds. On top of one of these platforms is a playground merry-go-round being swung back and forth like the motion of a washing machine. On top of the merry-go-round is a rocking chair that has its back cut off so another rocking chair, oriented at a 90-degree angle to the lower one, can sit on top of it. You're in the top rocking chair.

Each stage of this tower is remotely controlled by a 9-year-old boy. He is told to jerk his control back and forth in a manner calculated to produce the most discomfort in the passenger. He is told he is allowed to have no mercy, and that the passenger is his 6-year-old brother. Heavy metal music is being played at a deafening volume. This pattern needs to be sustained for about three days, so the 9-year-old may get bored and quit before then. But the sea won't.

We were on the radio to the famous Herb Hilgenberg of *Southbound II*, a weather guru who helped a lot of people, including ourselves, cross the Atlantic. We were saying to Herb, please make it stop. So he says to us, well, you sail this-a-way and that-a-way and in a day or so when you hit longitude 76, you should see some moderation of the conditions. Herb's a genius, almost, but he had told us we'd see 20-25 out there and we were seeing 30-35. Funny thing was, he seemed not to believe us. He had predicted 20-25, so as far as he was concerned that's what it was, and anyway you know how those sailor guys lie. But we were down to a double-reefed main with about four feet of headsail and *Maverick* was never seeing the south side of 8 knots, surfing to 12 and 13 and even 14. I think it was blowing a bit more than 20.

At least we were going fast. The first three days out of Grenada *Maverick* turned in days of 158, 177, and 170 miles. After leaving Aruba we did 204, 175, and on the third day, the last half of which saw us in somewhat lighter winds, 155 miles.

We're now anchored in the storied San Blas Islands on the north coast of Panama, at the very end of the Atlantic Ocean. We're also at the end of another phase of the voyage, one that had a little more adventure to offer than we would have liked. Our farewell to this side of the American continent will be celebrated in these beautiful islands with the people who inhabit them, often referred to as Kuna Indians.

In our first couple of days here we met Juan Iglesias, and this was a real stroke of luck. A native of the San Blas chain, he speaks fluent English and has a degree in anthropology from a university in Spain. He is writing a book on the history of his people and has not only shared with us a lot of knowledge about the tribe, but he has volunteered to act as our guide for a few days as we sail to some other islands he has chosen and take a dugout canoe trip up a river on the mainland. He refused our offer of money for his troubles.

We have been informed by Juan that *Kuna* is really a word for the dialect, not the people, who are more properly known as the Dule, (pronounced "doo-leh"), or Dules for all the different tribes together, and that Indians are from India, not from here. The land of the Dules is not Panama or the San Blas Islands but Kuna Yala. I think we'll stick with

San Blas Islands so as not to be too confusing to the folks back home, but we will be referring to our hosts as the Dule, and not the Kunas.

Dreamworld

8:30 AM local time, Saturday, March 08 (1330 March 8 UTC).
9° 20.585'N 79° 54.668'W
Temp. 84, Humidity 79%, Cloud Cover 30%.
At anchor in Colon, Panama, the entrance to the Panama Canal.

When you leave the highly civilized industrial world and set out on a small boat to explore the rest of the universe, the dreams that propel you are visions of places like the San Blas Islands. Most of our previous ports of call, even in Africa, were places that, if not thoroughly modern, had cash machines, Internet cafes, cell phones, and satellite dishes. But here in the San Blas Islands, the place the Dule call Kuna Yala, much of the population lives with only rare signs of post Iron Age civilization. Although fairly familiar in the reports of long-distance cruisers, the islands are not well known to the world at large.

There are about 50,000 of the Dule people inhabiting the shoreline and islands on the northeast coast of Panama. They are descendants of the Chibcha people who numbered ten times that many at the time of the Conquistadors, and represented the most highly organized society in South America outside of the Incan Empire. The Incan culture and traditions were crushed by the Spanish between the 16th and 18th centuries, but the stubborn Dules held on to theirs and in 1925 fought off yet another enemy, the Panamanian government, to win their current independence. They were assisted in the battle by the warship *USS Cleveland*, which arrived to take the side of the indigenous people at the direction of Calvin Coolidge.

Today the Dule people have a relationship with the Panamanian authorities that gives them just a bit more separation from the powers that be than our own Native American tribes enjoy. They pay their taxes not to Panama but to their own government body, yet Panama would defend them in the event of an attack by outsiders. But I asked Juan, our guide, what would happen if oil or minerals were discovered in Kuna Yala. He said, "We'd be screwed."

The people mostly live on 49 islands of the 365 of the San Blas chain, some man-made. Some villages also exist on the mainland, where the Dules control a narrow strip of shoreline. It is on the mainland that crops of sugarcane, bananas, coconuts, corn, rice, mangos, and breadfruit are grown on native plantations.

The houses of the Dules give the impression of being those faux, quaint thatched huts that serve as guest rooms in the tourist hotels you see all over the tropical world. But they're not for show. They are made of post-and-beam construction with walls of white cane that is cut from the river banks on the mainland and held together by vines, cloth, or twine. The roof is thatched palm leaves, and the floor is dirt.

There are two separate buildings to each household, one for sleeping and one for cooking, which is done on an open wood fire. Since many dwellings have no doors and the gaps in the cane in the walls are not filled, and since the whole family lives in one room, privacy as we know it is not a feature of Dule life. Furniture consists of hammocks, blocks of wood, and sometimes the molded plastic chairs like the ones we buy at the local Target store. Many islands have no electricity and the only illumination at night comes from a fire on the floor or a simple oil lamp with no chimney. It is pretty amazing that every village doesn't burn down weekly.

The islands are mostly small, inhabited by perhaps 30 families, but some are home to 1,000 people. Transportation between the islands is by the main watercraft of the Dule world, handled mostly by men but with equal skill at times by women: a dugout canoe propelled by oars, sails, or an outboard. The canoes are hand-hewn from cedar. The sailing canoes are spritsail sloops with a headsail but no keel or centerboard, so they are not particularly weatherly as they make a huge amount of leeway. The sails are made from bed sheets or tarps or whatever cloth is available. The local sailors go out in these things in 20 knots and three feet of chop, with a full load of goods and little in the way of either form or ballast stability. They will hike out holding onto a line attached to the masthead, not unlike what we would call a trapeze. I would be a bit daunted to try to sail one of these between the islands, which are often many miles apart, unless I had a native skipper.

On the islands, fresh water is obtained by sailing or paddling your canoe a couple of miles to the nearest river on the mainland each day and filling 5-gallon plastic containers, returning around dawn. For this reason only the islands reasonably close to a mainland water source are inhabited. As far as plumbing is concerned, around the island one sees short piers, and at the end of these is a little hut. The interested party goes out to one of these to "send a fax," or more currently, "send an email," according to Juan. The sea disposes of the sewage.

One gets the impression of friendliness, cleverness, and competence from the Dule. Unlike what many might expect to see in an environment so devoid of modern conveniences, the people are energetic, canny, and enterprising. It is interesting to ponder how much of this is due to the fact that they have maintained their freedom and independence for so long. Of course, you could argue the reverse, that they have remained independent because they are canny and enterprising. So many of the indigenous people we've seen seem apathetic and lethargic by comparison.

The Dule are also very beautiful. Their strong faces remind one of the pictures of Peruvian natives. They have a prominent nose, high cheekbones, and sharp, alert, hawk-like eyes and though they are slight, their physical impression is proud and even haughty. But their personalities are gentle to the point of shyness.

The island we anchored at when we first arrived is described by Juan as a "tourist" island, although I think few of those reading this would find the atmosphere too "touristy." You can get to the airport at Porvenir by means of a short flight from Panama City and the details can be found in the *Lonely Planet Guide to Panama*. But the Hotel San Blas on Nalunega, and others like it, will not have air-conditioning or cable TV. You may get a concrete floor and a bed as opposed to a dirt floor and a hammock, but otherwise your accommodations will be similar to those of the natives. There are no golf courses. On the other hand, the Dule know their market value. Molas and other native crafts are sold by their makers, and if you want to take a picture of the native women (about whom more in a minute) on the "tourist" islands it'll cost you $1 per photo per woman. One photo of three women, to do the math for you, is $3.

Juan sailed with us aboard *Maverick*, guiding us to two "non-touristy" islands in the eastern Gulf of San Blas. On these islands there was no electricity and the people were quite a bit shyer than on Nalunega, but fortunately we had Juan to help break the ice. The second island we visited is called Nellie on the charts but Soledad Mandiga by the natives. Ashore, our beards were the subject of much curiosity, and among those under ten months of age, terror, as no men (or women) in this society have facial hair. Taking pictures is forbidden without the consent both of the individuals involved and the chief of the island, but the goal of anyone with a camera is to take pictures of the women of the Dule, the most spectacularly attired women, in my experience, on our planet. Unfortunately, they are also the shyest and most likely to hide their face, or run inside, when a camera comes out of the bag.

With the help of Juan, however, we maneuvered ourselves into a position where people practically begged us to take their photos. We did this by taking pictures of people who didn't mind, and this included the island's chief. Returning to the boat, the Captain took out his Canon BJC-50 printer, which is not a very good printer but is only as big as a carton of cigarettes and runs on its own battery or 12-volt power. We printed out a picture of the chief and returned to the island with it. This caused a sensation. Next, the bolder women were willing to have photos taken of their babies, at times in their mother's arms. These were printed out and caused another wave of excitement, and after that the Captain had them lining up for photos. I'm afraid the really shy ones still couldn't get up the nerve, so we didn't get a shot of every woman and child on the island, but we got a lot.

Why are the women so photogenic? Of course it starts with their natural beauty. But the further key is their native dress. For the benefit of our female readers, and those male readers who from time to time enjoy wearing women's clothes, the Captain will describe how their colorful look is achieved. Starting from the top, the older women always, and younger ones usually, wear a bright red scarf of store-bought material, loosely draped over the head. The cheekbones are rouged with an orange substance from a local tree, and a stripe is applied down the center of the nose with makeup. I'll leave it to our readers to find appropriate substitutes in the cosmetics departments of their choosing. A blouse with puffy elbow-length sleeves, sewn from a store-bought print of any color, is worn, and the bodice, from the breast to the waist, is constructed of the famous *molas* of the Dule people. These are brightly embroidered panels made of two or more layers of cloth sewn in a reverse-appliqué method, a foot or so square. The commercial ones turned out for tourists are made in a couple of hours, but the ornate traditional ones may take a week or more to finish, using hand-powered sewing machines. The skirt is a wrap-around cloth of colorful store-bought prints, usually blue, and shoes are simple sandals from a store in the city. As to foundation garments, about which many of our readers are no doubt curious, the Captain quite innocently came upon the answer to this question and can say with some certainty that under this spectacular costume women sport the same sort of underwear that they do in Fresno.

The ensemble just described is extravagantly ornate and colorful, and by itself would be plenty striking, but accessorizing takes it to a different level. There are bracelets covering the lower arms from elbow to wrist, and leggings covering the calves from knee to ankle, made of tiny plastic beads strung together to form bright geometric patterns. The beads are sewn together around the arms and legs and not taken off until replaced, about every three months or so. Finally, as if more accessories were needed to spice up a drab outfit, the women often sport gold earrings, necklaces, nose-rings, and as many as eight finger rings, all made by Dule crafts persons. You might think that clothes designed to fit the tastes of "primitive" people wouldn't look fashionable or sexy to us, compared to the modern western clothes Britney wears. You'd be wrong, wrong, wrong.

The entire outfit, except for the jewelry, is a product of the desire of these women to show off their beauty in spite of the strict prohibitions of the missionaries who taught them that to display their naked bodies was a sin in the eyes of God. The patterns on the molas are copies of the original body paint the women used before the coming of Christianity with the Spanish. The Spanish also introduced cheap beads which provided a ready alternative for their traditional paint. It's a sign that the Dule women have been able to adapt to changing conditions, whether they're enforced by a new religion or accomplished through more extensive trade, without sacrificing their traditional standards of feminine beauty.

Amazingly, the women don't wear their costume just for special days or for tourist shows but dress this way at all times, while the men wear aging t-shirts and shorts, with baseball caps. I don't know whether the fact that this is a matrilineal society explains that or not. The women own the property and control the household finances, but oddly they do not participate in the political process of the tribe, which is controlled by a council of chiefs.

The Dules' ability to adopt elements of modernity without forsaking their traditional culture extends to their relationship to nearby Panama City. The islands we visited are about a half hour from the airport by the canoes with an outboard. The flight to Panama City takes about 20 minutes, and costs $30, the price of three *molas*. Alternatively, from the village on the mainland we visited by canoe, it's an eight-hour walk and then a $3.25 bus ride to the city.

According to Juan, most local people go to the city from time to time and have therefore been exposed to CDs, movies, television, and the rest of modern life. But they return to their peaceful villages and, unlike the Lau group in Fiji, do not seem to worry about corruption from the outside world. The owner of the San Blas Hotel, a native of the chain, is quite well off and owns several houses in Panama City. But he almost never goes there. Despite the fact that as in many places of the world, young people are moving to the cities to work, there is plenty of vitality here and no sense of being in the last stages of a society's history.

Maverick's excursion in the San Blas Islands under Juan's guidance took us to the tiny Carti Island group, and then to the equally diminutive Soledad Mandiga, the one where we took photos and did not have to pay the $1 fee. In the Carti Islands, there was a four-day celebration taking place, and as far as we could tell, there were two things being celebrated. One was the anniversary of the 1925 revolution against the government of Panama, and the other was the onset of puberty for two girls of the village. Maybe things have changed in America, but when I was a lad, the beginning of the menstrual cycle was a matter of mystery and embarrassment. The young woman in question may not even have felt free to mention its occurrence to her mother, much less her father, or horror of horrors, her brother or the neighbors. Men were often so ignorant of the entire process that women would shield them from any knowledge of it whatsoever, lest they faint.

But here it is different. Upon a girl's having her first period, the entire village is alerted and a two- or four-day celebration begins. The girl, or in the case of the celebration we witnessed, the two girls, are housed, actually confined, in a small thatched hut constructed just for the occasion. They can be visited and observed by anyone, even two white guys from California. They have their friends over and do a lot of giggling. Each mother comes in and bathes her daughter often, alternating fresh and salt water. We did not observe this part of the celebration.

Meanwhile, the adults gather in the *circa* or community center, where both religious and governmental functions take place. They've been fermenting *chicha*, which is made from sugarcane and is mildly alcoholic, and now they drink it, along with a more recent addition, rum. Rum, although also made from sugarcane, is not part of ancient Dule tradition.

Ship's Anthropologist Terry Shrode and the Captain attended the celebration in the community center. It's a large version of a Dule house, perhaps 60 x 40 feet, the peak of the thatched roof about 25 feet above the dirt floor. Even in daytime, it's pretty dark inside. Though we are obviously not locals, no one takes special notice of us. There is a *kantule*, the leader of the ceremony, lying in a hammock in the middle of the room who is singing in a rather non-melodic fashion, and his singing tells various stories of the mythology and history of the Dule, plus the history and situation of the two girls. I'm given the impression by Glomildo, another native who along with Juan acted as interpreter, that the lyrics the *kantule* sings describe the girls' current condition and their future wedded life in graphic detail.

A chicken that will be killed at the end of the ceremony is tied under the singer's hammock. A bowl full of incense burns near the chicken. To accompany the singing, men dressed in the ceremonial costume of a blue shirt, accessorized with a necklace of noisemakers, and a black hat that I would have called a pork-pie, dance a sort of crude jig. The dance seems to be impromptu, and men get up one at a time or in pairs, as the spirit moves them.

Even though it is a celebration, there is neither the festive air nor the solemnity that the word would suggest to outsiders. As it's four days long, there may be an ebb and flow, and we may have been there at a low energy point. Or maybe not. People sit around the dimly lit building talking quietly and paying little attention to the singer, apparently indifferent to the notion that their conversation may distract from the focus of the event. The women on one side and men on the other chat, walk around, or just sit and smoke cigarettes in silence while the singing continues. Although the *kantule* physically holds the position of honor in the middle of the building, I would not have called the mood towards him particularly reverential.

Mr. Shrode was informed that it would be showing good will to buy a couple of bottles of rum at $6 each for the assembled. The bottles were ordered and showed up, and at this point they are given to a sort of wine steward, who takes the bottle and a small cup and goes around the room pouring a shot for each person. In the end, people become fairly inebriated, but still not raucous, at least as far as we were able to observe. The party might have gotten wilder after we were gone. Or maybe not.

Our understanding was that later that evening, after we had returned to the boat, the girls would have been brought from their little hut into the room and would have had their noses pierced and their heads shaved bald. When their hair grows out, as mature women they will adopt the hairstyle of the grown-up Dule female, a Beatle-cut.

We visited a village on the mainland by canoe. It is said in the cruising guide that you can take your dinghy up the rivers on the mainland, but on the river we took, the Mandy Yala, you wouldn't have gotten very far. It was frequently shallow and full of fallen trees and submerged logs, and sometimes swift. It was very hard work getting up the eight or so miles to the village that was our goal, and fortunately Ubaldo, our boatman, and Juan were expert canoe handlers. Juan, whose full name is Juan Amado Iglesias, is, as we've said, an indigenous Dule and despite his familiarity with city life, tribal politics, and the history and mythology of the Dule, he is not so citified that he has forgotten all the skills learned in his youth. It was four hours of paddling, poling, and walking the canoe through the shallowest parts before we arrived at the village.

At one point I noticed some movement out of the corner of my eye and looked around just in time to see a wide, grinning mouthful of teeth submerge.

I asked Juan if that was a crocodile, and he said, no, it was an alligator.

I said, Juan, let me get this straight. We have for quite a while now been walking along, pushing the boat up a river that you now tell us is full of alligators? They don't, like, bite, do they?

He said, no, not usually.

I said, Juan, would it be too much trouble for you to get a little more specific about the use of the word "usually," as it pertains to not being chewed up by alligators in this river?

He said, don't worry, no problem.

Folks, when you travel around the world, no matter what country you go to outside of the industrialized nations, a universally used English phrase you never, ever, want to hear—a phrase that instantly makes the blood run cold even though it is always said with a big smile—is "no problem." In Tahiti, when we entered the channel to Papeete and called on 16 to request instructions on anchoring, the person on the radio had only one thing to say: "no problem." The full meaning of this phrase happened to be, in this context, "I don't care where you anchor. But wait until you meet the port captain. Compared to dealing with him, right now you have no problem." When you meet the port captain, you find that, although there are 206 bones in his body, none of them is a funny one. In Thailand, "no problem" means "What you're requesting cannot be done, so it doesn't inconvenience me in the least." In Egypt, "no problem" means "this is going to cost you a very large sum of money."

So when Juan said there was "no problem," it didn't slow my elevated heart rate one bit. What I had hoped to hear him say was that the alligators preferred smaller prey, like little children, and I was further hoping that plenty of little children were nearby.

As we proceeded along our jolly, alligator-infested way, we saw two men in a boat full of bananas headed downriver for market, and a young family harvesting coconuts and bananas. We bought four coconuts and the woman, dressed in the manner described above even as she waded through the river, took a machete and quickly hacked off a slice from each, leaving a hole we could drink the milk from. Then, when she and her husband had filled their canoe, she left him and headed up the river, pulling the boat, containing her small child as well, back to the village. Though we had four grown men aboard, we could not keep up with her. Juan said that she would be returning to her house, from her plantation. Her husband provided labor and help, but she owned the property.

When we arrived at the village, the air was dryer than on the islands. A few villagers had horses, but the canoe was the main transportation, up the same way we'd come. The houses were farther apart than they are on the islands, where space is at a premium, but otherwise the layout and construction were the same.

The chief of the village was ill the day we were there so it wasn't possible to get permission to photograph, but Juan said it was okay if I took a shot of a local house when no one was around. I took only the one photo so I didn't get any pictures of the inhabitants, but I can report that, as remote as they are, the women of this village wear the same everyday costume as their friends and relatives on the islands. And despite the fact that wading in a muddy stream may be a part of the day's chores, their clothes are neater, and considerably cleaner, than those of the Captain.

We returned in the afternoon to *Maverick*. Ubaldo carefully steered his outboard-powered canoe from the mouth of the river through the chop whipped up by a 20-knot northeasterly, so as to minimize the spray on the two old Merkis, or Americans. It was a reasonably dry two or so miles to our anchorage in the lee of Soledad Mandiga. The next day we sailed with Juan back to the island of Nalunega, about an hour's distance.

On the last day we were at the island, we had the honor of meeting the highest chief of all the Dule, who is a resident of Soledad Mandiga. After our meeting, word came to Juan that he and the chief were to fly to Panama City to greet a delegation from the indigenous people of Guatemala. They've flown off now, to the modern world.

To the end, Juan refused to accept any payment for his guide services, but we finally persuaded him to take a donation for the community, along with a fistful of photos from our printer and a thank-you note written in the Kuna dialect. Oddly, on our last night at anchor in the San Blas Islands, both Mr. Shrode and the Captain experienced vivid, intense, and disturbing dreams.

LET US CROSS OVER

8:30 PM local time, Monday, March 10 (0130 March 9 UTC).
9° 20.585'N 79° 54.668'W
Temp. 84, Humidity 73%, Cloud Cover 20%.
At anchor in Colon, Panama, the entrance to the Panama Canal.

We're sitting in a rather cranky anchorage inside the seawall at the northern entrance to the Panama Canal. Somewhere between 40 and 50 boats are anchored nearby, awaiting their transit like *Maverick*. There are a dozen more or so at the Panama Canal Yacht Club, and because of the backup, boats are biding their time for somewhere between one and two weeks to get through. If *Maverick* goes through on schedule, it will have been a ten-day wait since our arrival.

The reason it takes so much longer here than in the Suez or Corinth Canals is the lock system, which makes the transit a much more complicated and slower process, so there's a bottleneck. The way it works is that on the north side, for ships coming from the Atlantic, and the south side, for ships coming from the Pacific, in the morning all the very large ships go up, and, having crossed Gatun Lake in the middle, in the afternoon they go down. This is so that the ships, which are designed to be as big as possible and still get through the canal, can have daylight to see the two feet of clearance they have on each side. The Canal wants the yachts to go through in daylight as well, but many of us will not make it through the lake during the day because of, for example, a late trip up through the locks. So we may spend the night at anchor in the lake and wait until the next afternoon, when lock traffic starts down again. The yachts transit in the small space just aft of the big ships, in the same lock. During the night, less troublesome ships, such as freighters with plenty of clearance, will pass through the locks, as the locks are operated 24 hours a day.

All ships except yachts are kept from hitting the sides by locomotives, six on each side, that have steel cables running to the ship. A pilot with a lot of experience takes command of the ship and by radio directs the operators of the locomotives when to ease and when to tighten the cables. There is no computerized system for either advancing the locomotives or tensioning the lines; it's all done by judgment calls and it really doesn't seem like it would work but it does. In fact, although the locomotives are of a more recent design, the entire system works in the same way with pretty much the same equipment as it did when it opened in 1914. I won't go into much detail here, since I'm sure there is a website with pictures that explains the whole thing, but Ship's Historian of Engineering Marvels Terry Shrode and the Captain took the time to visit the first set of three locks the other day and it's an impressive piece of business.

All yachts are required to have four line handlers on board in addition to the helmsman, and there also will be a pilot on board to direct our movements. This means we've had to hire three local guys. You can do it with backpackers, but I was a hippie at one time in my life and so I have a pretty good idea what kind of job they may do. We also must have four lines 125 feet long, and those we rent. We actually might be able to come close to that with what's on board, but we'd have to cut a couple of anchor rodes. *Maverick* is also befetished with ten old tires wrapped in garbage bags acting along with our regular fenders to deal with unplanned but possible contact with things we don't want to contact.

All this costs money. The transit fee is $600 plus an $800 deposit, which can be handled by signing off on the $1400 with a Visa (but not Master) Card. They don't actually charge your account the other $800 unless something goes wrong. If you pay in cash, you have to fork over the entire $1400 and wait a couple of months for the refund. The line handlers are $55 per day per man and it often takes two days. (The pilot comes with the transit fee.) Lines rent for $60, and tires are $3 each, complete with bags. The anchorage is free, but they charge you $2 a day to use the dinghy dock at the yacht club.

My insurance company said I was insured from the Atlantic home to San Francisco, but then said "Oh, you're going through the Canal? That's an extra $160." Of course, it's probably another $1000 if you go around the Horn or truck your boat home. And since my insurance expires on the 15th and we leave on the 13th, if we get bumped a day, I have to get another endorsement, for another $160, for next year's policy to cover the 15th. The entire story is even more irritating, but you're bored already. The whole thing, counting the extra insurance but not the dinghy dock and the deposit, is $1180. With no insurance, using backpackers, and going to the dump yourself to find tires, you should make it for under $750. On the other hand, the big yachts use agents to do the paperwork, which although slightly tedious is really no problem, and the agents can cost $600 more. The fees for the big ships are quite a bit more impressive. Some pay over $200,000, but this is still far cheaper for them than the alternative, going around the Horn.

THE GREAT DIVIDE

11:30 AM local time, Friday, March 14 (1630 March 14 UTC).
8° 56.330'N 79° 33.487'W
Temp. 84, Humidity 73%, Cloud Cover 90%.
On a mooring at the Balboa Yacht Club, Panama City. In the Pacific Ocean.

A lot of people watched us go through the Canal via the Internet site for the webcam at the Miraflores locks. I realize that there are still some people who believe the Apollo landings on the moon were staged in a hangar in Arizona by the Disney people, and so the few on this list who continually accuse the Captain of composing his missives from a condo in Milpitas will probably remain unconvinced that we're actually doing this, but we can't do much more than be on the 21st-century version of TV to prove it. You can without scruple, it is my opinion, believe anything you see on the Internet.

Here's how the day went. We were told on the day before that we had a "pilot time" of 4:00 AM. This means that the pilot boat will deliver your "advisor" at 4 in the morning. The 4:00 time meant that we had to pick up our line handlers at the dinghy dock at 3:30, which meant we got up at 2:30 to get everything ready to go. When our sleepy-eyed line handlers came aboard, we thought we'd better hurry to get the dinghy up in time for the pilot, but they said that daylight would be soon enough and they were right about that. A call to "Cristobal Signal," the man on the radio who gives ships and yachts instructions on channel 12 about their movements in preparation for entering the locks, confirmed the suspicions of the line handlers; the pilot was now scheduled for 5:30. The line handlers took to the bunks below and napped. The advisor actually arrived about 6:30, so we'd been up a few hours too soon, but whatever. We immediately got the anchor up and headed directly for the locks.

Actually, we made one short stop. The pilot was told that we had no refrigeration and that all the ice we had gotten the night before to keep drinks cold for our guests had melted. He had us stop at a dock just before the locks, where he had called ahead to have someone waiting with a big bag of ice. They have their standards.

The procedure is to lash three sailboats together to transit the locks, and it was determined that *Maverick* would act as the center boat. The decision was based on the horsepower of the boats' engines. The Moorings Beneteau 403 on our right weighs, according to its delivery skipper, only about 11,000 pounds, and therefore little horsepower is required to push it. The small boat on our left also had a less powerful engine. *Maverick's* 45-horsepower Perkins 4-107 would be the workhorse.

Before we got to the first lock of the three Gatun locks that would raise us to the level of Gatun Lake, where the majority of the miles of the crossing would take place, our advisor told us to raft up with the Moorings boat and the other boat, the New-Zealand-flagged *Honey*. He instructed me to put the boat beam-to the wind, but I politely suggested that, as we had a bit of a breeze and chop, I thought we might be safer to be head-to-wind, and this was agreed to. During the raft-up, it became apparent that our on-board line handlers' knowledge of knots was not quite at the level of seamanship one might have hoped for, meaning that somewhat more attention had to be paid by Bosun Terry Shrode and the Captain to the proceedings. But everything got done as well as was needed, without any damage, as had occurred a couple of days before when one boat for some reason t-boned the center yacht on its approach.

My advisor had told me that I, your Captain, would be driving the three boats and controlling our speed and course with my throttle and helm. At this point it would have been a good idea if he had explained to the other skippers that, when needed, they might be called upon to help turn or slow the raft, but this wasn't done, occasioning some raised voices later on. I took the helm and drove the ungainly mess towards the first lock.

On the way up, you are positioned just aft of a gigantic container ship, and on the way down, just forward of a similar ship. When you motor into place, all three boats are put gently into reverse and you stop. Four on-shore line handlers toss monkey fists with light line to the boats, which are far below them, two to the starboard boat and two to the port boat. These lines are tied by the line handlers on the yachts to the stouter, 7/8" lines onboard, and then these are drawn up by the on-shore handlers and each looped around a bollard on the top edge of the lock walls.

The mighty gates then slowly close and water starts entering in holes at the bottom of the lock. As we rise, the line handlers take up the slack that occurs, keeping the raft in the center of the lock. The water raises us and the big ship at four feet per minute or so, and we are lifted about 27 feet in each of the three locks. When we reach the top, our lines are cleated off, the forward gates are opened, and the container ship moves forward to the next lock. Its own power is used for locomotion, so we are caught in the prop wash, but this puts less strain on the lines than one would have thought, and the advisors wait until it is well clear of us before having us release our lines.

What happens next is that the 7/8" lines are released from their bollards and tossed into the lock, with the ends still secured to the light lines that are retained by the on-shore line handlers. The on-board line handlers haul the big lines aboard. I am told to put *Maverick* in forward, and I drive us into the next lock and the process is repeated. As I drive, the four on-shore line handlers who hold the light lines walk along the lock and I am instructed to control my speed to match an easy walk. Since we are going up in the next lock, they will have to climb a flight of stairs between the locks, so when we get to the second one, they will be far above us.

When the third lock has brought us to the highest level, we can look back, which is really north, not east, and wave goodbye to the Atlantic Ocean. This is the last sight we'll have of it. The lock gates are opened and we motor just outside and untie the raft. At this point we are told to use the sails if we wish, and since it's downwind, we just unfurl the headsail. But as the wind is patchy on the Gatun Lake, we also motor to keep up a good speed. Our schedule for making it to the locks on the other side has been set on the basis of the speeds the sailboats say they can make at the time of admeasurement. It's best if you don't exaggerate because you don't want to tie up the whole Panama Canal.

The lake is quite a beautiful place. It's man-made and in the middle of a jungle and we see monkeys in the trees as we sail by one of the islands. Except in its relevance for classical history, when Corinth's isthmus played a more major role, Panama hosts arguably the most important isthmus on the planet. When North and South America split off from Pangaea at the end of the Mesozoic, South American marsupials, whose origins reach back into the Cretaceous, flourished with the separation from their placental predators. The earliest marsupial fossils are found not in Australia but in South America, around 65 million years ago. Then, when the same general group of tectonic processes that created the Sierra Nevada, the Andes, and the islands of the Caribbean finally sewed the last piece of Central America together at Panama in the Pliocene, say two to three million years ago, the placental mammals from North America crossed the new bridge to South America and eliminated almost all of the marsupials, four entire orders including a saber-tooth tiger, in a geological heartbeat. Extinction is just another day at the office for Mother Nature. The llama (*Lama glama*, believe it or not) of the Andes, the well-known relative of the camel, is one of the invaders. After coming south, they became extinct in North America. Among the small number of animals that came north and succeeded are the opossum, the armadillo, and the porcupine.

Back in the present, our advisor has confirmed our 3:00 PM time (noon California time) at the Miraflores locks, the last ones before the Pacific Ocean, so I get off an email to Theresa to alert all the folks on the email list about the webcam. Then, for a few hours the line handlers nap below as Mr. Shrode does most of the driving and the Captain takes photos and watches from the foredeck. The lake is well marked and we have an advisor, so there's not much danger in getting lost. After the lake, we go through the Gaillard Cut, 7.8 miles long, the part of the Canal that crosses the Continental Divide and the big ditch that required the intensive excavation that caused so much suffering and death in its construction.

The physical dimensions of the Canal establish a standard which ships crossing in either direction from the Atlantic to the Pacific cannot exceed, so naval architects have designed the Panamax vessels, which are down to the inch the largest ships that can fit through the Canal. The dimensions are length 965 feet, draft 39.5 feet, beam 106 feet. The lock chambers are 1000.5 feet long and 110 feet wide, leaving just two feet of clearance on either side. The draft is controlled by the locks but also by the depth of the channels in the lake and the Gaillard Cut, and in years of low rainfall this figure is reduced. Shipping companies are notified and must switch to vessels of less draft. This was not of any concern to the pilot of *Maverick*, however.

The amount of water used every time a ship is locked down is about 52 million gallons. The odd thing is that if you send one yacht down alone in a lock, no more water is taken from the lake than if you send a container ship down. This counter-intuitive fact was confirmed by our advisor.

The locks on the Pacific, or southern, side after the Gaillard Cut are separated into two tiers. At the top are the Pedro Miguel locks, a pair of basins that drop 27 feet or so. These are followed by the Miraflores locks, two pairs of basins dropping the remaining 54 or so feet. We raft up again in the same formation just before the Pedro Miguel locks, and again there is a protest about how the pilots plan to accomplish it, this time coming from the skipper of the (brand-new) Moorings boat. His suggestion was accepted by the pilots, and we eventually agree on a plan and get the raft made up. Once again, your Captain drives us into the lock, this time ahead of the container ship. It is just slightly disconcerting to pull up right to the front of the lock, as you are on the edge of a precipice and can easily imagine it being a waterfall.

From the second lock, we exited into the channel, which is contiguous with the Pacific Ocean, which is the same thing as being in the Pacific Ocean, the ocean we left at the Torres Strait on Tuesday, October 2, 2001. Since then we have sailed about 16,000 miles. Still, we're a long way from home, 3,000 miles of hard traveling, northwest as the crow flies. But of course, boats don't fly.

The Final Leg

Homeward Bound

3:00 PM local time, Thursday, March 21 (2000 March 21 UTC).
09 24 N 085 25 W
Temp. 89, Humidity 67%, Cloud Cover 20%.
Off the coast of Costa Rica, close-reaching in 8 knots.

We have elected to stay along the coast rather than take the offshore, "clipper" route back to California for a couple of reasons. One is that unlike most cruisers heading to the South Pacific from California, we did not go to Mexico first, have never cruised there, and this may be our only chance to sail those fabled waters. Although we've heard some good things about Costa Rica and El Salvador, current plans have us continuing northwest as long as conditions are favorable and fuel holds out.

Secondly, while we believe that *Maverick's* hull is sound or we wouldn't be out here at all, there is a small ding in the unalloyed faith we had in her before our little *contretemps* in Carriacou. As Mandy of *Rich Reward* said, "She'll have to prove herself to you all over again." Mandy is doing a solo circumnavigation in the company of a separate boat sailed by her parents. She and her husband had bought the boat and were outfitting her for a world cruise, but before the project was completed, he was diagnosed with cancer and soon died. She finished the work herself and now, at age 32, she's already been cruising for a few years and though she has been injured a few times, she is undaunted and bright-eyed. We left her and her parents at the end of the Panama Canal, where they were to head west.

Coastal cruising presents a different set of challenges from an ocean passage. Currents and winds change around headlands and capes; we may see land breezes and sea breezes; there is a lot of traffic; there are usually fishing boats and nets to look out for; navigation has to be more precise; you don't have the space to maneuver that you do at sea. On the other hand, it's possible to duck in someplace for shelter, and you can motor all you want knowing that you can fuel up along the way. The section we're on from here to San Francisco will be the longest coastal passage of the trip, longer than the Strait of Malacca or the Red Sea or even the Mediterranean. The majority of it is upwind and up-current. We're moving as far north as fast as we can now while the conditions are benign in order to buy ourselves some time later so we'll have the luxury of waiting for good weather to make progress.

THE OLD MAN AND THE SEA

12:15 PM local time, Wednesday, March 26 (1715 March 26 UTC).
14 30 N 092 45 W
Temp. 86, Humidity 70%, Cloud Cover 40%.
At the south end of the Gulf of Tehuantepec.

Since we left the Panama Canal on March 17, we have been traveling northwest along the coast of Central America. Stopping only once for a couple of hours for minor repairs and fuel in Costa Rica, we have passed the countries of Nicaragua (pronounced Nick-ah-rahg-yew-ah by the British), Honduras, El Salvador, and Guatemala, and this morning we find ourselves off the Mexican shores. Our intended landfall is the port of Huatulco, which cruisers favor, although sometimes all that means is that there is a yachtie bar with a lot of white folks drinking cheap beer. Not that there's anything wrong with that.

The sailing so far has been easy, what there is of it. We've not seen winds over 20 knots and often have a gentle sea breeze in the afternoon, accompanied by flat seas. The sea has put away her other moods and there is a notion of strength at rest. The only worry is the thunderstorms at night, as we have learned to respect the danger of lightning.

The area is busy with wildlife. We spot sea-turtles every few minutes, sometimes several at once and at times we have to turn the boat to avoid hitting them. Mr. Shrode spotted a manta ray swimming near them. Dolphins are more plentiful and exuberant than any we've seen elsewhere, leaping clear of the water or smacking their tail fins on the surface. We've left the ubiquitous frigate-birds and royal terns of Panama behind, but we have seen mysterious white birds that fly around the boat at night, appearing almost luminescent. I haven't figured out what they are, as it's difficult to make them out in the dark.

The most spectacular wildlife exhibition so far was occasioned by Ship's Ichthyologist Terry Shrode. Mr. Shrode was at his piscatorial best, drowsily lounging in the cockpit while the pole and the line and the hook did all the work, when we heard the "zzzzzzzzzzz" of the reel.

"Fish on!"

We jump up and look back. Behind the boat, just like in the movies, is a gigantic marlin jumping clear out of the water, the newest victim of Mr. Shrode's prowess. But not for long. After about 15 seconds, before he even got the pole out of its holder, there is a muted "snap" and the line goes limp. The marlin continues leaping, no doubt to try to make sure he's free of the line but also as if to say, "If you think you can catch me with that silly little city-boy gear, you're dreaming, pal." It's a good thing he didn't bite the hook on the other line, which is far more substantial. What would we do then? No doubt there are fishermen out there who would pay a lot of money to catch a marlin, but man, it's, like, bigger than our dinghy. Mr. Shrode and I, sportsmen that we are, wouldn't want to get anywhere near that thing unless it was in an aquarium.

We are motoring along in a flat calm heading out across the Gulf of Tehuantepec. This can be a nasty bit of business. We've been watching the faxes and studying this area ever since we were in Colon awaiting our canal transit, and from that time until now, there has not been one of the dreaded "Tehuantepecers" that sweep down from the Gulf of Mexico, gaining strength as they cross the land to emerge into the Gulf of Tehuantepec with storm force winds.

Sure enough, just to provide a little drama, the weather gurus have predicted one for this weekend, bringing winds of up to 60 knots and seas of 25 feet. We'll be fine and should be safe in Huatulco by then. If nothing goes wrong.

Here Today, Gone Tamale

12:30 AM local time, Saturday, March 29 (0530 March 29 UTC).
15° 44.952'N 96° 7.782'W
Temp. 84, Humidity 72%, Cloud Cover 50%.
Anchor down, Huatulco, Mexico.

We made it across the Gulf of Tehuantepec and didn't get killed as we arrived in Huatulco before the high winds kicked in. It was still ugly, though. What we had was, say 20 knots on the nose and the current of about a knot and a half with us. That meant wind against current, so the chop was so steep that our speed was sometimes down to 3.5 knots even with the current. Then the current turned around so the seas flattened out and we could sail faster, but the current was against us so we went slow. Ha ha ha! One lower shroud is going to have to be replaced, etc., etc., etc., the latter two of which etc.'s belong in the department of redundancy department but nevertheless I assume my drift is caught by you.

Mr. Shrode has gone ashore with some guys from another boat here so I'm alone on *Maverick*. There's some kind of festival of the sort that every Third World country seems to have so very often because their towns have still not gotten cable and there's nothing else to do. In addition, it's another way for them to avoid doing the things for *Maverick* that need to be done. What's to celebrate? It's probably some saint's birthday. I would so love to have Augustine come back and see a lot of women dressed up in elaborate clothes and some rather bad music in his honor. Maybe it's Patrick, though, who probably didn't mind a little mariachi.

Earlier I had been witness to a little parade in the town—not the town at the beach but another one a short cab ride in, that is the real town. The women and girls were spectacularly dressed in Mexican costume, perhaps even more colorful than the Dule, but the thing about the Dule women is that they wear that stuff every day so they rule, those Dules. Anyway, each troupe of women had a band and I think there were three or four troupes and since they weren't very large and there were no floats or horseback riders in the parade to act as buffers, by the time the last unit passed, you could still hear the first band, so you heard all four bands at once. They weren't very good to start with but had that out-of-tune Mexican charm, so hearing them all at the same time created something not distinguishable from chaos. To my ear. But I'm not an expert.

The Tehuantepecer is supposed to start blowing tonight and blow 60 knots for a couple of days and then 40 for a couple of days. We're kind of nervous as it's so close to here (the highest winds are predicted to blow not 50 miles away) but all the locals we asked say it'll be okay. The only cruisers we talked to about it were the ones Mr. Shrode is in town with, and they hadn't even heard about any stinking Tehuantepecer. It's very arcane stuff, unless you've ever read anything at all about cruising in Mexico. The weather fax shows 12-foot waves going perpendicular to the shore where we're anchored in a bay that's about a quarter-mile deep. If I can see 12-foot waves from where I am, I figure they can see me. I'd say, like, 5-foot waves, that's my absolute limit at anchor, and that's being liberal. There's a marina around the corner we could go into but maybe it won't be necessary or if it is, it will be too late.

We may be stuck here for a few days and so if we feel the boat is safe like the locals say it will be, we may rent a car and drive to Oaxaca in the mountains. I've heard of it but I don't know whether it's worth going to. I always liked it though because the word looks cool cuz it has an X in it and you pronounce it wa-HAWK-ah, which sounds cool, but the look and the sound are not related in any language I know, which is only one, excepting ancient Greek and Latin, which are not languages but stuff you have to learn in school so you'll be smart, but you won't know any languages. You'll pronounce Oaxaca "Oh, AGGS-ack-ah."

This is a resort but a Mexican resort, except for the passengers on the cruise ship that only stayed for the afternoon. The people swimming at the beaches and browsing in the shops are Mexican. It seems that the last thing Mexicans on vacation will eat is tamales, as you will only see steaks or shrimp on the menu. Although we did see a sushi bar. Thing is, I want Mexican. Last Mexican food we had was in Australia and it tasted just about like what you'd expect the food at a Mexican restaurant in Australia to taste like. Now here we are in Mexico but where are the tamales?

You probably have to go to California to get real Mexican food. That place down the street from the Palomino in LA on Lankershim, El Michoacano, for example, oh yeah. But there are people in the US who like fake gringo Mexican food with lots of sour cream to disguise the fact that the cooks don't have a talent for enchilada sauce and you know what I think the real secret is? Lard. Although there are probably others. But in Marin County, California, where famous seamen like Paul Cayard and your Captain live, it is probably illegal to import lard or own the animals it comes from, whatever they are, lardosaurs or something. Because, I don't know, what, it's not organic? Is Crisco vegetarian lard? But Crisco is probably also illegal in Marin, or at least it's something that you wouldn't be able to mention using, even in your support group. Even so, Crisco's not as good as real lard so what's the point of humiliating yourself? If you copped to using real lard, the shock value would far outweigh any embarrassment, and you'd be thought of as an in-your-face out-of-the-box kind of person. I think maybe lard made from free-range lardosaurs raised on organic barley or weeds or whatever they eat, now there's a product that has a future. Sea captain, Mexican food-seeker, marketing genius, a man for all seasons.

You'll Start Out Standing

2:45 PM local time, Sunday, April 6 (1945 April 6 UTC).
15 40 N 096 55 W
Temp. 91, Humidity 71%, Cloud Cover 10%.
Underway near Puerto Escondido, Mexico.

When one undertakes a venture such as ours, he perhaps holds out the hope that the experience may toughen him a bit, make more of a man of him, that sort of thing. He'll walk with a salty swagger and have a certain air that sets him apart from the ordinary man. The last thing one wishes is to be proven a weakling, a fool, a coward.

It's true that the Captain currently has a salty swagger but it has more to do with the fact that he's found the tamales and the question on his mind is "Dónde estan los baños?" than that he's got a few miles under his keel. And about his air, the less said the better, although it does do a rather good job of setting him apart from other men.

Daniel Patrick Moynihan once said that if you live life fully, it will break your heart, probably quoting an old Irish proverb. Similarly, it seems that if you sail enough miles, the sea will turn you into a poltroon. Just what you didn't want.

The crew of *Maverick* arrives at Huatulco where all the books say it's safe to wait out a Tehuantepecer. The Captain looks at the bay, which is not too deep, and the faxes, which predict 12-foot waves gliding oh-so-gently by only a short distance away. He recalls that waves have the property of refracting around things. (Even *particles* may act like waves and refract, exhibiting just the sort of duplicity that the Captain abhors in the universe and its miserable doings.) Looking at the headland that protects the bay, he hypothesizes thusly: Here lies the sort of thingamajig around which a wave, if it got a notion to, might refract, sending its mischievous energy into the harbor. The books say no, it's safe. Never one to be reassured by facts or evidence, the Captain has that particular talent of the coward, to be afraid.

Seeking reassurance he asks the port captain if the harbor is safe, if the mean old waves might refract into the harbor. The port captain pats his hand and looks meaningfully into his eyes, having seen his sort before. "No, it is very safe here."

So then the Captain goes to see the manager of the marina, Andrico, who has the sort of sporty name that tennis pros and ski instructors favor, and asks him the same thing. "No, not to worry," he says in his best bedside manner, as if reassuring a little old lady.

So the books, and the Port Captain, and Andrico, and the fishermen, and the indulging looks on the faces of all who are brave, say that the nasty waves will not refract around the headland.

But the waves refract around the headland.

On Sunday, when the Tehuantepecer is scheduled to start blowing to 50 knots, the right side of the bay, the one the locals said was safest, starts to look untenable and will be if it gets worse. We move to the other side of the bay and as usual make certain we've got the hook well stuck. Later, the other cruising boat in the anchorage follows.

On Monday, the winds reportedly gusted to 65 knots, hurricane strength, out in the Gulf, and we had gusts of up to 40 in the bay. Every vessel in the bay dragged its anchor, except *Maverick*. Okay, there were only three other vessels. But one was a 60-foot steel trawler, and another was a large barge. Both craft were anchored by professionals—members in good standing of the "nothing to worry about in this snug harbor" school of thought. The trawler crew was aboard and tried to re-anchor but couldn't and eventually settled for tying up to the pier, which, with the surge, was a very ugly solution. The barge fetched up on the rocks. A local tug attempted to stabilize it at the docks, but when that failed, grounded it on a beach. The cruisers were away in town, so when we saw their boat was dragging in the strong wind and chop, we got into the dinghy with three fenders and clambered aboard to try to keep the fenders between their boat and a huge channel buoy. As the boat dragged past it, we found some lines and tied two to the buoy, stabilizing the situation until the weather died down. They were not ungrateful; the boat would have foundered.

An exasperating fact is that most of the time, the dashing, devil-may-care skipper who throws out 30 feet of rode in 20 feet of water and says, "Who's ready for a brewski?" is going to be fine, while the silly crew of *Maverick* that spent FIVE HOURS before they were satisfied that their anchor was well set in Mykonos will look like fools. Most of the time even a poorly set anchor will not drag, the boat will not be broken into, the through-hulls will not fail, we will not lose our passports, the lighthouse will be working, the rig will not come down, the hull will not come apart, the navigation will be obvious, the chart will be correct, the oil cooler will not spring a leak, lightning will not strike, the boat will not swing onto the reef in a gale, and all your worries will seem the far-fetched scenarios of a guy with no self-confidence and no sense of adventure.

When we were in Lipari, I saw an excursion boat loading passengers for a day trip. Everyone was in a festive mood, the crew welcoming the visitors, handing out drinks, helping them stow their bags. Only one man stood apart from the rest, leaning on the rail with a worried look on his face, staring down at the mooring lines. Though he wore no uniform, I knew in an instant he was the captain.

It's a little humiliating to feel the need, or even the duty, to be a fussy worrywart. It's really not what you had in mind when you visualized yourself as Captain. There is no dignity in paranoia, when the movies teach us that the hero is like Butch Cassidy or the Sundance Kid, jumping off a big cliff and not getting hurt. On the other hand, in the book, *Little Big Man*, there is a story about Wild Bill Hickok that I assume is apocryphal, but nonetheless like many apocryphal tales it is a good one. As he approaches a bar to get a drink, a man at a bar stool on the end who seems to be passed out drunk lifts up his head and raises a gun to kill him. Hickok, prepared for that eventuality because he's paranoid, has his gun hidden behind the hat he holds in his hand, and blows him away. Little Big Man is amazed, and asks Hickok how he knew that guy had a gun, and Hickok replies that it was just a hunch, and when he gets hunches like that 99 out of 100 times he's wrong. "But it's that one time in a hundred that pays me for my troubles."

Two-Lane Blacktop

11:00 AM local time, Saturday, April 12 (1600 April 12 UTC).
16° 50.517'N 99° 54.265'W
Temp. 85, Humidity 76%, Cloud Cover 10%.
At anchor in Acapulco Bay, Mexico.

Having weathered the Tehuantepecer, Ship's Automobile Enthusiast Terry Shrode rented a car and invited the Captain along for a jaunt to Oaxaca. The car he chose was none other than the classic Volkswagen Beetle of our collective youth, which is still manufactured and sold in Mexico, not to be mistaken for the new, safer version made for our older, less daring selves. We got a red one, just a year or so old, and Mr. Shrode assumed the driver's seat, applied his foot to the pedal, and popped the clutch. Then he backed up and opened the door for the Captain. "Just wanted to see if I could do a wheelie," he said.

We headed up the coast a little from Huatulco and turned inland towards the Sierra Madre del Sur. It is this mountain range, which, ending at the Gulf of Tehuantepec, creates a barrier for the barometric highs in Texas and northern Mexico that causes the winds to accelerate through the Gulf to hurricane force on the seas to the south. The effect is a venturi like what we get on the San Francisco city front, but on a massive scale.

The road was paved all the way and in pretty good shape so that Mr. Shrode had little difficulty maintaining hull speed, and more often, planing speed. The Captain, however, having the previous evening taken advantage of the generous beneficence of the cruisers whose boat we had rescued, was feeling none too enthusiastic about the twists and turns of the roadway. We stopped in a small mountain town for gas, where it was decanted from plastic jugs, and in another for a remedy for the Captain's malaise: *tacos de pollo con salsa picante*, and a little hair of the chihuahua.

Proceeding up the precipitous curves and high ridges, we gained the high pass, for which unfortunately no altitude was given but let's say 6500 feet. From here we descended into a series of three very large valleys that exist at a similar altitude and have a similar feel to the high deserts of Nevada, minus the purple sage and the riders thereof. Leaving the mountains and their pine trees behind, we began to see a different display of vegetation. Although we were well south of the Sonoran desert, we recognized several plants common to that region. Among them were yucca and agave, both members of the order *Liliales* that includes lilies, asparagus, and the blue-eyed grass familiar to Marin residents. Different varieties of agave (the "century plant" we see in California) are used in the production of tequila, mescal, and pulque, a kind of beer. We saw forests of saguaro and prickly pear cactus. There was also an acacia with a brilliant purple flower, abundant and in bloom everywhere. Aside from the acacia, which was spectacular, I would have called the general effect scruffy, as it lacked the floral variety and striking austerity of the real Sonoran desert while maintaining its heat and dust.

After a long (for the Captain) seven-hour drive, we entered the city of Oaxaca, which occupies a central place at the junction of the valleys. Our correspondent Hank Strauss claims that the town was named after a spitting contest, but you won't hear the Captain repeating that one. On the other hand, no one is sure of the origin of the name or its meaning but it seems to come from the Zapotec language.

The outskirts of town may be scruffy and dusty but at the town square you meet a formal central park with a gazebo. On one evening Mr. Shrode and the Captain got a table on the balcony at one of the better restaurants overlooking the square. As we sipped good Mexican wine and mescal and dined on chateaubriand, we were serenaded by a brass band playing a medley of Stephen Foster songs such as "Oh, Susanna," "Camptown Races," "My Old Kentucky Home," and "Swanee River." Foster was one of those songwriters who sold his songs cheap and died poor. Except for the electric lights and the casual dress of the throngs strolling about the square, nothing gave a hint that one hadn't been transported to an elegant evening in 19th century America.

The main attractions of this area of Mexico are related to its being the cradle of the Zapotec civilization, one of the major pre-Columbian cultures in Mexico. Whether they like it or not, all these societies are grouped together under the name of a famous sailor from Europe who never even won an America's Cup. We visited Monte Alban, one of the few ruins of its type not called by an unpronounceable indigenous name. The main plaza was begun in about 500 BC, so was contemporaneous with classical Greece. The civilization centered here reached its zenith in about 800 AD, the time of the Vikings. It is set on a mountaintop area reminiscent of the type of acropolis found in the classical world, but it covers a larger area and contains more massive construction than, for example, the acropolis at Athens. The buildings are the familiar pyramidal type you've seen in photos of other Mesoamerican cultures. It occurred to me while I looked at them that before the invention of the arch or buttress, the only way to make a stable building as tall as those here or the even larger ones in Egypt, was by using the pyramidal structure. Perhaps it's this practical reason and not some magic formula that determined the shape of these buildings.

The people who inhabited this space and ruled the huge fertile valleys that they overlook were the Zapotecs. There is some evidence that at the time of their greatest strength, the climate was wetter and more suitable for agriculture than it is today. The Zapotecs used (and their descendants still use) the seeds of the heavenly blue morning glory in their religious rituals and for "curative" purposes. These seeds contain the psychotropic alkaloids D-lysergic and D-isolysergic acids. Evidence of the ensuing hallucinations is found in the remains of ancient art at the ruins, and also in the present day in brightly painted wooden carvings of bizarre and surreal animals sold by modern craftsmen. Like many of their contemporaries in this area of the world, the Zapotecs also practiced ritualized human sacrifice. Taken together, the drugs and violence bring to mind one of the ogres of the 20th century, Charlie Manson, who evidently was merely born in the wrong place and time for helter-skelter. The Zapotecs may have felt that he fit right in.

The ride back took us on a different route through cultivated fields of agave that couldn't help but remind us of the Napa valley. The vicinity of Oaxaca is apparently the major center in Mexico for the production of mescal, although not tequila.

We also drove by a man making adobe bricks by hand, so I yelled out the window, "Hey, the '60s are over, dude, time to give it up and get into raising free-range lardosaurs."

ACAPULCO

5:00 PM local time, Monday, April 21 (2200 April 21 UTC).
19° 3.404'N 104° 18.550'W
Temp. 86, Humidity 67%, Cloud Cover 50%.
At anchor in Manzanillo Bay, Mexico.

Leaving Huatulco, *Maverick* battled strong countercurrents and the chop produced by 20-knot headwinds around Puerto Angel. It took us 30 hours to make the 60 miles from Huatulco to Puerto Escondido, for an average of 2 knots. In order to make that average, for some very long hours we were going backwards. We set the hook in the treacherous anchorage at Puerto Escondido overnight so that we could replenish our fuel and so that Mr. Shrode could recover from a vicious 24-hour flu. There, we found our old friends from the Red Sea, the Med, and Morocco, the crew of *Nordic*. Frank and Mary and the kids sailed from Santa Cruz about five years ago, and as I write this, are celebrating crossing their outbound path at Manzanillo, completing their circumnavigation. Our friends on *Delphis* will finish theirs in Zihuatenejo. One of the peculiarities of *Maverick's* circumnavigation is that we will not complete it until we get to the shipping channel outside the Golden Gate. Technically, in order to say you've circumnavigated, you needn't have accomplished it all on the same voyage. Since both Mr. Shrode and the Captain have sailed up the coast from San Diego to San Francisco on *Maverick*, we will be entitled to claim ours in San Diego. But we won't.

We intended to sail from Huatulco directly to Zihuatenejo, but we didn't make it. After the quick stop in Escondido, we noticed the transmission was not reliably engaging in forward. That's no big deal at sea, but of course it will finally fail when you are maneuvering in close quarters in a harbor. We determined to head for Acapulco to see if repairs could be made. We're now veterans of the process of arranging for serious repairs in countries that may not have US-style equipment or access to parts. We would like to be out of this area of Mexico, or actually all of Mexico, by June 1 because of the threat of hurricanes. And of course, everyone calls Mexico "Manañaland." I feared the worst, as we still had a long way to go to San Diego.

We entered Acapulco late on Tuesday April 8 and anchored in about 70 feet. The harbor is a mushroom-shaped bay about the size of the central San Francisco Bay bordered by Angel Island, the Golden Gate Bridge, the City, and Treasure Island, and it's almost as pretty as ours. During the daytime, Acapulco seems a typical modern city with high-rises crowding the shore, but at night you see that the surrounding hills make a natural bowl, and the lights twinkling from the houses on the hillsides create a beautiful frame for a painting that features *Maverick* at anchor, right in the center.

The next day, Wednesday, we were referred to a mechanic named Oscar Rodriguez. We managed to track him down on his cell phone and made an appointment for Thursday for him to see the transmission. When he told us on Thursday that the engine would have to be removed and the transmission rebuilt, my heart sank. When could it be done? He said he would start it the next day (Friday) and could have it back in the boat the first of the week. I couldn't believe my ears, and although he seemed knowledgeable and honest, I had to ask him two or three times. I still didn't believe it.

But by Tuesday afternoon, we had completed sea trials and were ready to leave the next morning. The price was about $850. By comparison, the job of rebuilding both the engine and transmission, carried out soon before our departure by a respected shop in the Bay Area, had taken something like two months and the cost of the transmission rebuild was much higher. And of course, now both the engine and transmission have required major repairs since we left.

Other than that, the big deal in Acapulco was seeing the cliff divers. It costs $2.50, which includes a beer, and it's just about worth it.

By the time we arrived in Z-Town, as the cruisers call it, we didn't have the leisure to stay. But I saw one feature of the town that I've never read about. It's another mushroom-shaped bay, about a quarter of the size of Acapulco. The beaches surrounding the bay are chock-a-bloc with resorts, but higher, on the hills overlooking the bay where you'd figure the rich folks live, are plywood, one-room shacks that have the look of extreme poverty. Their occupants have a perfect view of the folks frolicking at the resorts and the luxury yachts in the harbor.

We left the next morning without going ashore and motored the entire 180 miles to Manzanillo. Here Mr. Shrode will get a respite from strict discipline aboard while the Captain takes shore leave with Theresa at Las Hadas. This is the famous and painfully expensive resort where the movie *10* with Bo Derek was made. The male star was Dudley Moore, who was about as tall as the Captain. Bo Derek isn't really as stupid as everyone said, but when she was asked to make the sequel, *11,* she had to be told that that was the next number. I have sent Theresa my instructions that she must bleach her hair blonde and put it up in cornrows, and I anxiously await her response.

T-Shirt Weather

7:30 PM local time, Monday, May 5 (0230 May 5 UTC).
24 46 N   112 15 W
Temp. 63, Humidity 85%, Cloud Cover 0%.
At anchor in Bahia Santa Maria, Baja California, Mexico.

When we got into Cabo San Lucas at the tip of Baja California, we spent about an hour and a half refueling and watering, and then headed up the coast. In that time we satisfied whatever curiosity we had about the place, but I suppose we didn't really give it a fair shake. Leaving Cabo, we soon passed 23 27 N, which puts us out of the tropics for the last time and as if the weather were conscious of this, the breeze immediately turned very cold. A low and the cold front it brought to Baja had us pulling our fuzzies and foulies out of the lockers they've lived in almost without interruption since we left home. I'm sure we haven't been this cold since a few days after we left, and since then when we said it was "t-shirt weather," we meant it was so cold we had to put a t-shirt on. Bye-bye to that.

We made another 180 miles before finally stopping to take a break here in Bahia Santa Maria after the six straight days from Manzanillo. The weather guru for this leg, Don from *Summer Passage* out of Ventura, said it would be windy, and last night it gusted up to the high 30s in the anchorage. This leaves us about 550 miles more of Baja before we make San Diego. West Coast sailors know that this passage is referred to as the Baja Bash, and justifiably so. It blows pretty consistently 20-25 on the nose with higher gusts, but the hardest thing for us to get used to was the cold.

Bahia Santa Maria is a beautifully desolate anchorage, with nothing here but a few frigate birds and pelicans. Although it's windy, the anchorage is secure so it's not bad at all. We probably won't stay long enough to launch the dinghy and do any exploring, but who knows. We have a few things to do, among which are stopping up all the leaks we discovered when we headed upwind, and drying out the stuff that got wet. As we haven't sailed upwind since the Red Sea, the chainplates need rebedding and new gaskets need to be put on the hatches. This and some other routine maintenance won't take long.

Next to us in the anchorage is 69-year-old Susan Meckley on *Dharma* from the Bay Area, who is single-handing down the coast with the intention of sailing to Phuket. She's looking for crew but for now handling it on her own. She's not completely alone, as she's accompanied by a Chihuahua named Bonita and a parrot named Sweetie Bird that has learned how to call the dog. She describes herself as 5'12" with lots of red hair, so she's not a small woman, and not a frail or timid one, either. She's a retired US Army Master Sergeant and even at her current age, I don't think I'd want to mess with her.

When she heard we had no refrigeration, she wanted to give us some cold stuff, like some frozen clams and a couple of cold beers. But we were too lazy to inflate the dinghy. She told us real men would swim over for a couple of beers, so that's how long it took Susan to figure out what everyone else already knows. So then she says she'll put the beers on a line with a float and try to send it to us, as we're downwind. She rigged up a bag and attached it to her fishing pole and sent it floating towards us, and we were waiting with a line to toss that had a hook on the end to grapple with. But there was a wind shift and the bag went drifting the wrong way, so we pulled up the anchor and motored over to it, picked it up and re-anchored. And you thought it was easy out here.

WITH GOD ON HIS SIDE

8:00 AM local time, Thursday, May 15 (1500 May 15 UTC).
27° 41.238'N 114° 53.455'W
Temp. 64, Humidity 67%, Cloud Cover 0%.
At anchor in Bahia de Tortugas (Turtle Bay), Baja California, Mexico.

We are about halfway up the coast of Baja, awaiting a weather window to go north. As we speak, it's a bit bumpy out there, and as is usual for this area, we have what one cruiser calls "strong noserlies." There are a few boats that have tried to make it out of here and returned with various problems, and among them is *Nordic*. These are friends of ours from Santa Cruz that we've been occasionally running into since the Red Sea. Skippers Frank of *Nordic* and Dennis of *Delphis* had been conversing with the Captain in Acapulco about being paranoid that even though we're so close, something might go wrong preventing us from finishing. Since then we have had to have the transmission rebuilt, and *Nordic* is now stuck with an engine problem. They've left the boat here at anchor and we don't know where they are.

There being an absence of other hard news, the Captain is reminded of the old saying, often applied to the circumstances of a seagoing vessel, that the devil has work for idle hands. Naval commanders throughout history have learned that if the crew is not given tasks with which to occupy themselves through the long and generally uneventful hours of a passage, fighting, gambling, dancing, singing, fiddling, and frolicking may result. The crew may forget its mission entirely and degenerate into a bunch of louts who are getting jiggy with it. The consequent lowering of the level of discipline and military readiness of the crew is not to be tolerated, and so they are ordered to polish the bronze and holystone the deck and sand and paint and varnish until everything aboard is ship shape and Bristol fashion, and then start over again. Since our readers are not in a geographical location that would make these types of chores on *Maverick* practical during this slow news period, the Captain has devised an equally onerous task to occupy the recruits in our Navy, which is the reading of what follows. It is our belief that this will effect a return to proper deportment and harden our crew for battle.

Just about a long stone's throw from the Captain's house in Marin County begins a boulevard that bears the name not of a Conquistador, nor a President, nor one of the founders of California, but of the greatest pirate in all of history. It is named after Francis Drake, a man of humble origins who rose to become the most celebrated seaman of the

Elizabethan Age and a favorite of the Queen—or one of the most dreaded villains in the world, depending on your point of view.

Beginning near the California State Prison at San Quentin, his boulevard heads through Greenbrae and past the College of Marin, then briefly visits the leafy lanes of Ross, one of the most affluent neighborhoods in the most affluent country in the world. No doubt there is a parvenu or two like Drake himself in residence there, which is not so much a crime in the Northern California of the 21st century as it was in the England of Elizabethan times, and therein lies a thread of the fabric of Drake's life and a wound he could not heal.

From Ross we cross the bustle of the town of San Anselmo, then, after passing through Fairfax, we come to a turn taking us to the quiet valley of Nicasio. In the late 19th century, a legend was found among the Indians dwelling there according to which some of them were descended from white men on a ship. One hundred years earlier, two different Catholic missionaries to the area reported that some among the Indians were tall, fair in complexion and hair, and bearded. From across the Atlantic Ocean in England, one of our sources says that after anchoring offshore, Drake's crew ventured inland and found, among other things, "many blessings fit for the use of man."

Continuing out Sir Francis Drake Boulevard—"Sir" because he was knighted for his activities—we travel through beautiful San Geronimo Valley through the towns of Olema and Inverness. Surmounting Inverness ridge, we encounter the dairy farms and the remote and isolated feel of the Point Reyes Peninsula, and after a long drive we come to the lighthouse at the end of the land. This lighthouse, when viewed from the sea, remains one of the most lonely and romantic visions of all the seascapes we have seen in our travels.

Looking back towards the coast from a vantage point above Chimney Rock, if the fog has lifted, we can view the dramatic shoreline leading up from San Francisco, and across the way, we can see the long beach at Limantour. Just to the left of the beach we see Drake's Estero, and the large body of water beneath us and enclosed by the headlands, where the crew of *Maverick* has many times set the anchor just about as Drake would have, is the bay that bears his name.

Drake's ventures as a young seaman involved piracy and plunder under the guidance of some older relatives in the nearby Hawkins family. His career from the start involved controversy, not so much because of the questionable legality of his pursuits as because of his character. Physically courageous to the point of recklessness, he could be at turns generous, ruthless, sensitive, violent, charming, greedy, vindictive, courtly, and devious. He shared his best qualities with the common seamen at his command and those defeated foes to whom he was magnanimous in victory, especially the rich ones. His worst qualities seem to have been exacerbated, in record if not in fact, by three factors: 1) His education was poor, and yet he came to have power over refined gentlemen who were jealous of a man who, born to inferior circumstances and lacking in polish, nevertheless had the better of them. They could write more effectively, and not a few sources of our information on Drake are from these sorts of men. But this won't suffice to answer all the questions about his character. 2) Drake's insecurities about his low-born status made him hypersensitive to just these kinds of rivalries and fueled his obsession to dominate those who harbored the least resentment of him. He magnified their treachery and punished them, if necessary by violence with a patina of legality. 3) He practiced a violent profession in a violent era.

Queen Elizabeth I, one of the few regents in history to have an age named in her honor, was a powerful, cunning, and enigmatic character who liked Drake and, while keeping a close watch on him, tolerated and surreptitiously encouraged his exploits. At the time, the line between state business and personal business was considerably more indistinct than it is today. The Queen would often personally invest in questionable private undertakings that served the purposes of England and at the same time enriched her and others involved, while publicly deploring the activities of "privateers" who raided her enemy's towns and ships. Likewise, private citizens would lend their ships and money to missions undertaken in the interests of the Crown, with the understanding that they would share in whatever booty might be captured. On further thought, maybe it's not so different from today. England's enemy was the Spain of Philip II, who had imperial ambitions and was clever and hardworking enough to achieve them. He had a worthy rival in Elizabeth.

Following Columbus' discovery of the New World, Spain wasted no time in exploiting the "Indyes," along with Central and South America. The great pre-Columbian civilizations quickly fell to Spanish might, and Spain became wealthy bringing their gold and silver back home. Columbus had been an Italian sailing for Spain. Another import, Magellan, who was Portuguese, also sailed under the Spanish flag and, hoping like Columbus to find a west-about route to the Orient, in 1520 discovered the strait at the tip of South America that bears his name. This allowed the Spanish to expand their domain to the ports of the west coasts of Central and South America during the first part of the 16th century.

Magellan continued his voyage and gained credit in the history books for being the first man to sail all the way around the world. But he didn't. He died in the Philippines, and Juan Sebastián de Elcano, the master of one of the other ships in Magellan's fleet and a person who had earlier been involved in a mutiny against Magellan, completed the voyage in

September 1522 with only one out of the original five ships. Elcano, not Magellan, deserves the credit for being the first one, but he wasn't the originator of the venture nor its original captain. You'd think that once it was done, the rush would be on for others to match the feat, but the next circumnavigation didn't happen for nearly 60 years and then it was accomplished by an Englishman.

Thanks in part to Magellan's new strait, the Spanish had gotten the jump on the English and others in South America, but they had barely enough time to settle a few of their people and "pacify" the native populations—converting them to Catholicism—before another plan to exploit the New World was conceived by Drake's mentors, the aforementioned Hawkins family of Plymouth, England. Sailing with them as a young man, Drake learned a faster and cheaper way to wealth. Why bother to conquer native peoples and manage gold mines? Arrrgh! Just take the stuff from them's that does it! For a quarter of a century, Drake and Hawkins plundered the Spanish Main with scant opposition until Philip finally was able to come up with some ways of defending his colonies from their depredations. By then, Drake was a very rich man.

It served England's national interest to have Spain weakened, and it served the interests of the investors and pirates to enrich themselves with the spoils of plunder. In addition, it served the political interests of the Queen to promote the Protestant faith that was in direct opposition to the Pope and his power, and to Catholic Spain. Elizabeth's father, Henry VIII, had split with Rome over the business of his separation from Catherine of Aragon, to marry Elizabeth's mother, Anne Boleyn. Henry's defiance of the Pope had less to do with theology than with power. By the time Elizabeth, who was third in line for the throne, was crowned, the official faith had gone from Henry's Church of England to his son Edward's Protestant faith to his daughter Mary I ("Bloody Mary") and her zealous Roman Catholicism. Mary was also married to Elizabeth's later rival, Phillip II.

The fact that Elizabeth survived during a shifting period when one's faith could mean the difference between having a head or not having one speaks volumes about her ability to, at a very young age, navigate intricate and dangerous waters. It also meant that when she assumed the throne as a Protestant, she was accomplished in the art of playing her religious cards carefully and to her best advantage. Maybe she was devout as well. It's possible. More likely, like many people, she made no distinction between God's desires and her own.

Some of the same can be said of Drake, who, throughout his career, practiced the trappings of Protestant religious ritual aboard ship with gusto. Yet when politically necessary, he could be conciliatory to the other side. But neither Queen nor pirate scrupled to use religion to foment and support a virulent hatred of both the Irish and the Spanish papists. The Catholic Church made itself a perfect whipping boy by supporting the Inquisition, a tool that had the effect of controlling both political and religious foes, and by declaring that followers of the True Faith owed no allegiance to heretical monarchs like Elizabeth. This justified Elizabeth's practice of executing persons suspected of treason by virtue of their confessed Roman Catholicism—not to mention their real antipathy for Elizabeth—like her cousin Mary, Queen of Scots.

For Drake, the stage was set to use God, Queen, and Country to provide himself with a metaphysical foundation and justification for actions that, in the absence of these high values, cannot be distinguished from vicious, rapacious, and profitable raids on defenseless Spanish towns and vessels at sea. In his mind, what he did was not at all criminal and he bridled when the word *pirate* was used to describe him. The Queen for her part pretended outrage and promised to pay restitution to the aggrieved parties, which restitution always seemed slow in coming. Aside from his religious war against the "antichrist," Drake had the Queen's wink and nod, and the Queen's money. He was the Oliver North of the 16th century.

Few criticize Drake as a sailor. He sailed without any of the modern tools of navigation, as had Columbus at the end of the previous century. There had been essentially no progress since then in navigation, with the exception of the fact that the Spanish had begun to chart the New World. Unlike Columbus and Magellan, Drake did not fancy the idea of sailing off to some uncharted never-never-land. Since English seamen had never sailed to most of South America, and the Spanish guarded their charts and sailing directions (*derroteros*) as though they were nuclear secrets, he therefore had a problem. But he solved it by use of the tools most familiar to him, of which he was now master. He simply captured a Spanish ship, imprisoned her pilot, confiscated his navigational papers, and pleaded, bribed, cajoled, or threatened him until he agreed to act as Drake's pilot for the specified waters. Maybe some torture was used. Problem solved.

Drake's fleet of ships, including his flagship which was not at the time called the *Golden Hinde* but the slightly more prosaic *Pelican*, left Plymouth November 15, 1577, on a voyage that would cement his place in history. It would have been no surprise to the crew to find they had signed on for a mission of piratical raids. Only the most naïve would not have known Drake's methods, yet later many gentlemen on the trip testified in court that they had no idea this sort of thing was in Drake's plans. However, word was circulated that this time they were headed for Alexandria in the Mediterranean. When they found themselves on a course for the Strait of Magellan, a destination that the Queen, with Drake's complicity, had kept secret, there were some people among those aboard who didn't feel they had been fairly used. There were rumblings of mutiny and a gentleman captain of one of the other vessels in the fleet, and by gentleman we mean someone to the manner born, was executed in an incident that many consider a black mark in Drake's biography. Yet Magellan had had similar problems and also authorized an execution on his voyage of discovery. The Captain of *Maverick* has yet to resort to like methods to maintain discipline aboard, and it is widely thought that this bespeaks his effectiveness as a leader of men.

The real purpose of Drake's voyage was kept secret from almost everyone, and even after it was complete, where he went and what he did was never fully disclosed. As of today, there is very little clarity on some parts of it. Certainly the primary mission was to distress and despoil any and all holdings of the King of Spain, and there is little doubt that this was accomplished. But it seems that the Queen and Drake conspired to keep the Spanish guessing at what else he was up to and what he may have achieved. They already regarded Drake with awe and terror, viewing him as having almost supernatural powers. Why not keep them in the dark about England's larger intentions? Sharing his discoveries with the enemy would not serve, and how better to discomfit Philip II than by intimating that Drake may have found a northern passage to the west coast of North America, or something else of great import?

The Spanish holdings on the west coasts of South and Central America were undefended, since it was thought that no one had the nautical or navigational ability to sail in those waters except the Spanish themselves. After he emerged from Magellan's Strait and gained the Pacific, the first Englishman to do so, Drake plundered at will and came away with an untold fortune.

As he sailed north from South America, however, details become increasingly vague, and no firsthand accounts of this part of the voyage have survived. Many materials and drawings have been lost, and what remains is often contradictory. Some reports seem to have been borrowed from accounts of other voyages to the New World and are not even relevant to Drake's. Unquestionably, much of this vacuum of information was by design. We know he stopped at Huatulco in Mexico where *Maverick* waited out a Tehuantepecer, but there is no mention of high winds in the accounts we have of Drake's voyage. He left Huatulco in April, and he seems to have reached his highest latitude, whatever it was, in June of 1578. On the way he undoubtedly did the Baja Bash himself. Earlier Spanish explorers had trouble with it just like today's sailors; in 1540 Francisco de Ulloa spent 65 days tacking between Isla Cedros and the Baja peninsula without being able to make any northing, which must be some kind of record.

One source claims that Drake reached 48 degrees north, almost at the Juan de Fuca Strait. It is more commonly believed that Drake made it to about Mendocino, then turned back southward and careened his boat, which had possibly been renamed the *Golden Hinde*, in what came to be known as Drake's Bay. (It may however be the case that the ship was only renamed after the voyage; *Pelican* was a name dear to Elizabeth and the politician in Drake would have seen the advantages of keeping it.) At this bay he named the land "Nova Albion," or New England, "in respect of the white bankes and cliffes, which ly towards the sea," reminding him of the white cliffs of Dover. The quote, one of the most telling pieces of the meager evidence of his stay at Drake's Bay, is from a book published 75 years after his return. He reportedly emplaced a metal sign on a post at this place, but modern metallurgical evidence has not tended to confirm the authenticity of the one "discovered" in the twentieth century and to my knowledge still kept at the Bancroft Library of the University of California. There is no evidence that Drake found San Francisco Bay.

The white banks and cliffs of Drake's Bay are striking and we will be looking, on our way north, for any other cliffs that may fit the quoted description. In Drake's Bay, the cliffs are composed of the sedimentary rocks sandstone and limestone, and in Dover they are chalk, which has the same chemical composition as limestone. Those at Dover are from the Cretaceous, while the ones in Drake's bay were deposited later, in the Tertiary.

Over the last 30 million years, the Point Reyes Peninsula has moved northward from its original position near Los Angeles on the western side of the San Andreas fault, and as it did, the movements associated with its northward course also caused vertical changes, with the result that for long periods of time the part we now hike on was submerged. It was during these periods that the original bedrock received the coating of light-colored marine depositions of sandstone, limestone, and other sediments, now elevated above the sea, that make up the white cliffs Drake saw from his anchorage in the bay.

At the point he careened his boat here, Drake probably did not know which route he would take home, although there is some evidence that he considered a circumnavigation from the start. He most likely intended to make some attempt to find a northern route across present-day Canada, at the time a sort of holy grail of navigation, but when that failed, he had three options. He could go back the way he came, but this presented the unhappy potential of trouble, as this time the Spanish would be well warned of his arrival and disposition. He could abandon the *Golden Hinde* in Panama and make the trek with his men and booty overland across the isthmus to the Atlantic, where he could capture a vessel to take him back to England. As amazing as that sounds, it was the type of thing that wouldn't have intimidated the indomitable Drake. He was fully capable of forcing his will on local resources and meeting formidable challenges of this sort. His third option, if successful, would however bring worldwide fame, would allow him to preserve the fortune he had acquired, and would hold the promise of further prizes. This was to head west to Asia and from there around the Cape of Good Hope to home. Once he reached the islands of the western Pacific, navigation routes were fairly well established by the Portuguese, although Drake would have to rely on his standard methods to acquire pilots and charts. This course, the boldest of the three very difficult options, was Drake's choice.

He arrived back in Plymouth in September of 1580. After his return, he was hailed as a hero, but the Crown's disinformation campaign circulated conflicting and confusing accounts of what he'd done. What is certain is that the trip, even taking time to explore unfamiliar seas, plunder, pillage, despoil countless villages and ships, and make necessary repairs, had taken less than three years—and that Francis Drake had become the first man to plan, command, and sail a voyage all the way around the world.

Abashed

8:00 AM local time, Wednesday, May 21 (1500 May 21 UTC).
31° 51.569'N 116° 37.546'W
Temp. 67, Humidity 78%, Cloud Cover 0%.
At Baja Naval marina in Ensenada, Baja California, Mexico.

As the careful reader will have noticed, we are in Ensenada. San Diego, California, USA is the next stop. This is the 119th foreign harbor we've visited, our final one before re-entering the United States. We took a slip here, the first one since the end of November when we were at a marina in Gomera before we left the Canaries for the Atlantic crossing, and so we enjoyed the first hot shower in about six months except for Las Hadas. The pleasures of a hot shower are vastly underrated.

Ensenada puts us beyond the worst of the Baja Bash. In all, it wasn't so bad. Most of it was sailed in 20-25 knots on the nose, and as I mentioned before, the most unpleasant thing was how cold it seemed. We stopped at Bahia Santa Maria, Bahia San Juanico, and Turtle Bay, and the trip to Ensenada was the last leg. All along we had been listening to a weather guru to try to get some miles under the keel in mild conditions, but in the end I don't think we could really tell the difference. We didn't see over 30 knots so I guess the windows were good ones.

Several cruisers waiting to leave Turtle Bay had professional weather routers they were in touch with on satellite phones, and on the day we left, the weather guy we listen to, Don on *Summer Passage*, didn't agree with the professionals, who are admittedly giving a more specific forecast for a particular passage. But actually, there are not too many variables. This time of year the wind blows from the northwest down the coast almost without exception, in the range of 10-30 knots. So the weather prediction is either you get the high end of that or the low end. Don said low, the other guys said high for the three days or so it would take to get to Ensenada in a sailboat.

One way to look at it is that they were both right. Or another way to look at it is that they were both wrong. Sometimes we had 12 knots, sometimes 25. About half and half. Is it really worth downloading all that stuff from the Internet and spending all that time analyzing it, when you could just flip a coin and get the same results?

We left with a pretty large group on Saturday morning, going with Don's promise of an easy passage. Besides the wind, another variable is the sea state. As it turned out, there was a gale near Catalina that sent some pretty good-sized seas our way. But there was another split decision here, as we had very calm seas for about 60 miles, but about 15 miles north of Isla Cedros, we began to encounter some fairly heavy going with seas at 10 feet and wind in the 20-25 knot range. The big boats who were faster than *Maverick* and so ahead of us all cracked off a bit to ease the boat's motion, but guess who didn't?

By dawn we had passed everyone, and of course this completely made up for the lack of sleep and consequent splitting headache. This kind of behavior may be the reason we broke the boat. At any rate, before this happened, we started to think we were going to get cheated on the Baja Bash and not get our share of bashing, but now we're happy. Some guys whined to Don about his forecast, but not us. Weathermen are not to be held to the same standards as other professionals. The reverse is also true, and if it weren't, we'd see automobiles with the wheels on the top, and toothbrushes that weigh 100 pounds and are made out of balloons.

Ensenada is pretty pleasant, by which I mean that if you walk up into town, chances are real good you won't be hit by some big wave. It's a nice feeling.

Jiggety-Jig

10:00 AM local time, Friday, May 23 (1700 May 23 UTC).
32° 42.568'N 117° 14.060'W
Temp. 68, Humidity 74%, Cloud Cover 100%.
At the public dock on Shelter Island, San Diego, California.

At 5:30 yesterday (Thursday) afternoon (0030 May 22 UTC), *Maverick* crossed into US waters at 32 degrees, 31 minutes north, 117 degrees, 11 minutes west. After 798 days and 29,524 miles, we were back in the USA, with less than 500 miles left to get home. I'm sorry to report to all you dreamers and malcontents, among whose number the Captain maintains a proud membership, that after all the places we've been to, America is still my favorite country in the world in almost every respect, usually by a considerable margin. I have missed it and as a matter of fact may never leave it again. Show me another country that can produce Jerry Lee Lewis, Muhammad Ali, Marilyn Monroe, and Little Richard without breaking a sweat, and still has someone left over who immediately answers your call on VHF 16 and knows what they're talking about.

Almost Homeboy

2:30 PM local time, Monday, May 26 (2130 May 26 UTC).
32° 42.568'N 117° 14.060'W
Temp. 71, Humidity 69%, Cloud Cover 70%.
At the public dock on Shelter Island, San Diego, California.

Upon reaching shore for the first time in America, I guess I forgot to kiss the soil, which in any case may not have presented a pretty picture to the strangers strolling along the waterfront. Instead, I found myself among them, looking out at the boats on San Diego Bay, where I took my first sailboat ride back in the '50s. As I walked, I saw a boat from our marina back in the Bay Area, *Radio Flyer,* on a mooring and looking neglected. The San Diego Yacht Club's *Stars and Stripes* was towed out to do some practicing or fundraising or whatever they do on that boat. Without being conscious of it, I had a big grin on my face from just being happy to be back, and I was saying hello to everyone who walked by. It took about a half hour for me to realize I was scaring people.

I went into a bar and restaurant that used to be the Kona Kai Yacht Club where I had played many gigs as a kid. Nothing seemed familiar so I went a little farther to Humphrey's, a bar that features a lot of music, and saw names like Taj Mahal and my old boss Maria Muldaur on the playbill.

Entering this establishment, I ordered a gin and tonic and then sat at a dockside table and engaged in a few meditations. Before long, a waitress came by, startling me out of my reverie, and asked if I needed another drink. I looked up and momentarily mistook her for the woman behind the bar from whom I'd ordered the first one. I was about to say, "Oh, it's you!" with the same kind of unnerving giddiness that my mind had locked into since putting my feet ashore, due to a non-drug-induced—and therefore in some peculiar way natural—chemical imbalance. But halfway through saying it, I realized that it wasn't the same woman at all and, improvising rapidly on the fly, my brain searched for an alternative. In mid-stride, I changed my greeting to "Oh, it's ME!"

The fact that the grin had not left my face could not have but added to the picture that this perky young thing beheld of a small, old, bearded man with the look of a manic homeless person who had just ecstatically succeeded in identifying himself. The problem for me then being, how to recover from such a statement, so in vain I searched for a remark to regain a small portion of dignity. Should I have said, "Oh, I didn't really mean it was ME, I mean it was YOU, but actually I had you mixed up with someone else!" Would that have made her feel a little more comfortable? I decided that prudence required me to comment no further.

Soon I was joined by Don Lovas, my oldest friend and the guitar player in the earliest bands I was in. I stayed at his house a couple of nights and marveled at his high-speed Internet and digital cable TV, both of which had improved greatly during my absence. We don't usually talk about old times but rather are still trying to figure out how things work in the here and now. He reminded me that we've gotten to the age where "the choo-choo is getting closer to the cliff." I talked for a long time with Don's daughter Tanya, who is every bit the super-fox that her mother is. Tanya's mother is Sandi, Don's ex-wife, who was the girl singer, cuz that's what we called them, of Sandi and the Accents, the most popular band in San Diego in the mid-'60s. Tanya wasn't born then but is now the wife of Mike and mother of Tristan, and is considerably older than her mother was when the band broke up. Time doesn't sail, it flies.

When Don was returning me to the boat Sunday morning, the car broke down. In the next five minutes, two motorists and a cop had stopped to offer assistance. Don called a tow truck on his cell phone and a man rode by on a bicycle and asked if we were okay. When we said we thought we had it under control, he shouted encouragement as he rode away. When travelers return from abroad and tell you the people were friendly over there in some strange land, don't forget that they're not so bad here either.

Then last night I had dinner with Ship's Stateside Medical Officer Frank Mannix. We dined at the Bali Hai, where my father used to take the family out to dinner 40-odd years ago. It is just as I remember it, except that the staff, who were grown-ups back then, are now just kids. It crossed my mind that almost two years earlier, Mr. Shrode and I had been anchored in French Polynesia near the Bali Hai of the movie *South Pacific*, the inspiration for this eatery.

I wanted Frank to give me a list of all his exalted accomplishments (among other things he is Professor of Emergency Medicine at the University of California) so I could pass them on to our readers, but he said, "Just tell them I'm your old bass player." Frank played bass and was the leader of Sandi and the Accents. If Frank is as good a doctor as he is a bass player, and I'm sure he wouldn't have it any other way, our medical advice was as good as it gets.

It's Memorial Day today, which was originally a holiday proposed by the southern United States to commemorate, in reconciliation, the dead soldiers of both the Union and Confederate Armies, and now the remembrance is extended to the dead among US soldiers of all wars. It's a day to feel gratitude for their sacrifice. It's a good day to be home.

The Boatmen Cometh

4:00 PM local time, Wednesday, June 4 (2300 June 4 UTC).
Latitude and longitude on a need-to-know basis only.
Temp. 66, Humidity 68%, Cloud Cover 80%.
Location undisclosed due to security considerations.

We had to stay an extra day in San Diego to wait for it to stop blowing hard in the wrong direction so we left Tuesday morning and made a quick trip of it up to Santa Barbara by Wednesday noon. We had some dense fog on the way after passing Catalina and spent a rather fretful night and morning dodging heavy traffic in the Santa Barbara Channel. We had three or four encounters with ships that passed within a half-mile or less that we couldn't see at all. I don't have any idea how we would have survived this without GPS and radar.

We've done little but see old friends in San Diego and Santa Barbara. In addition to Don and Frank, we were visited by Sandi of Sandi and the Accents, and her husband David. David was once involved in a project to drive jet skis to Hawaii from Southern California, and they almost made it. Sandi was one of the greatest female singers I ever worked with, so she's right up there with Carla Thomas ("Gee Whiz") and Mary Wells ("My Guy"). Sometimes I think I would trade the whole circumnavigation to be transported back to the '60s and play one more gig with Frank, Don, Gabe, Doug, and Sandi.

In Santa Barbara and San Diego, we were also visited by some Ericson 39 owners who had some questions. I changed the subject, since I had no idea what they were talking about. In Santa Barbara we hoped to meet Paul Moore, but what happened was this: Captain Paul was supposed to return to real life after he got *Okiva* through the Panama Canal—but he wouldn't go home! So he and Francis are headed for Fiji.

After Santa Barbara, we had an easy trip up the coast, if you like motor-sailing in the fog with no wind and calm seas. Considering the alternatives, it was peachy. From time to time at night, we could see the loom of familiar towns through the mist, and farther on, the fog lifted so that the 15-second beacon from the Point Sur Lighthouse was bright and cast a reflection on the glassy surface straight to *Maverick*. The last 20 miles or so we were treated to the very rare light southwesterly, blowing the diesel exhaust into the cockpit. Welcoming us to our home waters were thousands of By-the-Wind-Sailors (*Velella* sp.), also known as "Purple Sails." About two inches in diameter, these are the only sailboats in the animal kingdom, but unlike *Maverick*, they don't go to weather for beans.

You know, it's starting to look as though we might pull this thing off. I think it's about time we get back. In the short period since the crew left the US, there has been a stock market crash; a major terrorist incident; two wars; the A's, Giants, and 49ers all choked in the post-season; George Harrison and Little Eva died; and almost everyone got older. Never fear, America, help is on the way. We have stood our last night watch and entered the final waypoints in the GPS. *Maverick* is coming home.

As for the final approach to San Francisco, I can do no better than to quote that great American writer, the dauntless Captain of *Maverick*:

> *When a traveler approaches the Bay from sea, there is nothing at all to give a hint of the size and importance of the cities of San Francisco and Oakland. Sutro Tower is visible, and as you sail closer, you can see the understated Sunset District, which could easily be mistaken for a small coastal town, sloping towards the west. Otherwise, the cities are hidden by the coastal mountains and all the mariner sees is a rugged and undeveloped coastline, and in fact the Golden Gate is such a small opening that most early explorers failed to find it.*
>
> *But as the sailor approaches closer to the rocks and cliffs of Land's End and finally passes under what is now the Golden Gate Bridge, the whole mass of humming activity suddenly reveals itself. This is startling at night, when it is reminiscent of the scene in a science fiction movie where a dark cave leads to a small door, which, when opened, reveals a vast, obviously powerful, alien civilization.*

The Golden Gate

1:20 PM local time, Saturday, June 7 (2020 June 7 UTC).
37° 49.743'N 122° 27.604'W
Temp. 66, Humidity 66%, Cloud Cover 100%.
In San Francisco Bay.

At 1:15 PM *Maverick* passed under the Golden Gate Bridge. A little earlier, at 11:30 AM (1830 UTC), on a bleak, cold, and foggy morning, we had entered the San Francisco shipping channel, completing our circumnavigation. The only people there to witness this event were Mr. Shrode and the Captain. On a list beginning with Magellan in 1522 or Drake in 1580, depending on how you count it, the crew of *Maverick* is the most recent entry. We have joined the ranks of explorers, privateers, merchants, dreamers, heroes, blackguards, warriors, adventurers, champion sailors, desperados, housewives, grandmothers, teenagers, infants, dogs, cats, and parrots who have preceded us around the world. We tip our hats to them.

Both Sides Now

11:00 AM local time, Saturday, June 21 (1800 June 21 UTC).
37 57 N   122 31 W
Temp. 64, Humidity 58%, Cloud Cover 100%.
At home in San Rafael.

The first thing I did when I got home was to get sick. I hadn't had any but the most minor of health problems in places like Tonga, and Eritrea, and Morocco, but when I hit the home waters, I got a vicious and lingering cold.

Could it have been that unconsciously, I was resisting returning to normal life? I don't think so. I seem to be bathed in luxury in my old house, which Theresa had stocked with all my favorite stuff. To have a refrigerator, hot and cold running water, a TV, and all my records and books close at hand seemed like heaven. My leg still involuntarily gets ready to work the foot pump every time I go to the sink, but the water flows with no pumping! Old friends have stopped by and taken me out to lunch, sometimes generously promising, as Bob Spinner did, that they will be happy to pick up the tab "every time you finish a circumnavigation." The best thing of all, not counting Theresa, is that I've regained the ability to just pick up the phone and instantly annoy and berate any number of friends and relatives. I've really missed that.

There is a bit of the Rip Van Captain going on, because in the US things don't stay the same for long. More than one correspondent has written to say that we'll be returning to a harsher America than the one we left. My feeling is that as long as we ourselves don't become harsher, I can deal with it. But I've already been to a couple of A's games and started to get familiar with the new guys, and there's nothing that serves to reassure a lost soul that things haven't changed that much and all is right with the world, as much as a baseball game on a sunny afternoon.

So far, the weirdest thing about being back is that home seems so familiar that it is really very hard to believe that I've been where I've been the last two years. Was I really in Savusavu, and Kumai, and Salalah? That's very odd. Maybe it was someone else. Before we left, there were those who said, and no doubt hoped, that I'd come back a changed person.

Though it has been just over two years, it seems a very long time ago that we departed San Francisco Bay with dreams of sailing all the way around the world. At the time our imaginations were filled with fairy-tale images of exotic lands and palm-lined harbors, and as it turned out, we weren't disappointed. But it is more truth than rhetoric to say that even after completing it, the voyage seems scarcely real at all, no less dreamlike in remembrance than it was in anticipation.

We sailed to the fabled South Pacific beloved of Stevenson and Gauguin, where London made his ill-fated voyage to the Solomon Islands, Cook observed the transit of Venus, and Bligh made good his flight from the mutineers of the *Bounty*. Our first passage of nearly 27 days from San Francisco culminated in the elation of a tropical landfall in the verdure of the Marquesas. We found places with names of Polynesian fantasies, like Hiva Oa, Nuku Hiva, Opunohu, Rangiroa, Bora Bora, Savusavu, Malolo Lailai, Vanuatu. In Tahiti, we rescued *Maverick* from grave danger when a gale blew out the trade winds and she swung onto a reef in the middle of the night. With Captain Paul Moore of *Okiva*, we launched our own rum-fueled pirate attack in the waters of the Royal Papua Yacht Club in New Guinea, and our intended victims' lives were spared only by a timely outbreak of prudence on the part of his crew, Francis—and the authorities. We had a pleasure cruise through the feared Torres Strait and after crossing the Arafura Sea, reached Australia, the Land Down Under.

Somberly considering the government warnings and constant rumors about Muslim violence after September 11, we determined we would carry on as planned and would, unlike some who felt it was imprudent, fly the American flag. We found our way to the magic island of Bali, where sacred monkeys run wild in their own temple and the dancers and musicians bring word from a parallel universe. Sailing north into the Java Sea, one of the Seven Seas of Sinbad, we were treated with Biblical severity by a thousand miles of strong headwinds, adverse currents, and black thunderstorms that blew so hard you couldn't hear your own voice. In an attempt to take refuge from the punishment of wind and seas, we ran *Maverick* aground in the channel leading to the Indonesian city of Banjarmasin and spent a tough day kedging her off in strong currents, wind, and chop. Finally reaching the Kumai river of Kalimantan, we took a trip into the primordial jungle led by a Dayak warrior with a blowpipe and came face to face with the Wild Man of Borneo. After transiting the South China Sea and the Strait of Malacca, we blasted Conway Twitty at the mysterious hongs of Phang Nga Bay in Thailand. We sailed on to the tea plantations of Ceylon, where tuk-tuks shared the roadway with elephants and goats, and the Tamil Tigers were kept at bay with depth charges near *Maverick's* berth. We saw the sea turn white near Oman and foiled the pirates in the Gulf of Aden. We sailed up the Red Sea, watched a sunset on the Nile, and smoked sheesha with a Bedouin prince.

Emerging from the Suez Canal and sailing Homer's wine-dark seas where mighty Xerxes sent his ships against the Athenians, we made landfall in Turkey and walked in the footsteps of Alexander the Great.

We sailed past Cape Sounion in Greece and remembered the warriors of Argos returning with their beaked ships full of booty from the sack of Troy, as they spotted this landmark of their homeland. Many years later, a lookout here spotted the sacred ship returning from Delos and sent word to Crito telling him his old friend Socrates must prepare for the end. We imagined Saint Paul among his flock as we visited Perge and Athens and Corinth. We sat by the temple of Apollo at Delphi and looked down the steep hillsides of Parnasos where supplicants once traveled from far-off lands to hear the oracle foretell victory or defeat in love and war, and doom for the House of Oedipus. We found the island kingdom of Ithaca that Odysseus returned to, as his Penelope sat patiently awaiting her lost warrior and weaving and unweaving the shroud for his father, Laertes.

We clambered around the lava flows atop Etna and sailed through the Strait of Messina to Stromboli, whose volcano was a lighthouse to the ancient Mediterranean mariner and where the characters of Jules Verne's *Journey to the Center of the Earth* regained the surface. Both volcanoes erupted shortly after *Maverick's* visit. We left the Mediterranean by sailing between the Pillars of Hercules and, crossing the Atlantic Ocean, followed the route discovered by Christopher Columbus 500 years ago. The passage culminated with Mr. Shrode and the Captain working desperately to keep *Maverick* from sinking before she reached the boatyard at the island of Carriacou in Grenada. Sailing again after repairs, we encountered brutal sea conditions north of Columbia on our way to the San Blas Islands, where we visited a people still cheerfully living a stone-age life. We transited the locks of the Panama Canal as we crossed the Great Divide to rejoin the Pacific Ocean. Finally setting sail for America and home, we followed Elizabeth's pirate Sir Francis Drake back towards our beloved San Francisco Bay, still to my eyes the most beautiful in the world. Now from my window above the Bay, I look out on waters that are connected, unbounded, to all of our adventures.

Our faithful warrior *Maverick* lies in her slip with a battle scar or two of her own, weary but at peace with herself. On countless nights she protected us, safe and dry below, while she took it upon herself to suffer the violent pounding of wind and deadly sea. People will walk by her and pause, and she may hear them say, "She sailed around the world." Her rest is well earned, and her trials, for now, are over.

But perhaps one day soon you'll be aboard as Mr. Shrode casts off the lines and we turn her bows to the open sea. You'll hoist the main and we'll enter a waypoint for the land of come-what-may, which, according to legend, is found just outside the Golden Gate. Through our hearts will pass a shadow of trepidation as we leave friends and families, and the protection of our familiar bay behind. We know we'll face the gales and calms, the pirates and the shoals, and the other perils endured by the mariners of olden days. Yet we'll believe, as Slocum did, that a strong hope will master our fears, and that in the fullness of time we'll reach the safe and peaceful harbor of our desires that lies not far beyond the west horizon, at the edge of the sky. There we'll hoist our glasses in honor of those who came before to chart the reefs and take the soundings, and feel no small measure of pride in the knowledge that in our modest way, we have followed in their wake.

Until that happy day, may all the heavens from the North Star to the Southern Cross that have beckoned us since time beyond knowing, smile down on my fond ambition to have the honor of remaining,

Dear Friends,
Your Most Loyal and Humble Servant,
The Captain

Appendix

For more photos and stories see http://ussmaverick.net

FACTS

We broke no records.

Total time of the voyage: 812 days.

Number of miles: 29,993. To give you an idea of how much sailing this is, the average boat is sailed about 12 times a year, which works out to twice a month during the summer sailing season. If each sail is a pretty good day-sail around San Francisco Bay amounting to, say, 20 miles, the boat is sailed 240 miles a year. At that rate, it would take about 125 years to do the same amount of sailing *Maverick* did in the last 27 months. On the other hand, after over two years of very expensive and relatively grueling travel, we're actually right back where we started, so what's the point?

Number of miles sailed to windward (i.e., we had wind but we were not able to fetch our destination): About one tenth of the total, or about 3,000 miles. Of this, about 500 miles was motor-sailed.

Number of total miles under power: A little less than 1/6 of the total distance, around 4500 miles (counting the above 500 miles). Almost all of this was either in the Med or from Panama to California, the majority because of lack of wind.

Countries visited: 26, not counting the US.

Days underway: 252 (days being 24 hours, not an afternoon sail), which is about 31% of the time we were gone.

Average speed while underway: just over 5 knots.

Days spent in harbors (or out of the water): 560

Number of harbors visited: 124 harbors and anchorages. Of these, 16 were slips, 14 were med-ties, leaving 94 anchorages where we were on the hook or on a mooring.

Top speed on GPS: 17.7 knots. This is pretty danged fast for a boat that is not known for surfing.

Highest 24-hour run: 204 miles, an average of 8.5 knots.

Longest passage: 26 days, 23 hours, and 35 minutes (3512 miles, San Francisco to Hiva Oa, an average of 5.4 knots).

Highest sustained (12 or more hours) winds observed underway: 40 knots (full or fresh gale) with higher gusts. Three times from behind, near Bora Bora, at the bottom of the Red Sea, and leaving the Canaries, where we went fast, and once on the nose in the Red Sea, where we bore off and reduced sail. Days in the low 30s (near gale) were considerably less rare, however. We saw at least 30 such days at sea.

Highest sustained winds at anchor: 35 knots with gusts to 45 and above in Tahiti, Tonga, Fiji, Marsa Thelemet in the Gulf of Suez, and Mykonos (Greece). We didn't drag any of these times but the wind backed 180 degrees in Tahiti during a gale and we swung onto the reef.

Highest winds observed underway: 50 knots with gusts to 60 knots for about a dozen squalls lasting 20-40 minutes near Borneo, and 50 knots on the approach to Aruba.

Highest waves observed underway: Occasional 20-ft. seas during a gale near Bora Bora; again in a gale in the Red Sea; again in gale conditions after departing the Canaries. Although not pleasant, none of these were among the roughest seas we experienced, which were in the 8-12-foot range and were found in every ocean but mostly in the Pacific Ocean and Western Caribbean Sea. We did not experience particularly rough seas in the Red Sea or the Med.

Weather rarities: Sandstorm when underway in the Red Sea; three close-by lightning strikes: two with very minor damage in Malaysia, one with significant damage in Greece.

Other rarities: The sea turned white from horizon to horizon in the middle of the night from a bioluminescent algal bloom near Oman.

Groundings: Once on a coral reef in Tahiti, once in mud off of Borneo. We were able to kedge off without assistance both times, but it wasn't pretty.

Near-collisions with shipping, acts of terrorism or piracy (not counting the encounter off of Sri Lanka that begins this book), collisions with whales, or knock-downs: Zero.

Cost: Counting the original purchase price, about $115,000 was invested in *Maverick*. I kept decent records, so this is pretty close, but it doesn't count every stainless steel fastener I ran down to Whale Point Marine to buy and there were a lot of those. This is somewhat below average for world cruisers, but the million-dollar yachts are rarities for this kind of thing, as are the guys going around in 30-footers. The highest-ticket items in upgrading the boat before we left were new spars and rig from Ballenger and an engine and transmission rebuild, but the rest of the modifications, sails, emergency gear, spares, and electronics add up. Repairs underway were on the high side but not unheard of, if you keep in mind that the distance we traveled is not too much shorter than the distance put in on most five-year circumnavigations, and that we had a couple of fairly unusual problems, including the hull issue. Engine rebuilds or replacements are not what I'd call rare for world cruisers.

The total in repairs was in the neighborhood of $25,000 over the 28-month period, about 83 cents per mile, the biggest things being major engine work in Egypt and the hull damage repair in Carriacou. I know some people make it around on a modest budget and have few problems, but my guess is that they are in the minority on both counts. Which is not to say it can't be done, of course. Certain things, like the level of gear you equip the boat with, are under your control. Other things are not. Something that added to our expense was the fact that since we were on a two-year schedule, we could not always afford the time to shop around for bargains and cheaper ways to do things. However, this was balanced by the fact that we interrupted our gainful pursuits back home for a shorter time.

In addition to the above, our shared monthly expenses for food and fuel, berthing, canal fees, customs and immigration, meals out, and excursions averaged about $1000 each, or $2000 a month. (This doesn't count the expenses incurred when the girls showed up and the budget went out the window, but on the other hand, they generally kicked in all or some of the money for these trips.) We could have done it on less had either one of us enjoyed cooking, but we found that after making landfall, we ate out more often than not. I would guess that this level of expenditure is about average, but there are high-rollers who hit the hot clubs, play golf every day, and hire out all the boat work, and others who rarely eat out, stay in backpacker hotels when inland, shop very carefully for every $5 purchase, and pick up jobs on other boats when they can. It's probably a bell curve, but cruisers are as a rule pretty frugal, since, unlike people on short vacations, they are in for the long haul.

To sum up, the trip cost the Captain about $167,000 (not deducting the resale value of the boat, about $30,000, which of course is significantly less than the original investment) and Mr. Shrode about $27,000. Folks who are thinking about doing something along these lines usually like to know this sort of thing.

OPINIONS

I could make a list of at least half a dozen regions of the United States that equal or exceed in beauty anything we saw out there. If you haven't seen the US, it would make sense to go where they accept dollars and speak your language before embarking on an expensive trip to the South Pacific. The fact is that unless you make a special effort to get away from the normal tourist packages when you visit the tropics, your experience will be a typical expensive resort not appreciably more exotic than Hawaii or the Bahamas.

Top travel recommendation: Bali. Beautiful and weird in an interesting and charming way.

Least favorite stop: Egypt; there were no other contenders. The spectacular constructions of the ancients are a striking contrast to the shoddy workmanship and sleazy hustle of their modern heirs.

Best sailing venue: Fiji. Challenging, beautiful, friendly culture, countless great island anchorages. At the time of our visit, there was no large charter operation there, although there are quite a few independent operations.

Most disappointing sailing venue: the Med. You can't do anything to fight windless days except start the engine. Besides that, Europe seemed pretty white-bread compared to where we'd been, and if you're not careful, you can find yourself in some very expensive marinas. If you want to sail the Med, my advice, based on very limited experience of course, would be to do Turkey or the Balearics. We also heard good things about the Adriatic, but we didn't have time to go there. It's great being in Europe and there are wonderful harbors, so it's just the sailing that was disappointing.

Most challenging leg: The Java and South China Seas. We played the weather according to the books, but the window slammed shut six weeks early and we sailed 1000 miles to weather in strong winds. The Red Sea was tough in spots but we could work around most of them and it's an interesting place with great diving and exotic anchorages. The secret to making it up the Red Sea safely is relying on visual cues to navigation and being skeptical of charts and published waypoints. Most people came to grief not out in the heavy weather but in making risky calls when trying to escape it by getting through a pass into a reef with inadequate charts and/or visibility. We very narrowly escaped this fate ourselves.

Easiest and most attractive charter suggestion: the Moorings in Raiatea, French Polynesia. They've got you covered.

Most widely visible US products: Coke and Sprite, Windows 98, and McDonald's, with Coke and Sprite being by far the most ubiquitous commodities from any country. Detroit cars are rarely seen.

Most unexpected general observations:
Number one: Even though every corner of the Third World is less spiffy and efficient than what we're fortunate enough to enjoy in the First World, most of what we saw was quite a bit more civilized than I had visualized. You have to go to places even more remote than we did to find people who aren't familiar with cell phones and the Internet.

Number two: It was quite unsettling when I found myself actually waxing nostalgic for the energetic, inventive, and enterprising style of American culture. I'm not unaware that, by tradition, I'm supposed to come back to the States with a backward, romantic glance towards simpler, less stressful, happier cultures and a rueful grimace at our own rat race. But I just wasn't able to persuade myself that the attraction of such places was not the wistful fantasy of the ancient human desire for Eden, which, for those of you who are not Biblical scholars, is a place we humans got kicked out of, and to which we are not allowed to return.

GEAR REVIEW

In my life, I like the rush, the buzz, the ecstasies, the raptures, the reveries. Don't you? I try to maximize the time on earth I spend in the pursuit of these, and I pay only the most minimal attention possible to the real world, to serve the admittedly pedestrian motive of staying alive. The reveries are why I sailed, unless you count the honorable, age-old ambition of man to spend and re-spend countless thousands of dollars on crap that breaks. I wanted to put my own ears and eyes, my own physical presence at the scene of what I thought was waiting for me out in the beyond. Kierkegaard tells the parable of the grand banquet where, after the guests arrive and everyone is served, those in attendance speak with eloquence and at great length about the wonderful and sumptuous feast before them. But no one takes a bite. I didn't want to be one of those guys.

Unfortunately for those of my ilk, who were lovingly warned by their mothers that they had "stars in their eyes," sailing a boat for these distances can be an aggravatingly concrete undertaking. The times spent in dreamy contemplation of the power of the sea or the beauty of the landfalls or other deep and weighty matters are more than balanced by the moments spent in gritty grappling with the exigencies of the substantive, intractable, and irritatingly self-important material world. Every time my reveries were interrupted when something on the boat broke, I felt personally insulted, as it appeared that this little insignificant piece of metal had the temerity, and what's more, the wherewithal, to mess with my groove, bum my trip, or maul my buzz. I loved this little outrageously expensive item so much I bought it and have been good to it so it should be good to me, or so I felt. Otherwise, it's just not fair, and fairness is, like, a thing with me.

I'm not quite the only one that feels this way. There's circumnavigator Allen on *Celerity* who confided to me in Turkey that he wished that he could, just one time, make a landfall and not have some boat problem causing him to focus on the exasperations and not the pleasures of cruising. Or circumnavigator George on *Kemo Sabe* who, in the middle of an annoying repair, said with a steely smile on his face that he loves sailing, but "this boating sucks." I picked these two because they are both very funny guys who have been doing it for a while, not the grouches, who do exist out here, and maybe I'm one of them. Want to make something of it?

It's the rare skipper you can't get to go off after a beer or two and a few provocative questions, and I mean off, on some particularly expensive and exasperating boat problem he faced, like blowing out a sail at a bad time. Then someone else picks it up, and it's like that skit by

Monty Python, where it's, "Sails! You had sails? On our boat we had to climb the mast and hold our arms out!" And the next guy says, "Mast! You had a mast? We had to stand naked on the deck and hold our clothes out to catch the wind." And the next says, "Deck! You had a deck?..." and so on. It's enough to make one into a Gnostic, that old Greek religion that teaches that the soul is locked in an alien physical world that is really not its true home, which in the case of your Captain is La-La-Land.

Russell on *Blue Highway* and I discussed it in the Canary Islands. I said that although I'd prefer to meditate on the significance and poetry of the landfalls, I am otherwise occupied with missing the reefs and paying attention to depths—and also thinking, how the heck am I going to get the antenna tuner fixed—to have any poetry running around my poor little overburdened brain. So he says that, while that is how it is, we're building memories that will be enjoyed at our leisure. So I say, Russell, I'm an old man and I'd prefer not to wait, cuz you see, putting off pleasures and packing stuff in the bank so I could do something later is what I did for a long time so I could do what I'm doing now. I was under the impression that that process had now come to fruition and in fact now IS the leisure I looked forward to. I don't want to hear that the cycle has started again and it's fine if I'm not having fun now because I'm scoring points for later. What if it just goes on like that forever and you never get to the good part? Wouldn't that be like medieval Christianity, where you suffer for all you're worth here below, in this vale of tears, just so you can have fun when you're dead? Not that there's anything wrong with that.

Anyway I'm not going to, like some others who have written about cruising, try to advise you on what gear to buy or how to go about this or that in outfitting your boat as if I knew what I was talking about. It could not fail to be boring for those readers whose interests do not extend to bilge-diving in a seaway. And also, when I get going, I may start yelling like someone with Tourette syndrome cuz nobody knows the trouble I've seen. So the best you can do is to read *Practical Sailor*, which is not particularly helpful but do it anyway so you can laugh a hearty and bitter laugh at them later, as no matter how clever they are with their little tests, they just cannot recreate the conditions of long-term use at sea.

To make a brief summary of our experience with major gear from which it is wise not to extrapolate, since whatever happens to you will be completely different: Some of the stuff that stood up best was the stuff that took the worst beating: sails (Hood), blocks and deck gear (Garhauer, Ronstan), winches (Barient, Lewmar), and running rigging (Sta-Set and Sta-Set X). We didn't change sheets or halyards or blow out a sail the whole way around. Some of the bits of electronic gear that caused us no trouble were the radar (Furuno 1622), HF radio (ICOM M710 w/ tuner),

GPS (Garmin 128), the camera (Olympus D-460 digital), and the weather instrument/barograph (Speedtech). The last two are not major gear but I'm fond of them as they never had a hiccup. Some of these were damaged by lightning but you can't hold that against them. My favorite manufacturer of marine equipment is Garhauer. They are one of the most helpful companies I've ever dealt with in any context.

The biggest problems, aside from the hull, which isn't really gear, were the engine (freshly rebuilt Perkins 4-107), the transmission (freshly rebuilt Borg-Warner), the computers (Compaq), the autopilots (Navico), dinghy (West Marine/Zodiac), prop (Martec two-blade folding prop; but it struck a reef so we can't blame it), and outboard (Nissan, which had to be replaced). These are the big money ones, except the dinghy, which was more just an ongoing pain in the neck, dealt with by Ship's Inflatable Engineer Terry Shrode, and so qualifies.

Just about everyone seems to have engine problems, not infrequently major, on this kind of trip. Autopilot problems are also almost universal; those guys who do the Transpac races have been known to have as many as four backups, so little faith have they in their reliability. We had innumerable other problems but they were all less than $750, which does not mean that they weren't complicated and nerve-wracking to deal with.

I realize that some of the folks who manufacture boating gear, even with the best of intentions, have a good reason for not making stuff that doesn't break under this type of use. The fact is that the number of people doing long-distance cruising is entirely insignificant. I figure that substantially fewer than 100 boats from the US complete a circumnavigation per year. Compared to the number of sailboats in the US (about 1,600,000 in 2002, according to the Marine Manufacturers Association) this is less than 1/100 of 1%. To say that this segment of the market has a negligible effect on product feedback is to speak euphemistically. No matter what the manufacturers claim, how could it be otherwise? We are really not the people they're selling to. Since we all have to use stuff from the same manufacturers, everything breaks, even on rich people's boats. So when a salesman tells you that something is "bulletproof," think "Bulletproof when used as indicated, for the occasional sail on Lake Merritt—or better still, when not used at all, although even this will not prevent failure."

There is another possible explanation, and that is that human beings are, after all these thousands of years, not yet capable of consistently making things that will stand up to the sea.

I'll give you two points to cogitate, screamingly obvious but always in need of repeating to the prospective cruiser so he or she can ignore them like everyone else did before they left, including me: One, there is nothing that can't break. Two, there is nothing that can't break. Unless you really, in your heart of hearts, live just to fix things (and I've met two or three out of several hundred cruisers about whom this could truly be said), your patience with fixing things will wear thin. After reading this, you probably will tell yourself that the people who have had gear problems, the Captain included, were simply not prepared well enough to begin with, like you yourself WILL be when YOU go. Ah, it is with great fondness that I remember the days when I spoke that very sentiment myself.

But there are solutions! One is to buy a brand-new, high-end boat. This doesn't work, as you can prove to yourself by buying one, if you like treating yourself to very expensive lessons, like the sad man I met in Greece who had a two-month-old Hallberg-Rassy with a thousand problems, or Peter with his beautiful Oyster 71 *Oceans Free*, who put it on a reef after engine failure in the South China Sea. Another solution is purity and simplicity. The Pardeys and the Streets of the world advocate having boats on which nothing is aboard that cannot be fixed by the crew. I respect these folks a lot and their advice, really, really, really makes sense, but 1) It takes a lifetime of learning to be safe the way they do it. 2) They're not that safe. Can you fix an EPIRB or a GPS? You want a depthsounder? Don Street took *Iolaire* up the Thames in an adventure reported in a major cruising magazine. There were two non-trivial semi-disasters that could have easily been avoided had he an engine, and that's why so few people follow his example. Cook went high-tech for his time and if he did it today, he would have forward-scanning sonar, which would have kept him off of Endeavour Reef.

That's my gear knowledge in a nutshell. All the other stuff is just details. Having said that, if someone out there really wants to know how the crew of *Maverick* chose to outfit the boat, check out the chapter cleverly entitled "The Boat" back at the beginning of the book. It was written before we left, so it is refreshingly free of any knowledge born of experience.

Acknowledgements

The writing of these pieces was accomplished during the circumnavigation. Upon our return, a few people—just a few, let's not exaggerate—encouraged me to assemble them into book form. I dabbled at it, but unfortunately, I'm lazy. Yet eventually the deed was done.

The book was edited by Jill Kelly, and two other people were uncommonly generous in their wise reading of the text and their gracious and fortifying remarks. Barry Braverman reviewed the contents in exhaustive detail with discerning insight, and I also benefitted greatly from an exacting critique by my wife, Theresa. Additionally, Elizabeth Spinner, a professional in the English language, was of great help, and artist Phil Freyder corrected my bullfight terminology. If stupid, clunky, or incoherent passages remain in the book after their suggestions, it is because I was too obstinate or obtuse to heed their advice. Songsmith Don Kennedy lent his sharp artistic judgment to the cover.

The voyage itself was achieved in no small measure through the exertions of people back home. Among these none was more important than Theresa Fisher, who was incautious enough to marry me upon my return. She monitored and condensed all emails from our correspondents; tracked down, ordered, shipped, and sometimes personally delivered innumerable spare parts; and of course, offered her encouragement throughout the trip. Mr. Shrode's wife, Caroline Fernandes, allowed her husband to accompany me on this foolish adventure, and provided her support in countless ways, including contributing the title to this book.

Our shoreside staff was augmented by Jim Mead, who helped with weather and was responsible for much of the website organization, contributing chapter summaries. Technical wizardry for the design of the website was provided by Tim Eschliman. Medical consultations were courtesy of Frank Mannix, who managed to keep us alive by long distance, while, presumably, not neglecting any patients back home.

Tradewinds Sailing in Richmond, California deserves our heartfelt gratitude for teaching me and Terry about proper seamanship.

Finally, there is Mr. Terry Shrode. A man of many talents, his most remarkable quality is that rarest of abilities, to remain steadfast and positive in the face of unanticipated and profound reversals of fortune. We both routinely put our lives in the other's hands, and there is not a person on earth I'd feel safer entrusting with mine. *Maverick* has gone off to other voyages, but Mr. Shrode and I now own a modest Catalina 22, and remain the best of sailing buddies.

San Rafael, 2013

www.ingramcontent.com/pod-product-compliance
Lightning Source LLC
Chambersburg PA
CBHW071645090426
42738CB00009B/1425